Pension Fund Investments in Real Estate

Pension Fund Investments in Real Estate

A GUIDE FOR PLAN SPONSORS AND REAL ESTATE PROFESSIONALS

Natalie A. McKelvy

Q

QUORUM BOOKS
WESTPORT, CONNECTICUT • LONDON, ENGLAND

Library of Congress Cataloging in Publication Data

McKelvy, Natalie A.
  Pension fund investments in real estate.

  Bibliography: p.
  Includes index.
  1. Pension trusts—United States—Investments.
  2. Real estate investment—United States. I. Title.
  HD7106.U5M34   1983   332.6'7254   82-25542
  ISBN 0-89930-035-9 (lib. bdg.)

Library of Congress Catalog Card Number: 82-25542
ISBN: 0-89930-035-9

First published in 1983 by Quorum Books

Greenwood Press
A division of Congressional Information Service, Inc.
88 Post Road West, Westport, Connecticut 06881

Printed in the United States of America

10 9 8 7 6 5 4 3 2 1

For Charley

CONTENTS

Tables   ix

FOREWORD—Thomas J. Gochberg   xi

FOREWORD—David Shaw   xiii

Acknowledgments   xv

Introduction   3

Part One—The Pension Fund Business

1. A New Source of Capital?   9

2. Life in the Slow Lane—Investing Pension Fund Money for
   a Living   35

3. Legal Problems   68

Part Two—The Real Estate Business

4. A Story   103

5. The Real Estate Business in the 1970s and Today   109

6. The British   178

7. What to Expect from Real Estate Investments   186

Part Three—Pension Funds in Real Estate

8. The Commingled Funds   211

9. Direct Investing   248

   Bibliography and Other Sources   283

   Index   291

TABLES

1.1 Retirement Fund Investment Performance 1965–1979   17
1.2 Size of Pension Fund Assets by Type of Plan (year-end 1981)   21
1.3 Holdings of Private, Non-Insured Pension Funds
     (year-end 1981)   27
1.4 Holdings of Public Pension Funds (year-end 1981)   28
1.5 Holdings of Private, Insured Pension Funds (year-end 1981)   29
1.6 Real Estate Holdings of the 10 Largest Pension Funds
     (September 30, 1982)   31
2.1 Investment Managers Grouped by Total Tax-Exempt Assets
     under Management (year-end 1982)   45
2.2 100 Largest Managers of Tax-Exempt Money (year-end 1982)   46
2.3 10 Largest Managers of Tax-Exempt Money (year-end 1982)   47
2.4 10 Largest, Independent Managers of Tax-Exempt Money
     (year-end 1982)   48
8.1 20 Largest Managers of Real Estate Equities for Pension Funds
     (June 30, 1982)   215

FOREWORD

This is a timely book, for it describes a new investment arena: the investment of pension fund money in real estate.

It is not one book but three. The first describes the pension fund business for those in the real estate industry; the second explains the real estate business to those who manage pension fund assets; and the third describes the interplay between the two.

As an investment banker who specializes in real estate and the current president of the Pension Real Estate Investment Association (PREIA), I have been involved in both businesses for the last 15 years. When Natalie told me she was planning such a work, I applauded her energy and respected her masochism; she had set herself a difficult task.

The difficulties of explaining one business to the other, much less describing how they could work together are substantial. The people in each business come from different backgrounds, and their styles, perceptions of risk, and morality differ dramatically. Real estate has been the playground of the private entrepreneur; pension officers spend their lives in the more conservative end of the corporate treasurer's office.

If Natalie had written this book 10 years ago, it would have been premature. Then, these two investment worlds were not generally in contact with each other.

What changed and caused these two alien cultures to collide? For real estate, the economics of development and the sources of money changed, forcing developers and investors to look to pension funds for capital.

The early 1970s had been the heyday of the publicly funded real estate investment trusts, the REITs. They had lent to everyone on everything; transactions went quickly and simply. Most importantly, the REITs were pure lenders, and they would lend a developer 100 percent of his needed funds. He could build without putting any equity into the project, and he could retain full ownership when it was completed. Pension funds would have been hard-pressed to compete with REITs as anything but straight real estate lenders.

But the loose lending of the REITs combined with rising interest rates pushed the income property business into disaster in the mid-1970s. High inflation and climbing construction costs and cap rates added a finishing blow. Developers could no longer mortgage out their entire costs; they needed real equity.

Where would these equity funds come from as project costs skyrocketed? They could think of two sources: syndications of equity-limited partnerships—and pension funds.

On the other side of the investment world, pension funds were looking for higher yields, stability, and an inflation hedge, especially in light of their disastrous performance in the stock market during the mid-1970s.

The world of the private entrepreneur and the corporate treasurer met, and, given the need of each for the other, it appears their "shotgun marriage" will last.

Each is learning the other's business. Pension funds, in particular, are becoming more knowledgeable and sophisticated in selecting real estate money managers.

This book is the first serious treatment of this new field, and, as such, I expect it to become a classic.

Thomas J. Gochberg
Smith, Barney Real Estate Corporation
New York, New York

FOREWORD

Pension plan assets invested in real estate are on the increase, both in absolute and relative terms, and the amount written on the topic increases along with them. But this is the first book that analyses what is happening and suggests ways for different pension plans to invest in property. *Pension Fund Investments In Real Estate* is also the first book written specifically to explain the real estate business to pension sponsors—and the pension business to real estate professionals. It is one of the most delightful and informative instruction manuals I have ever read.

Pension Fund Investments In Real Estate should be required reading for pension fund officers considering real estate investing or real estate professionals interested in serving the pension community. The book will give each a vivid picture of the other's interests. Lawyers, actuaries, consultants, accountants, indeed, anyone involved in supporting the pension and real estate businesses should also benefit.

As a former pension officer and someone who has devoted his career to pension fund investment management, I can testify that McKelvy has truly captured the flavor of that business. From the beleaguered corporate pension officer trying to compete in the "investment performance Olympics" to the public fund administrator beating back the wolves who want to use his fund's assets for "social investments," the author has described it all.

She has also confirmed the dangers pension officers have only sensed when dealing with members of the real estate community. What we don't know can, indeed, hurt us. McKelvy points out that pension officers should not let their fear of the investment discourage them from investing in real estate. Instead, pension officers should try to learn about it and then do what is right for the pension fund involved.

The book is readable and often amusing. While reading it one night at the public library, I burst out laughing at one of her examples and endured some hostile stares for disturbing the peace. No one has ever broken into laughter over Benjamin Graham and David Dodd's *Security Analysis*. In its own way, this book is at least as instructive on pension funds and real estate as those gentlemen were on securities investing—and far funnier.

The author has a fine sense of the bizarre. No one should miss her chapter on the pension fund that financed a motel in the early 1970s and ended up in the motel business. The description of what those trustees went through is enough to chill the blood of anyone who has ever served as a pension fund fiduciary.

McKelvy has succeeded in balancing both sides in her presentation. She is uniquely suited to write the book; she worked for a series of mortgage banking and real estate firms from 1972 through 1976 and then wrote about the pension investing business for several years as a reporter for *Pensions & Investment Age* magazine.

This is a book that needed to be written. Retirement plan sponsors and real estate professionals clearly need to establish better lines of communication. This book will help bring that about.

David Shaw
Bankers Trust Company
New York, New York

ACKNOWLEDGMENTS

Much of this book is drawn from interviews and conversations with people in both the real estate and pension fund businesses. I owe them all a debt for sharing their time, their insights, and their good humor.

To protect their identities and privacy, I have not used their names when quoting them in the text. But I have listed their names here, except for those who requested anonymity.

Before listing those names, I would especially like to thank a number of people: Thomas Gochberg, president of the Smith, Barney Real Estate Corporation, New York; David Shaw, vice president at Bankers Trust Company, New York; and Meyer Melnikoff, actuary, Goldman, Sachs & Company, New York. All read the book carefully and offered valuable advice for improving it.

Stephen Berg, Julie Rohrer, and John and Gail Grossmann provided hospitality and help when I was interviewing people in New York. My husband, Charley; my agent, Barbara Neilson; and my editor, Lynn Taylor were sources of support and encouragement, as was my close friend, Judy Chapperon.

John English, vice president and chief investment officer, The Ford Foundation, New York, and Ernie Bianco, senior vice president, Meidinger, Inc., Chicago, wrote endorsements when I applied, without luck, for a grant to the Guggenheim Foundation to finish this book.

I would like to thank the following people for interviews and information:

Thomas J. Anathan, assistant vice president, Real Estate Investment Department, Aetna Life & Casualty Company, Hartford, Conn.;

Cecil J. Baker, chairman, The Pension Fund Property Unit Trust, London;

Gary Barth, Jones Lang Wootton, New York;

Robert Bitticks, vice president, United States Trust Company of New York, New York;

Donald H. Bodel, president, Richard Ellis, Inc., Chicago;

David Bowerman, vice president, Money Market Directories, Inc., Charlottesville, Va.;

Norman W. Bowie, consultant, Jones Lang Wootton, London;

Frank G. Burianek, national director of actuarial practice, Meidinger, Inc., Louisville, Ky.;

Kenneth D. Campbell, president, Audit Investments, Inc., New York;

Joseph P. Clancy, senior vice president, Real Estate Division, Opus Designers Builders Developers, Inc., Mt. Prospect, Ill.;

H. L. Cone, manager, Investment and Plans Financing, Exxon Corporation, New York;

William S. P. Cotter, president, American Agricultural Investment Management Company, Inc., Bannockburn, Ill.;

James S. Dailey, vice president, Real Estate Operations, Diversified Business Division, Aetna Life & Casualty Insurance Company, Hartford, Conn.;

Donald Davis, vice president, Real Estate Investments, Prudential Insurance Company of America, Newark, N.J.;

Nick Faulkes, Phillips & Drew, London;

James E. Foley III, Jones Lang Wootton, Houston;

James Foran, executive vice president, Real Estate Investment Management Group, Mellon Financial Services Corporation, New York;

Bulkeley "Buck" Griswold, manager, fixed-income investments, General Electric Pension Trust, Stamford, Conn.;

Barbara Haslanger, vice president, Gifford Fong & Associates, Chicago;

Dunbar M. Helsley, director, Employee Benefits Division, Aetna Life & Casualty Company, Hartford, Conn.;

Jack S. Jacobs, chairman of the board, Jacobs/Kahan & Company, Chicago;

Hugh R. Jenkins, director-general of investments, National Coal Board Superannuation Schemes, London;

Nathaniel B. Jones, vice president, J. H. Ellwood & Associates, Inc., Chicago;

Donald King, principal of the RREEF Funds, Chicago;

Robert Kinney, president, Real Estate Investment Management Group, Mellon Financial Services Corporation, New York;

William M. Lieber, pension tax counsel, U.S. Congress, Joint Committee on Taxation, Washington, D.C.;

John S. Lillard, president, JMB Institutional Realty Corporation, Chicago;

William Madden, senior vice president, Warburg Paribas Becker-A. G. Becker, Chicago;

Vincent F. Martin, Jr., managing partner, TCW Realty Advisors, Los Angeles;

Martin Myers, Jones Lang Wootton, London;

Jay Neuman, attorney, Securities and Exchange Commission, Washington, D.C.;

Allen Palles, president, APCO Financial Services, Chicago;

Harry Pierandri, vice president and portfolio manager, Equitable Life Assurance Society of the United States, New York;

Gary Pines, senior vice president, Meidinger, Inc., Chicago;

Jerry M. Reinsdorf, chairman of the board, Balcor/American Express Inc., Skokie, Ill.;

Samuel Zell, chairman of the board, Equity Financial & Management Company, Chicago.

Pension Fund Investments in Real Estate

INTRODUCTION

Since the late 1970s, pension funds have been investing more of their assets in income-producing real estate and could conceivably become one of the principal sources of capital for that business. Yet the pension investor does not understand the income property business, nor does the real estate community understand how pension funds operate. Each is only vaguely aware of the other's motivations and needs.

The result is they find it difficult and frustrating to deal with each other. Pension officers recall stories about real estate brokers who spent most of their presentations talking about the tax benefits of a special deal, not knowing that pension funds are tax-exempt entities and oblivious to the merits of tax deals. Real estate people will counter with tales about pension funds who refused to take advantage of positive leverage on a deal and insisted on paying all cash, thus throwing away 5 percent a year in additional return.

The misunderstandings between the two businesses stem largely from ignorance, but they also come from differing attitudes toward risk. The men and women who run pension funds are fiduciaries—trustees of their funds—and they are bound by law to run them prudently and exclusively for the benefit of the people in the plans. They can be sued for imprudent investing by those in the plan, so they invest the money as conservatively as possible. In the jargon of investment theory, they are the ultimate "risk-averse" investors.

The income property investor, on the other hand, sits on the opposite end of the risk spectrum. He is not a fiduciary. He invests for his own account or that of his employer, and he has one goal—to make money. He pays far less attention to the risks involved since he runs no risk of being sued for imprudent investing and can make a great deal of money if his investments do well. He is a risk-taker and an eternal optimist.

The pension investor either overestimates or fails to understand the risks of real estate investing, and the real estate investor chronically underestimates them. Both bring their unrealistic expectations to the bargaining table. In spite of confusion on both sides, pension funds continue to invest in income property and to become more directly involved in it. The progression has taken three steps. First, in the mid-1970s, pension funds invested in income-producing real estate entirely through commingled funds, which are pools of pension money run by investment managers. The most famous is PRISA, the Prudential Property Investment Separate Account, run by the Prudential Insurance Company.

In the second stage during the late 1970s, plans started putting money into commingled funds that had more specialized investment strategies, such as those that bought only properties in the Southeastern part of the country or specialized in writing mortgages. The third stage began in 1980 when some of the largest plans began investing in real estate on their own and hired investment managers to run individual accounts for them.

If pension funds are to continue to invest in property and do so more effectively, both they and the real estate community must learn more about the other's attitudes and investing practices. Otherwise, funds will be deprived of the top returns they can make by shrewd investing, and real estate investors will watch another possible source of capital dry up. Income property would never become more than the minor part of pension portfolios that it is today.

This book attempts to explain each business to the other and suggests ways that both groups might improve their relations and do more business together. The book is designed to be read in its entirety by both groups, but certain topics will interest one more than the other. Consequently, the work is divided into three parts: part one is for people in the real estate business, part two for those in the pension fund business, and part three should interest both.

In part one, real estate readers will find a description of the pension fund business and the funds' investment philosophy. There is also a chapter on the legal restrictions that funds face when they invest in property.

In the second section, the pension fund reader will find a short story about what can happen when a fund gets in over its head in a real estate deal. There is an explanation of how the income property business works, and a discussion of how British pension funds invest in property. A separate chapter describes the risks and returns funds can expect from real estate.

The third and final section examines commingled real estate funds and the ways that pension funds can invest in property on their own.

This book is designed primarily for corporate, government and union pension funds that have at least $50,000 or more to invest in property; it excludes plans with less than $500,000 in total assets. Plans under this benchmark have to invest in property through public and private real estate syndications, and a discussion of these vehicles is beyond the scope of this book. Nor are Independent Retirement Accounts or Keogh plans discussed. They are, for the most part, very small and have problems that differ substantially from those of formal, organized pension funds.

The real estate analysis concentrates only on pension fund investments in income property—that is, property that generates rental income. Such property consists primarily of shopping centers, office buildings, apartments, industrial buildings and hotels. It does not include raw land. Pension funds invest in income property by buying existing buildings, building new ones, or writing mortgages.

There are no sections on pension fund investments in farmland or residential mortgages. Farming is a different business than income property investing, and residential mortgages are considered bonds, not real estate investments.

There are many technical issues a fund would encounter in property investing, such as what it should look for in buying shopping centers or the exact wording of joint-venture agreements. These topics belong to experts in property acquisition and real estate law; they are not covered here. My approach is broader, and I hope to give the reader the flavor and some understanding of each business rather than a detailed description of how each works.

This book is not a comprehensive textbook on either the real estate or the pension fund industry. It is a series of essays that explores both businesses—a study that describes two, separate business cultures trying to work together for their mutual benefit but having a difficult time because of their many differences. I hope this book helps bridge that gap.

PART ONE

The Pension Fund Business

1 | A NEW SOURCE OF CAPITAL?

One million seconds equals 12 days.
One billion seconds equals 32 years.
> —*letter to the editor*
> Forbes
> *January 5, 1981*

A billion minutes ago, St. Peter had been dead 12 years.
> —*Senator Daniel P. Moynihan (D.-N.Y.)*
> Forbes
> *November 24, 1980*

THE LARGEST FUND

At year-end 1982, the pension fund of the American Telephone and Telegraph Company had $45 billion in assets, making it the largest pension fund in the United States as well as one of the largest pools of capital the world had ever seen. Its assets were greater than those of all but the largest of the *Fortune* 500 industrial companies and it used over 100 investment management firms to run its money.

At this writing, the AT&T fund is on its way into history. As part of AT&T's antitrust agreement with the U.S. Department of Justice, AT&T must spin off its 22 local telephone companies into seven regional companies; the AT&T pension fund must be split up, a process that will begin in 1984 and take several years. Nevertheless, for the purpose of illustration, the AT&T fund can be considered one, huge pension fund and one whose investment practices are typical of those of other large, corporate pension funds in this country.

Depending on the state of the stock and bond markets, the telephone companies' pension assets should grow at a compound annual rate of 8 percent and reach $75 billion by 1990, according to an estimate made by AT&T assistant treasurer David Feldman in June 1981.[1] "I can't see the point where we'd actually be the securities market in this country, because they're growing, too," one of the fund's investment directors once said. "But it does seem that we own 10 percent of everything."

That may be the case in the securities markets, but the fund is far less involved when it comes to real estate. Historically, the AT&T fund and the entire pension fund community have ignored income property investments in favor of stocks and bonds. Of the AT&T fund's $45 billion in assets at year-end 1982, 53 percent were invested in common stock and cash equivalents; and 38 percent were held in intermediate and long-term bonds. Only 7 percent of the fund's assets were invested in the ownership of real estate. Translating these percentages into dollars, the AT&T fund held $24 billion in common stock and cash, $17 billion in bonds, and $3 billion in real estate.[2]

These figures fail to show the fund's shift in investment policy. Historically, the percentage of the fund invested in stocks has varied from 50 to 60 percent of fund assets and the percentage in bonds from 30 to 40 percent. But the percentage of assets the fund holds in income property just increases—from 2 percent of assets in September 1980 to 3.5 percent in 1981 and 7 percent at year-end 1982. From September 1981 to year-end 1982, the amount of money the fund held in property quintupled. In 1980, the AT&T fund held $600 million in real estate investments.[3] Three years later, it held $3 billion. The fund had bought or written mortgages on $2.4 billion of real estate in less than three years.

That $2.4 billion, though substantial, is not that large by the standards of the AT&T fund. In the same period, the value of its common stock holdings increased $7 billion and its bond holdings by $8 billion. Nevertheless, the fund has been making a growing commitment to real estate.

The rest of the pension fund industry showed similar increases in the percentage of assets held in property. The funds were lured by soaring income property values. During the double-digit inflation of 1979 and 1980, real estate far out-performed stock and bond investments. Since institutional investors had become convinced that high inflation would plague the economy for at least 10 years, they became equally convinced that real estate was the ultimate inflation hedge. So they started buying it.

In the case of the AT&T fund, in June 1981 Feldman told *Pensions & Investment Age* magazine that pension funds as a whole would invest 10 percent of their assets in the ownership of real estate by 1990.[4] He predicted funds would "fill the gap" in the real estate market left by insurance companies, which at the time were cutting back on making commercial mortgages. Although he refused to predict what the fund's asset mix would look like in 1990, Feldman predicted that pension funds in general would have 60 percent of their assets in stocks, 25 percent in bonds, 10 percent in ownership of real estate, and 5 percent in international securities.

By early 1983, the AT&T fund held about 7 percent of its assets in real estate. The fund invested primarily through commingled funds: pools of money managed by investment advisors and made up of contributions from different pension plans.[5] Through its investment managers, the AT&T fund also bought property directly for its own account and started doing joint-venture deals with other investors. From no interest in property in 1979, the fund took great interest in it, as did many other pension funds.

At this writing, pension fund interest in property has cooled from the intense levels of late 1981. The recession that began in 1980 depressed property values, and returns fell or leveled off. Other investments showed better returns, in particular, the guaranteed-income contracts, or GICs, offered by insurance companies. These contracts promise a fixed return for three to seven years and in early 1982, GIC rates reached 15 or 16 percent. In late summer of that year, the stock market rallied and pension funds started channeling money into common stocks. At the same time, some pension funds had done so well with their real estate holdings that they had already reached their investment ceiling for that asset, typically 10 to 15 percent of assets.

It could be argued that this drop signaled the end of pension fund interest in property. It had just been a fad and real estate would revert to the investment sideshow it had always been. But if the comments of pension investors themselves are to be believed, this is not the case. They are making a long-term commitment to property.

Referring to an office building the AT&T fund was joint venturing with Coldwell Banker, Feldman told *Pensions & Investment Age* in July 1982 that "what happens over the next 12 to 18 months will not determine whether it is a good investment. It depends on what happens over the next 40 years."[6] This attitude toward property is not uncommon among pension funds although there is no way of knowing if it is the dominant feeling. But if the funds really act this way, they have the potential to become a major force in the income property business.

INVESTMENTS TO DATE

Although pension funds have the potential to become a major force in the real estate markets, they are nowhere near that point yet. In 1980 and 1981, the funds were a well-publicized source of equity and long-term money but only in a small corner of the real estate market—the market for prestigious, new income property that cost more than $10 million and was located in a prime area.

The largest source of money, life insurance companies, increased their purchases of property in 1980 and 1981 but cut back on new mortgage investing, preferring to invest in the short-term bond market with its high rates. By 1982, several large life insurers found themselves pressed for cash and were forced to sell property. This further cut the flow of money to real estate, and pension funds became one of the few sources left. Ironically, most of the money they invested in property at this time was invested through commingled real estate funds—many of which are run by insurance companies.

The pension funds were a well-known source of capital, but they did not invest a great deal of money in property, relative either to the size of pension assets or the size of the income property market. In the summer of 1982, a study by Peter Aldrich of the real estate management firm of Aldrich, Eastman & Waltch; and Richard Kopcke of the Federal Reserve Bank of Boston concluded that pension funds "are hardly even participants in the conventional real estate markets." They had little impact on the income property market, despite the publicity surrounding their investments, the authors wrote.[7]

A survey conducted in the summer of 1982 indicated how active the funds had been in property. The survey of 95 real estate investment companies that handled pension fund accounts showed that as of June 30, 1982, pension funds held only $19 billion in real estate equities, which is pension jargon for owning property.[8] This represents only 2.4 percent of total pension assets, estimated at $808 billion at year-end 1981. It is also a paltry amount, considering the immense size of the income property markets in this country.

Since the overwhelming majority of pension funds that invest in real estate choose to do so through a commingled fund or an investment management firm, this survey, conducted by *Pensions & Investment Age,* covered nearly all property owned by pension plans. It took the funds a long time to reach this level. At the beginning of 1980, the funds held $6.2 billion in real estate equities. In 2½ years, they had bought only $13 billion in income property.

Pension funds also invested in commercial mortgages by buying into commingled funds that wrote only commercial mortgages or hiring an advisor to run an individual account for them. At year-end 1981, they held about $4.5 billion in commercial mortgages.[9] But the plans' direct mortgage holdings were much less than what they held indirectly—through policy reserves at life insurance companies.

Sometimes a pension fund sponsor turns over the investment and administration of his fund entirely to a life insurance company, giving the company full discretion to invest the assets. The money is pooled with the life company's own assets in its own corporate account, known as the general account. At year-end 1981, life insurance companies were running about $186 billion of pension money in their general accounts. Of this money, about 3 percent, or $4.8 billion, was invested in real estate equities and 26 percent, or $49 billion, was invested in mortgages on income property.[10] Through no initiative of their own, pension funds run by insurance companies through their general accounts were important mortgage lenders.

When these general-account holdings are included, at year-end 1981 pension funds held a grand total of 3 percent of their assets, or $24 billion, in real estate equities and 6.7 percent of their assets, or $54 billion, in commercial mortgages. The pension fund industry's total real estate portfolio was $78 billion or 10 percent of fund assets. Although ten cents of every dollar was invested in real estate, only three of that ten were investments made by the plans through their own volition. The rest had been invested by insurance companies through their general accounts.

In contrast, pension funds held roughly 30 percent of their assets in common stocks; 30 percent in corporate bonds; and 30 percent in cash, government securities, and other investments. They held hundreds of billions of dollars in each of these categories, dwarfing their holdings in real estate.

The $78 billion that pension funds have invested in real estate is not a great deal of money considering the financing needs of the income property business in this country. The Aldrich-Kopcke study estimated that the income property business needed to raise $250 billion in long-term financing by 1985. The pension funds, which had bought approximately $13 billion of property in 1980 and 1981 and written roughly $16 billion in long-term mortgages, were hardly acting like financing powerhouses that could rescue the real estate business.[11] What was $29 billion in equity and long-term mortgage money when $250 billion in construction loans were coming due?

The funds are slowly increasing their holdings in property, but it will take them at least 10 years to become substantial participants in the income property markets.

POWER FROM SIZE

As pension funds move into real estate, the real estate business will change to accommodate them; in spite of their small participation in the markets to date, the funds are already starting to have an effect. Their potential impact stems from their sheer size. The funds are big and growing bigger. Fueled by contributions and reinvestment income, funds grow by 8 to 15 percent a year, a growth rate that should continue through at least the end of the century.

At their year-end 1981 value of $808 billion, pension funds had enough assets to buy almost two-thirds of the *Fortune* 500 companies. *Pensions & Investments* magazine called pension funds "the single most potent source of savings and investment in America, growing at $60 billion a year."[12] The amount of money flowing into pension funds is staggering.

There have been a number of models designed to project the total assets of pension funds by the end of the century. One well-publicized model shows that nongovernment, or "private," pension plans will have assets of $2.9 trillion by 1995.[13] Private plans made up only 61 percent of all pension assets at year-end 1981. Total assets for all pension plans should be far higher.

The study was commissioned by the U.S. Department of Labor in 1980 and used historical rates of return to project the funds' "likely" investment performance over the next 15 years. The study's authors also assumed that the economy would show an average real growth rate of 2.5 percent a year. Considering the real growth for the economy during the 1970s was 3.15 percent, this estimate is not unreasonable. If private pension funds do reach $2.9 trillion by 1995, they will own more than half of the country's common stock and one-third of its corporate debt. If they invested only 10 percent of their assets in real estate equities, they would own $280 billion of income property, in addition to the mortgages and property they owned but which were run as part of insurance company general accounts. From their sheer size, pension funds would be a power to reckon with.

LOOKING TO HISTORY

There is a parallel between pension funds' current attitude toward real estate and their approach to common stocks in the early 1950s, according to Meyer Melnikoff, former head of the group pension department at Prudential Insurance Company and now at Goldman, Sachs. The creator of the most successful commingled real estate fund, the Prudential Property Investment Separate Account (PRISA), Melnikoff is considered an authority on pension fund investments in real estate.

He argues that 1980 was the "threshold year" for pension fund interest in real estate, just as 1952 saw pension funds enter the common stock market with the formation of the College Retirement Equities Fund. Until 1952, pension funds held little if any stock, preferring the dependable returns of corporate bonds. But in 1949, the U.S. Supreme Court ruled that the amount of a worker's pension was subject to collective bargaining between union and management.

"Pension fund managers saw that wages would escalate and so would pensions," says Melnikoff. "They were worried about the effect of inflation on pension liabilities, too, so shortly after the Court's decision, they got into common stock."

Today, over 30 years after that historic decision, no one follows the antics of the stock market without considering the impact of these "institutional investors." As funds embrace property, 30 years from now, no one will follow the income property market without considering the funds' behavior.

In 1980, pension funds held common stock equal to 15 percent of the market value of all outstanding publicly traded and privately held stock. They do much of the trading on the New York Stock Exchange and invented "block" trading. In 1965, only 3 percent of all the trades on the New York Stock Exchange were "block" trades, that is, trades of 10,000 shares or more. By 1980, blocks accounted for 26.5 percent of NYSE trading and the percentage continues to rise. A study in the fourth quarter of 1980 showed that institutions, primarily representing pension fund money, accounted for 64.9 percent of the share volume on the NYSE.[14]

Pension funds are stockbrokers' biggest customers; in 1975, the funds were able to force brokers to negotiate their once-fixed commission rates, thus triggering a revolution in the securities industry that is still being felt.

Pension funds dominate the bond market. They held 43 percent of the book value of corporate and private-placement debt in 1980. Funds also developed a taste for U.S. government securities in the 1970s. By 1980, they owned 14 percent of all such securities outstanding, prompting more than one wag to note that the U.S. government could take a big step toward retiring the national debt if it nationalized pension funds.

Melnikoff and many other observers are convinced that real estate is next. Melnikoff is actively marketing real estate products to the funds, but disinterested observers of the pension fund business agree with his prediction: "I am convinced," he says, "that our pension funds will be like the European pension funds. They will hold 20 percent of their assets in real estate, though it may not be in my time."

OVER THE THRESHOLD TO WHAT?

If 1980 was the threshold year for real estate, what does that mean? In 20 years, pension funds will hold more real estate in their portfolios than they do now, and the real estate business will have adapted to its new participants. But how will it adapt, and how will funds choose to invest their assets in property? With pension fund interest in real estate so much in its infancy, it is impossible to draw firm conclusions about how both industries will change. But a few characteristics of these changes are appearing already.

It is probable that there will be fewer, private real estate investors able to compete with pension funds on the purchase of large, prime properties. The funds' competitors do not have and cannot afford to borrow the huge sums needed.

Real estate developers will continually change their operating practices to accommodate the needs of pension investors. Currently, this includes an inordinate preference by the funds for buying property entirely with cash, without a mortgage. Ten years ago, real estate professionals laughed at these all-cash buyers and their plodding ways. At this writing, it is required procedure, largely because the supply of favorably priced, long-term mortgage money has shrunk. Developers have to sell or finance on terms agreeable to pension funds.

A two-tier real estate market is developing. Pension funds and other institutions woo the developers of prime, income-producing properties while the owners of smaller, less-desirable properties struggle to finance and sell their developments.

Pension funds could become real estate developers themselves, taking over existing development companies or creating their own in-house staffs. With their financial clout, pension fund developers could drive the private developer out of business, simply because he had no other easily available source of money. Some British and Dutch pension funds have already done this and are major real estate developers in their own right. British development companies now build for the large pension funds and insurance companies, rather than for their own accounts, as has been customary in the United States. The British institutions simply refuse to lend developers the money to build their own projects.

The British developer was forced into the role of general contractor in the mid-1970s. Soaring interest rates and the real estate depression of 1974 bankrupted many developers and soured institutions on property lending. At the same time, inflation started to climb; since real estate was the only investment that was doing well, institutions decided it was an inflation hedge worth owning. They refused to cut the developers in on the equity. Having no other source of money, he was forced to work for them. Today in Great Britain, only the largest developers do their own deals and manage to retain ownership; the smaller ones are contractors for institutions. A similar trend is starting to appear in the U.S. income property market.

There are many other glimmers of trends and changes, but they are just glimmers. How much effect the pension fund community will actually have on real estate is still only speculation. Nor is it easy to extrapolate from pension fund experience in the stock market to their influence in real estate. The real estate markets in this country differ substantially from any other market in which pension funds have ever been involved.

They are far larger and more diverse than any of the organized securities markets. What's more, few managers of pension fund money have had any experience with real estate investing. They knew a great deal about stock investing before they ever entered that market. In the 1950s, pension funds moved easily into common stocks; a substantial move into real estate will be far more difficult.

THE INVESTMENT HORROR SHOW

In spite of the difficulties, pension funds are being pushed to increase their real estate holdings by one powerful force—the need to improve their long-term investment performance. The 1970s were an investment horror show for the funds, and the 1980s appear likely to generate a similar dismal record.

For the decade of the 1970s, pension funds showed a median, compound, total return on their portfolios of 4.3 percent a year, according to A. G. Becker, Inc., the leading firm tracking pension fund investment performance. The rate of inflation, as measured by the Consumer Price Index, was 7.4 percent a year during the decade; pension funds had a median return, after inflation, of −3.1 percent a year.

By definition, the word "median" means that half the funds bettered this return but half did worse. (See Table 1.1.) It also means that the little old lady in tennis shoes who left her money in a passbook savings account at the local savings and loan for all of the 1970s had a better return on her money than most pension fund investment managers. She at least made 5.25 percent a year. After management fees, they only made 4.3 percent.

The investment return on pension fund money for a longer period brought no improvement over the 10-year figures. For the 15 years from 1965 through 1979, sophisticated institutional investors had a median return of 4.1 percent a year. The annual rate of inflation was 6.2 percent; their real rate of return after inflation was −2.1 percent a year. The 1980s failed to bring relief. Soaring interest rates destroyed the value of pension fund bond portfolios.

Investment statistics can be misleading. Average numbers, like these median returns, mix the giant pension funds with the small and those with huge stock holdings with those holding only Treasury bills. To further explore these dismal, long-term investment records, Becker analyzed them by size of investment manager, size of pension fund, amount of money in the pension fund, investment strategy, and other criteria. They had a big data base to work with: by 1979, Becker was tracking 3,500 pension funds totalling more than $90 billion in assets.

Becker's conclusion was crushing. Over long periods of time, such as 10 or 15 years, most pension funds have the same investment performance—regardless of what they invest in; their size; how often they buy and sell their stocks and bonds; or whether they are managed by banks, independent investment counselors, or insurance companies. In the short term, such as a five-year period, pension funds might outperform the stock market indexes or the rate of inflation; but in the long term, it was futile.

Table 1.1

RETIREMENT FUND INVESTMENT PERFORMANCE 1965–1979

(Compound annual returns, in percentages)

	15 years 1965–79	10 years 1970–79	5 years 1975–79	3 years 1977–79	1979
Median Fund Performance					
Stocks	4.3	3.6	13.9	6.4	21.2
Bonds	4.6	6.8	6.7	2.1	1.4
Cash Equivalents	NA[a]	7.5	7.6	8.2	11.4
Total Fund	4.1	4.3	10.6	4.8	13.1
Market Performance					
Stocks (S&P 500)	5.6	5.9	14.8	5.4	18.7
Bonds (Salomon Brothers)[b]	3.3	6.2	5.8	-0.9	-4.2
Treasury Bills (3-month)[b]	5.9	6.4	6.8	7.6	10.3
Consumer Price Index	6.2	7.4	8.1	9.7	13.3

Reprinted by Permission. *1979 Tax-Free Fund Performance.* © A. G. Becker, Inc., 1980.

[a]Not available.

[b]Bond market returns for years prior to 1969 and Treasury bill returns for all periods shown have been obtained from Roger G. Ibbotson and Rex A. Sinquefield *Stocks, Bonds, Bills and Inflation: The Past and the Future.* Chicago: Financial Analysts Research Foundation, 1977.

In brief, nothing mattered.

In fact, it can be persuasively argued that Becker's conclusions for the 1970s can be applied to any 10- or 15-year period of returns for pension fund money managers. Each year, the firm studies long-term performance and comes to the same conclusion. Though they may do better over three- to five-year periods, the managers simply underperform market averages over the long term.

The 1970s were particularly fraught with traumas for the institutional money manager. No matter what he did during the 1970s, a large percentage of his pension fund clients still had the same poor rate of return.

The ranks of professional money managers are filled with some of the most highly educated and intelligent people in the country. If they could see the 1970s turning into a bad dream, why didn't they make aggressive moves to protect their clients' accounts from inflation?

Some did, but most did not. As will be shown in the next chapter, it would have gone against their grain as institutional investors. Over the long term, the pension business does not reward original thinkers. So money managers waltzed their clients' money among the limited number of moves they could make as "conservative" investors. They shifted their asset mix 10 percent one way or the other between traditionally defined portfolios of stocks and bonds, and they certainly didn't seriously consider investing in real estate, foreign stocks or oil wells.

The real problem with the investment managers of the 1970s was that they all had been investment managers in the 1960s. "Remember," says one, "we came through a generation of money managers in the 1960s where any idiot who was throwing darts at the wall would make money in the stock market. So, if somebody came to him and said he could make seven percent in a real estate commingled fund, he'd tell him he was crazy. The manager was making 30 percent in the stock market."

Unfortunately for all involved, inflation caused the returns on stocks and real estate to reverse in the 1970s, leaving a trail of distraught money managers and pension fund sponsors behind.

A WALK ON THE WILD SIDE

It is an edifying experience to walk through the 1970s as the horrified pension sponsors saw them. Following their good experience in stocks in the 1960s, corporate pension funds had invested as much as 75 percent of their assets in common stock by 1972. They then watched the stock market plummet in 1973 and 1974. By the time it hit bottom, the stocks that funds held in 1972 were worth only 55 cents on the dollar.

Many pension fund managers panicked and sold their stocks at the bottom of the market. They, of course, completely missed the big run-up in the stock market that began in 1975. So they jumped back in in 1976, and the market stopped going up. The stocks in the Standard & Poor's 500 Index, which is a mirror image of most pension fund stock portfolios, went nowhere. By this time, bond yields were increasing because inflation was picking up. So pension funds shifted gears and started loading up on bonds in 1977 and 1978.

Fund managers scratched their heads. Inflation was increasing, but the stock market was not. The old adage that the stock market was a hedge against inflation was not working. In fact, pension funds were losing money by holding stocks in the 1970s.

James Lorie, a professor at the University of Chicago Graduate School of Business, argued that stocks were no longer an inflation hedge in the 1970s for three reasons: company profits did not grow fast enough to outpace inflation; effective, corporate tax rates increased sharply during the decade; and stocks carried a risk premium relative to bonds.[15] All three acted to push stock prices down.

Lorie found that the stock market did worse during the 1970s than during the decade of the Great Depression. Between the end of 1969 and the end of 1979, the value of common stocks on the New York Stock Exchange declined by about 42 percent. From the end of 1929 through 1939 the market fell only 31 percent. If a pension fund had invested in all the stocks listed on the New York Stock Exchange in 1969 in proportion to their initial value and then reinvested all the dividends, it would have had an average annual rate of return for the decade, adjusted for inflation, of −1.5 percent a year.

"When stock market historians look back upon the 1970s," Lorie wrote, "they are likely to refer to what happened during that decade as the Great Crash."

Pension fund sponsors wondered if stocks were still a hedge against long-term and steady inflation. Perhaps stocks only did badly when inflation was accelerating, as it did in the late 1970s. This theory stumbled in late 1979 and 1980 when the stock market took off on what the *Wall Street Journal* called "one of the headiest runs in the last several years"—just when inflation accelerated into the double-digit range.[16]

Fund managers responded by pouring money into the stock market in 1980 and 1981, but they were baffled and shaken. Common stocks were supposed to insulate a portfolio against inflation, and bonds were the vehicle for safe, steady income. But the high and extraordinarily volatile interest rates of 1979 and 1980 were killing off the value of bond portfolios, and the stock market proved that it and the rate of inflation often walked radically independent paths. In the pension community, the feeling grew that their guidelines for conservative, prudent investing simply no longer held. It is a fear that continues to grow.

How can a fund sponsor pay pensions that are tied to wage levels if the pension fund can't make a decent rate of return on its portfolio? A sponsor must protect the fund from inflation or contribute ever-increasing amounts of money to keep it financially sound. Out of desperation, fund sponsors started to explore untraditional pension investments.

The experience of the few funds that did have real estate holdings enticed their pension colleagues. The handful of real estate investments offered for pension funds by banks and insurance companies outperformed the efforts of stock managers in the 1970s. Stock portfolios run by banks for pension clients were up a total of 61.1 percent for the decade, while bank-run commingled real estate funds were up 131.5 percent. Many of these pooled funds were not even organized until the middle of the decade.

It was actually fortunate timing. The mid-1970s were absolutely the best time to buy property in years. The commingled funds picked it up at the bargain prices that prevailed following the 1973–74 real estate collapse. When income property ran up in value in the late 1970s, the commingled funds showed big returns. The result was a definite pickup in pension fund interest in real estate, an interest that continues to grow today.

THE PENSION FUND UNIVERSE

Knowing that pension funds hold 3 percent of their assets in real estate equities is much like knowing that, on average, the year-round temperature in Chicago is 59 degrees. It doesn't help on the day it's five below zero or 95 above.

The pension fund industry is not some $808 billion titan lumbering at a steady gait through the capital markets but a collection of different types of plans. Anyone who wants to do business with pension funds must learn these distinctions; they affect the plans' attitudes toward real estate investing.

The first immediate qualifier is that not all funds that are listed as pension plans are true pension plans. Roughly $70 billion in assets belong to profit-sharing funds. A profit-sharing fund will only pay retirees what is in their accounts at the fund when they retire. The retirees collect only what has been contributed to the fund by themselves or their employer, plus the investment results credited on such contributions. Hence, profit-sharing plans are called "defined-contribution" plans.

A true pension plan, on the other hand, will pay retirees fixed, monthly benefits when they retire, regardless of what has been contributed to the fund. The retirees' pensions are based on the average of their pay over the last five to ten years before retirement. Because benefits are fixed, pension plans are often called "defined-benefit" plans.

Some plans have elements of both defined-contribution and defined-benefit plans; others are clearly one or the other. Most have similar investment strategies, in spite of the different nature of the benefits they pay. Sometimes, all types of pension and profit-sharing plans are grouped under the heading "employee benefit funds" or "tax-exempt funds"; except in highly unusual circumstances, pension funds pay no taxes on their investment income. In this book, unless noted otherwise, the terms "pension funds" or "pension plans" will be used to refer to all pension and profit-sharing plans set up by corporations, government bodies or unions.

The term does not include the millions of Individual Retirement Accounts (IRAs) and Keogh plans that individuals and self-employed persons set up for their own retirement. The problems of these plans are beyond the scope of this book. Most IRA and Keogh accounts are small and capable of investing only $5,000 to $10,000 in property. They have no other choice but to invest through publicly offered real estate syndications or private syndications arranged by their tax lawyers. The problems of real estate syndications and these tiny investors differ from those of pension funds with $50,000 or more to invest in property.

Beyond the simple distinction between defined-benefit and defined-contribution plans, there is a whole taxonomy of pension plans based on the organization that set them up, that is, "sponsored" the fund, and how the fund's investments are managed. (See Table 1.2.)

Private Pension Funds

Pension plans sponsored by corporations or by joint trusts of labor unions and corporations are the largest sector of the pension industry. Such plans had $495 billion in assets as of year-end 1981 and made up 61 percent of all pension fund assets.[17]

These pension plans are also commonly known as "private" pension plans, to distinguish them from "public" funds, which are sponsored by state and local governments. Private pension plans are further divided by how they are administered and their funds invested. $186 billion of private pension funds were "insured" in 1981, meaning their assets were invested and benefits paid entirely by a life insurance company. The qualifier, "insured," does not mean that the retirees' benefits are insured, nor does it have anything to do with the Employee

Table 1.2
SIZE OF PENSION FUND ASSETS BY TYPE OF PLAN
(year-end 1981)

Insured private pension funds	$186 billion ⎫	$495 billion
Non-insured private pension funds	309 billion ⎭	
State and local government pension funds	225 billion	
U.S. government employee pension funds	87 billion	
Railroad Retirement Funds	1 billion	
TOTAL	$808 billion[17]	

SOURCES: *Flow of Funds Accounts: Assets and Liabilities Outstanding 1957–80,* Division of Research and Statistics, Board of Governors of the Federal Reserve System, September 1981, pp. 27, 31.

Flow of Funds Accounts, Second Quarter 1982—Annual Revisions, Division of Research and Statistics, Board of Governors of the Federal Reserve System, September 1982, p. 25.

Life Insurance Fact Book (1982), American Council of Life Insurance, pp. 50, 51.

NOTES: Common stock holdings included at year-end market value, corporate bond holdings included at book value.

Insured figure includes $6 billion in IRA/Keogh plan money. Other categories do not include such accounts.

Retirement Income Security Act (ERISA). Insured pension funds are simply those managed entirely by insurance companies.

Pension funds run by any other type of money manager or run in-house are called "non-insured" pension plans. Most pension sponsors hire outside managers, typically banks and money management firms, to run their funds' assets. Life insurance companies can also be hired to invest part of a pension fund's assets. Under such conditions, they are considered outside money managers.

The non-insured, corporate pension funds are the leaders of the pension industry when it comes to trying out new investments—or rather their investment managers are. The money managers talk the funds' trustees into trying new investments or hiring consultants to analyze their portfolios. The funds, which held $309 billion in assets in 1981, are often the only subjects of research studies purporting to investigate "the pension fund industry." The reasons are simple. Because they are funds that try new investments, corporate plans have investment strategies that are more interesting than those of public funds; more data exists on corporate plans than on any other sector of the pension fund community, both from the government and their own consultants. Private pension plans, both insured and non-insured, are the only plans covered by ERISA, which requires them to file reports on their investments.

On the whole, private, non-insured pension plans are the best-managed funds, and it is their sponsors who have the most interest in real estate. Greenwich Research Associates conducts an annual survey of the pension investing practices of the nation's largest corporations.[18] Of the more than 1,000 corporations it surveyed in 1982, Greenwich found that more had invested in real estate than ever before: 37 percent had invested in real estate equities compared to 35 percent in 1981, 22 percent in 1980, and only 10 percent in 1976.

The greatest enthusiasm was coming from the largest funds, those with assets of more than $500 million. Of these funds, 72 percent had invested in real estate equities by 1982, compared to 70 percent in 1981 and 54 percent in 1980. Interest faded as fund size decreased. Sixty-two percent of funds with assets of $251 million to $500 million held real estate investments during 1982. But only 18 percent of plans with assets between $16 million and $20 million held property. The 1982 Greenwich study also showed that though the number of corporate pension plans investing in real estate was increasing, it was increasing at a slower rate than in previous years.

Most pension funds that invest in property do so through commingled funds. In 1982, returns on these pooled funds dropped from the 16 percent levels they had shown in 1981 to below 10 percent. Nevertheless, the number of corporate pension plans that started to invest in property increased slightly. Even if corporate pension funds cut back on their real estate investing, it is unlikely that they will ever stop investing entirely.

Public Pension Plans

The pension funds of state and local governments or "public" pension funds make up the other large segment of pension fund assets. In 1981, these funds held $225 billion, or 28 percent of all pension assets. They are less interested in real estate than private plans, though some of the largest public funds are starting to invest.

It is important to understand which funds are considered part of the "public fund" universe and which are not. Public funds include only the pension funds of employees of city and state governments and the employees of agencies of these governments, such as the local sewer district or water works. They also include the pension funds of police, firefighters and teachers.

Public fund statistics do not include the $87 billion which made up retirement funds for federal employees in 1981 or the $1 billion in funds of the Railroad Retirement System. (Table 1.2.) The railroad system is a quasi-government pension fund and a category unto itself, as is the federal employee retirement system. The reader is not missing much by not considering these funds' investment strategies. The railroad funds make up only a small percentage of the assets in pension funds, and most of the federal employees' pension funds are invested with a considerable lack of imagination: they hold only Treasury securities. The federal government guarantees that those pensions will be paid so fund assets do not need to be well-invested.

Nor are the assets of Social Security included in any discussion of public pension funds, partly because the government refuses to label it a pension system, but largely because Social Security has no assets. Social Security is funded on a pay-as-you-go basis, a method of pension funding that ERISA forbids private funds to use. With such funding, the money moves from the pockets of contributors to Social Security directly into the hands of retirees. The stray billions that appear as the system's assets are really just cash that will be paid out shortly as benefits.

The quality of administration and investment management for public pension funds varies more widely than for private funds. Generally, public funds are considered the poor cousins of the pension industry. Those state and local government employees who manage the funds are paid less than their counterparts in private industry. The funds are often backward in their investment practices, both because they are hamstrung by statute in how they can invest and because of their proclivity to take the low bidder on everything they buy, including investment expertise. Public fund sponsors often try to bargain over investment management fees; some of the most successful money managers, who can afford to be picky, will not solicit their business.

There is no ERISA requiring sponsors of public funds to fund their plans, stick to a specific vesting schedule, and promise pension benefits they know they can afford. Understandably, they do not; many smaller funds have not had an actuarial study in years. Public pension funds are notorious for increasing pension benefits to employees without computing the cost. They improve early retirement or give retroactive increases in pensions, using a funding schedule that is not professionally accepted by actuaries and inadequate to pay the promised benefits. Some funds pay larger pensions than their retirees made in salaries while they were working.

Automatic cost-of-living adjustments on pensions are rare among private retirement plans; the costs of indexed pensions are unpredictable and high. This has not stopped some of the public pension funds from indexing their pensions to the Consumer Price Index, though on rare occasions they are forced by fiscal reality to rescind such a lavish benefit. This is difficult to do.

In 1980, the citizens of Los Angeles voted to cancel the automatic cost-of-living adjustments the city paid on pensions to its police and firefighters. The voters had approved the adjustment in 1971, basing it on the Consumer Price Index, but in 1979, when the CPI in the Los Angeles region soared 17.5 percent, everyone had second thoughts. The mayor claimed the adjustment would bankrupt both the city and the $780 million police and firefighters fund, particularly since the fund held 80 percent of its assets in bonds and cash. The fund had had a compound annual rate of return of 5.66 percent for the previous nine years, but the CPI in Los Angeles had compounded at 7.59 percent for the same period. Additionally, Proposition 13 had cut tax income to fund the plan.

The plan was labeled a "fiscal time bomb" and a city councilwoman went aloft in a gas balloon to publicize the soaring cost of pensions. She should have stayed aloft. Although the public voted to limit the adjustment in November 1980, the police and firefighters successfully maneuvered to preserve it. A year after the referendum, the cost-of-living adjustment still flourished. It was not until June 1982 that the voters were able to cap it by imposing a 3 percent limit on benefit increases. To do so, they had to vote to amend the city charter.

For at least 10 years, there has been talk about a law like ERISA that would cover public pension funds and hold them to the same strict financial accountability that their private counterparts endure. But the talk has gone nowhere. It could take another 10 years before a public-fund ERISA—a PERISA—is passed in even a watered-down form. Some observers believe it will take the collapse of a major public fund system before these funds are taken to task for their behavior. It took the bankruptcy of Studebaker and its failure to pay its pensions that finally turned ERISA into law after years of talk.

Congress is reluctant to meddle in the affairs of state and local governments, and the public fund administrators are strongly opposed to PERISA, although many worry about their funds and privately talk about "the crisis" in public plan funding. They would prefer that the state rather than the federal government do something about public pension fund regulation.

If catastrophe occurs in the public fund area, Congress may be forced to move and pass a PERISA with teeth. This might occur sooner than we think, according to a 1980 study of public funds conducted by the General Accounting Office.[19] The GAO found that under present funding practices, the financial condition of public funds is "likely to deteriorate." A major problem is that the ratio of retirees to workers is increasing, and with it the cost of funding the plans.

The GAO also found that, as in the case of the Los Angeles fund, fiscal irresponsibility is not confined to small-town plans. Although large public funds were generally better funded when viewed as a whole, there were wide differences among them, and some had serious problems. The GAO concluded that the few, fully funded public plans would remain healthy, but the numerous poorly funded plans could expect financial difficulty in this century.

The largest public pension systems range in quality of management from the exemplary retirement system of the state of Kansas to that of the state of Arizona where the system's best investment managers resigned in late 1980 when the state cut investment fees. The Arizona system suffered an earlier embarrassment when the chairman of the board of trustees was found to be stealing money from his employer, the Diocese of Tucson.

The $2.6 billion Illinois Teachers' Retirement System was managed and invested almost entirely by one bank in the state capital, the Springfield Marine Bank, for 42 years. The fund was the bank's entire trust department. In 1980, for example, the bank reported to Money Market Directories that it managed $2.45 billion in tax-exempt assets for 210 clients.[20] One client, the state teachers fund, had a $2.2 billion account at the bank, and the other 209 clients had an average portfolio of $1.2 million each. Giving an essentially rural bank a $2.2 billion portfolio to run was not the wisest investment strategy.

A study commissioned by the governor found that the teachers fund had had an average annual rate of return of 5.4 percent for the five years through June 30, 1981 when other funds across the country averaged an 8.6 percent return. A second study showed that the plan was dramatically underfunded. The governor pressured the fund to clean itself up by threatening to balance the state budget by cutting pension contributions.[21] The trustees were finally persuaded. In July 1982, they took much of the money away from Springfield Marine and gave it to seven other managers.

With such an approach to fund management, it is no surprise that many large public funds manage their portfolios badly. Often it is not the fault of the fund administrator, who is a government employee in charge of overseeing the fund. Local politicians view the pension fund, its administrator, and its investment managers as pawns in their political wars. Fund assets are moved from manager to manager, based on the whims of the current clique in power.

Other funds are severely limited by state and local laws as to what they can invest in. Some are forced to invest in what they would normally avoid. The New York City funds were forced to buy the bonds of the Municipal Assistance Corporation in the 1970s to save New York City from bankruptcy. This is an extraordinary example, but other cities require their pension funds to hold tax-exempt municipal bonds as a matter of course. Pension funds are exempt from income taxes; with municipal bonds, the funds receive a return below that paid on taxable corporate bonds in exchange for tax-free income the funds do not need.

In 1980, the New York Employees Common Retirement Fund, then the fifth-largest of all pension funds, was still prohibited by state law from owning real estate with a partner. This restriction greatly frustrated Madelon Talley, who was then chief investment officer of the $13 billion fund. "We want equity," she complained.[22] The fund did not want the risk of investing in real estate on its own, so the state law "prohibited us from one of the best investments in the country, commercial real estate," she said.

Mrs. Talley should have been grateful. At least the New York Fund was permitted to hold 20 percent of its assets in common stock. Until late 1980, the $4 billion Florida State Retirement System was prohibited by state law from holding more than 10 percent of its assets in common stocks. In 1979 and 1980, when bond values crashed and inflation took off, the Florida State Retirement System had 84 percent of its assets in fixed-income securities, primarily corporate bonds. The Florida legislature acted, and as of this writing, the fund now can invest up to 40 percent of its assets in common stock; it can also invest in real estate equities. The fund had no plans for how it would handle real estate. It will be interesting to see if they botch the job as badly as they have handled their other investments. The Florida fund is a political football, and the average tenure of investment directors there in recent years has been measured in months.[23]

If public pension funds mishandle their stock and bond investing, the bread-and-butter holdings of the pension business, how sophisticated will they be in their real estate investments? Some are even forbidden by law from investing in commingled real estate funds, which are the principal vehicles pension funds use to invest in property.

Many public funds will never consider income property investments. They are too conservative or restricted by law to do so. Ironically, though, when it comes to investing in home mortgages, there is a great deal of activity in public fund circles. At this writing, growing numbers are being forced by local politicians to make below-market home mortgages to government employees or state residents, or to engage in other poor-paying "social investments" in real estate.

This is not real estate investing; it's coercion. Politicians placate the voters or some other constituency by having the pension fund make them loans. It is only coincidental that such loans involve real estate, and for many public funds this is as far as their "real estate investing" will ever get.

The Asset Mix

Given the differences in management style between public and private, non-insured pension funds, it is not surprising that they have different attitudes toward investing. Public fund sponsors are more traditional, heavily weighting their portfolios with bonds and other fixed-income securities. They do so either from their natural inclinations or, as we have seen, because of restrictive state and local laws. Private funds hold far heavier concentrations of common stock. In fact, public and private pension funds have allocated their portfolios among stocks, bonds and cash equivalents in almost exactly opposite ways. They have, in pension fund jargon, different "asset mixes."

At the beginning of 1981, private, non-insured pension funds held 59 percent of their assets in stocks and 20 percent in corporate bonds. (See Table 1.3.)

Table 1.3
HOLDINGS OF PRIVATE, NON-INSURED PENSION FUNDS
(year-end 1981)

	$ billion	percentage of total assets
Total Assets	$309.3	100.0
Demand deposits and currency	2.0	
Time deposits	12.1	
Corporate equities	183.1	59.2
Fixed-income (i.e., debt)	105.5	34.1
Treasuries	30.6	
Agencies	9.3	
Corporate bonds	61.7	19.9
Mortgages	3.8	1.2
Miscellaneous	6.6	

SOURCES: *Flow of Funds Accounts: Assets and Liabilities Outstanding 1957–80,* Division of Research and Statistics, Board of Governors of the Federal Reserve System, September 1981, pp. 27, 31.

Flow of Funds Accounts, Second Quarter 1982—Annual Revisions, Division of Research and Statistics, Board of Governors of the Federal Reserve System, September 1982, p. 25.

NOTE: Common stock holdings included at year-end market value. Fixed-income included at book value. Figures do not add up due to rounding.

Public funds held roughly the reverse: 23 percent of their assets in common stocks and 46 percent in corporate bonds. (See Table 1.4.)

Because public funds favor fixed-income securities, they have always had an interest in commercial and residential mortgages, which they view not as real estate but as bonds. Public funds held 5.6 percent of their assets in mortgages at the beginning of 1982. Although this is not substantial, it is still more than the 1.2 percent of assets in mortgages held by private, non-insured funds. Neither public nor private, non-insured funds owned enough real estate to even have the category, real estate equities, included in their breakout of assets, shown in Tables 1.3 and 1.4 from the Federal Reserve System.

Insured pension funds, on the other hand, own more real estate and hold more mortgages than any other class of fund. (See Table 1.5.) At the beginning of 1981, the funds held 26 percent of their assets in mortgages and 2.6 percent in real estate equities. But, as noted earlier, they are the most aggressive of pension real estate investors by default. They have no control over how their assets are invested since they have turned them over in their entirety to a life insurance company. The life company pools the money with its own corporate assets in the general account.

At this point, a more detailed explanation of insurance company terminology is in order since insurance companies dominate pension fund investing in real estate.

For years, life insurance companies pooled assets from all sources into one,

Table 1.4
HOLDINGS OF PUBLIC PENSION FUNDS
(year-end 1981)

	$ billion	percentage of total assets
Total Assets	$225.4	100.0
Demand deposits and currency	4.6	
Corporate equities	51.5	22.8
Fixed-income (i.e., debt)	169.3	75.1
Treasury Issues	27.0	
Agencies	21.7	
State and local obligations	4.2	
Corporate bonds	103.7	46.0
Mortgages	12.7	5.6

SOURCES: *Flow of Funds Accounts: Assets and Liabilities Outstanding 1957–80,* Division of Research and Statistics, Board of Governors of the Federal Reserve System, September 1981, pp. 27, 31.

Flow of Funds Accounts, Second Quarter 1982—Annual Revisions, Division of Research and Statistics, Board of Governors of the Federal Reserve System, September 1982, p. 25.

NOTE: Common stock holdings included at year-end market value. Fixed-income included at book value.

huge account—the general account. But in the 1960s, the companies started offering new insurance products, such as variable annuities. These annuities were backed by a common stock portfolio, and the annuity payments depended on the performance of the underlying stock. The law limited the amount of common stock the general account could hold, so insurers had to set up a new account, called a separate account, to fund these new annuities. All the assets of the separate account could be invested in common stock.

Insurance companies found that separate accounts had other uses. In the 1960s, the companies started marketing their services as investment managers to pension funds. A fund could hire the insurer to run an individual stock or bond account for it, just like it would hire any other investment manager. The insurer would then set up a separate account for the client's money.

Insurance companies eventually began using separate accounts to pool the stock and bond portfolios of their smaller clients or to allow clients to invest in "special investments," like direct bond placements or real estate. Pension funds that wished to invest only 1 or 2 percent of their assets, or several million dollars, in real estate could do so through a special separate account. These accounts were just like the pooled funds run by banks and other investment managers for their pension clients; all were considered commingled funds.

The largest commingled funds that invest in real estate today are separate accounts run by insurance companies such as PRISA, run by Prudential Insurance; Separate Account Number 8, run by Equitable Life; and the Real Estate Separate Account (RESA), managed by Aetna Life.

Table 1.5
HOLDINGS OF PRIVATE, INSURED PENSION FUNDS
(year-end 1981)

	$ billion	percentage of total assets
Total Assets	$186.3	100.0
Demand deposits and currency	1.5	
Corporate equities	17.1	9.2
Fixed-income (debt)	150.2	80.6
Treasury issues	2.9	
Agencies	5.1	
State and local obligations	2.6	
Foreign Government and International Agencies	3.6	
Corporate bonds	69.6	37.4
Mortgages	48.9	26.2
Policy loans	17.5	
Real estate equities	4.8	2.6
Miscellaneous	12.9	

SOURCES: *Flow of Funds Accounts: Assets and Liabilities Outstanding 1957–80,* Division of Research and Statistics, Board of Governors of the Federal Reserve System, September 1981, pp. 27, 31.

Flow of Funds Accounts, Second Quarter 1982—Annual Revisions, Division of Research and Statistics, Board of Governors of the Federal Reserve System, September 1982, p. 25.

1982 Life Insurance Fact Book. American Council of Life Insurance, Washington, D.C.

NOTE: Common stock holdings at year-end market value. Fixed-income holdings at book value. Above breakout of pension reserves is based on the percentage breakout of the total assets of life insurance companies at year-end 1981. Excludes pension assets in real estate equity and mortgage separate accounts, but includes pension assets in other separate accounts. Figures do not add due to rounding.

A Top-Heavy Industry

In 1982, there were more than 500,000 private and 6,000 public pension plans in the United States. They ranged in size from the $45 billion AT&T pension fund to the $50,000 funds of small-town police departments across the country. But the largest public and private funds dominate the pension fund industry, and they get the most attention from marketers and suppliers of real estate investments.

The pension fund business is top-heavy. The 1,000 largest public and private pension funds had $622 billion in assets in the fall of 1982, according to a survey by *Pensions & Investment Age*.[24] At this writing, a figure for the assets of all pension funds in 1982 was unavailable. But in 1981, the top 1,000 funds held $519 billion or 64 percent of the entire $800 billion in pension assets in that year.[25] The percentage for 1982 should be similar or even larger. Because of employer contributions and appreciation of their assets, the top 1,000 funds grew by $103 billion, or 20 percent, from 1981 to 1982.

The 200 largest pension funds cut an even more impressive swath. In the fall of 1982, they held $469 billion: 127 held assets of $1 billion or more. Again, a 1982 figure for total pension assets is not available, but in the fall of 1981, the 200 largest funds held 55 percent of all the assets of public and private pension funds. Their assets equaled those of the 16 largest *Fortune* 500 industrial companies in 1981.[26] More than 3.2 million people worked for those 16 giant companies, but it took only several thousand to manage the money for the top 200 pension funds: administrators, money managers or an in-house investment staff, and a battery of clerks processing monthly retirement checks.

In the fall of 1982, the 200 largest pension funds consisted of 67 public, 117 private, and 10 union or jointly trusteed plans; also included were six miscellaneous funds belonging to the United Nations, the World Bank and various churches. The infamous Teamsters Central States Pension Fund, with its $3.7 billion in assets, is a constant member of the top 200, ranking number 26 in 1982. The Teamsters fund long had the dubious distinction of being the pension community's most aggressive real estate investor. In the mid-1970s, the fund held about 80 percent of its assets in real estate, much of it in property allegedly controlled by organized crime.

The Teamsters fund held the mortgages on several Las Vegas casinos, including Circus Circus and Caesar's Palace, and the mortgage on the building housing the IRS in Austin, Texas. The fund's typical strategy was to lend on some risky venture and then be forced to foreclose when the borrower defaulted. In this way it acquired, among other properties, a hotel in the Virgin Islands, an ice rink in Las Vegas, a truck stop in Michigan, boat slips, a defunct pail factory in New Mexico, vacant condominiums, and a cemetery. Under pressure from the U.S. Departments of Labor and Justice, the fund's real estate holdings were cut from 80 percent of assets in the late 1970s to 12 percent in the fall of 1982. With 10 percent of its assets in mortgages and 2 percent in real estate equities, the fund's asset mix now resembles that of a public pension fund.

Including Teamsters Central States, 105 of the 200 largest pension funds owned real estate totaling about $12 billion. The pension funds that owned the most property were the AT&T fund with an estimated $2 billion, the Ohio Teachers Retirement System with $809 million, and the Exxon Corporation fund with $564 million. Of the 200 largest pension funds, 68 held mortgages totaling $23.7 billion. The figure includes both commercial and residential mortgages and offers no insight into how active the funds were in commercial mortgage lending.

The 200 largest pension funds are a formidable force in the capital markets, but the 10 largest pension funds are investment empires unto themselves. As AT&T assistant treasurer David Feldman once said of the fund, "Whatever the securities market is, I think we're it." Since the largest of the large funds have the most money and staff to seriously invest in real estate, it's instructive to look at their current real estate holdings in detail. (See Table 1.6.)

Even in these rarified regions, the real estate investment trends hold. The corporate pension funds concentrate on owning property. The public funds invest primarily in mortgages.

Of the 10 largest pension funds, corporate plans held 2 to 6 percent of their assets in equity real estate and little if anything in mortgages. Only General

Table 1.6

REAL ESTATE HOLDINGS OF THE 10 LARGEST PENSION FUNDS
(September 30, 1982 Estimates)

Fund	Total Pension Assets	Percentage in Equity Real Estate	Percentage in Mortgages	Total Assets in Real Estate
AT&T/Bell System	$40.1 billion	6[a]	NA	$2.4 billion
New York State Common Retirement	17.0 billion	0	16	2.72 billion
New York City Systems	16.0 billion	0	1.0	160 million
General Motors	13.8 billion	3.0	0	414 million
California Public Employees	13.5 billion	0.6	22.1	3.1 billion
New York State Teachers	10.0 billion	NA	13	1.3 billion[+]
General Electric Company	7.4 billion	3.0	13	1.2 billion
Texas Teachers	7.3 billion	0	3.1	226 million
California State Teachers	7.3 billion	0	23.4	1.7 billion
IBM Corporation	7.0 billion	2.0	0	140 million

SOURCES: *Pensions & Investment Age Magazine*, January 24, 1983, "Profiles: The top 200;" and January 18, 1982, "Profiles of the top 200 employee benefit funds." New York State Common Retirement Fund, "The Fourth Annual Analysis of Common Retirement Fund Investments as of March 31, 1982."

NOTES: "NA" means the fund did not report this holding to the magazine, so total real estate assets are most likely understated by a small amount—hence, the "+" after these funds' total real estate asset figures.

Assets of savings plans are not included since they can be withdrawn by plan participants at any time and the participants can often choose how they want the money invested. Savings plans rarely invest in real estate. Only pension and profit-sharing assets are listed here.

[a]Includes both equity real estate and mortgages.

Electric's pension plan had a significant amount of mortgage holdings, most of which were landsale-leasebacks on income property leased to high-quality tenants. The large public funds were substantial mortgage lenders, but held little if any of their assets in equity real estate. The public funds are both commercial and residential lenders. In the fall of 1982, the New York State Common Retirement Fund held $2.7 billion or 16 percent of its assets, in mortgages. Of those mortgages, about 80 percent were conventional mortgages on commercial income property.

The California Public Employees and Teachers Retirement Systems are two of the country's largest holders of residential mortgages, with a combined mortgage portfolio of $4.7 billion in September 1982. The systems are the largest buyers of single-family home mortgages in the state of California. Until mid-1981, the California system held only $5 million in real estate equities, consisting of the land under some of its mortgage holdings.

The law forbids many public funds from owning property. Others prefer mortgages to equity real estate investments because mortgages are easier to make and involve no property management. The California system is the only one of the largest public funds to change its investment strategy and buy property. In 1981, the system hired an investment advisor and announced that, over time, it would invest 5 percent of its assets in real estate equities. The fund had committed its first $75 million by March 1982, and in July of that year announced it would acquire another $600 million in income property either directly or by using convertible mortgages. In its move to own real estate, the California system is an exception in public fund circles, although a few funds are starting to express interest in ownership.

Pension funds of all types will continue to increase the amount of money they invest in real estate, but the real estate community should not overestimate what the funds can do for them. Pension fund sponsors have some peculiar ideas about property investing.

NOTES

1. Clare Minick, "Three sponsors peer into 1990," *Pensions & Investment Age* (June 22, 1981), p. 45.

2. AT&T Public Relations Department, telephone conversation, February 11, 1983.

3. "$472 billion in top 1,000 funds," *Pensions & Investment Age* (January 19, 1981), p. 16.

4. Minick, "Three sponsors," p. 45.

5. Note on terminology: The term "commingled fund" is used throughout this book to denote any pool of money made up of contributions from individual pension funds: the money is held in trust and run by an investment manager or general partner. The manager of the fund is always a fiduciary under the general law of trusts, but may not be subject to the fiduciary standards of the Employee Retirement Income Security Act (ERISA). The pension plans in the commingled fund are always passive investors and have no control over how the money is invested.

Technically, only pooled funds run by banks are "commingled funds." Insurance companies run "separate accounts," investment managers run "group trusts" or "real estate investment trusts," and general partners run limited partnerships. But everyone in the pension industry lumps them all under the name "commingled fund."

6. Steve Hemmerick, "AT&T, Coldwell joint venture in L.A.," *Pensions & Investment Age* (July 19, 1982), p. 1.

7. Mark Westerbeck, "Banks face potential realty crisis," *Pensions & Investment Age* (September 13, 1982), p. 3.

8. "Real Estate Advisor Profiles," *Pensions & Investment Age* (September 13, 1982), p. 23.

9. Ibid. *P&IA* shows pension fund commercial mortgage holdings at $16 billion. This number includes mortgages run in some insurance company general accounts. The number used here is the sum of the mortgage holdings of the individual real estate advisors. It excludes general account holdings. Although the statistics are dated June 30, 1982, they should be close to those of December 31, 1981, since pension fund interest in real estate slipped in early 1982.

10. American Council of Life Insurance, *Life Insurance Fact Book (1982)* (Washington, D.C.: American Council of Life Insurance, 1982), pp. 5, 53, 68, 87. These numbers are derived from data on the pages listed above. Pension reserves, exclusive of assets in mortgage and real estate separate accounts, make up about 35.9 percent of insurance company general accounts. General accounts held $136.3 billion in commercial mortgages and $14.4 billion in real estate equities. Therefore, pension funds invested through the general account held $48.9 billion in mortgages on income property and $5.2 billion in real estate equities.

Life company asset figures include assets of separate accounts (p. 87). The assets for real estate and mortgage separate accounts were deducted from total asset figures for real estate and mortgages (p. 68) in order to arrive at the holdings in the general account alone.

11. The amount of money put out in long-term mortgages by pension funds in these two years is underestimated. To my knowledge, accurate statistics do not exist since data is only collected for funds that invest in mortgages through general accounts at insurance companies.

Insurance company data is provided by the American Council of Life Insurance, *Life Insurance Fact Book (1982)*, p. 71. The Council lists new investments made by life companies by year and investment category.

Data on the mortgage activity of private and public pension funds during 1981 has been collected by the Board of Governors of the Federal Reserve System and printed in its *Flow of Funds Accounts, Second Quarter 1982, Annual Revisions* (September 1982), p. 25. The Flow of Funds numbers only show changes in outstanding balances on pension fund investments at the end of each quarter. The numbers do not show acquisitions and so they underestimate pension fund activity in mortgages. In spite of the underestimate, and with the exception of pension funds invested through insurance company general accounts, pension funds are not a significant source of long-term, commercial mortgage money.

12. Advertisement for *Pensions & Investments* (July 7, 1980). *P&I* used its own estimate, based on numbers computed annually by the U.S. Securities and Exchange Commission. (*Pensions & Investments* was the earlier name of *Pensions & Investment Age*).

13. Les Stern, "$2.9 trillion in pension assets by 1995," *Pensions & Investments* (June 9, 1980), p. 1.

14. "NYSE trading by plans doubled in four years," *Pensions & Investment Age* (December 7, 1981).

15. James H. Lorie, "The Second Great Crash," *The Wall Street Journal* (June 2, 1980), editorial page.

16. Charles J. Elia, "Stock Market Scored One of its Headiest Runs in Several Years in First 9 Months, Data Show," *The Wall Street Journal* (October 2, 1980).

17. Estimates of pension assets, particularly those of private pension funds, are notoriously inaccurate. The Securities and Exchange Commission and the Federal Reserve Board each analyze pension assets and investment data using numbers collected by the SEC and various trade groups. But the Fed and the SEC analyze the data differently; their results are incomparable in some categories.

The data collected by the SEC appears to be incorrect. In 1981, the Labor Department double-checked SEC data for 1979 by going over its own reports—the Form 5500s that private plans are required to file with the department. The DOL reviewed forms filed by 37,500 plans and found that the SEC had underestimated private pension plan assets by $100 billion. In 1979, total private plan assets should have been $386 billion, not $286 billion.

Another study of pension data, conducted by Salomon Brothers in early 1982, concluded that the SEC data was so inaccurate that relatively little could be determined about the holdings and activities of the funds.

I use the year-end 1981 figures for pension assets computed by the Federal Reserve Board in September 1981 and 1982. Statistics on insured plans are from the *Life Insurance Fact Book* (1982) published by the American Council of Life Insurance. The Fed and the Council provide the most up-to-date and complete statistics on pension assets currently available. At this writing, the Fed has not adjusted its data to take account of the $100 billion in extra private pension assets discovered by the Department of Labor's study. Private pension assets should probably be $595 billion instead of $495 billion, and total pension assets closer to $908 billion than $808 billion. Pension assets are likely to top $1 trillion by 1983.

18. Linda Sojacy, "Real estate was hottest investment field in 1981," *Pensions & Investment Age* (December 21, 1981), p. 15, and "Greenwich releases corporate plan study," *Pensions & Investment Age* (January 10, 1983), p. 9.

19. "Financial woes hurt public plans," *Pensions & Investments* (March 17, 1980), p. 4.

20. *Money Market Directory (1981)* (Charlottesville, Va.: Money Market Directories, 1980), p. 626.

21. Linda Savage Ruhe, "Illinois Teachers fund reallocates its assets," *Pensions & Investment Age* (July 7, 1982), p. 2.

22. Daniel Hertzberg, "New York State Pension Fund Director Plans Fundamental Shift in Investing," *The Wall Street Journal* (July 22, 1980).

23. Neil Cavuto, "Bailey resigns; cites 'political interference,'" *Pensions & Investment Age* (July 6, 1981), p. 3.

24. "Top 1,000 fund assets surge to $622 billion," *Pensions & Investment Age* (January 24, 1983), p. 1.

25. "Profiles of the top 200 employe [sic] benefit funds," *Pensions & Investment Age* (January 18, 1982), p. 11.

26. "The 500 Largest Industrial Corporations," *Fortune* (May 3, 1982), p. 260.

2 | LIFE IN THE SLOW LANE— INVESTING PENSION FUND MONEY FOR A LIVING

> In selling real estate to pension funds, you tend to run into what the Catholic Church calls "invincible ignorance." They talk and talk with you, but won't do a thing.
>
> *—a real estate manager for pension funds*

> The trouble with pension funds is that half of them think real estate is the bond business; the other half think we're all crooks.
>
> *—another real estate manager for pension funds*

"INVINCIBLE IGNORANCE"

Real estate people unfamiliar with pension funds are often confused by what they view as the strange behavior of fund sponsors. For example, a corporate pension officer will spend tremendous amounts of computer time and his own energy analyzing real estate strategies for his fund. He'll meet with representatives of real estate firms, dine with them, and ask dozens of questions.

He and his board of trustees will agree with the logic of all the arguments for real estate investments. But when the discussion turns to initial investment, fees to the manager, and timetables for cash disbursements, the pension officer stops returning phone calls. Finally, he tells the real estate company that the board has pulled him off the real estate project: for the next six months, he is doing an in-depth analysis of bond immunization techniques. If he is a young man, when the real estate company calls him back later, they find he has been replaced with a fresh-faced but similar young man with an MBA from the same East Coast school. His predecessor has gone on to marketing in the pet food division, and this one knows nothing about real estate.

And the whole process starts from scratch again.

Or real estate people will read in *Pensions & Investment Age, Institutional Investor,* or one of the other pension magazines that a large fund is looking for a real estate manager; the fund wants to develop properties for its own portfolio. One developer actually called the pension officer who made numerous such statements in the trade press. He asked the pension man what projects his fund was considering. It turned out the pension officer only had authority to buy passthrough securities issued by the Government National Mortgage Association ("Ginnie Mae").

When faced with such situations, most real estate people wonder if pension funds are run by unbalanced men or if they themselves did something wrong. Assuming that the real estate ideas or products were worthy and their presentations clear and well-reasoned, why should so many fund trustees agree at first and then become indifferent? Why do funds behave aggressively and then retreat?

The problem is that procrastination and second-guessing are built into the way pension funds invest their money. Corporations supposedly conduct their business to maximize their profits. Pension funds conduct their affairs to minimize their chances of being sued by an angry plan participant. This is a big difference; it is the chief reason pension officers behave so strangely.

How did it ever get to the point where such a giant pool of capital was managed with such a perverse investment goal in mind? Surely, investing money to avoid lawsuits is not the most profitable use of that money, either for the companies sponsoring pension plans or the participants who will collect their pensions from that fund. What happened?

MONEY WITHOUT A MASTER

One of the major causes of this situation is that no one really knows who owns the money in pension funds—the organization that sponsors the fund or the people who will collect their pensions from it. The fund is a trust that must be run only for the benefit of the plan participants. The pension money they receive when they retire is definitely theirs—once they retire. But if ownership of an asset is defined as having control over it, then plan participants do not own the fund, and neither do the companies that sponsor and pay into it. From the day a worker is covered by the plan to the day he retires and actually collects his pension, there is a large gray area of confusion.

A number of books and articles have come out since the mid-1970s, arguing either that pension funds are owned by their participants or should be controlled more directly by the union whose members' pensions they fund. Peter F. Drucker, the well-known business consultant and professor of social science at the Claremont Graduate School in California, wrote a well-publicized and thoughtful book on the subject in 1976. The book was entitled *The Unseen Revolution: How Pension Fund Socialism Came to America*. In it, Drucker argued that because pension funds own at least 25 percent of all outstanding common stock, and the stock funds the employees' pensions, the employees own the stock. Therefore, they actually could control many corporations if they wished; the United States is actually the first truly Socialist country in the world because the workers own the means of production.[1]

The AFL-CIO and several individual unions are pushing for more worker control over pension fund assets, reasoning that since the assets fund their pensions they must be their money. Other groups argue that pension funds should be invested for "social purposes," which usually means a purpose the group making the charge finds politically useful but that probably won't have much of an investment return. A favorite complaint is that a state pension fund is not investing enough in small companies doing business in that state. Rhetoric about "social investing" is usually leveled at public pension plans and infuriates the funds' administrators.

Most fund sponsors take a dim view of arguments for worker control or social investing, especially when their companies and governments pay tens of millions of dollars into pension plans annually. In their view, the fund is not some pool of deferred salary payments belonging to the workers and set aside for their retirement. The typical sponsor attitude was once voiced by an administrator of the Bell system pension funds: "The money in our pension fund belongs to AT&T." But if it was absolutely clear whom the money belonged to, such arguments would not flourish. Critics may charge General Motors or U.S. Steel with not investing their company's money for social purposes, but no one will question who actually owns those companies. The stockholders do. No such clear-cut line exists in the pension community.

All pension fund assets are required by law to be invested "solely for the benefit of the plan participants." A plan participant can sue the fund's trustees if he thinks the fund is being invested imprudently. But if he would rather see the money for his pension invested in stocks instead of bonds, he has no power or right to enforce his wishes on the plan sponsor. Because he has no control over how fund assets are invested, a participant does not "own" any pension assets, although he "owns" the right to a pension. Some profit-sharing plans do give participants two or more choices as to how their accounts can be invested and will pay them the money in their accounts under certain rigid conditions. But no defined-benefit pension plan permits a participant to take the money out of his account any time he desires to buy a new car or home.

On the other hand, the organization sponsoring the pension fund does not own the money either: it is held in trust for the benefit of the participants and the sponsor is the fund's trustee. Although he can hire another trustee to invest the money, the sponsor is still ultimately responsible for the plan's financial health. He is a fiduciary charged by law with carefully husbanding the resources of the fund until its participants retire and collect their benefits.

If the sponsor really thinks the fund could make a fortune investing in operating oil wells off Venezuela, he probably would not make the investment. For some compelling reasons, that is not the kind of investment trustees make, as we will see shortly. Like the participants, the sponsor does not really control the fund's investments in the sense that he has complete discretion to invest them the way he wishes. Because he lacks total control, he doesn't own the assets either.

In stable economic periods, it makes little difference to the health of the fund's portfolio who owns the assets. The trustee can make money for his charges by sitting still and buying high-quality bonds and other traditionally conservative investments. But in difficult and inflationary times like our own, such trust arrangements are disastrous for the fund's financial health. An investor must change his whole attitude about investing when inflation runs at 12 percent instead of 2 percent. He must move quickly, take risks, and perhaps make investments he would not have touched only five years before. Most trustees appear incapable of such flexibility. Although their job is to guard and invest their fund's assets, they are more concerned with showing how responsible they are as fiduciaries than how shrewd and adroit they are as investors. The trustees make their investment decisions by committee and the natural conservative bent of their committees restrains them from making drastic changes in investment direction, even when they should be made.

Neither plan sponsors, trustees nor plan participants own the pension fund, in the sense that they have total control over how it is invested. So no one behaves like an owner. No one makes the difficult decisions, the decisions to invest the fund in something radically different, and then takes the responsibility if it does not work out. No trustee can make these decisions and still feel comfortable with "the prudent man rule," the ultimate touchstone and guide to pension fund investing.

THE WORLD OF PRUDENT MEN

Pension fund sponsors are "fiduciaries," or caretakers of the plans' assets. For private plan sponsors, this is a heavy burden. Under ERISA, they can be held personally liable for any breach of fiduciary responsibility regarding the plan. If a company's director of marketing behaves foolishly and loses a fortune for his company, he can be protected from the stockholders' wrath in the courts because the corporation is legally liable for his actions. He may only lose his job. But if the pension fund officer invests pension money and disregards his role as a fiduciary of the fund, the courts can go after him personally. His house, car and children's college money are at stake. Understandably, plan sponsors are quite concerned with what the proper duties of a fiduciary are, particularly in how the funds' assets should be invested.

Under ERISA, Section 404(a)(1), the federal government spelled out how fiduciaries of pension plans should conduct themselves in the investment world: They should "discharge their duties solely in the interest of the participants and beneficiaries of the plan."[2] The plan assets should be invested only to provide benefits to pensioners and defray administrative expenses. Fund investments should be diversified to "minimize the risk of large losses."[3] The plan sponsor may delegate the investment of his funds to outside money managers, who then also become fiduciaries of the fund under the law.

Section 404(a)(1) also describes how a fiduciary approaches any investment. He must invest the money "with the care, skill, prudence and diligence under the circumstances then prevailing that a prudent man acting in a like capacity and familiar with such matters would use in the conduct of an enterprise of like character and with like aims."[4] In pension circles, this is called "the prudent man rule." But just how would a "prudent man" invest his money? According to this definition, he would invest it with the care and diligence that other prudent men in the investment business would invest it. A prudent man invests like a prudent man. The definition defines nothing.

So pension sponsors diligently follow the dictates of the prudent man rule. They carefully, diligently and with great skill handle the investment of their pension fund money by investing it the same way all the other, supposedly prudent, pension fund colleagues invest their money. Unless a substantial number of these other pension fund sponsors invest in antique porcelain, old coins, or real estate, neither will the prudent pension fund sponsor. Instead, he will follow the herd. The prudent man rule explains the fund sponsor's near obsession with not wanting to be the first fund to make a new type of investment. If no one else is doing it, there is no certainty that it is a prudent investment.

The U.S. Department of Labor, which is charged with interpreting and enforcing the prudence clause of ERISA, has attempted to give fund sponsors some guidance about what it all means, but the results are far from satisfying. At this writing, the department's major accomplishment is a 1979 regulation stating that each individual investment in a pension portfolio does not have to be ruled prudent for the fund's portfolio to be considered prudently run. Just because a certain investment is riskier than the traditional blue-chip securities trustees normally buy does not automatically mean the investment is imprudent, the department said. The asset should be judged only in the context of the role it plays in the overall portfolio. If the fund buys the stock of a small new company rather than that of blue-chip companies, the investment "may be entirely proper under the Act's prudence rule," the department said in the regulation.[5]

On the surface, this makes sense. A billion dollar pension fund should not be restricted to investing all its money in traditional and prudent securities with mediocre returns. It could help the fund's overall investment performance if it held a small percentage of risky and unusual assets that could potentially make a big return for the fund.

But what does this prudence regulation really mean to the fund sponsor? Unfortunately, it is not helpful. The regulation does not tell him if his fund should be the first to invest in antique cars or venture capital situations. The Department of Labor refuses to rule on whether specific investments are prudent or not, claiming "no such list could be complete."[6] That is certainly true. What the regulation really means is that a fund sponsor can make an untraditional investment. But if he's challenged on it by a plan participant, he has no idea what the Labor Department, or the courts, might rule. The investment may or may not be prudent and appropriate, but no one will tell him if he made the wrong choice until after the fact.

The well-intentioned regulation is counterproductive in a perversely subtle way. Before, a pension sponsor could stick to traditional, blue-chip stocks and not feel too badly about their mediocre returns: that was just the type of investment trustees made. Now, he feels guilty if he is not out "studying" some new investment, even though he is as confused as ever about whether it belongs in his portfolio under the prudence rules.

Being rational men, fund sponsors respond by trying to share as much of the responsibility for investing fund money with outside money managers as they can. If they hire a well-known, institutional money manager that other large, well-known, and prudent fund sponsors have hired to run their money, they will be deemed prudent fiduciaries themselves. If the manager's investments do poorly, that is not as important as the fact that the fund sponsor behaved prudently by hiring him in the first place.

This attitude explains why pension funds have waited in line to get into real estate commingled funds run by the Prudential Insurance Company or the Equitable Life Assurance Society rather than give their money to equally competent but less well-known real estate money managers. Equitable and Prudential are the two largest managers of pension fund money in the country. Fund sponsors do not know how to judge the competence of other real estate managers, so they give their money to the large, well-known advisors. "No one could fault a pension fund for giving money to the Pru," salesmen of other less-blessed commingled funds often complain.

The necessary implication of the prudent man rule is that making money for the pension fund is far less important than behaving like other pension fund sponsors. This atmosphere hardly generates exciting or profitable investment ideas. It also explains why fund sponsors could stomach the poor performance records of their well-respected pension fund managers in the 1970s. Everyone else had similar records.

Pension sponsors, particularly corporate fund sponsors, seem to care more about their investment performance relative to other pension funds than they do about earning a real rate of return on their portfolios. This appears to be the case even though sponsors know their investment performance significantly raises or lowers their pension costs. Instead of concentrating on aggressively protecting their funds from inflation, pension officers are more concerned with having an investment record equal to or slightly better than that of the average pension fund of their size and asset mix. That is why a fund sponsor could actually be pleased with a 5.5 percent compound annual return for the decade of the 1970s. The median pension fund performance for the decade, as computed by the A. G. Becker Company, was 4.1 percent.[7] Therefore, the fund of the sponsor in question had "excellent" performance compared to his colleagues. Fund sponsors also measure the prowess of their managers by comparing the performance of their stock portfolios against the performance of the stocks in the Standard & Poor's 500 Index. Most pension fund stock portfolios are almost exact copies of the conservative holdings in the S&P 500; following the index is a good proxy for following other funds' stock performance.

An entire industry of "performance monitoring" has grown up around the measurement of pension fund investment returns. Pension funds pay millions of dollars in consulting fees each year to find out in excruciating detail how much better or worse they did than "the universe" of funds that had their size or asset mix. As one real estate manager for pension funds pointed out, "These fund sponsors would rather have long-range plans, charts and graphs than money in the bank. The big institutional money management firms, like Equitable and Prudential, play to that love of numbers." The funds' investment managers and plan sponsors do not compete with the inflation rate to get a real rate of return on their portfolios. They compete with each other in an investment fantasy world of their own making. The fund sponsor may pontificate about the importance of an investment return that betters the rate of inflation, and he really believes it. But his eye inevitably focuses on what his neighbor is doing.

"What's the incentive of any agent of a pension fund to be aggressive in his investments?" a former banker who ran pension fund money says. "If he follows the pack, he's got a rate of return between x and y that his principals, who are his customers, deem acceptable. If he makes more for them, his principals will think he's lucky. But if he makes less, he'll get kicked."

"Pension fund officers," this man concludes, "are in the mistake-avoidance business. They're so afraid to make mistakes, they don't do a very good job representing the funds."

For a pension officer, to do a superior job is to be given a pat on the back; to do a bad job is to be fired; but to do a mediocre job is to be given peace, quiet and job security. What kind of men (there are few women in the business) are attracted to such a role? What do their corporate employers think of them? The answer is, unfortunately, "not much."

THE SECOND-CLASS CITIZEN

Many presidents of major U.S. corporations have worked their way up through their own company's ranks. Some come to the top job after careers in marketing, manufacturing, or finance or after running the company's largest overseas subsidiary. But no one who has spent most of his career primarily running the pension fund has ever become president of a major corporation. If the president came up from being chief financial officer, he undoubtedly spent time running the pension fund when he was an assistant treasurer. Typically, that was years before when he was being rotated through the treasurer's office.

The pension officer slot is a low-level job. But there's more to it than that. According to Stephen Gross, a principal of the pension consulting firm, Evaluation Associates, pension officers are almost second-class citizens.[8] It's unlikely that someone who stays in such a job for more than several years could ever land the top job.

"I am convinced," the ex-banker quoted in the previous section says, "that no one really cares about the pension fund. It's just money for a bunch of laborers who need it when they retire." Managing money for "a bunch of laborers" simply pales when compared to heading a marketing program for a new product or working on the firm's next corporate acquisition. There, an executive can be aggressive and win recognition from top management. The pension officer wins recognition from no one, unless he is unlucky enough to get involved in some lawsuit for breach of fiduciary responsibility or to show an investment return on the fund that underperforms other funds. Then, he will get dark stares from his boss. For the most part, there is little glory in pension land.

The actual investment of the fund's assets is usually handled by outside investment managers, but at home, the fund is directed by the old and sleepy or the young and inexperienced. The older pension officer has sat in his job for years and is going nowhere: he is just resting until retirement. The young officer is usually fresh out of an MBA program and wants to get out of the job as quickly as possible and on to something more exciting. Time at the pension fund is just one stop in his training. Managing the pension fund is not, as Gross says, "a clearly defined future management path for bright people."[9]

The pension officer is a low-ranked employee in the treasurer's office and may or may not have a staff to help him with the fund. He may be called an assistant treasurer, a director of investments, or a pension fund supervisor, but his duties are the same. He tracks the fund's current investments and plans what it should do with future cash flow. He studies all the different consulting, record-keeping and evaluation services available to see if any of them can be used. He talks to the money managers and lets them know what the trustees expect out of them. If the money managers are inept, he must tell the fund's board of trustees and begin the elaborate and time-consuming search for new ones. Every month or quarter he must brief the trustees, who are usually top executives in the company, about the status of the fund's portfolios and what he thinks should be done. Then he and his staff get to do it, under management's ever-critical eye. Management views the pension fund as a bleeding sore on the corporate body, one that can never be healed. They are not naturally sympathetic to a pension officer's pleas that more money should be spent on investment, evaluation and supervision of the fund.

The pension officer handles only fund investments. Another employee, usually working in personnel, will handle benefit payments and claims. He will bear the title "benefits manager" or "administrator," and sometimes will be a woman. The benefits manager rarely talks to the pension officer or may have never met him, though one handles cash coming in and the other cash going out of the same pool of money. This is a slipshod way to manage a pool of assets that may drink up an annual pension contribution from the sponsoring company of as much as 20 percent of pretax profits a year.[10] The pension fund can cost as much as the chemical plant the company decided to build in Houston after months of corporate soul-searching. The plant gets man years of attention. The pension fund gets none.

"It is inconceivable to us how management, by neglect or design, fails to recognize this huge absolute and relative cost," says Gross.[11] He concluded that top management must not be aware of how much the pension fund actually costs. Otherwise, they would give the pension officer the same real authority and status as other corporate officers who are responsible for 20 percent or more of corporate earnings. So far they have not. The pension officer can be overruled by anyone on the board of trustees or anyone above him in the treasurer's office. His hard-won conclusions about investment strategy for the fund, made after months of study, will be thrown out the window. DeMarche Associates, a pension fund consulting firm, captured the flavor of the situation exactly in a Christmas card they once sent to their clients. The cover of the card was a sketch of a pension officer sitting at his desk, which was buried under piles of reports. His boss stands in front of him and says: "Forget the asset mix project. The chairman's barber just convinced him to go 100% bonds."

Needless to say, a man who can be overruled by the chairman's barber is not well-paid compared to the earnings of other corporate officers who control similarly expensive projects. Top management really views the pension officer as a clerk. Gross decided management does so because "a misconception still exists that, like death and taxes, nothing can be done to change the inexorably increasing pension cost."[12] All you need is someone to keep track of how much money has been thrown away on it already. This view of the pension fund and its staff is not universal, says Gross. Each year more firms wake up to the true cost of pensions. But for the most part, he says, this attitude of indifference prevails.

Consequently, the pension officer feels little pressure to cut pension costs or seek out new investments. Management does not particularly care, so why should he? He can spend long hours filling out government forms required by ERISA, monitoring money managers, and keeping track of his portfolio's dividend payment dates. He can also go to lunch with all the salesmen of investment management firms trying to add his fund to their stable of clients. Constant streams of such salesmen flow through the office of a pension officer each year; the attention they lavish on him, the first line to the all-powerful fund trustees, is the only "perk" the pension officer gets. In his quiet corner, he can also explore all the new, untraditional investments that investment managers pitch him, such as real estate, financial futures, stock options and venture capital programs. He knows his board of trustees is incapable of quick decisions and does not particularly care about innovations in pension management, so why not? Learning when there is no pressure to put it to use can be a pleasurable experience.

"People running pension funds just love to talk to you whether you're talking about options or real estate," says one exasperated pension sales manager for a large life insurance company. "They'll sit and talk to you forever, because it's a whole new element of their jobs, a new learning process." The typical industry meeting for pension officers reflects this attitude. A great number of the presentations deal with untraditional investments, investments that the sales manager just cited calls "sideshows that get more attention than they're worth." But no pension officer wants to miss the latest fad. "Of all pension assets, 85 percent are invested in publicly traded securities," the sales manager says. "But everybody already knows everything about stocks and bonds."

Eugene B. Burroughs, director of investments for the International Brotherhood of Teamsters, scolded his pension fund compatriots on their fickleness, in a speech to the 1980 annual meeting of the International Foundation of Employee Benefit Plans. "It's no longer prudent just to shovel money into an investment simply because it is considered safe," he said. "Everyone is talking about what a great investment real estate is but only 1 percent of the total pension assets in this country are invested in real estate," he said. "Why? Inertia. It's easier to talk about it at a cocktail party than it is to really make a commitment."[13]

It is also easier to talk with the sales representative of a firm that manages investments like stock options as opposed to real estate. The stock-options salesman looks like the men the pension officer deals with at other investment management firms. He is selling a product that is a security and is traded on public exchanges. Even though the two men are discussing an investment new for the fund, they feel comfortable with each other because they talk the same language.

Pension officers and real estate people, on the other hand, do not talk the same language, although they often use the same words. For example, take the word "leverage": it has a good connotation for real estate people. A leveraged piece of property is one with an attractive mortgage on it, which means that the owner will make a better return on his own cash in the project than if he had built or bought the entire project with only his own money. Leverage means you can borrow money to make money and that is good.

Pension officers instinctively cringe at the word. To them, "leverage" conjures up visions of selling common stock short, that is, borrowing stock in order to sell it. The short-seller then hopes the price of the stock will fall so he can buy it back for less than he sold it; he then pays back his borrowing and pockets the difference as profit. Now, that is risky. Relative to short-selling, writing a mortgage on a well-run property is much less risky. But pension people do not make that distinction. Going short is bad; therefore, all leverage is bad.

Pension fund officers also feel uncomfortable with people in the real estate business because real estate firms have not had a tradition of investing pension fund money. A limited circle of money management firms runs pension assets. There is an easy two-way street between them and pension funds, and the staff from one regularly finds jobs in the other. In our analysis of pension culture, it is worthwhile to take a brief look at the world of traditional money management.

THE MONEY MANAGERS

The Players

The business of running pension fund money for corporations, unions and governments is a complicated and sophisticated one that can only briefly be touched on here. But it is worth some comment, not only because pension officers and their money managers often switch places, but because these investment advisory firms are the real catalysts of the pension fund business. They dream up new investments, package them, and send salesmen on the road for two years to sell them to their pension fund clientele. The investment advisors created all the products and investment techniques pension funds now use in real estate; real estate people should have at least some sense of who their competition is.

According to *Pensions & Investment Age,* which conducts an annual survey of money managers, more than 600 firms managed pension accounts in the United States at year-end 1982.[14] The money management industry is even more top-heavy than the pension business. The 200 largest pension funds held about 55 percent of all pension assets, excluding those of federal plans. But the top 200 money managers ran 91 percent of all the tax-exempt money that pension sponsors had managed by the 604 surveyed advisors.[15] (See Table 2.1.)

The 604 managers polled by *P&IA* ran $770 billion of pension, endowment and foundation money in 1982, of which the vast majority was pension money.[16] Assuming pension funds had at least $900 billion in assets in 1982, money managers ran nearly 85 percent of all pension assets, with the remainder run in-house by the funds themselves or belonging to the federal government's pension plans.

Money managers also run endowments for universities and charitable foundation money. Much of the $60 billion in endowments and foundations is run in-house by the organizations themselves, but if it is managed by outsiders, it is managed by the largest advisors. Like pension funds, foundations and endowments do not pay income taxes on their investment income, and all three are often lumped under the heading "tax-exempt assets." Their money managers are consequently known as "tax-exempt advisors."

Pension sponsors favor the largest tax-exempt advisors. These large advisors watch their accounts multiply, not only because they sign on new pension clients, but because the money they already manage is essentially reproducing itself: a

Table 2.1
INVESTMENT MANAGERS GROUPED BY TOTAL TAX-EXEMPT ASSETS
UNDER MANAGEMENT
(year-end 1982)

Managers ranked from:	Average tax-exempt assets managed by each firm		Total tax-exempt assets managed by this group
1 – 10	$20.9 billion		$208.5 billion
11 – 100	4.3 billion	$593.3 billion[a]	384.8 billion
101 – 200	1.1 billion		108.7 billion
201 – 604	0.2 billion		68.0 billion
		Total	$770.0 billion

SOURCE: *Pensions & Investment Age,* April 4, 1983; pp. 1, 24.
NOTES: "Tax-exempt assets" include all pension fund, endowment fund and charitable foundation assets. There was approximately $60 billion in endowments and foundations at year-end 1982.
[a]Includes an estimated $40 billion in foundation and endowment assets and $553 billion in pension money.

large pension account generates a large cash flow from its investments which, in turn, the advisor automatically reinvests. Money begets money with a vengeance in this business. The more pension money an advisor runs, the more attractive he will look to potential clients, regardless of his investment record—compliments of the prudent man mentality.

Who are these tax-exempt advisors?

They are banks, life insurance companies, and privately owned, independent counseling firms. As shown in Table 2.2, of the 100 largest money managers, banks run more tax-exempt money than either of their two classes of competitors. Historically, banks have served as trustees for all types of personal and corporate accounts; it is only natural they would manage and serve as trustees for pension funds. It is also considered good business to give a corporation's major lenders a piece of the pension fund to manage. Since ERISA, this practice has died down, but it still exists.

The life insurance companies are the monoliths of the tax-exempt investment business. Seven of the 10 largest pension managers in the country are life companies. Prudential Life and Equitable Life between them ran nearly $60 billion in pension fund money at year-end 1982. (See Table 2.3.) Although there are only 18 life insurance companies listed among the top 100 pension advisors, the average amount of pension assets run by each is more than twice that run by the average of the 43 largest bank money managers. Certain life insurance policies and deferred annuity contracts are really pensions, and life companies have been involved in the pension business since its infancy.

Independent investment advisors are the third category of tax-exempt money managers, and they make up in numbers what they lack in accounts. Of the 604

Table 2.2
100 LARGEST MANAGERS OF TAX-EXEMPT MONEY
(year-end 1982)

Investment Manager	Number of firms	Average Assets Per Firm	Tax-Exempt Assets Managed
Commercial banks[a]	43	$5.1 billion	$218 billion
Life insurance companies[b]	18	11.2 billion	201 billion
Independent advisors	39	4.5 billion	174 billion
Total	100		$593 billion[c]

SOURCE: *Pensions & Investment Age,* April 4, 1983.
NOTES: "Tax-Exempt Assets" include assets of pension funds, endowments and charitable foundations.
[a]Includes commercial banks, trust companies and affiliated managers.
[b]Includes $25.1 billion in assets of Teachers Insurance Annuity Association/College Retirement Fund. TIAA/CREF is a unique insurance company that invests retirement assets for teachers, academics and the employees of certain non-profit institutions.
[c]Includes an estimated $40 billion in foundation and endowment assets and $553 billion in pension money.

Table 2.3
10 LARGEST MANAGERS OF TAX-EXEMPT MONEY
(year-end 1982)

Investment Manager	Tax-Exempt Assets Under Management
Equitable Life Assurance Society of the United States	$32.6 billion
Prudential Life Insurance Company of America	27.4 billion
TIAA/CREF[a]	25.1 billion
Aetna Life & Casualty Company	23.9 billion
Metropolitan Life Insurance Company	21.1 billion
Morgan Guaranty Trust Company	19.3 billion
Bankers Trust Company, New York	18.8 billion
Travelers Insurance Company/TIMCO	14.3 billion
Alliance Capital Management	13.2 billion
CIGNA Corporation	12.7 billion
Total	$208.5 billion

Reprinted by Permission. *Pensions & Investment Age,* April 4, 1983, "The nation's leading advisors," p. 1. © Crain Communications.

NOTES: "Tax-exempt assets" include pension fund, endowment fund and charitable foundation assets. There were approximately $60 billion in endowment and foundation assets at year-end 1982.

Total does not add due to rounding.

[a]Teachers Insurance Annuity Association/College Retirement Equity Fund. A unique insurance company that invests retirement assets for teachers, academics and the employees of certain non-profit institutions.

investment advisors in the pension business, 421 are independents; they dominate the list of money managers on the low end of the asset scale. Most of the 199 advisors who run less than $100 million in tax-exempt money are independents. The independents range in size from the largest private manager in 1982, Alliance Capital Management of New York, to dozens of small firms such as Noddings, Calamos & Associates, Chicago. Alliance is the ninth largest pension manager in the country, running $13.2 billion in tax-exempt money in 1982 with 35 portfolio managers in several offices. Noddings, Calamos ran $38 million in pension money with four portfolio managers working out of one office in Chicago.

Unlike banks and insurance companies, the names of independent investment counselors are not household words anywhere but in the pension community. To acquaint the reader with some of their names, Table 2.4 lists the 10 largest independent firms. With the exception of Fayez Sarofim and Batterymarch Financial, the top 10 firms are established, traditional counseling firms with a long history of managing pension portfolios. The Sarofim and Batterymarch firms are

Table 2.4
10 LARGEST, INDEPENDENT MANAGERS OF TAX-EXEMPT MONEY
(year-end 1982)

Firm	Tax-Exempt Assets Managed
Alliance Capital Management Corporation New York	$13.2 billion
State Street Research & Management Company Boston	10.1 billion
Jennison Associates Capital Corporation New York	9.0 billion
Chase Investors Management Corporation New York	8.5 billion
Fayez Sarofim & Company Houston	8.5 billion
Batterymarch Financial Management, Inc. Boston	7.9 billion
Loomis, Sayles & Company, Inc. Boston	7.5 billion
T. Rowe Price Associates, Inc. Baltimore	7.1 billion
Scudder, Stevens & Clark New York	6.6 billion
Brown Brothers, Harriman & Company New York	5.8 billion

Reprinted by Permission. *Pensions & Investment Age,* April 4, 1983, Page 56, © Crain Communications.

NOTE: "Tax-exempt assets" include pension fund, endowment and charitable foundation assets.

tributes to how high-powered marketing and good investment records can pull an unknown operation to the top in five years, whereas with the other firms, it has taken decades.

For the most part, the men who work in middle-level pension investing jobs at banks, insurance companies and independent firms are understated and cautious, just like their pension officer counterparts. The management firm makes its investment decisions by having an investment committee draw up a list of 100 to 300 stocks and a number of bond issues they deem acceptable for pension clients. All portfolio managers must then build their portfolios from securities on that list; most pension portfolios look alike at any given firm, and usually the differences in portfolios among firms are equally small.

Portfolio managers are often intelligent and highly educated: many hold law degrees or graduate degrees in finance from good business schools. They are usually older, 38 to 50 years of age, leading to what pension consultant John Casey calls "a generation gap" in money management.[17] During the 1970s, the poor performance of the stock market and the merger or dissolution of many brokerage firms frightened young business school graduates from Wall Street careers. And as of this writing, they have not yet started to return.

Portfolio managers have a great talent for numbers. Some of the best were once engineers or computer systems analysts. All can provide pension officers with the computer-printout sheets and fancy graphs of investment performance the officers love. Using performance monitoring jargon, heavily laced with terms like "Bayesian-adjusted betas," the man in charge of client relations at any decent money management firm can demonstrate that even if it appears his firm has had a poor investment record over the last five years, they have actually had a superb record recently. They were "in the top Becker quartile," as the jargon goes, for the most recent nine months, six months or quarter.

A Fee Business

Money management is a fee business with compensation figured as a percentage of the market value of assets under management. Fees are computed on a sliding scale; the more money a pension client leaves with a manager, the smaller a percentage of assets he pays as a fee.

Some independent money management firms charge as much as 1 percent of assets a year to run a portfolio, and some banks will charge as little as 0.2 percent or less on the amount of an account in excess of $100 million. That 0.2 percent still comes to a $2 million fee on a $1 billion portfolio. That fee may not cover all the expenses the manager charges the client: securities trading costs are absorbed by the client's account, as are some administrative costs.

The rule of thumb for the break-even point for a traditional investment operation is $100 million of assets under management, although this varies depending on factors such as the manager's fee structure, the number of portfolio managers, and the amount of investment research the firm carries on. Some managers prosper on $10 million of pension fund accounts while others closely watch costs until they top the $250 million mark. Beyond the break-even mark, managers enjoy efficiencies of scale. It takes as many portfolio managers to run $400 million as it does $200 million; the firm may have to add only one more professional manager when it passes the $800 million mark. Money management is not a capital-intensive business. All a young, independent firm needs is an office, a telephone to call stock and bond traders, and some computer terminals to keep track of the market and run analyses of their own portfolios.

Consequently, money management can be lucrative. The partners in successful, independent money management firms can become millionaires. Their portfolio managers will make $75,000 or $100,000 a year—twice or three times what a corporate pension officer makes. Banks and insurance companies pay more in line with typical pension officer salaries. But at higher levels, they pay more, too.

Big fees and big salaries are clear incentives for money managers and even clearer signals to pension fund officers, particularly those of large funds. Many sponsors realize that if they use their own pension staff, they could probably do as good a job as an outside manager and save the management fees. Surveys show that funds run in-house have an investment record similar to that of funds run by external managers, but administrative costs are lower because in-house staffs have fewer professionals and no overhead. The telephones and desks are already there.

Pulling money in-house requires a big effort and a commitment from upper management to cut pension fund operation costs, a commitment, as we've seen, missing from many U.S. companies. Nevertheless, in 1982, 121 of the 200 largest pension funds ran $199 billion of their money in-house.[18] The U.S. Steel and Carnegie Pension Fund, for example, has run its $5.4 billion portfolio in-house for years. Each year, more plans join it.

Splitting the Fund

Over the last 10 years, the trend among plan sponsors has been to split the management of the fund's assets among several, specialized money managers in an attempt to diversify the fund and to improve its investment return. Today, a sponsor will hire a number of common stock managers, a bond manager, and perhaps one or two all-purpose managers, or "balanced" managers, who run both stocks and bonds. To this basic collection, a larger fund will add managers that run portfolios of international stocks, stock options, real estate or some other unusual investment.

To date, splitting the fund's management has not helped long-term investment performance. As mentioned in chapter 1, A. G. Becker's long-term performance figures show that over 10- or 15-year periods, most pension funds experienced the same investment performance, regardless of whether they were managed by banks, insurance companies, independent firms or a combination of all three. From the long-term viewpoint, it makes little sense to switch managers at all, unless they are dishonest or totally inept. Few are. But plan sponsors continue to fire their old money managers and hire new ones every three or four years. Most sponsors believe they can improve a fund's investment record by doing so.

Often, a sponsor will dismiss a manager because he has a poor two- or three-year investment record. The fund will then hire an advisor with a good record for that period or one with a strategy that is the latest style in pension circles. Ironically, the newly appointed manager will often sign on just before his investment performance starts to deteriorate. Pension officers joke that they should dismiss all managers who have had strong records over the last two years; it must be time for their luck to sour.

A manager can be dismissed because the board of trustees needs a scapegoat for its own mismanagement of the fund's affairs. More often, a manager will go because he cannot convince the board of trustees that his firm is really doing something for the fund. In the trade, this is called "a communication problem." Pension sponsors want service. If the portfolio manager does not fly out for quarterly meetings with the board, if he does not return phone calls promptly, or if his firm does not provide up-to-date lists of the market value of the fund's portfolio or records of every transaction, he can be fired.

Pension officers carry this too far at times, but they have their reasons. The posting dates on stock and bond transactions, dividend credits, or payments to retirees can make a difference of hundreds of thousands of dollars to a large fund. In the 1960s and early 1970s, for example, some large banks were debiting their pension clients' accounts immediately for pension checks written to retirees. The bank had the use of the funds before the check cleared, not the pension fund; there were many nasty scenes between pension disbursing agents and pension officers before the practice died out.

Changing money managers is expensive and time-consuming. Fund sponsors often call pension consultants whose sole expertise is their professed ability to analyze money management firms. These consultants will conduct a full-scale "search" for money managers. In selecting three or four managers for a $200 million fund, they can easily run up fees and expenses of $80,000 or more. This does not include the cost of the time the pension officer spends listening to investment presentations by the 10 to 15 firms the consultant finally recommends he interview. It often takes a full year to pick new money managers from the time the decision was made to start the search until the new ones are hired. While the search is on, the pension officer is courted by all the managers in the competition. That is a significant reason for him to encourage that new managers be hired in the first place.

A Growth Business

Today, institutional investment management is a growth business. Pension funds generate billions of dollars a year in cash flow that needs to be invested and there are only 600 managers to handle it. Large funds rarely like to have their account at any one manager equal more than 10 percent of that firm's assets. Once they reach the limit, the fund will direct its new cash flow elsewhere. Before AT&T agreed to break up its pension fund, the fund administrators talked of running out of competent money managers over the next 10 years; they planned to bring money in-house.

The biggest pension managers will always dominate the institutional money management business. But small, new investment firms have a chance, assuming they can talk two or three of the larger and more innovative pension funds into giving them some money to run. They can then use their initial client list to convince other pension funds to invest with them. Getting the first client is the trick for these new money managers, especially if they are selling an unusual investment for pension funds—such as real estate.

It was far easier, though by no means effortless, for Prudential Insurance to persuade some of the first pension funds to invest directly in real estate over 10

years ago. A small real estate firm, unknown in the pension industry, could not
have done it. Pension fund sponsors trust the large traditional managers, even
if the sponsors themselves know nothing about the investment their managers
are pushing. Meyer Melnikoff, the mastermind behind PRISA, Prudential's real
estate fund, recalls what it was like to approach sophisticated, large pension
funds about real estate investing in the early 1970s. "Most of them knew so little
about it, they would frequently ask us what questions they should ask," he
remembers. "We'd give them our discussion and they would say, 'That sounds
interesting. Now if I knew more about it, what would I ask you?' "

Most innovations in pension investing come from traditional pension managers,
who then "educate" plan sponsors to their use. Real estate has been no exception
to this rule. But to educate, a teacher needs a pupil who is receptive. Although
bouts of high inflation and poor investment performance have made sponsors
more receptive to real estate than ever before, they appear to have an inbred
dislike for the investment and distrust of the people who are involved in it. Many
sponsors want Prudential, Equitable and other trusted managers to serve as their
trusted intermediaries between them and the real estate world—forever.

THE HOSTILITY TOWARD REAL ESTATE

Cold Feet

With the exception of a few portfolio managers at life insurance companies,
money managers and pension officers know nothing about real estate investing.
"Most American pension funds are run by people who are securities-oriented,"
says a real estate manager for several large pension funds. "They've grown up
in stocks and bonds as opposed to the real estate mortgage or equity business;
they don't know real estate nor do they understand it. They've never felt the
need to move into it because there's been no impetus for them to do so."

But that impetus exists now. Generally speaking, real estate has been a better
investment than stocks and bonds over the last 10 years. If inflation becomes a
persistent problem, the common opinion among investors is that real estate will
continue to be a good investment. This means a pension officer or money manager
is going to have to learn something about it and actually use that knowledge. It
may be fun to chat about real estate over cocktails at an investment seminar,
but it is another thing entirely to try to make an investment in property.

How is the typical, middle-aged money manager or pension officer most likely
to respond to this challenge? Not very well, according to a former investment
advisor. Most money managers and pension officers who run stock and bond
portfolios have an investment record sitting squarely in the middle. They are no
better nor worse at what they do than their colleagues. Suddenly, stocks and
bonds are out and real estate is in as the investment of the 1980s. "It's like being
a lawyer all your life and having someone completely change the commercial

code when you're 45," says this portfolio manager. So what does the investment man do?

"Well," says this manager, "he thinks to himself, 'I spent 20 years learning the stock and bond business, and now it doesn't mean anything anymore? I'm supposed to become a real estate expert? I'm not going to do that. For goodness sake, I'm going to retire in 10 years.' "

It is a powerful impetus to hate real estate. In addition, pension officers and tax-exempt advisors have an unfortunate, innate dislike for the people in the real estate business: it is a classic case of personality conflict. The world of the institutional investor is slow, conservative, and filled with well-bred people who could just as well have had careers as successful bankers or government officials. As bureaucrats at heart, they do not like the aggressive entrepreneurs who populate successful real estate development companies and brokerage firms. They can deal with the real estate staffs of life insurance companies; the insurers are also the largest pension fund managers in the country and can be trusted. But in a pension officer's eyes, the rest of the real estate industry is peopled with hustlers, looking to make a buck with his fund's money. This attitude prevails even though some of the largest and most successful real estate companies are as bureaucratic, conservative and "prudent" as any tax-exempt advisor.

Much of this distaste can be traced back to the prudent man mentality that pervades institutional investing. There is a sense among pension officers that it is beneath their dignity to worry about making money. Their goal is not to be successful, shrewd investors but to prudently husband their funds' assets. Pension officers know that their funds, particularly the undefended public funds, are viewed as the fatted calves of the capital markets. Whenever anyone comes up with a harebrained scheme that needs money, he often tries to convince pension funds to invest in it; pension officers are expert at dodging such persons.

No business suffers more for lack of capital than real estate. Brokers and developers are constantly on the prowl for money to finance their dreams. One real estate developer started his own commingled real estate fund for pension funds expressly for that purpose. "I'm a real estate man; I need the money to do my deals," he says. "I don't care where the money comes from, and if I have to get it from pension funds, so be it."

This attitude terrorizes fund sponsors. The pension funds who have gone into this man's commingled real estate fund have done well, but he certainly would never bluntly voice this motive to his clients. Compared to what they make on other investments, pension funds could make a fortune going into a joint venture or partnership with such a successful real estate man, but they will not do it. They would rather be "prudent" and broke with someone who looks like them than rich and successful with someone they consider a boor.

The Lawyers

There is no indication that this hostility will diminish soon. Pension officers are reinforced in it by their lawyers. Because upper management views the pension fund as a legal problem, the corporate attorney must clear every new type of investment a pension officer suggests for the fund. "The lawyers decide what pension funds are permitted to invest in because the investments must meet the tests of prudence," says Melnikoff. "The lawyer is going to try and anticipate what some other lawyer, who is now a judge, is going to decide."

When he was selling the Prudential commingled real estate account, PRISA, to pension funds in the early and mid-1970s, Melnikoff experienced first-hand the tremendous opposition U.S. lawyers have to investing pension money in real estate. "We had to persuade the lawyers of many fine corporations, as well as outside counsel from top-flight law firms, that it would not be imprudent to put a part of the pension fund into property," he says. "It was pretty tough in many cases. They were very much impressed by the debacle with the real estate investment trusts (REITs) in 1974. We used to spend a fair amount of time distinguishing PRISA from a REIT."

This attitude bothers Melnikoff. He was particularly struck by it when he attended a meeting of the American Bar Association in 1979 to watch a panel discussion on untraditional investments. Real estate was included. "After I thought about it a bit," he says, "I started to wonder how in the world property got to be an untraditional investment in the United States when for most of history it was the primary source of wealth. Even today, in most of the world it represents the only form of wealth: after all, there are no securities to speak of in Pakistan."

The attitude of U.S. lawyers contrasted with that of the European and British institutional investors Melnikoff had visited when Prudential was considering starting PRISA in 1970. The Europeans ridiculed the suggestion that real estate was not a traditional investment; one of the elder statesmen of the German insurance world told the Prudential delegation that during the German hyper-inflation of the 1920s only property maintained its value, regardless of how badly the currency was debased. All the owner needed, was another source of income to pay the property taxes and the ability to maintain the property's physical condition.

So why is real estate "imprudent" in the eyes of U.S. lawyers? Melnikoff still is not sure, but he did get a response from one lawyer who heard of his distress with the legal profession. "The reason you think real estate is prudent for pension funds," this lawyer told him, "is that you never attended an American law school."

The MBAs

The nay-saying services provided by corporate attorneys are augmented by the company's financial staff, who actually are in charge of the pension fund. "Financial officers today," says Melnikoff, "still come largely out of the ranks of MBAs; they don't have courses about real estate investment in business schools. They have courses on securities."

Who needs to know about real estate? Corporations want to hire young business school graduates who know something about the capital markets. As members of the financial staff, they will devote their careers to raising money for the company in the securities markets as well as through banks. If the company needs real estate expertise, perhaps to buy a site for a factory or relocate corporate headquarters, it hires outside real estate brokers. If the company buys property often, it might have its own one-man real estate department. He has probably never seen the inside of a business school, though he has bought and sold millions of dollars of property throughout his career. He and the financial department will have few, if any, dealings with each other; the financial staff secretly looks down on him because he does not have an MBA from a good school.

This will change, says Melnikoff. As corporate pension funds become more interested in real estate, corporate financial staffs and business schools will accommodate them by offering courses on property investing. "A subject does not become institutionalized and taught in business schools until institutions take an interest in them," he says. Real estate will then come out of what he calls "the secret world of the entrepreneur" and be considered as much an appropriate pension investment as stocks and bonds. The same thing happened with common stock investing in the early 1950s, he says. As more pension funds embraced common stocks, more courses were taught on securities investing: the once "risky" investment became prudent and traditional in the eyes of fund managers.

Of course, it took 20 years for attitudes to change. It will certainly take at least that for real estate to lose its dark, risky reputation. Most business schools still lack real estate courses, although all offer investment courses that study mostly stocks and bonds. Real estate is mentioned only in passing, as if it were some freak sideshow to investments and not the nation's greatest source of wealth. Young MBAs are still left with the impression that anything they need to know about real estate can be gleaned from reading one of the dozens of books published annually on how to make a fortune in apartment properties "with no money down." Is it any wonder they think so little of the investment?

Chorus of Complaints

Lawyers, MBAs, pension officers and money managers dislike real estate and it is easy for them to find fault with it. If a manager receives too many inquiries from pension clients about when he is going to start a real estate program, or a pension officer gets pressure from his board of trustees about when he is going to look for a real estate manager, both pension officers and managers can launch into a ritual litany of the problems of investing in real estate for a pension fund. They will concede that, for the sake of diversifying the portfolio, pension funds should invest 5 percent of their assets in one of the large commingled funds run by the large insurance companies. But that is it.

Like two frogs in a pond, they can engage in endless choruses about the problems of real estate, a chant that goes something like this:

- All real estate is risky. Look what happened to the real estate investment trusts in 1973 and 1974.
- Most real estate people are unethical and will bilk any investor they can.

- Outside of a handful of banks and insurance companies, there are no real estate investment managers for pension funds that have a track record. How can they be trusted? All their management fees are too high anyway.
- There is no publicly traded market in property, like the New York Stock Exchange for common stocks. How can I know what my property is worth from day to day?
- Who has the time or staff to monitor a portfolio of real estate investments? Who even knows what to monitor?
- It is all overpriced because the foreign investors are buying it.
- It is all overpriced because investors who can use the tax advantages of real estate dominate the market and push up the prices. Pension funds do not need these tax benefits; we always overpay.
- Real estate is an inflation hedge. If inflation drops to 5 percent a year, real estate is not worth owning.
- You cannot sell property fast if you need to, like a stock. It can take months to find a buyer and close a deal.
- There are no sophisticated theories about how to pick property. Should I buy the office building in Dallas or the shopping center in Los Angeles? How do I know I have made a good deal?

Certainly, each of these complaints surrounds a grain of truth, and some are more accurate than others. Much real estate is risky. Many developers are crooked, and there is no readily available pool of time-tested managers standing by who will take all the headaches of managing individual properties out of a pension officer's life. These are real problems that must be handled. But fund sponsors and their advisors often take them to extremes. They become particularly distressed that they cannot exactly determine the market value of a piece of property from month to month: many pension officers view this as the biggest problem with real estate investing.

The Investment Olympics

Pension officers need market values on their portfolios for a number of reasons. ERISA requires private plan sponsors to value their funds by taking into account the market value of the assets in some way. Just how they are to do this is left up to them, and a variety of techniques for evaluating stock and bond portfolios flourish. How to value real estate is anyone's guess. A fund must also have a market value so that pension officers can compute the fund's rate of return. Without that magic number, a sponsor doesn't know how his fund is doing compared to everyone else's—the pension community's favorite obsession and the chief measure employers use to gauge the competence of their pension staff.

But most importantly, the fund sponsor needs to know how much the portfolio is worth in order to determine his annual contribution to the plan. If the market value of the fund's assets are falling, the sponsor may have to contribute more money to the plan. Market values are important numbers. Stocks and bonds have known market values at all times. Real estate does not, and that is enough to frighten off many pension investors.

Consider, for example, a pension officer who buys a stock for $10 and sells it for $20 a year later, during which time the stock pays no dividends. The pension officer doubled his money. He had a 100 percent annual rate of return. If he did not sell the stock, perhaps betting it would go still higher, he could still say that he doubled his money during the year even though he did not sell the stock and "realize his appreciation." He could collect that money by merely telephoning his broker and telling him to sell. Because he can sell at a moment's notice, the "unrealized appreciation" is as good to him as the cash he would realize when he sold the stock; his supervisor is just as pleased with his subordinate's investment abilities. If the fund holds the stock indefinitely, the supervisor can figure the investment return by merely looking up the stock's price in the *Wall Street Journal*.

Now consider the same example applied to real estate. A pension fund buys an office building at 10 and sells it at 20 a year later without collecting any income from it in the meantime. The fund doubled its money on the building, just as it did on the stock that it sold at 20. But if some buyer offers the fund 20 for the building after a year and the fund does not sell, the situation changes. Once that potential buyer leaves the scene, the fund cannot turn around, call a broker, and sell that property to someone else for the same price only a week later. A new buyer may take months to find and most certainly would offer a different price.

What is the market value of the office building after one year if the fund does not sell it? What is the value if someone does not even make an offer on it? And how is the supervisor of that money manager or pension officer going to compute the fund's investment return and market value? He cannot. And the investment performance Olympics come tumbling down.

There is no table in the *Wall Street Journal* listing the daily sale prices of office buildings in Dallas. Even if there were, and there have been attempts at creating such indexes, they would be useless, or worse, misleading. Each piece of property is unique; it cannot be compared with other properties on the basis of sale price. In fact, the reported sale price of a building is often the least important fact about the transaction. The way the buyer financed the sale, the structure of the leases, and whether the buyer or seller had to pay for the new roof are far more important in figuring how much a seller made on a property. Even if this data were available, there is no generally accepted way of computing a rate of return on real estate; it is anyone's guess what the yields on real estate announced in the business press really mean. The real problem is there is no such thing as "unrealized appreciation" on a real estate investment. The investor never knows what a property has earned him on his original investment until he actually sells the building.

This is anathema to pension fund investors. They want to know what they are making. So, commingled real estate funds for pension funds created their own version of "unrealized appreciation." Each quarter, the staff appraiser for the commingled fund estimates how much the fund's properties have appreciated

over the previous three months. This "unrealized appreciation" figure is added
to the actual cash return the properties earned during the quarter; the result is
the "total quarterly rate of return." The problems with this system will be discussed
in chapter 8, for this total return number is misleading. The unrealized appreciation of a commingled fund's real estate is in no way similar to the unrealized
appreciation of the stock and bond markets.

But it is the same term used in securities investing, and that comforts a pension
officer. He calmly posts the unrealized appreciation of his commingled fund real
estate holdings as part of his fund's investment performance for the quarter or
year. This obsession with investment performance numbers is a natural outgrowth
of the prudent man mentality. If a pension officer is challenged on his investment
choices, he can pull out his detailed records on the fund's investment performance
and prove his case.

This need to justify everything he does in a court of law also explains why
pension funds hold so little of their portfolios in such assets as real estate or
private placement securities: these assets are difficult to find buyers for. In case
the pension officer is told that a particular investment is imprudent, he wants to
be able to dump the offending holding as quickly and easily as possible. This
is why a billion dollar pension fund will hold 95 percent of its assets in publicly
traded stocks and bonds that can be purged from the portfolio with one call to
the trading desk. It perplexes outside observers why such a giant pool of assets,
needed to fund long-term pension liabilities, should be invested as if it must
always be possible to liquidate the entire portfolio overnight. It is another case
of prudent man fallout.

In the pension officer's eyes, then real estate has two strikes against it. First,
it is difficult to compute rates of return on; second, it can take months to sell.

What's the Beta of This Building?

The third strike against real estate is its total lack of elegant theory. Pension
officers do not appreciate the beauty of the financing of a Chicago office building,
pasted together in 14 layers to provide tax benefits to all the partners involved.
Instead, they want theory.

Consider the sophisticated statistical models that embrace every aspect of
securities investing. The organized capital markets in this country generate enough
annual data to fill miles of computer tapes and boxes of computer discs. Trading
volume, stock prices, stock movements after a dividend announcement—all these
and much more can be sifted out. Academics dedicate entire careers analyzing
these numbers, spinning theories, and creating models about how to make money
in the stock and bond markets. Pension officers and money managers pay religious
attention to all of it.

The academics gave the pension business the efficient market hypothesis, the
capital-asset pricing model, and modern portfolio theory, ("MPT" to the well-
versed). They introduced index funds, alphas, betas, R^2, risk-reward ratios, time-
weighted and dollar-weighted rates of return, and the Black-Scholes Options

Pricing Model. Pension officers and money managers drop these terms in conversations, though few know what they mean. The academics also created the elaborate statistical backbone of the pension fund performance monitoring business. Never have so many three-color transparencies and investment charts been used to give so much legitimacy to investment returns lagging the rate of inflation.

What can real estate offer to compete with this? "Deals" scribbled on the backs of envelopes? There is no general, elegant theory which explains how the real estate market works. There is no accurate data to work with and, as mentioned, no uniform way of computing a rate of return. It is unlikely this will change. Real estate is too complex and unpredictable to be tied up in one comprehensive theory; attempts to do so fall flat.

In fact, trying to be a sophisticated financier in real estate transactions can actually hurt. One woman who holds an MBA from the University of Chicago opened a successful condominium development firm and found she had to "unlearn" much of the financial theory she had picked up in school. "The real estate people I was dealing with had never even heard of discounted cash flow analysis," she says. "That's just not how deals are done." Though it has become popular among insurance companies and other institutional real estate investors to use discounted cash flow analysis, it is nearly always used to justify overpaying for a deal. The cash return going in is too low, so the analysis, or a model based on it, is used to show how the cash flow will improve dramatically in five years. It is all subterfuge: good deals shine on their own and need no embellishment from discounted cash flow analysis.

Real estate's lack of elegance distresses pension officers. It is only a short step in their minds from being annoyed that there is no data or theory about real estate to believing that it must be imprudent to invest in it because such figures and models are missing. ERISA does not say it is imprudent to invest in real estate. And no pension officer, when asked, will say he would violate his fiduciary obligations by investing in property. But in his heart, he's not convinced.

TEMPERING THE HOSTILITY

Should We Give Up?

Faced with such hostility from the pension community, real estate people often feel the urge to give up and leave sponsors to the handful of commingled real estate funds they adore. Such pessimism is certainly understandable: most snails move faster than fund sponsors. But as much as pension officers dislike real estate, they are being forced into it because of pension costs and the perseverance of real estate people. Sponsoring corporations now spend an average of 20 percent of pretax profits a year in contributions to their pension funds; some estimate it will increase to 27 percent by the end of the decade.[19] Management cannot trim pension benefits to trim pension costs. Unions and employees would scream. The only real way to cut costs is to improve the fund's investment return.

"Most corporate executives would be shocked to learn what the impact on earnings per share would be if the rate of return on the pension fund increased 2 percent," says Stephen Gross of the pension fund consulting firm Evaluation Associates.[20] The trade-off varies. Most actuaries estimate that for each 1 percent increase in long-term investment return, say over a 40-year period, an employer can reduce his pension contribution by 20 percent. This means if the pension officer increases the fund's investment return from 6 percent a year to 8 percent and can hold it there for 40 years, the corporate pension contribution would fall from 20 percent of pretax earnings to 12 percent. This is a rough example, but it does show that management has a handsome incentive for improving investment return.

In the past, management has not paid much attention to pension costs or the real rate of return on the pension portfolio. But the situation is changing. The Financial Accounting Standards Board is working on an appropriate way to include pension costs and liabilities on corporate financial statements. As of 1982, pension costs were relegated to cryptic footnotes in annual reports. Eventually they will show up on the statements themselves or in detailed disclosures. Once the stock analysts, the investing public, and the banks know the true amount of pension liabilities, the company will be hit where it counts—in the price of its stock and the cost of borrowing money.

In fact, pension costs have caused more than one carefully crafted corporate merger to be restructured or to fall apart. Someone asks for details about the unfunded vested liability of the pension fund or the corporation's liability to a multiemployer pension plan. Suddenly, millions of dollars in unknown expenses come out of the closet and onto the spread sheets. There are other forces pushing up pension costs. Inflation, the problems of Social Security, and the average American's belief that he is entitled to retire in his old age will make it more expensive than ever before to run a private pension plan.

"Real estate cannot perform CPR on a pension portfolio," a real estate advisor once said, but it can help improve return and lower costs. If real estate people are willing to work slowly and adapt themselves to prudent manhood, in five years they can have a good working relationship with sophisticated fund sponsors. Some powerful tail winds are pushing them together.

Inflation

The most powerful force pushing pension funds into property is inflation. Inflation not only erodes investment performance, it also eats up the purchasing power of the fixed-dollar pensions retirees receive. The less their pension buys, the harder retirees and current plan participants will fight for pensions that automatically increase with the cost of living. Such fully indexed pensions would cost corporations a fortune.

In 1980, only 5 percent of all private pension plans had automatic cost-of-living adjustments: that handful restricted the adjustment to about 3 percent a year, according to Barnet N. Berin, director of professional standards for William

N. Mercer, the nation's largest pension consulting firm. "Not a single profit-making company indexes pensions fully to the CPI (Consumer Price Index)," he wrote in an article published in the *Wall Street Journal*.[21]

Companies use Band-Aids to repair the damage that inflation wreaks on pension benefits. Many large corporations have given their retirees one-time cost-of-living increases, although they had no legal liability to do so. Another approach was tried by Inco, Ltd., a nickel-mining company. Inco set up an "escalator annuity" savings plan in 1980: financed with both Inco and employee contributions, the supplement boosts a pension by 6 percent a year for 15 years from age 66 on. The number of companies with a plan like Inco's can be counted on two hands.

As inflation continues, indexed pensions will become a bigger issue, and unions will start bringing them to the bargaining table. Organized labor's biggest victory in the 1970s was the automatic cost-of-living adjustment or "COLA" on wages, won by the United Auto Workers. A COLA on pensions is the logical next step. Management has not taken this step on its own because at even modest inflation rates, fully indexed pensions would double pension costs, according to Berin's calculations. In the same *Journal* article cited above, he estimated that companies spend 5 to 15 percent of total annual payroll on pension costs. The average is 8 percent of covered or total payroll.

"If fully indexed to the CPI," he wrote, "costs would find a new plateau, probably from 7 to 30 percent of payroll."[22] Depending on the fund's actuarial assumptions, for every 1 percent increase in the cost of living, pension managers would have to increase their pension reserves by 6 to 10 percent. This means that if inflation was 5 to 10 percent a year, over a period of time, pension assets would have to grow by 30 to 100 percent over their current levels to fund the new benefits. This is a worst-case scenario. It is unlikely that employees or unions can force many companies to fully index pensions, though they can bargain for richer benefits because of inflation. Management will not cripple the company to protect retirees.

But they may be forced to pay more in pensions, anyway, because of the serious problems now facing Social Security. When Social Security has problems, so does the private pension system. The two systems are completely entwined; many companies adjust a retiree's pension based on what he is collecting from Social Security. There are growing indications that the federal government wants more control over the private pension system and wants to integrate it more fully with Social Security. No federal laws exist to this effect, but various federal commissions and regulators have concluded that the private pension system should pick up more of the responsibility of paying for an individual's retirement. Not only do unions, employees and retirees pressure their companies for better benefits, the federal government has started in, too.

No pension officer wakes up one morning and says to himself, "My God, pension liabilities will destroy our corporate balance sheet in 10 years. The pension plan must make more money on its investments." Instead, his boss starts pressuring him to pay more attention to costs, a pressure that eventually leads to pointed questions about why the fund's return is so low. Why not investigate inflation hedges like real estate? And so the pension officer goes off to examine commingled real estate funds.

Disguise Yourself as a Money Manager

Any real estate firm that understands how pension officers and their supervisors view real estate is miles ahead of the firm that approaches them as they would any other source of capital. Pension officers may look like commercial bankers, but as we have seen, they live in a world of their own. The more a real estate firm can put a pension officer at ease, the better off both will be. Consequently, it makes sense for a real estate firm to look and act as much like a traditional pension fund money manager as possible—pin-striped, understated, with an office full of early American furniture and pictures of ducks.

A real estate firm should also hire salesmen with a pension background to market the firm's services. One company considered going into a partnership with a Midwestern bank. "The only thing those bankers would be is a front for us," said the man in charge of the venture. "They'll market our services to pension funds, but they won't have a thing to say about how we invest the money."

Those who do not want a bank as a partner can take on one prominent member of the pension community as a partner, or hire him through some incentive program to market the firm's services. The Chicago syndication firm of JMB Realty did this when they reached an agreement with John Lillard; he became president of a new JMB subsidiary that runs commingled real estate funds for pension funds. Lillard had been a partner with the large money management firm of Scudder, Stevens & Clark, heading their Chicago office. He had sold traditional investment services to pension funds for more than 20 years when he decided that real estate was the investment of the future for pension funds. After months of talking to real estate firms, he decided to work with JMB Realty; together they started a commingled fund for pension funds. Lillard knew little about real estate and JMB knew little about pension funds. Although each has learned from the other, they keep to their own areas of expertise. Lillard sells the funds and handles the pension clients, JMB invests the money in property, and the funds are doing well.

The Dilemma

The only problem with such an arrangement is the shortage of prominent pension advisors who wish to abandon successful careers at their peak and start out on something new. The John Lillards of the world are in limited supply.

It is, of course, possible to hire younger, unknown marketing men, and one that has had several years' experience selling to pension funds is a better choice than one just off the street. But even with experience, they will have an uphill fight selling sponsors on the real estate services of a firm unknown to the pension community. The pension officer is expert at fending off the advances of investment salesmen; a salesman's name is likely to end up in a pile of pink message slips with the names of 50 other real estate firms unknown to the pension officer.

There are simply a lot of people out there selling pension funds the same thing—a commingled real estate fund structured exactly like Prudential's extraordinarily successful PRISA. Understandably, pension officers feel they should not have to settle for a PRISA copy if they have a chance to get into the real thing, or one of the handful of other well-known funds that resemble it. Commingled real estate funds differ little in structure or strategy. The two things that distinguish one from another are the abilities of their staffs to do deals and to manage property. These are difficult skills to measure, particularly since most funds have been in existence for less than five years and have no track records. One sponsor estimated that in mid-1982 there were 135 commingled real estate funds, with a new one springing up each week. If a real estate firm offers something different than a commingled fund, it will be even more of an uphill fight. Not only will the pension officer not know the firm, he will not know what the firm is selling: that is two strikes against them instead of one.

This dilemma plagues attempts to interest pension officers in a wider variety of real estate investments. If it is not a commingled fund like PRISA, they do not understand or want it. If it actually is a commingled fund like PRISA, 55 other salesmen have been there already. Or worse, a PRISA salesman showed up.

A growing number of funds are branching beyond commingled funds by hiring real estate managers to handle individual accounts for them. But this is more expensive and risky than investing through a commingled fund. Although it is becoming popular with the larger funds, those with assets of $100 million or more, it is unlikely to catch on with the majority of pension funds. Most funds will never get beyond investing in real estate through commingled pools. It is simply too difficult. The commingled fund diversifies pension portfolios into income property without saddling the pension officer with the responsibility of managing buildings.

Sponsor interest in commingled funds has percolated down from the largest pension funds to the medium-sized funds. "Now we're starting to get the dumb questions about real estate from funds in the $10 million to $100 million range," says a marketing man for one of the giant commingled funds. Prudential, Aetna Life, Equitable Life and Rosenberg Capital—some of the most successful commingled fund managers at this writing—cannot manage all the money that will go into commingled funds. Medium-sized pension funds do consider investing in lesser-known commingled pools; these pension funds already use regional banks and smaller money managers as investment advisors and are comfortable with them.

The drawback with these medium-sized pension plans is that their pension officers and trustees know nothing about real estate. A commingled salesman who is not with a well-known fund can spend months selling them on his fund.

It is difficult to fill up a commingled fund with the $100 million in assets needed to make a profit for the manager if the salesman has to spend six months getting each $1 million contribution.

Of course, a firm can abandon the commingled fund treadmill by offering pension sponsors real estate products the pension officers consider safer than commingled funds. These include Ginnie Mae passthroughs, mortgage-backed bonds, and the common stock of conservative, publicly held REITs. Pension officers view these more as securities than real estate, though sometimes, when asked if their fund invests in real estate they will answer "of course," the fund owns some Ginnie Maes. But Ginnie Maes and other mortgage-backed securities are part of the bond business, and the big investment and securities firms have this market locked up. Pension fund sponsors can buy Ginnie Maes and mortgage-backed bonds in carloads from Merrill Lynch, Salomon Brothers, and a host of other firms. They do not need other sources. And pension fund stock analysts have already picked apart all four REITs a fund would ever consider buying.

What actually can a real estate firm sell to pension funds? For many firms, the answer is nothing directly. Many developers and brokers would be better off doing business with the managers of the successful commingled pools than attempting to go directly to the pension funds themselves. They have no credibility in the eyes of fund sponsors; unless they attach themselves to a traditional money management firm, they will never get it. For example, the first two commingled funds created by Coldwell Banker had to be sold to pension funds by Smith Barney, Harris Upham. It was only with the third fund that Coldwell had the credibility with the pension community to sell to them directly.

Nevertheless, dealing with commingled funds has its problems, too. As of this writing, there are less than half a dozen that have any real assets to commit— that is, they can come up with $10 million or more at a time. And everyone sends them deals.

Those real estate firms who insist on selling directly to pension funds anyway, have a number of options. They can create and sell variations of commingled funds: several firms now offer commingled funds that make mortgages with equity participations or buy only apartments. The Coldwell Banker funds develop property, and several banks offer funds that invest only in the Northeastern, Western or Southern United States.

A real estate firm can also become a consultant on retainer or an investment advisor for larger pension funds. The Real Estate Management Group of Mellon Financial Services, New York, successfully writes mortgages with equity kickers or buys property directly for its pension clients. Other firms are trying to set up consultant relationships with pension funds, collecting fees only when they bring in suitable investments. But all such one-to-one relationships between funds and consultants are in their infancy.

Firms with experience in syndications can consider getting into a completely different niche of the pension market—pension funds with less than $10 million in assets. There is a real shortage of good real estate product—or good investment product at all—for small pension funds. The smaller they are, the more problems they have. Commingled fund salesmen do not usually call on plans with less than $1 million in assets; only the the local life insurance salesmen seem to care about them at all.

The minimum contribution a commingled fund will accept from a pension fund averages about $250,000, though some, like PRISA, will accept contributions as low as $50,000. If the sponsor of a small plan wants to invest 10 percent of his plan's assets in real estate, he must have at least a $2.5 million plan and be happy to put all of his real estate money into one commingled fund. A real estate syndication or commingled fund that would let such a plan contribute $50,000 or less would offer this market a real alternative.

Most pension funds with less than $10 million in assets belong to small businesses. Those with less than $1 million are often retirement plans for partnerships of doctors or lawyers, or the plans of single, well-to-do individuals. All are normally run in a haphazard fashion by the plan sponsor: he either buries the fund in a corner of the trust department at the local bank, where it is neglected, or turns it over entirely to an insurance company, where he is overcharged. Sometimes the sponsor tries to run it himself, relying heavily for his investment advice on the stockbroker who does the fund's securities trading.

If a firm is good at real estate syndications and lines up a major stockbrokerage firm to sell its products, it could sell to these funds. The Balcor Corporation of Skokie, Illinois has had success selling wraparound mortgage syndications designed specifically for small pension funds. The minimum contribution is $5,000.

Pension funds could invest more money in income property in more lucrative and innovative ways than they do now. The biggest obstacle is the attitude of the men who manage the funds: unless a real estate investment is cloaked in a commingled fund or a Ginnie Mae passthrough, they dread it. Many secretly pray that the stock market will embark on another 20-year boom so they can drop the whole topic. Although 37 percent of the 1,000 largest corporate pension funds invested in real estate as of 1982, 63 percent did not, Greenwich Research found.[23] In all categories of pension funds, more funds avoid real estate than jump in.

At this writing in early 1983, a recession has depressed rents on all income property and hit the new office market hard in certain cities. Commingled funds have been big buyers of new income property, particularly office buildings, and the funds' 1982 returns have fallen by 50 percent or more from their 1981 levels. Commingled funds posted 15 and 16 percent returns in 1981; 1982 returns are closer to 7 or 8 percent.

Falling returns and negative publicity have cooled pension fund interest in property. Although good estimates are not yet available, it appears that pension funds invested less money in property in 1982 than they did in 1981, but it is unclear how much they cut back. At this writing, the stock market is six months into a bull market that shows no signs of stopping. If the market continues to boom and commingled funds post two or three years of 7 percent returns, pension funds will direct more money to stocks and away from property. On the other hand, many economists predict that bouts of high inflation and continuing capital shortages will plague the country over the next 20 years; despite periodic shake-outs, the value of existing income property should rise strongly.

In either case, pension funds will become a growing part of the real estate market. Sponsors and their money managers may slow their investing in real estate when returns are down, but when they start to climb, the plans will come back in quickly.

To survive, those in the real estate business must know how to deal with pension funds and their commingled managers. Funds can own, buy, sell, develop and mortgage property, but a number of laws and regulations limit how deals with pension funds can be structured and how managers and consultants can be paid. Since few funds aggressively invest in property, no one knows exactly what all the legal restrictions are: the questions have never been raised. The existing restrictions do not seriously hamper real estate investing, and it is unlikely major restrictions will be unearthed in the future. But anyone involved in investing pension fund money in real estate should know that there are legal and regulatory limits to what he can do.

NOTES

1. Peter Drucker, *The Unseen Revolution: How Pension Fund Socialism Came to America* (New York: Harper & Row, 1976), p. 1.

2. U.S., Department of Labor, Pension and Welfare Benefit Programs, *The Prudence Rule and Pension Plan Investments Under ERISA* (Washington: Office of Communications and Public Services, Pension and Welfare Benefit Programs, 1980), p. 7.

3. Ibid, p. 7.

4. Ibid.

5. Ibid, p. 12.

6. Ibid, p. 8.

7. A. G. Becker Inc., *1979 Tax-Free Fund Performance* (Chicago: A. G. Becker, 1980), p. 3.

8. Stephen C. Gross, "Neglect by superiors, ho-hum corporate attitude are problems for inhouse advisors," *Pensions & Investments* (August 18, 1980), p. 34.

9. Ibid.

10. Ibid.

11. Ibid.

12. Ibid.

13. "Real estate key for 'eighties,' " *Pensions & Investments* (December 8, 1980), p. 42.

14. "Profile statistics at a glance," *Pensions & Investment Age* (April 4, 1983), p. 24.

15. Ibid.

16. Ibid.

17. "Investment field needs younger blood: Casey," *Pensions & Investments* (June 23, 1980), p. 48.

18. "Profiles: The top 200," *Pensions & Investment Age* (January 24, 1983), p. 54.

19. Gross, "Neglect by superiors," p. 34.

20. Ibid.

21. Barnet N. Berin, "Indexing Pensions?" *The Wall Street Journal* (June 9, 1982), editorial page.

22. Ibid.

23. "Greenwich releases corporate plan study," *Pensions & Investment Age* (January 10, 1983), p. 9.

3 | LEGAL PROBLEMS

> Given my tax background, I love to sit and read regulations. But I
> can't get through ERISA and the prohibited transactions regulations.
> They put me to sleep.
> —*a tax attorney who managed an $80 million pension fund*

THE SCOPE OF THIS CHAPTER

ERISA—the Employee Retirement Income Security Act of 1974—is the principal
law governing the management and investment of private pension funds. Public
pension plans are not covered by ERISA, but nearly every other type of employee
benefit plan is, from profit-sharing to welfare plans.

ERISA has been called the most complicated law ever written in the United
States, a bit of hyperbole that nevertheless has some basis in fact. The law is
extraordinarily complex, badly written, and contains enough vague commands
and caveats to keep batteries of pension attorneys busy for years. And they keep
very busy. Lawyers regularly write pages and pages of interpretations of the law
and its regulations. Most start with a solemn intonation of what the law says
and then proceed along to a discussion of some fine point, similar in breadth to
the theological question of how many angels can dance on the head of a pin.

Nine out of 10 pension attorneys, said one commingled fund manager, will
read the law and tell you how it limits you in what you want to do. The 10th
will ask you what you are trying to accomplish and then explain how to maneuver
through the law so you can do it. This chapter is written in the spirit of the 10th
attorney; it does not provide one-stop shopping for legal advice. Instead, it gives
some reference points so when pension fund and real estate people talk to their
attorneys, they know if they have one of the nine who won't let them do a thing,
or that one in 10 who will make it all work.

The problems pension sponsors and real estate firms have with ERISA depend
on how they structure their relationships. Those structures determine whether or
not the real estate people are fiduciaries of the pension fund under ERISA. If
they are, they are subject to the prudent man rule and its heavy burden of liability.
ERISA's rules against self-dealing by fiduciaries, called "prohibited transactions," also hang over their heads. If the real estate people are not fiduciaries,
ERISA has no power over them. They may have a few problems with "indirect"
prohibited transactions, but those are ultimately the fiduciary's responsibility,
not theirs.

So the legal questions are, just what is a fiduciary under ERISA and how does a real estate person become one? And, if he is a fiduciary, what problems does he face and how serious are they?

The problems imposed by ERISA will not keep a real estate person from doing good deals for his pension fund client, but they will make it more difficult to do business. Because pension sponsors insist on such a passive role in real estate investing, hiring others to invest for them, the legal problems of pension fund investing in real estate are more the problems of the fund's outside investment managers than of the sponsors themselves. Therefore, most of the comment in this chapter is addressed to real estate people who happen to find themselves lurching into "fiduciaryhood" because of their pension clientele. If funds start to invest in real estate using their own in-house people, they will have to grapple with these problems, too. But such independence appears to be years off, if it ever occurs at all.

Beyond the problems of being a fiduciary—which will take up the bulk of the chapter—there are two minor legal issues everyone involved in investing pension money in real estate should be aware of. One is the rule on valuation. The second is the law on unrelated business income.

ERISA requires pension funds to place market values on their portfolios periodically; funds need to make an estimate of how much their real estate is worth. In 1980, the Internal Revenue Service issued regulations on acceptable valuation techniques under ERISA. Pension sponsors and their real estate advisors should be aware of these rules. The second minor legal issue is the tax law on unrelated business income. Until it was amended at year-end 1980, the tax law made it difficult for pension funds to buy mortgaged property; it required the funds to pay taxes on the income from that property. If the property was mortgaged for 75 percent of its value, the pension fund had to pay income taxes on 75 percent of the property's net income. Today, within a few loose restrictions, pension funds can buy any property they wish, mortgaged any way they want.

The chapter concludes with a brief discussion of how ERISA deals with real estate investments made under the banner of "social investing." How these "social investments" are permitted under the law is a lesson in how erratically the federal government enforces and interprets ERISA.

Before discussing the legal problems pension funds have in investing in real estate, I would like to recap the history of ERISA. In doing business with pension funds, it helps to know what Congress was trying to accomplish with this law and how the IRS and the Department of Labor became involved in enforcing it. Any real estate company that becomes a pension fund fiduciary will become accustomed to dealing with both ERISA and the government agencies that enforce it.

WHY CONGRESS PASSED ERISA

In 1964, the Studebaker Corporation closed down its big plant in South Bend, Indiana. The president of the local chapter of the United Auto Workers estimated that only currently retired employees and men over 60 would receive any pension benefits. Of the 7,200 members of his local, whose average age was 54, only 1,100 were eligible for a pension; the plan was not scheduled to be fully funded until 1989.

Studebaker was the big name in the pension fund scandals of the late 1960s. The demise of that fund was a good example of the incredible power employers had over their pension plans in the pre-ERISA days. Pension plans were creatures of the tax law and the IRS was in charge of regulating them. Federal pension law was a patchwork of laws and regulations that had been drafted piecemeal since the passage of the 16th Amendment, which permitted Congress to levy income taxes. One tax attorney, Daniel Knickerbocker, Jr., wrote of pre-ERISA pension law:

Congress articulated, and the administrators refined, an elaborate structure of exemptions, exclusions, deductions, income characterizations, and accounting rules, which had the effect of prescribing to one degree or another, the designs of most plans and the ways in which they were operated.[1]

The IRS was more interested in describing how a pension plan should be structured to qualify for its tax-exempt status than how it paid and funded benefits. The Department of Labor (DOL) had the authority to look into the administration of pension plans, but only to investigate complaints of criminal activity by plan sponsors or trustees, such as forgery and embezzlement. Otherwise, it was powerless to investigate the fund.[2] Critics charged that no state or federal agency was effectively regulating the day-to-day administration of pension funds. A plan sponsor could underfund his plan or terminate it if he wished, leaving the participants with no benefits and no recourse to recover them. The sponsor could even allocate the plan's assets for his own use, and run little risk of being detected or held accountable.[3]

Although most pension plans were well-run and cared for by their plan sponsors, a growing number were not. It took Congress 10 years to deal with this problem. Studebaker employees lost their pensions in 1964. The Employee Retirement Income Security Act was not signed into law until Labor Day 1974.

Congress did not start from scratch in drafting ERISA, but based it on the existing law in the tax code. The new law set up minimum vesting and funding standards for employee benefit plans. It set forth the prudent man rule as the investment guideline for pension managers and defined who plan fiduciaries were. The law required plan sponsors to provide certain information about the status of the fund to the participants and spelled out how a plan participant could sue his plan fiduciaries if he felt the fund was being mismanaged.

ERISA also required the government to set up a new federal agency, the Pension Benefit Guaranty Corporation. The PBGC would resemble an insurance company, collecting premium payments from all private pension plans and using the money to pay benefits on plans that had to be terminated because of a sponsor's bankruptcy. Congress did not want to see a reenactment of the Studebaker bankruptcy where workers received no pensions at all.

Because both the DOL and the IRS claimed jurisdiction over pension funds, Congress gave it to both of them. The DOL and the IRS would administer the law jointly and both were given great latitude in developing regulations. Not surprisingly, dual administration did not work. The two agencies kept colliding with each other, each interpreting the same part of the law differently. As a result, in 1979 President Carter signed an executive order, splitting the duties more specifically between the two agencies. But dual jurisdiction still does not work as well as the two agencies or the pension community would like; each year, a number of bills are introduced in Congress giving all pension authority to either the IRS, the DOL, or a third independent agency.

Until such legislation is passed, if ever, the interpretation of ERISA is a two-agency show. The sections of the law on vesting, prudent investing, and prohibiting transactions, among other issues, are regulated by the DOL. The IRS handles tax matters: it decides if a plan has an appropriate structure to qualify for tax-exempt status and enforces funding requirements. It also enforces prohibited transaction decisions made by the DOL, by levying excise taxes on the erring fund fiduciaries.

As a result, anyone dealing with legal matters affecting pension plans will find himself talking to the IRS on one day and the DOL on the next. For the most part, advisors and plan sponsors interested in real estate investing will deal with the Labor Department. The DOL interprets the fiduciary and prohibited transaction sections of ERISA: these sections have the biggest effect on real estate decisions.

FIDUCIARIES

To be or not to be a fiduciary under ERISA is the biggest decision any real estate advisor dealing with pension funds is called on to make. If a real estate person finds himself a fiduciary of his pension clients, he is subject to a number of restraints on how he can deal with them. He is personally liable for the money they give him to invest; he is subject to the prudent man rule and constrained as to how he charges the plan for his services; and he is limited in his investment decisions by ERISA's prohibited transactions rules, which were designed to prevent self-dealing and conflict of interest by plan fiduciaries.

In drafting the fiduciary standards of ERISA, Congress wanted to be certain that if another debacle like Studebaker occurred, or if a fund was shown to be mismanaged, it would be clear who was responsible and hence who would have to come up with the money to repair the damage. So Congress tried to describe just who was and who was not a fiduciary. Generally speaking, under ERISA, a fund's fiduciaries are the people who are responsible for making decisions about how a plan's assets are invested and how the fund is administered. To be a fiduciary, one must have discretionary control over the fund or part of the fund.

There are two types of fiduciaries—named and delegated. Named fiduciaries are actually listed in the documents setting up the pension plan. Named fiduciaries usually include the pension officer, the board of trustees for the fund or the "pension investment committee" as they are sometimes called, and the corporation's board of directors.

Named fiduciaries are the only persons who can delegate legal responsibility for the plan. In fact, they can relieve themselves almost entirely of their fiduciary responsibility by hiring investment advisors, as defined by ERISA, and delegating the investment responsibility to them. The investment manager is a delegated fiduciary and is responsible only for the assets he manages. If the named fiduciaries use prudent judgment in hiring an investment manager and then closely monitor his performance, they are not liable for his actions. The named fiduciaries are still ultimately responsible for the plan's health, but they now have a layer of protection. If this system were not in place, all fiduciaries could be ruled responsible for anything done within their sphere of influence.

The authors of ERISA did not want to burden named fiduciaries with the heavy responsibility of selecting an investment manager on their own. So ERISA provided guidance. If the named fiduciaries hired an advisor who was a plan asset manager as qualified in Section 3(38) of ERISA, they would be deemed to have appointed a delegated fiduciary; they would be free of responsibility for that advisor's individual investment decisions. The named fiduciaries could still hire advisors who were not qualified plan asset managers (QPAMs), and those managers would be fund fiduciaries. But the named fiduciaries would still be responsible for each investment decision those managers made. Consequently, though pension funds will hire managers who are not qualified plan asset managers, they prefer the latter; most investment advisors prefer to be qualified plan asset managers.

ERISA is specific about who is a qualified investment advisor. The advisor must meet three criteria: First, the manager must have the power to manage, acquire or dispose of any asset entrusted to him. Second, the manager must be registered as an investment advisor under the Investment Advisors Act of 1940 or else be a bank or insurance company as defined by ERISA. Finally, the investment manager must acknowledge in writing that he is a fiduciary of the plan.

The Basic Rule of Thumb

Until the DOL makes further rulings, it is still unclear as to exactly when a real estate firm or person is a fiduciary under ERISA of a pension plan it is doing business with. This issue will be dealt with in more detail later on in this chapter. But the basic rule of thumb is that investment managers are fiduciaries under ERISA and consultants are not. The key is control over assets. If the real estate people have the power to invest the assets according to their own ideas, they are fiduciaries.

For example, a real estate firm approaches a pension fund and offers to find real estate for the fund to buy. But the fund trustees must decide whether or not they will purchase a specific property. That real estate firm is acting as a consultant, not as an investment manager; it is not a fiduciary. The firm recommends and the trustees decide.

Now consider another real estate firm that approaches the same fund trustees and offers to invest some of the fund's assets in real estate. The real estate firm will pick the properties and decide whether or not they are appropriate for the fund, perhaps subject to approval by the board of trustees on some of the large purchases. Here, the real estate firm is an investment manager; it is a fiduciary of the fund.

The Final Words on "Prudence"

All ERISA fiduciaries are subject to the prudent man rule, which, as we saw in chapter 2, is the principal investment direction ERISA gives. Fiduciaries must invest plan assets as a "prudent man" would. In the case of delegated fiduciaries, such as investment managers, this means the manager must invest the assets in his care "for the exclusive benefit" of the plan participants. He must diversify the investments he makes for the fund "to minimize the risks of large losses" unless the named fiduciaries have told him not to.

Beyond the instruction to diversify, the prudence regulations tell an investment manager nothing about how to invest: they merely state that he be careful, professional, and exercise good judgment in his investments. Because he makes poor investments does not mean that he has invested imprudently. If he can show that he has carefully examined the investment before making it and had good reason to believe that it would do well, he cannot be held responsible for its failure. It is highly unlikely that a conscientious, reasonable plan sponsor or investment manager will ever stumble into the land of imprudent investing. This can be shown by sampling some of the lawsuits that the DOL has filed and won on this issue.

For example, in June 1980, the DOL sued the Glass/Metal Association and Glaziers and Glassworkers Pension Plan in Hawaii for violating the diversification requirement of the prudent man rule. The fund trustees wanted to use 23 percent of the fund's assets as a loan to the Holiday Country Club, a time-sharing resort. DOL sued to stop them and won.

In another case in early 1981, the department sued the Alaska Teamster Employer Pension Trust, Local 959, for violating the same diversification requirement. The $220 million fund had 80 percent of its assets in loans or other holdings secured by Alaska real estate. The DOL won a consent order, barring the fund from making further loans in the state.

In both the Hawaii and Alaska cases, the funds were clearly making unwise investments, on any basis one could care to name. How could any investor risk 23 percent of a pension fund's assets on something as risky as a time-sharing resort? In the Alaska case, the fund trustees were investing 80 percent of their assets in their own, tiny economy. What would happen to their portfolio if the state's economy started to slide? Clearly, the prudent man rule as enforced by the DOL is designed to protect fools from themselves and the pension plan from criminals. It was not designed to discourage plan investments in real estate or other new investments, or to inhibit the way these investments can be structured.

Compensation, ERISA and the SEC

Real estate people are accustomed to being paid for their services based on how much money they make for their clients. Their compensation is tied to the performance of the property they buy or the deals they do. At best, they receive a small piece of the equity. At the very least, they receive incentive compensation in the form of a share in the property's cash flow once the client has received a certain minimum level of return. But the pension fund business pays for investment help differently. The vast majority of real estate advisors for pension funds are paid only a fixed fee based on the amount of money they run for their clients.

There is some question whether a fiduciary under ERISA can take a piece of the deals he does for his clients or collect an incentive fee. ERISA does not forbid an investment manager from doing so. But the DOL, which interprets the law, is not certain it should allow such practices; under ERISA it appears to be generally illegal for an investment advisor to benefit from an investment he advises a plan to make.

The DOL is currently studying whether it should allow real estate managers of pension funds to pay themselves incentive fees. A handful of commingled funds and investment advisors already do; there were no regulations that said they could not. The Smith Barney Real Estate Fund, the Coldwell Banker funds, and an apartment fund started by JMB Institutional Realty all pay incentive fees to their managers.

The incentive compensation issue is further clouded by the fact that most real estate investment managers for pension funds register as investment advisors with the Securities and Exchange Commission under the Investment Advisors Act of 1940. The SEC forbids investment managers from collecting incentive compensation, in most cases. Certain mutual fund managers, for example, are permitted to collect incentive compensation. At this writing, the SEC is reconsidering its whole approach to incentive compensation, particularly since so many real estate advisors have registered with the agency.

Real estate managers do not have to register with the SEC. They run real estate, not securities. But they register for two reasons: to help their marketing and to be certain they are qualified plan asset managers (QPAMs) under ERISA. A pension fund's independent stock and bond managers, that is managers that are not banks or insurance companies, are required to register by both ERISA and securities laws. Real estate managers register so they can look like the fund's securities advisors and thus gain respectability in their pension clients' eyes.

Real estate managers also register so they can be sure that they are qualified plan asset managers. The DOL cannot decide if an independent real estate manager, that is one not a part of a bank or insurance company, must register with the SEC to be a qualified plan asset manager. So managers register to be safe. At this writing, the DOL is talking about requiring real estate advisors to register with the SEC. The Labor Department is short of staff: it can stretch its existing manpower by having other regulatory agencies police certain pension managers. But the department has not yet made this decision. If it does require advisors to register, and the department and the SEC decide to forbid real estate advisors from paying themselves incentive fees, most of the best people in the real estate business will avoid running pension fund money. They can make more money in other areas of the real estate business.

Before commingled real estate funds for pension funds existed, the real estate business had never seen an investment advisor who worked for a client for a fixed fee. Certainly there were consultants and brokers who worked for fees, but they worked on individual projects for a client and did not run his entire real estate portfolio. Banks had run real estate for their trust clients for a fee, but bank trust department officers are not part of the mainstream of the real estate business.

Fixed-fee compensation may be new to the real estate business, but it is the only thing the pension business knows. Pension sponsors manage their fund assets by farming them out to investment advisors: under current regulations, the SEC forbids these advisors to collect any type of incentive compensation. Investment management fees are a certain percentage of the market value of the assets under management per year. Stock and bond managers make less than 1 percent of assets a year, but real estate managers are the high-priced advisors of the pension fund business, making anywhere from 1 to 2 percent of assets under management. The fee depends on whether the manager is running pension money in a commingled fund or managing individual accounts for specific funds. Obviously, the more money an investment advisor runs, the more money he earns. The largest commingled fund, PRISA, which at this writing has over $4 billion in assets, pulls in more than $40 million in fees each year. Investment managers who run smaller commingled pools or who manage accounts individually for smaller funds would probably make more money without registering with the SEC and by taking a piece of the deals they do.

Those interested in the incentive compensation issue should contact The Pension Real Estate Investment Association (PREIA), a non-profit, educational organization of pension fund real estate managers. Members of this group closely monitor the regulations issued by the DOL, SEC and IRS to see if they affect pension fund investing in property. The group's address is listed in the bibliography.

Commissions

In the real estate business, it is common for those involved in any deal to collect commissions for arranging the sale, leasing or financing of the property involved. But ERISA forbids fiduciaries of pension plans from paying themselves commissions; the SEC also prohibits its advisors from such a practice. The DOL can sue the offending real estate advisor for conflict of interest, and it will sue any trustees of the fund that agreed to pay the commissions. The ban on commissions is only one of the many prohibitions against self-dealing by investment advisors set out under a section of ERISA entitled "prohibited transactions." Advisors must take care in how they structure any dealings with plans, or they will run into this legal swamp.

PROHIBITED TRANSACTIONS

Parties in Interest

Mention the words "prohibited transactions" to a manager of a commingled real estate fund or a plan sponsor who really wants to invest his fund's money directly into real estate and you will hear screams about "quagmires" and "the idiots and dodos" at the DOL who handle the regulation of these transactions. Bring up the same topic with a Labor Department attorney and he will talk about how the "P.T. regulations," as they are called, have saved hundreds of pension funds from being plundered by their corporate or union sponsors. They may be nearly impossible to enforce, but if they are enforced, they do work.

No one is comfortable with the prohibited transactions regulations. Section 406 of ERISA prohibits fiduciaries from engaging in "certain transactions" with persons who are "parties in interest" of the pension plan. Many of the problems pension funds have with real estate investing stem from Section 406 and how it defines parties in interest.

It seems nearly everyone who sets eyes on the plan or knows its fiduciaries can be construed as a party in interest. Among others, the list includes: the sponsoring employer of the pension plan, people who provide services to the plan, unions whose employees are covered by the plan, and of course, other plan fiduciaries. In addition, the law prohibits the relatives, subsidiaries, major shareholders, or joint-venture partners of these people from dealing with the plan. They, too, are parties in interest.

A plan and a party in interest cannot sell, exchange or lease property to each other; loan or extend credit to each other; or furnish services to each other. A party in interest is forbidden from using plan assets for his own benefit. Section 406 also prohibits fiduciaries from engaging in self-dealing, receiving kickbacks, or getting involved in conflict-of-interest situations. "What Congress was trying to do with this section," says a former DOL attorney who has dealt extensively with Section 406, "was to keep plan sponsors from using the pension fund as their own private bank."

It is a worthy goal, especially when one hears the stories about how corporations, particularly small, undercapitalized ones, drain the pension fund of money to buy a new lathe or meet the payroll taxes. For example, one Maryland corporation had its profit-sharing fund make its sponsoring company a low-interest loan equal to 99 percent of the fund's assets. Small funds are by no means the only problem. The same Alaskan teamsters fund referred to earlier, the fund that the Labor Department sued for investing 80 percent of its assets in Alaska real estate, also found itself in violation of the prohibited transactions rules. In 1981, the department sued the fund, charging it had bought an airplane for its union sponsor.

How could such a well-intended and important section of ERISA contain problems for ethical real estate advisors and their pension fund clientele?

Actually, the prohibited transactions themselves do not cause investment advisors their biggest problems. If the transactions had just been flatly banned by law, that would have been it. Pension funds could do nothing that smelled of conflict of interest; their investment horizons in real estate would have been severely limited. But sponsors and investment advisors are allowed to file for exemptions from prohibited transactions and here is where the trouble lies. The piecemeal way these exemptions are granted confuses everyone as to what the real limits are on plan dealings with parties in interest.

The Exemptions

After Congress wrote the prohibited transactions section, the law was so sweeping the lawmakers felt they would have to allow exceptions. Not everything that plan fiduciaries and parties in interest of a fund did hurt the plan. Some actions that would be self-dealing under a strict interpretation of the law could actually benefit the plan; Congress decided that there should be exemptions to the prohibited transactions rules.

A few of these exemptions are actually written into ERISA and are called "statutory exemptions." These are narrow, specific exemptions that permit pension funds to do things like lease space for a plan office from a party in interest. One statutory exemption does affect pension fund investments in residential real estate. Under certain conditions, the exemption permits pension funds to loan money to participants or beneficiaries of the plan. Union pension funds argue that this exemption, listed in Section 408(b)(1), gives them the legal right to make home mortgage loans to their own participants. Such loans are real estate investing only in the loosest sense of the word, falling more easily under the category of "social investments."

In addition to statutory exemptions, Congress also authorized a second type of exemption. Congress realized that there would be many individual cases where a specific transaction would be prohibited under a strict reading of the law, but not if the transaction was carefully reviewed. So, Congress gave the DOL and the IRS the power to jointly grant an exemption from the prohibited transaction rules for a particular transaction. Such an exemption is called an administrative exemption.

For example, a plan sponsor may wish to contribute a piece of property to the fund in lieu of his annual cash contribution. If it is a valuable piece of property and an excellent asset for the plan, there is no reason that it should be prohibited merely because a literal reading of the prohibited transaction rules would show that it was self-dealing by the plan fiduciary. Under the administrative exemption procedure, the company could apply to the DOL and the IRS, requesting permission to contribute the property. If both agencies thought it was a good deal for the fund, they would approve it; the company could contribute the property. The administrative exemption procedure sounds deceptively simple, but in fact, it drives the Labor Department, the pension funds and fund real estate advisors mad.

The Administrative Exemption Procedure

The first problem with the exemption procedure is that Congress never designed one. All ERISA did was order the IRS and the DOL to write the rules and regulations for granting these exemptions, a project which took months to get going.

The second problem was that ERISA required both agencies to approve each exemption: people seeking exemptions had to file their request with each agency. Naturally, hardly any exemptions were ever approved since the two agencies would disagree on interpretations of the law. In each agency, the request had to pass the approval of the most timid civil servant who had been assigned to administrative exemptions. It took over a year to get the most simple exemption through, if it went through at all. From the end of April 1975, when the first regulations on administrative exemptions came out, until the end of 1978, about 3½ years later, only 609 cases were closed and only 47 exemptions granted.

The situation was intolerable. Routine prohibited transactions, such as contributions of property to a pension fund, were taking months to be approved. Dual administration of ERISA by the DOL and the IRS was not working, and it was at its worst with prohibited transactions. Consequently, in 1979 President Carter split up agency jurisdiction more clearly, giving the DOL complete authority to rule on exemptions. The pace of exemption-granting has picked up since then; the DOL is proud that in the first nine months after it received jurisdiction, it was able to close as many cases and grant as many exemptions as were processed in the first 3½ years under dual administration. The DOL closed 505 cases and granted 60 exemptions in that nine-month period.

But pension sponsors, investment advisors, and other fiduciaries and business contacts of the funds still find the process a terrible nuisance. It is important to realize that it makes no difference whether a transaction is reasonable and fair to the plan, or even more than fair to the plan. If it is a prohibited transaction, the fiduciary and parties in interest involved cannot proceed unless thay can get an administrative exemption from the DOL.

In a speech reprinted by the DOL in 1979, Ian Lanoff, then administrator of the Pension and Welfare Benefit Programs at the Labor Department, gave the following advice on how one should apply for an administrative exemption. The application must:

. . . be as complete as possible. Copies of all contracts, leases, appraisals, and other material documents should be submitted with the original application. The application should include a detailed description of the transaction or transactions involved, identifying all the parties to the transaction and specifying their relationship to the plan and each other.[4]

If all the above are not enclosed, the department will dismiss the application for being "procedurally insufficient," Lanoff said. If the parties apply for an exemption for an "ongoing transaction," such as a long-term lease or mortgage, the department will be more inclined to grant it if the parties hire an independent fiduciary to monitor the investment and protect the plan's best interests. Independent fiduciaries can be "hired and fired" like anyone else, Lanoff conceded. But "the presence of an independent fiduciary is a most persuasive factor in considering exemption applications of this type."[5]

The Labor Department decides to grant or reject the exemption based on the sketchy criteria set out in ERISA for deciding such exemptions. The DOL can grant an exemption only if the transaction is "administratively feasible, in the interests of plan participants, and protects their rights."[6] This basically means the DOL can approve or reject anything it wishes. The Department is making investment judgments about whether or not a specific deal is a good one for the plan. As the final blow, before the DOL can grant any exemption, ERISA requires they publish the details of the request in the *Federal Register*; some interested person might want to comment on it.

If a plan fiduciary takes one look at this involved procedure and decides to do the transaction anyway, he has technically violated the law. If he is caught, the IRS will levy an excise tax, based on the amount of fund money involved. This is less onerous than it first appears, but the threat of a penalty tax is another nuisance.

There are minor transactions, occurring in the normal course of administering a real estate portfolio, that force plan fiduciaries to seek exemptions from the prohibited transaction rules. Some fiduciaries, rather than deal with the expense and aggravation of seeking an exemption, simply will not conduct the transaction, to the detriment of the plan.

A good example involved an $80 million profitsharing fund that owned an old building leased to the telephone company at an extraordinarily low rent. The pension officer wanted to clear the lease out of his fund's portfolio, but the telephone company was not interested in buying the building. The fund's sponsoring company stepped in and offered to purchase the building at twice what it was worth as an accommodation to the plan. This was the good news; the bad news was that the sale was a prohibited transaction. The pension officer estimated it would take six months to a year for the DOL to process his application. It would cost the fund double what the property was worth to hire a lawyer to draft the application or to have the pension officer do the work, figuring his time was equally as valuable. Needless to say, the telephone building and a few other marginal assets are still sitting in that fund.

This type of story is still rare because pension funds rarely manage their real estate themselves. But if funds become more active real estate investors, they will want to do business with the friends and partners of people they already know. That means prohibited transactions problems. If a pension fund does a joint venture with a real estate developer and then does another joint venture with a friend of that developer or a partner of that developer on another project, that is a prohibited transaction. The pension sponsor must seek an exemption.

The DOL personnel who work on exemptions are learning more about real estate investing. But at this writing, the department has no one who handles real estate transactions exclusively.

The Nuisance Multiplied

The prohibited transactions rules occasionally trouble individual pension funds. But they really affect investment managers who run real estate for pension clients—either as individual accounts or in commingled funds. Think of all the potential conflict of interest situations a commingled fund manager can fall into. If he has $50 million from 50 pension funds in his commingled account, he has 50 independent sources for prohibited transactions problems. Not only is the manager subject to the self-dealing laws in his capacity as the manager of the commingled fund, but he cannot deal with the 50 sponsors of the pension plans that have given money to the fund.

For example, assume a commingled fund buys an office building. Six months later a division of one of the companies whose pension plan has money in the fund independently decides to rent an office in that building. The fellow in charge of renting office space in that corporate division does not know anything about his pension plan's investments. He couldn't care less who owns the building: all he wants is office space. But under ERISA, he is a party in interest. Before the manager of that commingled fund rents to him, he must get an exemption from the DOL.

In another situation, assume a commingled fund managed by a real estate firm owns a hotel. An employee of one of the companies whose plan is in the fund wishes to stay overnight at that hotel. Unless the fund manager has received an exemption from DOL, that employee will have to spend the night elsewhere. The fund would violate the law if it rented to him. If a commingled fund wants to borrow money from the bank that happens to be the trustee of one of the pension plans contributing to the fund, it runs into another prohibited transaction.

The DOL has the authority to grant class exemptions, exempting a broad class of transactions from prohibited transactions. But so far, the department has granted only a handful. It granted a class exemption to commingled funds run by banks and insurance companies, permitting them to lease space to parties in interest; the amount of the lease must be less than $25,000 or 0.5 percent of the fund's value, whichever is greater. These funds can now rent trivial amounts of office space to parties in interest. Another class exemption permits banks and insurance company commingled funds to buy property management services from bank and insurance company affiliates. The cost of the service must not exceed what an outside company would charge. Still another class exemption permits employees of bank and insurance company funds or parties in interest to stay in the hotels that the commingled funds own.

This skimpy list basically exhausts the class exemptions designed to make it easier for the funds to invest in real estate. Note that they deal with only trivial situations, yet the department requires the commingled funds to keep detailed records of any transactions they engage in under these exemptions. Also note that the exemptions apply only to funds run by banks and insurance companies.

When the DOL was considering the class exemptions for bank and insurance company real estate funds, they were asked to extend the exemption to commingled funds run by independent investment advisors. The department refused, arguing that banks and insurance companies are subject to additional government regulation. Besides, they could not figure out whom to include under the class of "independent investment managers." As a result, to date, only banks and insurance company funds have class exemptions. The independent managers of commingled real estate funds continue to apply for class exemptions; at this writing, a few funds, such as those run by JMB Institutional Realty, have received individual exemptions.

Prohibited transactions regulations can have a major effect on the investment policy of any commingled real estate fund. A case in point involved the commingled real estate fund for pension funds, known as RESA, run by the Aetna Life Insurance Company. Aetna bought 10 regional shopping centers from General Growth Properties and wanted to put all 10 into RESA. "It was our policy to let RESA have first crack at anything we were buying," said James Dailey, who was head of the real estate division at the time. "We did that to minimize any conflict of interest problems." He called the General Growth properties "seasoned shopping centers" with old mortgages on them, five of which were held by Aetna. Because of the prohibited transactions rules, RESA could buy only the five centers that carried mortgages made by Aetna's competitors. The five with Aetna mortgages had to go to Aetna's general account.

Why he had to do this befuddled Dailey. "It's ridiculous," he said. "Those organizations with whom we have long-term relationships in origination of mortgage loans are all people who are active as developers and builders. It would be perfectly logical and normal for them to talk to us when they wanted to sell. But even our affiliated companies are prohibited from buying from them."

This means that Urban Investment and Development Company, one of the nation's most successful shopping center developers and an affiliated company of Aetna, can sell its wares to the Prudential pension account, PRISA. But Urban can not sell to Aetna's pension account, RESA. Aetna, Prudential, Equitable Life—all the insurance companies that run major commingled real estate accounts for pension funds—are also the major sources of long-term real estate investment capital in this country. Yet the pension law prohibits them from using their contacts with the real estate community to buy properties they are already familiar with for their pension clients.

"It's inconceivable," said Dailey, "that some sort of mechanism couldn't be devised to reflect that the transactions are absolutely arm's length. Otherwise our RESA is simply prohibited from looking at real estate that we've encumbered at one time or another. I can't say we run into this type of situation frequently," he said, "but when we do, the only losers are those beneficial interests in the pension funds we're buying for through RESA."

I mentioned this situation to a DOL attorney who is involved in prohibited transactions. He defended the law, arguing that Aetna would have found itself in a conflict of interest if it had put all 10 of those properties in RESA and one had gone bad. Whose interests would have been defended? Those of the mortgageholder, Aetna itself, or those of the pension funds, which owned the property?

It is hard to think he could seriously believe that a well-run regional shopping center with a paid-down mortgage is ever going to cause RESA much trouble, but that's the way the DOL thinks. They bring every case down to the lowest common denominator. "What if," he asked, "instead of Aetna Life doing this, we had Fly-by-Night Insurance Company? Every time they made a mortgage on a property and it looked like it was going bad, they'd have their commingled real estate account buy the property. The pension funds in that account were really keeping Fly-by-Night from going bankrupt." He has a point.

The Labor Department's View

For every legitimate exemption application the DOL receives, it receives dozens of astonishing requests. It is no wonder only a small percentage of requests for exemptions are granted. "We can't believe what some people want to do with their pension funds," says the DOL lawyer referred to above. "They ask us for exemptions on transactions that just make us laugh, they're so preposterous." Someone will want to use the corporation's $150,000 pension fund to make low-interest loans to the company, one of its subsidiaries, or the chairman's brother-in-law. Others will send in incomplete applications that fail to explain who the parties in interest are and what the transaction is: the DOL staff must telephone to find out.

Some applicants try to negotiate with the DOL staff. "Well," one will argue, "if I can't use 50 percent of the plan assets on that loan for the new lathe, how about 30 percent? What can I get?" This is a common practice which the department discourages. "I am impatient with applicants who view the filing of an application as the opening round of a negotiation," Ian Lanoff, head of DOL's pension department at the time, told an audience in 1979.[7] The problem is the pension sponsor's attitude. He clearly looks at the pension fund as a private source of capital for his corporate or union operations.

In the process of weeding out the predators from those truly trying to invest for the plan's benefit, the DOL staff finds it must make investment decisions about the transactions it reviews. "It's a very big problem for us," says the DOL attorney. "Many of these transactions coming in for an exemption are very complex. You have to figure them out." The staff is becoming more sophisticated about investments, the attorney says. But as more funds invest in real estate and other complex investments, how will a civil servant be able to separate the good investments from the bad? Pension funds hire professional investors to manage their money; the DOL is second-guessing them when it analyzes prohibited transactions.

If it takes six months to a year to get such an exemption, that is sometimes as good as banning the transaction outright. A developer might not wait around six months for his potential buyer to get DOL approval, especially if he can sell the property to someone else more quickly. And what if, after waiting so long for the results, the parties find the department denies the exemption? That is money and time out the window.

The DOL has no intention of issuing class exemptions that would permit pension plans or commingled real estate funds to deal with partners of their parent companies or the parent companies themselves. The prohibited transactions rules appear here to stay. The DOL is trying to protect plans from inappropriate transactions with parties in interest. If the plan must pass up a great investment because someone at the Labor Department did not understand it, that is the price it pays for protection. The exemption procedure is a nuisance for conscientious investment managers and pension sponsors, but a necessary nuisance.

The Legal Problems of Passive Investing

Real estate firms will only have trouble with prohibited transactions and incentive compensation if they manage real estate for pension funds as investment advisors. In that case, the pension funds remain passive investors and the real estate managers make the investment decisions. The managers are fiduciaries of the fund under ERISA. But if a real estate company sets up a partnership with a pension fund and both parties are general partners, then the real estate company avoids becoming a plan fiduciary; the two parties are partners and equals.

This distinction appears to be straightforward. Show that a company is a fund's investment manager; that company is a plan fiduciary under ERISA. Show that the company and the fund are merely partners in an investment; the company is not an ERISA fiduciary. But how does one distinguish between investment managers and partners? The question is deceptively simple—and still unanswered.

For example, if a pension fund buys IBM common stock, are the IBM directors fiduciaries of the pension fund under ERISA? The directors are running IBM on behalf of the shareholders and could be said to be trustees and investment managers for the shareholders. The pension fund is a shareholder; therefore, the IBM directors are trustees and fiduciaries of the fund under ERISA.

Clearly, this is a ridiculous situation. Corporate directors should not find themselves ERISA fiduciaries of pension funds just because some fund bought their stock that morning. But how can the situation with IBM be distinguished from that of a thinly traded real estate company where most of the shareholders just happen to be pension plans? Are the officers of that company plan fiduciaries under ERISA? If so, what distinguishes their corporation from IBM?

These are the types of fiduciary questions the Department of Labor has been grappling with since ERISA was passed in 1974. The department has written that ERISA clearly did not intend that every time a pension fund invested in a business the assets of that business should be considered plan assets and its officers, fiduciaries.[8] But how should the distinction be drawn? At this writing, the question remains unanswered. The Department of Labor proposed a regulation defining plan assets in 1979. Although the present head of the Labor Department's pension division has promised a final regulation soon, none has yet been issued.

The department is particularly confused about how to handle real estate investments. The proposed regulation distinguishes between a real estate company that uses pension money to develop and manage property and another that uses pension money to buy and hold existing property. The department wrote that the company that developed property was an operating real estate company. The pension plans probably bought into the company as an investment, just like they would buy a share of IBM. Therefore, the company's owners were not fiduciaries of their pension investors' money under ERISA: the owners were not running plan assets.

But the company that bought and held real estate as an investment was a fiduciary of its pension fund shareholders, the department said. Because it merely bought and held property on behalf of its shareholders, the company was their investment advisor. It is an investment company: its assets should be considered plan assets and its managers fiduciaries of the pension plans that are shareholders.

But as every real estate investor knows, no clear-cut line can be drawn between a company or partnership that builds property and another that just buys it. What happens if a real estate company uses pension fund money to build a property and then just keeps the property as an investment? Do the company officers become fiduciaries under ERISA because they have become passive investors in the Department of Labor's eyes? What if they buy some properties and build others? The distinction between operating and investment company does not hold up.

To avoid this problem, the DOL is also considering using a percentage of assets test as part of the final regulation. If a company invested in real estate and 75 or 80 percent of its assets came from pension funds, then it would be deemed to be running plan assets and would be a fiduciary under ERISA. If it ran less than that, it would not be a fiduciary. But again, at this writing, the department still is not clear on what the final plan assets regulation will be.

In the meantime, there are a number of vehicles that investment managers are using to allow pension funds to passively invest in real estate. No one vehicle has come forth as the ideal method to pool pension money for property investing. Pooled funds have been set up as group trusts, tax-exempt corporations, limited partnerships and real estate investment trusts. The insurance companies run their pools as separate accounts, and the bank and trust companies run commingled funds and common trust funds. The name "commingled fund" that is applied to all these different pools comes from the name of the pooled accounts run by banks.

The vast majority of commingled fund managers are fiduciaries under ERISA and must concern themselves with prohibited transactions. Some have filed for and received exemptions that allow them to invest a certain percentage of assets in deals that involve the parent companies of their investors.

But few pooled fund managers are not ERISA fiduciaries of the pension fund money they manage. For example, the commingled funds run by Coldwell Banker in Los Angeles are set up as limited partnerships. Coldwell is not a fiduciary of the funds under ERISA, though it bears the fiduciary responsibility that any general partner has toward its limited partners. This stand has certainly not hurt the funds' marketing efforts. Coldwell Banker runs one of the largest collections of real estate commingled funds in the pension business, and its funds are lumped together with all those run by banks and other investment managers under the category "commingled funds." Because it is not a fiduciary under ERISA, Coldwell Banker is not subject to the prohibited transactions regulations. It does have an advisory committee made up of its pension clients to review any transactions that might be construed as self-dealing. But this committee is Coldwell's own creation.

Coldwell's example shows that not all managers of commingled funds must automatically consider themselves fiduciaries under ERISA, though most of them do. Once the Department of Labor issues the final regulation on the subject, it will still take months to devise interpretations that can be securely applied. Those real estate companies that want to do deals with pension funds as passive investors—which is nearly every deal done with a fund—need a very good and flexible pension attorney to guide them through this area.

If a real estate company finds itself a fiduciary of a pension plan under ERISA, the company is subject to the prohibited transactions rules. It cannot collect commissions on the sale and purchase of property for that fund, and the officers of the real estate company are personally liable if they are sued for imprudent investing by one of their client's plan participants and lose. These restrictions are uncomfortable but not reasons to always avoid becoming a fiduciary under ERISA. The sales commission income is not that great, and it is highly unlikely that a real estate advisor will be sued for imprudent investing, much less lose. Finally, the penalties for engaging in prohibited transactions are not that serious, assuming that a real estate advisor gets caught in the first place, which is unlikely.

The Penalties for Prohibited Transactions

The Department of Labor is responsible for determining if a prohibited transaction has been committed; the IRS then levies and collects an excise tax on the guilty parties, or "disqualified persons," as the law calls them. The excise tax is 5 percent of the amount of money involved in the prohibited transaction for each taxable year, or part of a year, that the transaction exists. The tax stops accumulating only when the prohibited transaction is "corrected" and ends. Unless the guilty correct the transaction within a specified time, the tax rises to 100 percent of the amount involved. The fiduciary responsible may also be held personally liable under the prudent man rule for any losses incurred by the fund on the transaction.

The IRS appears to have the power to interpret the law on penalties. But at this writing, it has not defined what some key terms mean, such as "correction," "amount involved," and "correction period." In effect, writes Daniel Knickerbocker, in an excellent piece on prohibited transactions, "no prohibited transaction can die until the tax authorities sign the death certificate. The prospect is a frightening one . . ."[9]

The prospect may be frightening, but the reality is something else. In the first place, it is not totally clear that the IRS has the authority to levy the tax. It might share some with the DOL. Second, "the rules (for levying this tax) may be simpler to state than to apply," writes Knickerbocker.[10] As an example, he cites a trustee of a pension fund who receives a favorable personal loan from a local bank for depositing the fund's short-term deposits there: the penalty excise tax would be 5 percent of the amount involved. But what is the "amount involved"— the plan's assets or the amount of the loan?

If a property sale is involved, the amount involved would be the greater of the selling price or the value of the property. The penalty would be 5 percent of the price or value, and that could be substantial. But if the prohibited transaction is a lease or a loan, the amount involved is the rent or interest that had been paid up until the transaction was caught—or the market rate which should have been paid—again, whichever is higher. In the first year of a 10-year lease or loan, 5 percent of one year's payments is simply not much money. A prohibited transaction involving a lease or loan generates only a small penalty, assuming the DOL even catches it to begin with.

Knickerbocker points out that although the IRS has retained great powers to enforce the DOL's rulings on prohibited transactions by levying this excise tax, there are few signs that it is using them. He writes:

Will the prohibited transaction excise tax be a threat or just a vestigial curiosity? To this writer, Section 4975 is a clear danger—but not much of a present one—for those involved with employee benefit plans.

Lacking manpower and agents familiar with the section's scope, the Service has so far given it little attention.

There are hints that the holiday is nearing completion. But we are still a long way from an all-out enforcement effort. The snail-like pace in that direction reminds us of the medieval saint who prayed, "Oh Lord, make me pure, but not yet."[11]

According to Knickerbocker, excise taxes on prohibited transactions may never be enforced. "Short on manpower as it is," he writes, "the Service may never get around to taxing more than a fraction of all prohibited transactions."[12]

The Labor Department is not in much better condition to spot these prohibited transactions, although the department is making an effort. Each year, the several hundred thousand employee benefit plans covered under ERISA file a Form 5500 with the DOL. The 5500 is actually the pension fund's tax return, and on it is the question, "Is your plan engaging in any prohibited transactions?"

Unless a plan sponsor is dumb enough to write in, "Yes," it is unlikely the department would spot a prohibited transaction. The 5500 is a complex form; it takes the department months to organize them into boxes, much less review what is in them. It is likely that the statute of limitations would run out before the department could spot a violation, prompting Knickerbocker to call the statute of limitations the surest protection from the excise tax.[13]

If the prohibited transaction is an ongoing one, it could be discovered each tax year. But again, this is unlikely. The pension division of the DOL suffered staff cutbacks in 1982. One field investigator told *Institutional Investor* magazine that at present field staff levels, the average pension plan is likely to be audited once every 2,000 years.[14]

There is always the chance that the sponsor's auditor could discover a prohibited transaction and report it to the DOL or force his client to file for an exemption. There is also a chance that a plan participant, angry over the administration of the plan, would charge the trustees with breach of fiduciary responsibility; in the course of an investigation, a prohibited transaction could be unearthed. But most plan participants seem to care so little about the administration of their pension plans that this is a highly unlikely scenario.

Even if a fund is caught in a prohibited transaction, it does not necessarily mean that the "disqualified persons" must pay an excise tax. If they can show the DOL that they used prudence in selecting the investment and did not know they were engaging in a prohibited transaction, the DOL has the authority to grant them a "retroactive exemption." Then, they would not have to pay an excise tax. The DOL "is not wild about retroactive exemptions," as one department attorney put it, and has granted few. Ian Lanoff, a former head of DOL's pension division, has spoken out against them, noting in a 1980 speech that the "department expects to be able to avoid transactions before they happen," and that such exemptions "disrupt the equitable administration of the tax laws." A party in interest who enters into a prohibited transaction without first securing an exemption from the DOL "does so at peril," he said.[15]

But then, Lanoff softened his tone. If the department ultimately finds that the prohibited transaction originally met all the criteria for an exemption, the department would grant one retroactively.[16] To qualify, the transaction must have been administratively feasible, for the benefit of the plan participants, and protective of their interests. "The problem is," said Lanoff, "that with few exceptions, cases do not meet those standards."[17]

The transaction under question may also be poorly documented and possibly part of schemes to embezzle plan assets. If a well-done and documented transaction, obviously of benefit to the plan, floats into the DOL's net, it is a shock to the department staff. They assume the parties in interest made a well-intentioned mistake in reading the prohibited transactions laws, and they will be likely to grant them a retroactive exemption. If the transaction did not work out well for the plan, the parties would have a bigger problem justifying their reasons to the DOL, but it could be done.

By all counts, it appears that a pension fund and its real estate advisors could engage in prohibited transactions, not file for exemptions, and probably not get caught. If they did get caught and could show their transaction benefitted the plan, the DOL would be inclined to give them retroactive exemption. It is an attractive idea, but why risk discovery, no matter how improbable? A firm's pension clients would be greatly offended and upset if their manager was caught in a prohibited transaction. Such transactions are bad customer relations.

But if a specific transaction is a borderline case, the firm does not have to run to the DOL to talk about it. Assume it is not a prohibited transaction, get a reputable pension attorney to agree to write such an opinion, and then do it anyway. The firm has the documentation and has researched the transaction. Wait until the DOL comes after you, which is likely to be never.

One plan officer runs his profit-sharing fund exactly this way. The sponsoring company is in the investment business and is privately held; the pension officer has access to investments that most other pension plans would never have a chance to see. "Should I stay away from them because someone related to us said this is a transaction that may make sense for us?" says the pension officer. "My answer is 'no.' "

So he walks a wire. If it is obviously a prohibited transaction, he either avoids it or files for an exemption. But there are investments he will make where it is unclear that a prohibited transaction is involved, such as the following:

Our parent company does a lot of equipment leasing with company X. In our parent's transactions with X, X pays the company a rental which is about 50 percent of the fair profits. It could be construed as a partnership between our parent company and company X. Now, I work for a subsidiary company, and the subsidiary pension fund has loaned money to company X, secured by railroad cars at a very nice interest rate.
It's a successful and viable transaction but everyone here was tearing out their hair trying to determine if it was a prohibited transaction.

Did he call the Labor Department to find out? Certainly not. He called a pension attorney who wrote an opinion that it was not a prohibited transaction. If the investment sours and someone calls the DOL, he can defend his position with that opinion and his own and his colleagues' analysis of the deal. If the investment works out, it is unlikely to be challenged at all.

"The threshold I've crossed," he says, "is I can defend as prudent, as being a viable transaction, every transaction I've entered into in terms of financial feasibility, desirability, and due diligence in investigating it. I expect to be able to defend those transactions if I'm ever challenged."

Nevertheless, in spite of his reasoned attitude toward the risks in prohibited transactions, they do restrain his investing. "The thing that keeps us out of a much more substantial portfolio of real estate is the conflict we'd have with our sponsoring company. We have all sorts of self-dealing problems and must be very, very, very careful."

It would be misleading to leave the reader with the idea that plan sponsors and money managers are deliberately breaking the law on prohibited transactions or stretching it inappropriately. This man's knowledge of prohibited transactions is rare among pension plan officers, a June 1981 Labor Department study found.[18] In a survey of 1,000 plan officers, the department found that the majority claimed prohibited transactions rules had no effect on their pension plans. Few could cite any they had fallen into. But then most of the respondents who lived such a carefree life could not define the key terms in the prohibited transactions law.

"The absence of such awareness of understanding suggests the possibility that the law may sometimes be violated out of ignorance," the study discreetly concluded. The pension officers have so little technical knowledge of prohibited transactions, that "a pattern of serious abuse probably does not exist," the study said. This is the "ignorance is bliss" school of law enforcement. The government agencies cannot figure out the prohibited transactions law. The pension officers act as if it did not exist, and that handful of investment professionals and real estate people who do understand the law have substantial and unofficial leeway in how they interpret it. They might as well use it.

SOME COMMENTS ON VALUATION AND THE UNRELATED BUSINESS INCOME TAX

Next to the prohibited transactions rules, other legal problems facing pension fund investing in real estate seem anticlimactic. Nevertheless, there are two that should be mentioned: valuation and the unrelated business income tax.

Valuation

In the case of valuation, neither ERISA nor the regulatory agencies create problems for pension funds; the pension community generates them itself. There has been a great deal of nonsense perpetrated about how pension funds should value their property holdings. Most of it is spread by managers of commingled real estate funds, and most of their message is that pension funds need to know what the value of their property is each quarter and to the penny. It is implied that ERISA requires this, when in fact, ERISA requires no such thing.

Pension funds are not required by law to value their real estate holdings each quarter or even every year. But banking laws require managers of open-end commingled funds to post market values quarterly. It is easy to put a market value on a stock or bond commingled fund, but quarterly numbers on real estate funds are meaningless. Nevertheless, commingled fund managers compute them.

Quarterly valuations are a convenience for commingled funds and their pension clients. Pension plans need to add and withdraw money from the funds; quarterly valuations enable them to do this four times a year. Pension funds also base their internal accounting on different fiscal years, and each needs a market value number at a different time. Quarterly valuations provide one. Finally, the commingled managers pay themselves management fees each month or each quarter, based on the portfolio's most recent market value.

The practices of commingled funds have nothing to do with how pension funds that own property themselves should value that property. Pension funds actually have great latitude here. As one actuary put it, it is "wide-open" how they choose to value their real estate.

"ERISA devotes about 30 words to valuation," this actuary pointed out. The law does indeed require pension sponsors to periodically set a market value on their portfolios. But the only reason such a value is required is so the fund's actuary can use it to calculate how much the plan sponsor must contribute each year to keep the plan adequately funded. There is no other reason to "mark to the market" often. Pension fund sponsors should have investment horizons that stretch out 20 years into the future; there is no need for frequent, detailed valuations under such conditions. ERISA requires defined benefit plans to undergo an actuarial valuation every three years, and defined contribution plans, such as profit-sharing funds, must receive one every 12 months. But most plans revalue annually.

In figuring the fair market value of a pension fund's assets, the actuary ignores year-to-year fluctuations of the fund's portfolio. He needs to develop a stable figure for annual corporate contributions to the fund, a figure that does not change every time the stock or bond market moves. So the actuary smooths out the peaks and valleys of the fund's investment performance, spreading the effects of this performance on sponsor contributions over a 20- or 30-year period. He often works not with the fund's annual market value, but a five-year moving average of market value.

"The wise actuary," says the one quoted earlier, "doesn't spend a lot of time worrying over the value of the fund. He makes a reasonable estimate and works from that."

On November 10, 1980, the IRS issued a final regulation defining "reasonable actuarial methods of valuation" for pension funds. The regulation explained how pension funds should put a "fair market value" on their assets using a "corridor."[19] On a given day, the portfolio market value used by the actuary must be within 20 percent of the portfolio's actual market value on that day. The official value must be within that "20 percent corridor." If the actuary uses a five-year average figure for the fund's value, the official market value must be within 15 percent of the actual value. The IRS tightened the figure to 15 percent because averaging already takes into account some of the year-to-year fluctuations.

One actuary used the following example of how corridors work. Assume a pension plan contains only AT&T stock worth $65 a share on the market. But the next year, the value of that stock drops to $50 a share. The regulation says the actuary can value that portfolio, when the stock is $50 a share, as much as 20 percent above that amount, or at $60 a share. He can also take the five-year average price of AT&T common stock and be within 15 percent of that as his official valuation.

There are several other restrictions. The valuation method must be used consistently, stated in the actuary's report, and be performed on the same date each year, or every three years, as the case may be. The method cannot be designed to produce a result that is consistently above or below the actual fair market value. Within these restrictions, pension funds have and use a wide variety of methods to value their assets.

The regulation exempts "certain bonds and indebtedness" from the market value rule.[20] Since many funds hold bonds to maturity, pension funds can carry these assets on their books at cost. The regulation also exempts insurance company contracts from "marking to market" until the IRS figures out how to value them.

But there is not a word on real estate. Most actuaries, when valuing pension plan holdings in commingled real estate funds, use the value the commingled fund manager reports to his clients. With mortgages, an actuary will use the outstanding balance of the mortgages as his market value number. If the pension fund owns a piece of property directly, there is no precedent on how to value it, other than the regulation that the value must be within 20 percent of the actual price the fund will receive on the day it sells the property or 15 percent of the average value.

The simplest method of valuing property would be to hire a real estate appraiser to reappraise it each time the pension fund undergoes its actuarial valuation. The fund could also list the value of the property on its books at cost, assume that the property appreciated each year at some fixed rate, and then post that new value as its market value. Once every three years, the fund could commission an appraisal to correct this number. This simple valuation process is a far cry from the detailed reports on market value that commingled fund managers provide their investors with each quarter. It's not ERISA, but the needs of the commingled funds and their clients, that require such reporting.

The Unrelated Business Income Tax

Historically, pension funds and their commingled managers have paid for any real estate they bought entirely with cash. If there was a mortgage, they often paid it off. They did this because prior to 1981, the federal tax code stipulated that if a pension fund bought a piece of mortgaged property, it would have to pay taxes on part of that property's income. This tax was called the "unrelated business income tax."

At the end of 1980, Congress changed the law regarding this tax. Under certain conditions, pension funds can now buy mortgaged properties without incurring this tax. But many pension sponsors now believe there is something risky and illegal about buying any property with a mortgage on it. In reality, it can be argued that the history of the tax shows it was applied to pension investments in mortgaged real estate by mistake: the tax was never intended to inhibit legitimate pension investing in real estate, only to stop certain tax abuses.[21]

Generally, any tax-exempt organization, like a pension fund, is taxed only on income from trades and businesses that are unrelated to the organization's exempt purpose. In the case of pension funds, the funds were created to be investment trusts for retirement assets, not to own and operate businesses. Before 1969, some exempt organizations had found a loophole through which they could avoid the unrelated business income tax. A pension fund could "buy" a business and its assets, with the seller financing the transaction. The fund would then make regular "loan payments" to the seller. The sale was a sham and the pension fund was really a conduit to pass the profits of the seller's business back to him, tax-free. A pension fund could be used to assemble a business empire, tax-free.

To cut off this possibility, Congress added the Clay-Brown provision to the Tax Reform Act of 1969. Clay-Brown provided that an exempt organization's income from "debt-financed property," which was not used for its exempt functions, would be subject to tax in proportion to the amount in which the property was financed by debt.[22] If a pension fund bought property mortgaged 75 percent of its value, for example, the fund would pay income taxes on 75 percent of the property's income.

Unfortunately, Clay-Brown lumped together all leveraged real estate acquisitions. If a pension plan bought a piece of mortgaged real estate simply as an investment, it was assumed to still fall under the Clay-Brown provision. The new law stopped tax law abuses; it also frightened pension funds away from investing in mortgaged real estate. Ironically, due to an oversight, the Clay-Brown provision was never applied to commingled real estate funds run by banks and insurance companies. Though they often chose not to, they could have bought mortgaged property without incurring the unrelated business income tax.

Commingled funds run by independent money managers, on the other hand, were covered by Clay-Brown. Thomas Gochberg, president of the Smith Barney Real Estate Corporation, wanted to buy mortgaged properties for his pension clients. But the law had to be changed to permit it, which took three years. Gochberg was the only witness to appear before the House Ways and Means and the Senate Finance Committees in support of the bill. The amended law removes the tax triggered by the purchase of mortgaged property, but only under certain conditions.

From an investment viewpoint, the conditions do not make sense; they actually work against the plan's best interests. The law was amended not to encourage pension funds to buy mortgaged property but to keep them from abusing their new privilege to do so without paying unrelated business income tax. The IRS did not want plan sponsors and parties in interest using this new exemption to bring back the tax abuse problems it had stopped in 1969. Nevertheless, the amended law is a vast improvement over the old.

Under the amended law, real property includes not only a pension fund's, or commingled fund's, ownership of a piece of property but also interests they might hold in real estate joint ventures or partnerships. To be exempt from the unrelated business income tax on mortgaged real estate, a pension fund must hold the property subject to the following five conditions:[23]

1. The purchase price of the property must be fixed before the day the fund buys the property.
2. The price or payment schedule cannot depend on future revenue from the property.
3. The fund cannot buy property and then lease it back to the seller or a related party.
4. The fund cannot acquire property from or lease it to certain persons who are parties in interest.
5. To help the fund buy his property, a seller cannot provide the fund with nonrecourse loans that either bear an interest rate significantly below market or are subordinated to other debt on the property.

By requiring the property's price to be fixed, the first two conditions restrain pension funds from buying properties and then using the now tax-free income from the properties to pay for the purchase. The clauses keep funds from using their tax-free status to assemble huge portfolios of self-financed property. They also limit a fund's ability to negotiate for property. A fund is unable to buy a property with a questionable future and tie the price to its future performance.[24]

The third condition prohibits seller-leasebacks: the plan sponsor or another seller cannot use the pension plan to shelter income from a given property. The tax reason is apparent, but the clause limits a fund's options on structuring its real estate investments.

The fourth clause restrains pension funds from acquiring property from or leasing it to certain parties in interest who are related to the plan sponsor. Such persons could sell the property to the plan at a bargain price or else contribute property to the plan at a deflated value. The real estate would then be listed on the plan's books at the depressed value and the sponsor would be able to increase his annual pension contribution since the plan's market value has been understated. Because pension contributions are tax-deductible, the sponsor could claim a bigger deduction than he was entitled to. He could also increase his contributions by leasing property from the plan at an inflated rent. This clause discourages tax abuse, but from an investment viewpoint it hurts the plan. The clause inhibits a plan from acquiring some good properties at bargain prices or from collecting some lucrative rents.

The fifth and final condition forbids pension funds from allowing the seller to help finance the property's sale; it is the heaviest of the five conditions to bear. It prohibits pension funds from using favorable financing provided by a seller. If a seller offers to allow a pension fund to pay off $10 million of a $100 million shopping center over time and at a below-market interest rate, the fund cannot accept it without incurring the unrelated business income tax.

Again, there is tax logic behind it. The clause was designed to keep a seller from inflating the property's purchase price; he would then agree to accept payments on part of it, over time, at a lower-than-market rate of interest. Because the purchase price was inflated, the seller would show on his taxes that most of his gain from the property came from its appreciation in value. This would be a capital gain. If instead he had lowered the price, but charged a market interest rate on his financing to the pension plan, he would have received more of his gain in the form of interest-income payments from the pension fund. The tax rates on interest income are higher than those on capital gains; the IRS wants to make certain the higher tax rates apply.

These five restrictions show how much pension funds are creatures of the income tax code, sometimes to the detriment of their investment strategies. But they are also the only restrictions limiting the purchase of mortgaged properties by pension funds: they still leave considerable room to structure deals.

The amended law does not tax pension funds for buying properties that carry mortgages with "equity kickers." Such mortgages give the lender a piece of the ownership of the property, in addition to his interest payments. If a pension fund is involved in a joint venture or partnership that holds mortgaged property, the unrelated business income laws apply only to the pension investor's share of the debt. The other partners are not affected.

The amended law on unrelated business income and mortgaged properties has started what one observer called "a slow revolution" in how pension funds acquire property. The funds can more easily participate in joint ventures and development projects that involve mortgaged properties. Pension funds will also be able to stretch their purchasing power: by leveraging instead of buying for cash, they will be able to control two or three times the amount of property they do now. The benefits of the amended law far outweigh the five restrictions attached to it.

SOCIAL INVESTING

"Social investments" are pension fund investments made for reasons other than the plan's financial gain. Many of these investments involve real estate, particularly residential real estate. For example, a city employees pension fund may start making home mortgage loans to the local home buyers "to help the housing market." Or a plumber's union pension fund may make loans to local builders who use union labor in order "to help out the construction industry."

Real estate loans made for such social reasons are not true real estate investments as discussed in this book. They are made not to provide the pension plan with the highest return at the least possible risk, but to further some other goal. Social investments involving real estate are sometimes included in legitimate real estate investing programs of pension plans. They are often cloaked in rhetoric about how profitable they are for the fund as well as being socially responsible.

ERISA severely restricts social investing by private pension plans through its prohibited transactions rules, its ban on self-dealing by plan trustees, and its insistence that the fund invest its money "prudently." With few exceptions, if a private pension plan, usually a union plan, wants to engage in social investing, the plan trustees must apply to the Department of Labor for an exemption from the prohibited transactions rules. The DOL rules separately on each individual request. It can grant an exemption from the self-dealing ban, but it cannot exempt the trustees from the prudence requirements of ERISA. The social investment must be a good, prudent investment from a financial viewpoint and bear a market rate of return for the fund. A below-market-rate loan from a union pension plan to build a day-care center at a local factory would never make it past the DOL.

The Department of Labor established a policy on social investing that was first voiced by Ian Lanoff in 1979. Lanoff testified in Senate hearings on pension investment policy that the DOL would permit pension funds to make social investments only if it had been determined that the potential investments were equally desirable based on traditional economic analysis.[25] The investment had to make economic sense. Only then could a pension fund bring in other untraditional considerations in its investment decision.

Public pension plans, since they are not covered by ERISA, are not required to justify their investments under its strict rules. Consequently, most social investing is confined to public pension plans. The most popular forms of social investing are programs in which the fund makes home mortgages to local residents or to the participants of the pension plan. For years, the state of Hawaii pension fund had been the only state fund directly making home mortgages. But dozens of other public pension plans adopted mortgage programs in 1980 and 1981 when mortgage rates hit record highs. The funds' administrators were under tremendous political pressure to help their local housing markets.

The mortgage programs assumed a variety of shapes. The state pension funds in South Carolina, Massachusetts and Texas agreed to buy mortgages issued in their states and packaged by the Mortgage Guaranty Insurance Corporation (MGIC). Alabama's fund bought mortgages packaged by the Government National Mortgage Association (GNMA). California's public retirement system bought from mortgage bankers, and the Hawaii and Oregon funds bought from local financial institutions. Financial institutions in North Carolina went one step further: they set up their own mortgage corporation to package and sell North Carolina home mortgages to the state employees' pension fund.

All these programs received great amounts of publicity in spite of the small amounts of money they were actually investing in home mortgages. For example, in early 1980, the Texas and Massachusetts funds announced that they were each investing $20 million in local mortgages, prompting one man in the savings and loan business to point out that that was "peanuts." Home Federal Savings and Loan in California, then the largest savings and loan in the country, could lend that in one day, he said.

Having 1 percent of the fund assets in local home mortgages would not hurt any pension fund; single-family home mortgages are one of the safest investments a fund can make and could certainly be part of any pension fund's real estate program. But under the banner of social investing, making money for the fund is a secondary consideration. The state of Connecticut announced in the late spring of 1981 that its employee pension fund was offering $40 million of 30-year, fixed-rate mortgages at 13¾ percent interest to Connecticut residents. The fund was offering this rate even though local lenders were charging 18 or 19 percent on mortgages. State Treasurer Henry Parker explained that the fund was offering such a low rate because existing rates were "artificially high." He said, "We've decided that 13¾ percent is the market rate."[26] Connecticut also announced that over the next five years it would make $450 million in mortgages to state home owners. This was substantially more money than other public funds had proposed investing. By 1986, the Connecticut fund should have 16.3 percent of its assets in residential mortgages. This program benefits the home owners of Connecticut at the expense of the participants in the state pension plan and the taxpayers. The taxpayers will pay for it in increased pension contributions.

Most public plan administrators involved in home mortgage programs were able to sidestep the below-market-rate trap. They offered mortgages at the existing high interest rates. If a home buyer could not afford an 18 percent home mortgage from his local bank or savings and loan, he could not afford it from the state pension fund. The pension plan just became another source of high-priced mortgage money, but these first programs did start a trend of home mortgage lending by public plans.

California's public pension plans are some of the few that have branched beyond home mortgages in their social investments. In 1982, about 10 state, county and city pension plans announced they would invest $930 million within California. Of this amount, $280 million was allocated to Small Business Administration loans and another $650 million to loans on residential, commercial and industrial real estate. None of the loans will be made at below-market interest rates. At this writing, the breadth of California's program is the exception rather than the rule. Though they may branch out in the future, most public funds confine themselves to residential mortgage programs.

Unfortunately, home loan programs are not confined to public pension plans. In spite of ERISA, there is one loophole in that law that permits private plans to make home mortgages—in some cases at below-market rates. Naturally, the AFL-CIO, which has been pushing for more union control over union pension plans, found it. The loophole is a statutory exemption to the prohibited transactions rules; it is actually written into ERISA. It permits pension plans to make loans to plan participants and beneficiaries under certain conditions. The loans must be available to all participants on "a reasonably equivalent basis." The highly paid employees cannot receive preferential treatment, and the loans must be adequately secured and bear "a reasonable rate of interest."[27]

In July 1980, Robert Georgine, head of the Building and Construction Trades Department of the AFL-CIO, wrote to the Department of Labor and asked them to define what "a reasonable rate of interest" would be on mortgage loans to plan participants.[28] Georgine was also chairman of the National Co-ordinating Committee of Multiemployer Pension Plans, a trade group representing many union plans. In January 1981, Ian Lanoff answered and said such a mortgage loan program must be viewed solely as a plan investment and not as an extra benefit to plan participants. The loans must be prudent, and the rate charged must be "commensurate with the prevailing rate" offered by other mortgage lenders.

But the pension plan could be "flexible" about its interest rate. The rate could be lower than that offered by other lenders, depending on such considerations as the security offered, the term of the loan, and the amount of the borrower's equity. If the loan bore less risk to the pension fund, the fund could charge a lower interest rate; the Department of Labor would consider that a "reasonable rate of return."[29]

Georgine immediately told United Press International that the department had "really given us a green light" to make below-rate home mortgages with union pension fund money.[30] He predicted a boom in home building and better investment returns for union pension funds, which had suffered from the same miserable investment performance as other pension funds during the 1970s.

The Department of Labor denied that it had blessed below-rate mortgages.[31] It immediately battled with an operating engineers pension fund in Ft. Lauderdale over the issue. The operating engineers fund trustees wanted to offer a home mortgage program and the DOL tentatively approved it. True to its statement to Georgine, the DOL said the fund could offer mortgages at rates below those of other lenders if the trustees knew the participant's employment background well enough to judge that the applicant was an exceptionally good credit risk. The participant could also get a lower rate if he secured his mortgage loan with his vested pension benefit.

The pension fund would have to consider each loan on a case-by-case basis. The operating engineers did no such thing and started making below-market-rate mortgages to all participants who wanted one. The DOL sued the fund and the engineers sued back. At this writing, no final decision has been reached but there will certainly be more cases. There is also talk in Congress about loosening the prohibited transactions regulations as they apply to pension fund investments in home mortgages. The National Association of Homebuilders and the National Association of Realtors are strong supporters of such proposals, a few of which have actually made it to the floor of Congress.

Outside of home mortgage programs, the department has had to deal with some other investment programs that could be called social investing schemes. In 1976, the department issued a class exemption for building trade pension funds that wished to loan construction money to local builders.[32] These pension funds had traditionally invested some of their assets in construction loans to employers who contributed to the plan. The funds did so to generate work for plan participants.

The exemption was a narrow one. Nine restrictions limited the amount of the loan and required that it be made by a bank, insurance company or savings and loan association on behalf of the fund. The bank, insurance company or savings and loan must have discretionary authority to direct the plan's investments, complete authority to negotiate the loan, and the loan must satisfy the financial institution's own underwriting requirements. The builder must also have permanent financing arranged. No one can abuse the pension plan under restrictions like these.

The pension funds of some building trade unions have started foundations to help them finance or acquire property built by union labor. Trustees from the various funds attend meetings sponsored by these foundations and listen to presentations of real estate investments. The trustees of any attending fund may or may not decide to invest; they are under no obligation.

In January 1981, the Department of Labor wrote one such foundation in Southern California and said that as long as the fund trustees invested in these various projects solely on the basis of "economic considerations," it would be permissible for them to invest in projects built by union labor.[33] They would not violate their fiduciary responsibility, providing they used these investments as a way to diversify their portfolio and not as the sole source of their investments. Similarly, the Department has approved commingled funds, run by Prudential Insurance Company and others, that invest only in union-built real estate.

Union pension funds will continue to push for more power to invest for the union's own ends, but the Department of Labor and ERISA have a tight clamp on them. Unless the law itself is changed, it is unlikely "social investing" will become prevalent among private plans.

NOTES

1. Daniel C. Knickerbocker, Jr., "Prohibited Transactions Excises After Reorganization: Ticking Time Bomb or Just a Dud?" *The Tax Lawyer* 34 (Fall 1980), p. 147.

2. Murray Teigh Bloom, "Is Your Pension Safe?" *The New Republic* (October 31, 1964), p. 15.

3. Ibid.

4. U.S., Department of Labor, Pension and Welfare Benefit Programs, *Standards for Exemptions from ERISA Prohibited Transactions Provisions* (Washington, D.C.: Office of Communications and Public Services, Pension and Welfare Benefit Programs, 1979 and 1980), p. 1.

5. Ibid, p. 10.

6. Ibid, p. 2.

7. Ibid, p. 8.

8. U.S., Department of Labor, Pension and Welfare Benefit Programs, "Rules and Regulations for Fiduciary Responsibility; Proposed Regulations Relating to Definition of Plan Assets and to Establishment of Trusts," *Federal Register* 44 (August 28, 1979), p. 50364.

9. Knickerbocker, p. 179.

10. Ibid, p. 175.

11. Ibid, p. 185.

12. Ibid, p. 182.

13. Ibid.

14. Diane Hal Gropper, "The Ordeal of Jeffrey Clayton," *Institutional Investor* 16 (August 1982), p. 115.

15. U.S., Department of Labor, *Standards for Exemptions*, pp. 10–11.

16. Ibid, p. 11.

17. Ibid.

18. "Prohibited Transactions: Study of Impact of Provisions on Plans Issued by Labor Department," *BNA Pension Reporter* No. 344 (June 1, 1981), p. A-3.

19. U.S., Department of the Treasury, Internal Revenue Service, "Income Tax; Taxable Years Beginning After December 31, 1953; Minimum Funding Standards-Asset Valuation," Federal Register 45 (November 12, 1980), p. 74716.

20. Ibid.

21. "Miscellaneous Revenue Act P.L. 96-605," *U.S. Code Conqressional and Ad-*

21. "Miscellaneous Revenue Act P.L. 96-605," *U.S. Code Congressional and Administrative News* 6 (96th Congress, Second Session, 1980), p. 7316.

22. Ibid, p. 7315.

23. U.S., Senate, "Legislative History of Miscellaneous Revenue Act of 1980, P.L. 96-605," *Report No. 96-1036* Section 109 (December 13, 1980), p. 11612.

24. "Miscellaneous Revenue Act P.L. 96-605," *U.S. Code*, pp. 7317–18.

25. Howard Pianko and Robert R. Bitticks, "Socially Responsible Investment and Union Involvement in Pension Investment," *Legal Issues in Pension Investment* (New York: Practising Law Institute, 1981), p. 362.

26. "Ct. starts $450 million instate program," *Pensions & Investment Age* (June 8, 1981), p. 1.

27. James D. Hutchinson and Charles G. Cole, "Legal Standards Governing Investment of Pension Assets for Social Investing," *University of Pennsylvania Law Review* 128 (1980), pp. 1378–79.

28. "Washington Update—NCCMP proposes guidelines for mortgage loans to plan participants," *I.F. Digest* 17 (September 1980), (Brookfield, Wis: International Foundation of Employee Benefit Plans).

29. "DOL says plan's home loan mortgage program may charge lower rates than other lenders," *Legal Legislative Reporter News Bulletin* 15 (March 1981), p. 6, (Brookfield, Wis: International Foundation of Employee Benefit Plans).

30. United Press International, "Union Pension Fund Home Loans Okd," *Washington Star* (February 1, 1981).

31. "Pension Plans Allowed to Offer Participants Cut-Rate Mortgages," *The Wall Street Journal* (January 30, 1981).

32. Hutchinson and Cole, "Legal Standards," p. 1379.

33. Ian D. Lanoff, Administrator, Pension and Welfare Benefit Programs, U.S. Department of Labor, letter to Cox, Castle & Nicholson, attorneys for Construction Industry Real Estate Development Financing Foundation of Southern California (January 16, 1981), p. 1.

PART TWO

The Real Estate Business

4 | A STORY

A BAD DREAM

The following is the sad but true story of one fund's attempt to invest in real estate on its own in the early 1970s: it is every fund sponsor's bad dream about real estate come true. The fund involved was a large public pension plan. Public plans are particularly easy to take advantage of since the boards of trustees can change each time there is a city, state or union election. No one knows who is responsible for major fund decisions.

The names of the fund, the participants and the property have been changed to protect all parties from further embarrassment. "The newspapers in the city where the fund is located had a field day with this story. They were printing things like: 'Trustees squander policemen's pensions on out-of-state deals,' " said the real estate consultant who eventually cleaned up the mess. Call him Tom Jones. "The property became a real sore spot for the trustees, even though the fund had lost far more money in the stock and bond markets over the years than was even at risk here," said Jones. And he told the following story.

THE PARABLE OF THE SULTRY NIGHTS MOTOR LODGE

Jones works for a real estate advisory firm in New York. In 1974, the trustees of the fund approached his firm, asking for help with a real estate investment the fund had made. They had made a construction loan to a high-flying young developer to remodel the Sultry Nights Motor Lodge, which was located in the suburbs of a major East Coast city. The fund had loaned him $1.2 million to completely redo the motel, but he kept coming back and asking for more money to finish the project. The trustees were getting suspicious. Not knowing what to do, they approached Jones's firm and he was assigned to help them.

"Little did we know what we were getting into," recalled Jones. "It was a sad situation. Fraud was certainly committed by the developer on the fund, but it was never proven, and no one ended up doing time. As often happens, the snakes got away, and we were truly dealing with snakes here."

Jones and two of his colleagues flew out to look at the property, meet the developer, and report back to the board. "We told the board it shouldn't put another penny in that place," he said. When the developer heard this, he changed his tune; he dropped his request for extra construction money and asked for a long-term mortgage instead.

"We told the trustees they had the option to give him the loan or not, and we told them absolutely not to do it," said Jones. The trustees followed Jones's

They foreclosed on the loan in the spring of 1975, and Jones found himself supervising the operation of the motel, a mangy establishment like the thousands of run-down, independently owned motels that line this country's expressways.

"I wear the scars of that motel today," said Jones. "There were tremendous physical problems. The motel consisted of 20-year-old wood buildings that had been abused by all four operators who had run the place. The last guy did nothing but cosmetic work.

"We had some other problems, too, including cars being blown up in the parking lot and people's lives being threatened."

But I am getting ahead of the story.

The pension fund had made the construction loan on the Sultry Nights about three years previous. A real estate broker had approached the fund on a cold call, after finding the fund's name in the *Money Market Directory,* which lists the names of thousands of funds and of the men who run them. The broker pitched the board on lending money to a young developer who was making a name for himself remodeling motels. A major New York bank had already lent the developer money to refurbish at least five other motels, using funds from the bank's real estate lending division. In the late 1960s, the *Wall Street Journal* had included the developer in a story on the 10 richest young men in America; the final touch was the MBA he held from the Harvard Business School.

The developer presented the board with a glowing appraisal of the Sultry Nights's value, an appraisal he himself had paid for. It had been made by a certified professional appraiser, a Member of the Appraisal Institute, or MAI, as such appraisers are known in the business. "That appraisal," recalled Jones, "bore absolutely no relationship to the true facts. The appraiser was an MAI, but he really prostituted himself." The board did not know that. It was also unaware that the engineer the developer would hire to report on the progress of the remodeling would simply lie. "He would certify everything had been done according to the plans and specs when it certainly had not been done," said Jones.

With the developer's pedigree, his connections and his reputation, the trustees believed they were making an excellent investment by lending him construction money. They had been reading about what a good investment real estate could be; the real estate investment trusts appeared to be making fortunes for their shareholders. Here was their chance to make their first, small move into real estate. With the professionally done real estate appraisal and a competent engineer making on-site inspections regularly, they felt they were in good hands.

"Unfortunately," said Jones, "the board looked to professionals, even though they were retained by the developer, to give straight answers. It did not get straight answers. No one was doing any hard underwriting on the loans the fund made to this guy."

The true nature of the man they were dealing with did not come out until after the foreclosure. While digging through the motel's old file cabinets one day, Jones unearthed a memo from the developer to his motel staff, a memo Jones called "a blueprint for fraud." When the developer had asked the fund for a permanent loan, the trustees had flown out to inspect the property before making their decision. The panic-stricken developer wrote his staff members a memo instructing them how to prepare for the overnight visit of the trustees. It made shocking reading for the board, accustomed to the genteel mores of the pension investing community.

The memo started out with an instruction that the motel grounds "should be in 110 percent repair." Everything should be clean and neat. The trustees should have the best rooms in the place, "even if you have to completely refurbish the rooms to make them look beautiful." Be sure to give them bathrooms with "noiseless fans," and a bottle of liquor and baskets of cheese and fruit should be placed on their nightstands.

Only good politics, so far: the instructions of a borrower anxious to get on his lender's good side. But then the young developer took off. "It is imperative," he wrote, "that the cocktail lounge and the dining room be loaded that night with people. Additionally, it would be very wise to arrange to have the meeting rooms and banquet rooms in use on the days they are here." The developer then instructed his staff to hire an extra bartender and cocktail waitresses "with good figures and personalities" to handle the "crowds" they intended to have in the lounges. Another minion should invite some of the town officials to stop by and say a few good words about Sultry Nights and the developer. "It must be done so it looks totally sincere, however," he wrote.

He then moved on to espionage. Other staff members should contact any friends or relatives who worked at Jones's firm "to at least get an understanding of his personality." The developer said the visit of the trustees would make or break Sultry Nights and a string of other motels he had hoped to pitch the fund on. It was imperative that they "neutralize" Jones's negative report on the motel or they could be left without permanent financing on a number of other motel properties. But just in case their mission failed, he instructed the broker who had approached the fund in the first place to do some more research on pension funds: maybe another one would make the loans. "We should try and lean on other pension groups throughout the country which might be less sophisticated and more willing to take a smaller return than the knowledgeable investor or the insurance companies," our young entrepreneur advised.

When the trustees showed up, the Sultry Nights Motor Lodge was hopping with enough staged activity for even them to know that something was wrong. Several of them asked the real estate broker who was shepherding them around, "Where did you get these people? Did you have to hire them?"

"The guy only laughed," recalled Jones.

Noiseless fans and fulsome cocktail waitresses were not enough to placate the trustees. They foreclosed. But unlike a poorly performing stock, which could be sold off the next day and removed from the fund, the Sultry Nights was a nightmare that would haunt them for the next four years. Eventually, the trustees sold the property at a loss, but not until they had spent what Jones called "a ridiculous amount of time" trying to straighten out an asset worth only 0.2 percent of their total portfolio. Why didn't they bite the bullet earlier?

"One of the things about real estate is that you become emotionally involved with it," said Jones. The trustees were determined to make the motel work. They had been elected to their positions and were getting pages of bad press on the Sultry Nights. The papers were saying they did not know what they were doing and should not be running the pension fund.

It certainly did not help that the fund had foreclosed in 1975 when the real estate investment trusts were lying in ruins and the income property business itself was stumbling out of its worst period since the Great Depression. High-quality projects were sitting without buyers. Who would want to buy a 20-year-old, decrepit motel, without a franchise name, sitting on an expressway during a gasoline shortage? Investors could not find mortgage money to buy Sheraton franchises in prime areas, much less something like the Sultry Nights. The trustees were eventually able to sell the motel; they were lucky they could find anyone to buy it in any type of market. They also went through hell before they finally were able to unload it.

Among the highlights of their tenure as motel owners was the fight they had with the man who ran the motel's food and beverage operation. Through Jones, they fired him. "We later found out that his nickname in the area was 'The Torch,' " said Jones. "As it turned out, the person responsible for making certain complaints against The Torch had his car blown up the next night. It just happened to be pure coincidence it was blown up in our parking lot."

Jones also discovered that The Torch had owned three restaurants prior to becoming food and beverage manager at the Sultry Nights; two of them had mysteriously burned down the day before he planned to sell them. At least that is what The Torch told the insurance companies when he tried to convince them that the proposed sale price was actually the true value of each fire-gutted restaurant.

The escapades of The Torch were only the first of the fund's problems with the motel. Sultry Nights was located on a major expressway; as the price of meat rose, the motel had a number of trucks hijacked from its parking lot. A homosexual desk clerk created a minor stir by inviting his friends to spend the weekend and charging everything to their rooms. The cleaning staff stumbled across a suicide now and then. "I never realized that people prefer to commit suicide in some place like a motel, which is devoid of anything they know or feel," said Jones. Once they make the decision, they do it in a dump, not in a Hilton.

The 1973 Arab oil embargo basically killed off traffic to the Sultry Nights; Jones and the on-site staff were looking ahead with great relief to the Bicentennial Celebration in 1976. The historic East Coast should really attract tourists, and the motel's business should revive. Instead, the motel had its worst summer in three years. "The Bicentennial was the party nobody came to," said Jones. "The East Coast celebrated the Bicentennial by proceeding to scare the American populace out of ever coming out here by year-in-advance threats of overcrowding in motels and highways and food shortages. It was a disaster."

The crowning indignity was the condition of the east wing. The motel was in poor physical shape, but the rooms in the east wing were so badly deteriorated "that we would have objections from the general public at $15 or $17 a night," said Jones. "Teenagers wouldn't even rent these rooms for casual sex, they were so bad."

To generate some income off the east wing, Jones rented the entire block of rooms to a medical research group that tested drugs on human guinea pigs. Students off from college or young men waiting to go into the service would rent their bodies to this group for two to four weeks; the researchers would use them to test the effects of depressants, tranquilizers and other drugs on humans. The kids would then loaf in front of television sets or read, staggering off to get their blood pressure and other vital signs checked every few hours.

Often 40 or 50 of them would be wandering through the halls and rooms of the east wing. Jones finally forbad them to eat in the motel's main dining room because they were scaring the customers. Instead, they got special catered meals in a separate room. "It was really very frightening," he said. "You'd walk into the motel and see somebody who hadn't been awake in two weeks."

All this mayhem had a tremendous impact on the board. Since the time the ill-advised construction loan had been made, there had been a number of elections, and only two of the original trustees remained. "It was very difficult for them to comprehend the terrible problems we had with the food and beverage operations and the general problems of running a non-franchised motel," said Jones. "The whole thing was anathema to them."

Finally, Jones took them on a field trip to the motel in January 1979. "One of the trustees had to sit in his room in the east wing with his overcoat on because he couldn't get enough heat. The place was hot in the summer, cold in the winter, and had no soundproofing. You couldn't manage around that," Jones said. That visit did it; the trustees decided to sell. They and Jones had spent far too much time fiddling with a $1.2 million asset that would never have a chance at revival unless someone made a large investment to completely rehabilitate the buildings.

As luck would have it, the board was able to sell the motel in December 1979 to a veterinarian. One of his brothers owned and operated motels for a living; another was a building contractor; and all three were looking for tax losses. They would have to strip down and completely redo each room of the Sultry Nights, but they knew how to do it. They got a good price from the fund, borrowed their construction money elsewhere, and began paying off the fund in dependable monthly installments.

After the fund's experience with the Sultry Nights, the board was disillusioned with real estate. But there was a happy ending: Jones and his colleagues were able to convince the trustees that not all real estate investments resembled the Sultry Nights. Jones now manages a $70 million portfolio of high-quality commercial mortgages for this fund. The mortgages have equity kickers and the mortgage portfolio has substantially outperformed the fund's stock and bond holdings. At this writing, the trustees are talking about buying some income property.

Whatever happened to the Harvard MBA who brought them seven years of bad luck in the first place? "Well," said Jones, "a New York bank foreclosed on the five properties it had lent him money on about the same time we foreclosed. The *Wall Street Journal* did a followup piece on the 10 richest young men—10 years later. He could not be found. The notation on the story was this man was last assumed to be in the Mediterranean, but I think he is back in the country." Perhaps, he will pull out his *Money Market Directory,* flip it open to any page, and strike again. Real estate has generated great interest in the pension community; his timing could not be better.

The moral of the story? "There aren't any more crooks in the real estate business than there are unscrupulous stockbrokers," said Jones. "But some people in this business have no ethics at all; that's why a fund should not be investing in real estate on its own. They should find someone they can trust and work through him."

TRUST ME?

How can a pension fund sponsor find someone he can trust to invest money in real estate for him? Certainly he can hire the traditional, big-name money managers that now run his stock and bond portfolios. Many of these firms are now setting up commingled funds to pool their pension clients' money together and invest it in real estate. But are these money managers any better at managing real estate than they are at running stocks and bonds? Or will pension funds have to settle for poor to mediocre real estate returns just like they earn on their securities holdings?

If a pension sponsor does want a better return from a real estate portfolio, how does he know what it would take to make that return? Could he be a more aggressive investor without spending 90 percent of his time on 1 percent of his assets? How would he avoid getting trapped in a Sultry Nights Motor Lodge?

These are difficult questions, and no one has ready answers. But before he can begin to answer them, a pension sponsor must first try to understand the customs of the natives. Once he removes himself from the gentle world of traditional money management, he enters the totally unfamiliar one of real estate. Like the pension fund business, it has its own culture and set of values. The real estate business is complex and confusing, but there are some underlying principles and forces that drive it. If a fund sponsor understands these, he can decide if he can become comfortable dealing with real estate people or if he should stay on more familiar, but less lucrative, ground.

5 | THE REAL ESTATE BUSINESS IN THE 1970S AND TODAY

> I finished my presentation to a group of pension fund trustees and one of them asked, "What's the difference between a wraparound mortgage and a net lease?" Why didn't he ask me the difference between a wraparound mortgage and a football field?
>
> —*a real estate syndicator*

WHAT IS REAL ESTATE?

Mortuaries and Mortgages

Any building and the land under it, or a piece of raw land itself, can be considered a real estate investment. Single-family homes, mortuaries, apartments, ranches in Colorado, breweries, farms, shopping centers, the White Hen Pantry on the corner, nursing homes, hotels, burned-out warehouses, and a railroad right-of-way that stretches 20 feet wide and 300 miles long through Kansas— all can be considered potential real estate investments.

Some real estate investments are obvious, such as a cornfield owned by a local developer who plans to build on it within two years. Other investments are not so clear. A hotel can be considered a real estate investment, but it is also a business enveloped by a building. The business is renting beds and space and selling food to travelers and conventions. Sometimes farms are considered real estate investments. But most people in the real estate business know nothing about farming and consider it an offshoot of the commodities business.

Real estate investors themselves do not have one view of what real estate is. When the head of real estate investing at a major life insurance company was asked how much real estate his company held in its general account, he replied, "Not much, maybe 2 percent of assets."

Yet this company held 42 percent of its assets, several billion dollars, in mortgages on shopping centers, warehouses, and office buildings. The man simply did not consider mortgages to be real estate investments. Only buildings and land that the general account owned were real estate, and that amount was small. Mortgages were fixed-income investments.

But another real estate professional, who makes mortgage loans on commercial properties, chided me for asking him how much was held in mortgages and how much in real estate. "Mortgages are real estate," he insisted. "You never know how much they are real estate until you have to foreclose on one."

Clearly, any discussion of real estate investing will collapse into generalities unless the participants define their terms. What is the real estate that receives such publicity as the ideal inflation hedge and the investment a pension fund should want to hold?

A Visit from a Real Estate Salesman

When asked this question, the manager of a commingled real estate fund or a real estate salesman will give a pension officer a standard one-line answer: Pension funds should buy high-quality, income property in prime areas, diversified by property type and location. Income property, he will say, includes commercial, industrial, and office space which, if he is more specific, means shopping centers, industrial warehouses, and office buildings. If he is adventurous, he will add hotels and apartments to this list. He will then note that his firm or commingled fund is investing mostly in shopping centers these days, since office buildings are "overpriced"—or vice versa.

What a compact world of investment! Unfortunately, in real estate, saying you invest in quality income property is like saying that pension funds buy stocks and bonds. It is simple, true and obvious. Everybody buys "quality income property."

What should a pension officer ask next? Why shopping centers instead of almond groves in California? Or—what type of shopping center? Or—what is income property? All are excellent questions.

The visitor will answer that his firm buys shopping centers not because it would not know an almond grove from an orange grove (which is probably the case), but because almond groves are "too specialized an investment." Instead, he says, his firm buys "small regional centers in secondary markets with good demographics."

The pension officer is stuck in jargon again. Asked for examples of such small regional centers, the real estate man will start dropping names of shopping malls in cities 700 miles away. Unless he is consciously trying to be clear, he may lapse further into real estate jargon and start talking about "deals." The deal is the basic unit of professional real estate investing, much like the share is the basic unit of common stock. For example, the visitor will not say his firm bought the Oakwood Shopping Center with an insurance company providing the money and both of them splitting the profits. Instead, he will say his firm "did the Oakwood deal" with an insurance company that "got a piece of the deal for coming in." That means that they put up the money, or at least some of it, in exchange for part ownership.

The salesman may then embark on a monologue on the Oakwood deal laced with terms such as "cap rate, cash-on-cash into the deal, and expense stops" with perhaps some chuckling comments about "optioning the land across the street to finesse the center's owner into a sale." He will drop names of retailers the pension officer has never heard of and call them his "anchor tenants." Or else he will identify the tenants in the shopping center by the names of their parent companies when the pension officer has no idea which conglomerate owns which retail chain.

The visitor will be vague about what his firm and its insurance company partner expect to make on the Oakwood deal. He will be impossible to pin down and may claim much of what his interested listener wishes to know is "privileged information" as are, apparently, all useful details on any deal. If the pension officer asks this man any questions about what he is talking about, he will look surprised and wonder how anyone could be so uninformed.

Any pension officer serious about understanding the real estate business must ask real estate people many questions they will consider stupid. Short of jumping into the business itself, it is the only way to learn. A pension officer will find he must be pushier and more insistent that his questions be answered than he normally would have to be with a stock or bond manager. A suggestion that the officer would not consider committing money to real estate until he fully understood it may loosen the flow of such privileged information.

It is more likely, though, that a pension officer will be visited by a salesman for a commingled real estate fund specifically designed for pension funds, rather than a pure-bred real estate broker or developer looking for his own money. The fund salesman will have charts and graphs and projections and anticipate questions before the pension officer even asks them, reeling out answers about how, of course, real estate is the best inflation hedge around. He knows his audience does not understand the real estate business, and he probably does not understand real estate either. He is simply selling his employer's real estate "product" for pension funds.

This man's performance is as irritating and uninformative as that of his glib predecessor. If a pension officer wants to ruffle him and glimpse the organization behind the facade, a former commingled fund manager suggests he ask to see the details on the worst deal in the portfolio—the dog where they totally miscalculated and it will take 10 years to just break even, if they ever do.

One pension officer asked this excellent question and was refused an answer by three or four of the major commingled fund managers, proving they are as skilled at avoiding pointed questions as their unpolished competitors. And it is possible the rougher one would be the better to do business with anyway. Maybe he has been too busy doing deals and getting his money from elsewhere to learn how to shop deals to pension funds.

In this matter of appearances, pension officers should recall the poor investment performance of their big bank money managers in the stock market in 1974. Similarly, the most prestigious real estate firms with the longest lists of blue chip clients also can be staffed by incompetents. Several of the real estate investment trusts that went under in 1975 were sponsored by major banks, and one directed by the Chase Manhattan Bank was among the worst.

How can a pension officer learn how to sense such disastrous liaisons before he commits his fund's money? Beyond peppering the real estate men who come to his office with questions, he can sign up for a real estate course at the local community college.

If he is lucky enough to work for a firm with a corporate real estate department, he should make friends with the staff. A pension officer can learn a great deal about real estate by just wandering around after these people as they negotiate leases for a distribution center or plan the construction of a new plant. Watching one of them threaten a contractor for installing cheap insulation but billing the company for the more expensive brand brings home the importance of "controlling the cost of construction" more effectively than any book or lecture.

But in the absence of such real estate friends and teachers, books and articles are all a pension officer has to work with.

At the Bookstore

The pension officer, eager to learn about real estate, goes to his local bookstore and finds several shelves devoted to the subject. The majority of the books sport titles such as: *How to Make a Million in Real Estate and Retire to the South of France—With No Money Down*. The book is a testimonial to how the author built a real estate empire of six-flat apartment buildings and small warehouses in the suburbs without ever using his own money.

He started 10 years ago by borrowing $10,000 from the local bank and buying a vacant lot outside his hometown. He then sold the lot for $15,000 six months later, using the proceeds as a down payment on a three-flat in town and borrowing the rest from the bank. He then sold the three-flat nine months later for $70,000, and on and on.

And now he is rich. The book explains what to buy, where to find it, and most importantly, how to convince your banker to give you the money so you, too, can be rich.

The pension officer cannot fathom how this has anything to do with his situation. His pension committee has ordered him to put $5 million in real estate, and a collection of six-flats and small warehouses is hardly what they had in mind.

He is right. The *How to Make a Million* books have little to do with the type of real estate investing the pension committee is interested in.

The real estate business falls roughly into three parts: the income or investment property business, residential real estate, and everything else. The pension officer is interested in the income property sector, but the hundreds of how-to books are written for those interested in residential property, a vast number of readers. The residential real estate business serves the millions of Americans who own their own home or two-flat or, perhaps on a more ambitious scale, a 24-unit apartment building in the suburbs or a small warehouse or store. The value of such small holdings makes up most of the value of real estate in this country, and the pension officer, if he owns a house, is a member of this army of small investors.

This army has an army of real estate people serving its needs—residential appraisers, title insurance companies, homebuilders, mortgage bankers, savings and loans, government home mortgage programs, and real estate brokers. When someone says he is in the real estate business, he is most likely dealing in residential property and other small holdings.

Consider the National Association of Realtors, the trade group which represents real estate brokers and salesmen—the people who work as agents for property owners, trying to find buyers. In residential sales, the agents collect 6 percent of the sales price if the sale goes through. The NAR is the largest trade association in the country with about 600,000 members. But 85 percent of these people handle only residential sales and know nothing about investment property above the size of a 12-flat.

The residential business dwarfs the income or investment property sector of the real estate business, consisting of several thousand people who make their living buying, selling, developing or operating large pieces of income property— say those worth at least $5 million. Strictly speaking, income property is any piece of property, other than a farm, which generates a cash flow to the owner from rents. This is different from raw land or a house that, unless rented out, throws off no income to the owners.

Although the term "income property" embraces many types of real estate, people involved in this sector normally include only shopping centers, office buildings, hotels, apartments, and general purpose industrial property as "income property." The rest is "special purpose" property and not of much interest to an investor. For example, consider a building leased to a mortician who goes out of business. Who wants to own a building with four parlors and a Gothic chapel on the first floor and an evil-smelling workroom in the basement? Tenants for such a building would be difficult to find and would drive a hard bargain. But there are many potential tenants for an office building or a simple warehouse.

People in the investment property business do things like set up a joint venture to develop a $200 million office park or assemble investors to buy a $25 million shopping center. The community that is involved in the very largest and so-phisticated deals is very small—"about 60 people," quipped one developer. And that number includes investors, developers, lenders, real estate brokers, and mortgage bankers. "There are only four good commercial real estate brokers in the country," noted another large shopping center developer. And he named them.

The pension officer at the bookstore may find three or four books on investments in income property. Equations, lists, and dummy rent rolls and income statements fill page after page, interspersed with commentary about how an owner should prelease his major office building before seeking a mortgage or the importance of keeping your shopping center common area free of teen-agers.

It reads like an owner's manual for a new car. It helps someone run the car and fix it when it breaks, but it will not explain the theory of the internal-combustion engine.

Shopping centers are as complicated as any car and like them, there are certain principles underlying their operation. In this chapter, I will try to isolate the principles behind the income property business. I leave the detailed discussions of how to analyze specific properties to the textbooks on income property investment listed in the bibliography.

Income Property Versus Residential

Pension sponsors are more interested in investing in income property than in the residential market for a number of reasons. The major one is that, to date, the only way an institutional investor can easily participate in the residential markets is to buy a package of home mortgages assembled by the Government National Mortgage Association (GNMA) or a private company. These are fixed-rate mortgages and are just like any other bond investment a pension fund could make. They offer no inflation protection to the lender. When a home appreciates in value, the homeowner, not the mortgage lender, benefits.

However, if a pension fund owns income property, it can claim all the property's appreciation, and it is easy for a fund to make such investments. It simply buys into one of the many commingled real estate funds now available.

Nevertheless, it is sobering to realize that the millions of small owners in the residential market have done far better with their real estate holdings than the professionals in the income property sector. The small property holder has watched the value of his home or apartment building increase steadily along with the growth of the economy after the Second World War and the continual inflation which set in in the 1970s.

On the other hand, the investment property sector has been plagued with periodic losses of billions of dollars. In his excellent history of real estate collapses, Alan Rabinowitz describes the losses suffered by holders of overvalued real estate mortgage bonds and stocks in the 1920s and 1930s and those sustained by investors in real estate syndications and large urban developments in the 1950s.[1] He also describes the busts in large land development corporations in the late 1950s and 1960s, housing syndications in the late 1960s through the mid-1970s, and finally—the collapse of the real estate investment trusts (REITs) in 1975.

Rabinowitz marvels that "so many billions of dollars have been lost so often in investment property at the same time that so much money is made by practically all the holders of small scale properties."[2]

Unfortunately the small investor has always been attracted to larger income property, and invariably he suffers for it. He reads about the fortunes made in regional shopping centers and wants a piece of the action himself. But how can a small investor with $10,000 participate in a $35 million deal? Real estate developers are always looking for money, and the result has been a stream of syndications, partnerships, real estate investment trusts, pooled funds, and other vehicles designed to invest the public's money in income property.

The dark shadow on this perfect marriage has been that, as one type of vehicle became popular and the money streamed in, more and more promoters would enter the field and the quality of the real estate deals purchased would drop. The promoters would make money, not through the real estate investments they made, but by the fees they could earn for putting the deals together. Acquisition fees, brokerage fees, management fees, and sales fees all added up. The rule of thumb is 30 cents out of every dollar an investor would put into a public syndication would go to fees to the promoters and managers.

The promoters would make borderline deals just to collect the fee income. But reality would eventually catch up with them. A recession would hit, the income property market weaken, and all the borderline deals would crumble. The small investor in those deals would lose his money.

All the worst excesses in the history of real estate finance, concludes Rabinowitz, started out as modest attempts by honest entrepreneurs to improve the flow of capital to real estate by allowing the public to buy in.[3] And all these excesses, or busts, in the last 50 years have two things in common, he says.

First, the investors were all one step removed from the property they owned. They owned interests in the property through stocks, bonds or partnership certificates, and knew nothing about real estate. They would buy into syndications that a knowledgeable investor would not touch.

Second, the promoters of these syndications and corporations became so preoccupied with high finance, taxes, and pleasing the investment public that they did not pay attention to what was really going on in the real estate market and with their properties. They had already made their money in upfront fees, and they did not care if the deals turned bad. They did deals that would sell to investors, not deals that made financial sense.

The similarities to pension fund attempts to invest in real estate are striking. Pension fund officers know little about the medium. They entrust their money to "advisors" or managers of commingled funds who in turn contort their accounting and payout schedule—not to fit the nature of the real estate business, but to fit the needs of the pension funds. After all, the pension funds are the customers and they are paying the fees. So most fund managers give them what they want.

Certainly the major investment advisors are sincere in what they are doing for their pension clients in real estate. But as all are finding out, income property does not always appreciate. Consider all the downtown shopping districts that have fallen on hard times in the last 20 years or the community shopping centers in the suburbs that lost their business to the regional malls. There is no guarantee that a shopping center will quietly appreciate in value over the next 10 years. Or consider the more recent examples of new office buildings in overbuilt markets.

To understand why an income property's value can dry up and blow away, one needs to understand what makes it worth something to begin with.

WHAT GIVES INCOME PROPERTY VALUE?

Cash Flow

Much has been written about how income property values are tied to all sorts of things such as the rate of inflation, the cost of new construction, or a city's growth rate. Much of the writing on real estate implies an almost magical relationship between these forces and real estate values, as if the very presence of high inflation, climbing construction costs, and a growing population push up the value of a piece of property—or give it value to begin with.

This is definitely not the case. These forces do increase the value of income property but only for one prosaic reason—they tend to increase the property's rents and thus the cash flow from the building. This makes the property increase in value.

Inflation pushes up the cost of all goods and services, and so it pushes up rents—and the owner's cash flow. Climbing construction costs push up the rents on new buildings and if space is tight, the rents in existing buildings climb along with them—increasing the owners' cash flow. Income real estate in a fast-growing city must increase in value because the population needs stores and offices. The landlords can raise the rents—and thus increase cash flow.

Cash flow. Cash flow. Cash flow.

"When all is said and done," says one real estate investor, "real estate values are a function of how much cash a building throws off and what rate you cap (capitalize) it at."

This means that a property selling today for half of what it would cost to replace it with new construction can still be a bad deal. It all depends on the amount of cash it generates. Such a simple truth is often lost under the rhetoric about real estate as an inflation hedge, so consider this example. In the early 1970s, a wealthy investor purchased a beautiful new apartment project in Austin, Texas. Austin was and is a growing city, and there was a shortage of housing, so the project was always full. The buildings were located in a lovely part of town close to the University of Texas, so tenants included some students but mostly professional and career people.

The investor got a good price on the buildings. It would have cost at least a third more to rebuild those buildings at the time he bought them. So two of the three favorable forces referred to above were in his favor—growing population and a climbing cost of replacement.

Unfortunately, the project was surrounded by vacant land which other developers soon bought and covered with apartments. At the same time, the cost of gas and electricity soared because of the Arab oil boycott in 1973. The local utility companies were basically unregulated and immediately passed along their increased costs to the customer. In this case, the customer was the landlord. All landlords in the city paid their tenants' utilities. Naturally, the tenants ran the air-conditioners day and night, and the first landlord who tried to push utility bills on his tenants would watch them cross the street to his competition if he was not careful.

In the meantime, there had been so many apartment buildings constructed that many of the professional and career people living in the project left. They wanted a swimming pool, which the project didn't have, and they did not want to live with students. No tenant wants to live with students, nor does any landlord want to rent to them unless the option is an empty apartment. More and more students filled up the building. They were noisy and irresponsible. They defaced apartments and signed nine-month leases since they always had the alternative of moving back to the dormitory if the landlord did not like it. He, in turn, scrambled to find tenants for the three-month summer break, but was lucky to find even summer school students to fill the place. He could not increase his rents to meet his costs, competition was so bad.

How much is this property worth? It is still beautiful, since the landlord insists on maintaining his apartments in spite of student vandalism. It would cost two and one-half times the cost of original construction to replace the building today. Austin is still growing. But who wants a building with climbing maintenance costs, sagging rent levels, and nine-month leases? (The landlord managed to pass on his utility costs, but it cost him a fortune to put electricity and gas meters in each unit).

The amount and quality of cash flow—from this very beautiful project—stink. It is a true dog as an investment. The owner will be lucky to sell it for what he paid for it originally—and will probably have to sell for less.

This example, besides pointing out the importance of cash flow—reliable cash flow—illustrates the great effect competition can have on investment property. In fact, competition is the biggest force affecting a property's cash flow and hence its value as an investment. The luckless investor would have had a wonderful investment in his apartments if the whole town had not suddenly blossomed with new rental construction. The students could not have afforded his rents and would have been forced to live in their dormitories.

Competition

"You give me a building in an area where there's no competition," a major Chicago developer and investor says, "and I'll make a fortune no matter what the inflation rate is. Even if it's zero. But give me a building with lots of competition and a 20 percent inflation rate, and I won't make 5 percent on that building.

"Competition," he concludes, "is all that counts."

Competition, not inflation, determined what happened to the Austin apartment project. If that investor had only looked at the vacant lots next door, he would have known someone would build apartments there and that more competition meant rents would flatten. The only way he could continue to make money on his building would have been if he had bought the buildings at well below their reproduction cost. Then he could have charged lower rents than all his competitors who had put up brand new buildings.

Inflation does affect real estate values. As it forces up the prices of everything, it forces up a landlord's costs and hence he raises his rents. But if inflation is 10 percent a year for the next 10 years that does not mean that rents will follow. They lurch forward or fall, depending on the supply and demand for space. Since most landlords sign three-to eight-year leases with their office, commercial, or industrial tenants, the landlord typically has only one chance every three to eight years to catch up with his costs and raise his rents. If lease renewal falls when there is a lot of other space available, he has lost out until the leases expire again, no matter what the rate of inflation is.

The Chicago developer quoted above gave an excellent example of this phenomenon. His firm built a 628,000 square foot office building in Los Angeles, opening it in January 1974. Until the middle of 1976, he and his staff pleaded, begged, and gave away space to tenants just to fill up the building, at a cost of millions of dollars in time, grief, and tenant improvements. Finally, they leased the whole building at rents that averaged $9.50 per square foot.

They had signed five-year leases, and by 1979 some of the leases came due. 1979 happened to be a year when office space in Los Angeles was scarce, so the developer was able to roll over leases he had signed at $7 a square foot into leases at $24 a square foot, an "enormous hit," as he calls it. But if those leases had come up at a different time, he could have been stuck with $11 rents and would have had to wait another five years for the wheel to turn.

The same is true everywhere. In Chicago or New York, 10-year office leases signed in 1969 would have come due in 1979—when tenants were clamoring for office space. The owner would have made a "big hit" on his rents. But if he had signed 10-year leases in the same cities in 1965, he would have been forced to renew in 1975 when the markets were glutted with office space. He would have lost badly. The skill in real estate investing is being able to predict when such big rent jumps are likely to occur.

If an owner signs a five-year lease today and assumes that the rate of inflation will be 10 percent a year over that period, he has to be able to increase his rents more than 50 percent when the leases expire just to match the inflation rate. If office buildings go through a boom and he finds his high rise surrounded by similar office buildings, he loses. If space is tight, he wins. In the interim, no one can measure the performance of that property as an investment. The leases have to roll first.

Prices for income property are merely investors' guesses as to what the future "hit" on that property will be when the rents come up for renewal. They are buying futures, just like stock market investors buy a stock expecting the company to make money and its stock to rise. However, with stocks, an investor can look in the *Wall Street Journal* each day and see if he guessed right. With real estate, he must wait five years until the leases come up. With real estate, a good investor can sense how he is doing even though the final verdict will not come in until the leases come up and new ones are signed.

When someone in the income property business announces that his competitors are "overpaying" for a property or that an area is now "overbuilt," he is really saying he disagrees with them about what will happen to rents over the next 5 to 10 years. Those who are supposedly overpaying and overbuilding obviously think rents will go up more than he does. That is, they believe competition will not be that bad.

The Chicago developer cited above thinks many commingled funds have "massively overpaid" for property, but in the next breath he adds that it is really all a matter of perspective. He points to the case of a pair of 20-year-old office buildings in downtown Chicago that he bid on but were eventually purchased by a commingled fund for $71 million. He had offered $51 million. A good case could be made that the buildings were worth more than $51 million because a number of the major leases were coming up for renewal in the next five years and the Chicago office market was strong. It was likely the new owner could get substantial rent increases. But there were also a fair number of new office buildings going up, so competition was increasing.

The developer believed that both he and the commingled fund manager were expecting to make the same amount of money on the buildings once they bought them—roughly a 15 percent annual cash return over the next 10 years. It is just that the commingled fund manager was more optimistic than the developer about how much rents would jump. If the developer had bought the buildings for $51 million, he figured he would have an 8 percent cash return going into the deal. At $71 million, he concluded the commingled fund was making 5.5 percent. He could see no way that rents would climb so high that this investor would earn a 15 percent compound yield—after going in at 5.5 percent. They would have to more than triple rents when the leases came due. In his mind, they overpaid. Only the status of the office rental market five years from the date of the sale would prove who was right or wrong. What the competition decides to build in that time will determine the outcome.

Competition determines rents, rents determine a building's cash flow, and cash flow determines the value of a piece of income property. But how is cash flow translated into a price tag for a building?

Introducing the "Cap Rate"

Cash flow has a very specific meaning in the income property business. The building owner collects his rents. He then pays the building's heating bills and other expenses and makes his mortgage payment to his lender, or "debt service" as it is known in the trade.

What he has left is "cash flow" as traditionally defined in the income property business. This is real money, hard cash. There is no tinkering with the cash flow number to allow for "equity buildup" because part of each mortgage payment goes toward reducing the mortgage principal outstanding. Unless an expense costs him money out of pocket, it will not be included in the building's expense statement for figuring cash flow, nor will depreciation or reserves for repairs, for the same reason.

If the owner wants to sell the building, he will take his cash flow number, make an educated guess at how much investors or other building owners would want to earn on any money they had invested in a building like his, and then price it accordingly. For example, assume he owns the building "free and clear," that is, without a mortgage, and that his cash flow from the building is $500,000 a year. He thinks investors want to make 9 percent on their cash invested in such a building so he puts a $5.56 million price tag on the building ($500,000 ÷ .09).

Now assume he owns another building, much larger than the first, which has a $6 million mortgage on it. After paying debt service, the building's cash flow is the same as the first, $500,000, and the owner still thinks investors would want to make 9 percent on money they invested in such a building. So he prices the building at $5.56 million plus the balance of the mortgage for a total price of $11.56 million. An investor who buys either building will initially make 9 percent on his money, regardless of the fact that the price on one building is $5.56 million and $11.56 million on the other.

That 9 percent is the capitalization rate, or "cap rate," as it is known. And that is how income property is priced—from a $100,000 storefront office in a small town to a $50 million shopping center. Take the cash flow and divide by the cap rate. No one starts with the price and works backward. He always starts with the cap rate.

The seller will try to show that the cash flow is really higher than it looks. He will underestimate or lie on expenses. He will have tables showing estimated cash flow when the building addition is leased or when the county puts in the new road and the merchants in the building get more business. He might calculate cash flow that includes the "equity buildup" in the mortgage—or excludes the debt service. All sorts of numbers are called "cash flow" that are not. Potential buyers cut right through it all when they analyze the building. In the language of the trade, they "back out" all the owner's adjustments and optimistic estimates, calculate the cash flow the building actually "throws off," and "cap it."

In fact, the owner is allowed just one cash flow adjustment that buyers will not back out. He can show the cash flow assuming the building is fully rented, which to real estate people means that only 5 percent of the space is vacant. Buyers assume they can always find more tenants if actual occupancy is slightly less than 95 percent, so cash flow at 95 percent is used in computing sales price.

The entire value of the investment is expressed by capping the cash flow. There are no adjustments for extra appreciation. Commingled real funds add "unrealized appreciation" to the investment returns they post for their pension clients, but in the eyes of the real estate community this is nonsense.

In a perceptive article in the Spring 1975 issue of the *Real Estate Review*, the successful real estate developer Samuel Zell has this to say on the topic:

Some literature inviting real estate investments refers to "unrealized appreciation," which appears to be some sort of esoteric increase in value. This presently unmeasurable and indeterminate increase is sales puff rather than fact.
The valuation of unleveraged real estate is solely by a multiple of cash flow. Attempts to impute additional value in excess of the current income stream are not realistic.[4]

The cap rate baffles those not in the real estate business because they cannot figure out where it comes from, yet people in the income property business talk about it as if there were a sheet published each day, telling them what it is. No one sets the rate. No one knows where it comes from. It varies with no major financial or economic index like the Dow Jones Industrial Average or the Consumer Price Index.

Yet the going cap rates for various types of income property are easily discovered as shown by a Minneapolis developer who wanted to sell a piece of income property he owned in Milwaukee. He called six potential buyers, mostly insurance companies, asked for the real estate department, and asked what they were buying and what cap rate they were looking for on his type of building. They told him over the phone. All quotes were close and five prospects were interested in his building. He sent them the property's income statements and some photos of the building and eventually four companies made offers. Travelers gave him a slightly better deal, so he sold to them; but if Travelers had backed out at the last minute, he would have had three other people to make the deal—maybe not as profitable as what Travelers offered but close.

Cap rates do behave in some predictable patterns. Big flashy office buildings in major cities sell at lower cap rates than smaller buildings elsewhere. Institutional buyers are chasing the big deals because they are prestigious and seen as a higher quality investment. So buyers must take a lower return, and cap rates must fall. Industrial, office and shopping center properties have lower cap rates than apartment buildings for the same reason. They are more desirable. Apartments are difficult to manage, and there are fewer buyers interested in them, so the seller has to sell at a higher cap rate. Cap rates also vary by region. An office building in Atlanta will bear a different cap rate from the same building in New York City.

Cap rates are always expressed in fractions: $9\frac{1}{2}$, $5\frac{1}{4}$, $6\frac{5}{8}$—down to the $\frac{1}{8}$ distinction. No one will quote a cap rate of $7\frac{5}{16}$ or 5.138, and no one will add the word "percent" after their quotes. It is "cap it at $8\frac{1}{4}$," not "$8\frac{1}{4}$ percent."

The initial cap rate quoted between buyer and seller is only the jump-off point for negotiations, a marker thrown out on the table so both know they're at least talking prices in the same range and a deal is possible. When they finish, the final cap rate may be no different from the number they started with, so it appears they ran in circles. This is not the case. The cap rate the building sells at will set the value of a property for the market, but it does not tell how much an investor is really making on a specific building. That is determined by something the business calls the "cash-on-cash return."

Two identical buildings can have the same cash flow, and sell at the same cap rate—but one can be poor and the other a tremendous investment because the cash-on-cash returns to the owners differ.

Cash-on-Cash Return

This is the ultimate measure of profitability for a piece of income property, much like return on shareholders' equity is the ultimate measure of the profitability of a company. To compute a cash-on-cash return, the investor figures out how much cash he has in the deal. This includes the cash he used as a down payment when he bought the building plus any capital improvements he made that he paid for with cash. He then divides his cash flow by his cash in the deal. The resulting number, expressed as a percent, is his cash-on-cash return.

When someone buys a property, his cash-on-cash return is the same as the cap rate, by definition. The cap rate is really the ratio of the annual cash flow the buyer expects to make from the building to the amount of cash he has invested in the deal. It measures how hard his cash is working for him, and since cash is scarce among real estate investors, this ratio is crucial.

Once the buyer owns the building, he can substantially push up his return on his cash, his cash-on-cash return. He can, for example, increase the total cash the building throws off by forcing up rents as high and quickly as possible, or turning down the heat, or using the money set aside to fix the roof to pay himself a cash return.

Although owners aggressively do all this, historically this has not been the way they pumped up their cash-on-cash return. Instead of increasing cash flow from the building, they worked on decreasing their cash in the deal, which was far easier to do. They just arranged the biggest mortgages they could get on every property they owned. If they bought that great rarity, a property without a mortgage, they immediately went out and negotiated the biggest mortgage a lender, usually a life insurance company, would give them. And they took their own cash out of the deal.

If they bought a building with an existing mortgage, they ran to the lender, again probably a life insurance company, arguing that the building was worth more than what it was worth five years ago when the lender made the original loan. Hadn't they, the new buyers, just purchased it for more? Besides, the mortgage had been paid down for five years, so shouldn't the lender increase the mortgage? He did, or else the buyers would go to his competitors for the money.

Every owner tried to "finance out" his deals—to get as much of his money out of them as possible. In some cases, he was actually able to get all his cash out—to do "100 percent financing," as it is called—without tipping off the lender that he had no money in the deal.

How Leverage Works

A buyer did not need 100 percent financing to push up his cash-on-cash return. All he needed was a big, long-term fixed-rate mortgage—one for 75 or 80 percent of the property's value—that was "positively leveraged." That is, the annual mortgage payments, as a percentage of the mortgage's outstanding balance, had to be a smaller number than the cap rate on the building's annual cash flow, before the mortgage payments were deducted.

For example, if the ratio of the mortgage payment to the outstanding mortgage balance was .0815 (called the mortgage "constant"), and the cap rate on the building's entire cash flow before debt service was 9½, there was positive leverage.

This looks confusing at first, but it is not in practice. Positive leverage is that most simple of financing principles: buy a building to yield more than what you pay to borrow the money to buy it with—and you'll eventually get rich. Real estate people sigh when positive leverage is mentioned, much like pension officers fondly remember when the stock market only went up. Positive leverage sired many of the world's great real estate fortunes and it is easy to see how.

Consider an office building that was just recently completed and has no long-term mortgage or "permanent financing" as it is often called. The developer needs cash, so he decides to sell. The building is fully leased and throws off $1 million in cash flow a year. An investor agrees to buy the building entirely for cash at a cap rate of 9½. So the investor pays $10.5 million cash for the property (1.0 ÷ .095).

Three years later some leases come due, and the investor raises rents. By also watching expenses, he is able to increase his cash flow from $1 million to $1.1 million. So his cash-on-cash return rose from the 9.5 percent he was earning when he bought the building to 10.5 percent (1.1 ÷ 10.5).

What would have happened if he had used a mortgage? Assume that instead of paying all-cash for this building when he bought it three years ago, the investor went to a life insurance company and convinced them to give him permanent financing (i.e., a mortgage) on the property equal to 75 percent of the price. So, although the building cost $10.5 million, he put up $2.6 million of his own cash and the insurance company supplied the rest, $7.9 million, as a first mortgage.

The lender gave him a mortgage at 7 percent interest, amortized over 29 years and payable monthly. The mortgage constant was .0807. He was buying at a 9½ cap rate. The cap rate was higher than the mortgage constant so he was positively leveraged.

Out of his $1 million income stream from the property, the new owner paid $637,000 a year in debt service. That left him $363,000 in cash flow to line his own pockets. He had only $2.6 million of his own cash in the deal, so his cash-on-cash return going into the deal was 13.9 percent (363,000 ÷ 2.6 million), as opposed to the 9.5 percent he would have earned if he had bought the property entirely with cash.

Three years later, the owner raised his rents and cash flow before debt service increased from $1 million to $1.1 million. In the all-cash purchase, this improved his cash-on-cash return from 9.5 percent to 10.5 percent. But with positive leverage, his cash-on-cash return increased from 13.9 percent to 17.8 percent. He had increased his cash flow $100,000 in both cases, but he had so much less of his own money in the leveraged deal ($2.6 million as opposed to $10.5 million) that his cash-on-cash return skipped higher faster for each extra dollar of cash flow he could squeeze out of the building.

As a building generates more cash flow, it is worth more. For the all-cash owner, this means when he sells the building, he will probably get more than he paid for it. But for the mortgaged owner, it means he can get his money now. The more cash flow the property generates, the more it is worth and the larger a mortgage it can support. The leveraged owner will refinance the building, using the proceeds of his new, fat long-term mortgage to pay off his older, smaller long-term mortgage. The cash he has left from the refinancing is all his—most likely to be used to buy another building with positive leverage. Another real estate fortune is in the making.

Clearly, the all-cash buyer makes far less on his real estate investments than the one who uses a mortgage with positive leverage. This is one of the great, immutable truths of real estate investing.

But positive leverage could work against the owner, too. In the above example, he was paying $637,000 of his $1 million annual income from the building as debt service, leaving only $363,000 in cash. What if his heating bills tripled, his major tenant went bankrupt and stopped paying rent, or the building was not generating enough money to pay its debt service? He would either have to come up with the money out of his own pocket or lose the building in foreclosure.

Technically, these would be the alternatives; but in reality, it is a situation that could be avoided. First, it would be highly unlikely that a landlord would lose roughly one-third of his cash flow overnight, assuming the property was well-located and well-run. Secondly, in the halcyon days of positive leverage, insurance companies and other lenders were not interested in owning property, only in holding mortgages on it. If a borrower was having trouble, a lender would prefer to restructure the loan at a lower rate or extend the term for repayment, rather than go through foreclosure and actually take over the property. If a lender did choose to foreclose, he could only go after the property itself and not the borrower's other assets. Mortgages are "nonrecourse" loans secured only by the property itself. If an owner was not doing well on a property, he could simply walk out of the deal and leave it to the lender, losing only the money he had in it.

With positive leverage, a developer or investor could make a great deal of money if his building did well and only lose the small amount of money he had in it if it did poorly. Positive leverage was certainly the goose that laid golden eggs for the real estate business.

At this writing, it is difficult to find good, positively leveraged deals today, as will be shown shortly. But when they do exist, the wise real estate investor snaps them up. Yet, in spite of the clear logic supporting positive leverage, pension fund sponsors and money managers continue to believe that leverage of all kinds is risky. By buying for all-cash, they argue, they avoid the risk of foreclosure if the property hits hard times. So, they reason, they have less risk.

In fact, they have more risk than if they had used leverage. Their logic is completely backwards, as shown by Zell in the article on pension fund investing cited earlier.[5] Buying a property for all-cash is more risky than buying mortgaged property because an all-cash building with problems loses its value faster than the identical building with a mortgage. If it takes $500,000 in cash to buy a problem building with a mortgage, and $7 million to buy an identical building without one, the first will sell more quickly and at a higher price than the second. There are more investors with $500,000 in cash than $7 million, and someone who is taking the chance of buying a problem property wants to invest as little as possible in it.

The all-cash owner suffers another serious disadvantage. When potential buyers analyze a building, they cap its cash flow assuming 95 percent of the space is rented. This is considered optimum occupancy. If a building's occupancy has dropped to 75 or 80 percent, the building is considered a bigger risk and investors demand a higher return, that is, a higher cap rate. But if the higher cap rate is applied to the optimum cash flow of an unmortgaged building, its value drops dramatically.

Zell has his own example, but for continuity's sake, I will apply Zell's logic to the example I have been using, the building with the $1.1 million cash flow.

Assume disaster does strike. The owner's principal tenant goes bankrupt, stops paying rent, and moves out. Cash flow falls from $1.1 million to $500,000. The owner does not have a mortgage on the building, so the building is still throwing off a positive cash flow, albeit much less than before. The owner decides to sell the building in its half-empty condition and a year later he finds a buyer.

Since he bought the building four years ago, the market for his type of building has gotten better and the going cap rate for those with 95 percent occupancy has fallen to 8½. (It was 9½ when he bought it.) However, because his building is half-empty, no buyer will touch it for anything less than 13. The $1.1 million optimum cash flow capped at 13 gives a total price of $8.5 million. Having bought the building four years before for $10.5 million in cash, the owner will lose $2 million of his own cash if he sells.

Now assume the owner had mortgaged the building when he originally bought it and now finds himself in the same situation—the building half empty, the cash flow plunging. His income from the building before he makes his mortgage payments is $500,000, but his mortgage payments total $637,000 a year. It has taken him a year to find a buyer, so in the meantime, he has had to pay $137,000 out of his own pocket to meet the mortgage payments. The building is now losing money at the rate of $137,000 a year.

Because the building is half-empty, he must settle for a cap rate of 13. The optimum cash flow from the building, after debt service, is $463,000. Capping that cash flow at 13 means the buyer must come up with $3.6 million cash and assume the balance of the mortgage to purchase this property. But the owner only had $2.6 million of his own money in the building to begin with, plus the loss of $137,000 he ran to keep the building afloat while he looked for a buyer. His total cash in the deal then, is roughly $2.7 million. If he sells, he makes a $900,000 profit. If he had been in exactly the same situation, but the building had been unmortgaged, he would have lost $2 million on the sale. Clearly, the mortgaged property was a better investment.

However, owning mortgaged property does have its drawbacks. The break-even income is higher than on an unleveraged property, and the owner always runs the risk of foreclosure. These two conditions make it riskier than buying a property for all-cash. In the example just given, the property's cash flow dried up and if the owner did not have the money from another source to make the mortgage payments, he would have lost the building to the lender through foreclosure. But he did have the money—and he was able to find a buyer for the building—so he more than made up for his loss.

Pension funds are more likely than an individual to have the extra money needed to keep a building out of foreclosure and with good real estate advice they will be able to efficiently sell off properties that develop serious problems. So in spite of the risks of foreclosure, for a pension fund, owning mortgaged real estate makes more sense than buying all-cash.

Pension officers argue that they can avoid the entire possibility of foreclosure by buying for all-cash. When they buy a building for all-cash, they will hold it forever, never selling it, even if its return drops. But this is much like holding on to a bond, bought to yield 6 percent 15 years ago, when the going rate in the market is 12 percent. The investor is still getting his coupon yield, but his bond is only worth half of what he paid for it. If he never sells, he will never realize the loss, but he is paying for it anyway in lost opportunities—what he could have earned with the money now tied up in that 6 percent instrument if he'd had it to invest at 12 percent.

Of course, the bond market could come back and rates fall so that the 6 percent bond is worth something again. An all-cash investor can simply hold on to his poor property investments, trying to bring them around to full capacity with new tenants. But why buy all-cash in the first place when mortgaged property—no matter which way occupancy goes—is a better deal with higher yields and lower risk? Zell says of buying mortgaged properties: "These investments produce the kinds of yields that have made real estate investing glamourous and attractive. Leveraging not only produces a substantially greater annual yield in an inflationary economy, but also maximizes return on resale, both as a percentage and in absolute terms."[6]

In fact, there is only one time when leverage works against an investor, and that is when he uses negative leverage. So far, the discussion of leverage has only involved positive leverage—that is, the situation in which the buyer purchases a property for a cap rate that is higher than the constant on the mortgage. Negative leverage occurs when someone buys a property at a cap rate that is below the constant on the mortgage. If he buys a building at a 9½ cap rate and finances part of the purchase with a long-term mortgage at 11 percent interest, he is actually forcing his cash-on-cash return below 9.5 percent.

In our previous example of positive leverage, if the interest rate on the mortgage had been 11 percent instead of 7, the initial cash-on-cash return would have been 3.6 percent instead of 13.8 percent, assuming the lender was foolish enough to lend the same amount of money as before. (Mortgage payments at 11 percent would have eaten up 91 percent of the property's cash flow.) This buyer would have been better off buying the building entirely with cash. At least he would have had a cash-on-cash return equal to his cap rate of 9½. With negative leverage, the more he borrowed, the worse his return.

In the past, bouts with negative leverage were short, lasting two or three years at most. For the most part, positive leverage has ruled the investment property arena during the last 30 years. From roughly 1965 to 1975, the federal income tax structure was also extraordinarily favorable to real estate investing and there was a ready source of capital available to finance investment property. Insurance companies would make mortgages of 90 to 95 percent of a property's value. They were so anxious to put out money in long-term mortgages that they would prohibit their borrowers from paying off the mortgage early. They would write a 10- or 15-year "lock-in," as it was called, into their mortgage.

By 1979, high interest rates had caused long-term lenders to reverse their attitude on loans. It made no economic sense to make 30-year, fixed-rate loans that could not be paid off for 15 years. Instead, the lender wanted the right to call the loan due after five years. He began to question whether it made any sense to be a conventional mortgage lender at all, and many stopped making such loans almost entirely.

The Long-Term Mortgage Disappears

In 1979, long-term lenders began dropping out of the traditional mortgage market after finding themselves stuck with billions of dollars of 30-year, fixed-rate mortgages yielding 8 or 9 percent—when the going interest rate was 14 percent. While the mortgage lender, typically a life insurance company, was collecting such a return, the borrower had been making 25 percent or more a year on his property investments, compliments of positive leverage and a general run-up in property values in the late 1970s. The lender was bearing all the interest-rate risk. But the borrower received all the benefits. Not only did he enjoy positive leverage, he collected all the proceeds of the property's appreciation when the property was sold.

It was too much for the lenders to bear. In 1979, they started asking for and getting a piece of the deal, too. Insurance company lenders would lend a developer money at below-market rates, charge him only interest for five years, or structure any number of below-market-rate mortgage deals. But, in exchange, they wanted 20 to 50 percent of the property's cash flow—an equity "kicker." They wanted to be a developer's joint venture partner, not his lender. Because mortgage money was scarce, the developers and other owners were forced to agree.

For about three years, long-term lenders could demand and get substantial equity kickers on any loan they did. But as interest rates fell in the latter half of 1982, the mortgage market began to revive. Throughout 1982, insurance companies had been taking in money from pension funds anxious to lock up high interest rates in the insurers' guaranteed income contracts (GICs). With a GIC, the insurance company agrees to pay the pension fund a fixed rate of return on its money for 3 to 7 years or even longer.

As long-term bond rates fell, insurance companies turned to the mortgage market to invest this money. They began offering mortgages with maturities that roughly matched those of their GICs. The mortgages, dubbed "bullet loans," ran from 7 to 12 years with 30-year amortizations and bore a fixed interest rate which, at this writing, is 12½ percent for borrowers with good credit. Most importantly, bullet loans have no equity kickers.

Also in 1982, developers who had borrowed money from insurance companies when rates were high and the kickers substantial began trying to prepay those loans and refinance them with cheaper bullet money. At this writing, mortgage prepayments by developers should start funneling money back to insurance companies and give them more money to lend. In their competition to reinvest this money, the traditional 30-year mortgage—without a kicker—could be on its way back.

This scenario depends on what happens to interest rates and inflation because they control the supply of money to the long-term lender and govern his willingness to commit himself to long-term, fixed-rate investments. At this writing, it appears that the revival of the traditional 30-year mortgage, if it occurs at all, will be short-lived. The general consensus among economists is that both inflation and interest rates will start to rise again in 1984 or 1985. If that happens, the 30-year, fixed-rate mortgage will disappear again and will not come back in force until interest rates come down and stay down for several years at a time.

But unless interest rates stay high for years, the traditional long-term mortgage will be back. It is the classic tool for financing income property and has been so since the Depression because it solves the needs of both borrower and lender. It keeps the borrower from having to refinance every five years, possibly at times when rates are unfavorable and could force him into insolvency. It provides the insurance company lender with a long-term investment with a stable income stream, without the need for the insurer to actually own and manage the property.

Income property financing is actually a battle between borrowers and lenders. Sometimes the fates and the economy favor the borrower, as they did in the late 1970s, and sometimes they favor the lender, as they did in the early 1980s. But eventually the wheel turns. The recession turns into economic recovery or interest rates change direction and suddenly the party that had been structuring deals its way finds that it is now losing its clout and the other's fortune is rising.

At this writing, the developer and other potential borrowers have been beaten to the ground. But as mortgage money has started to reappear, their fortunes are improving, though it does not appear that 1983 will be the real time for their comeback.

One of the problems in this duet between borrowers and lenders is that when the music changes, some people are still playing by the rules that governed the last piece. At this writing, with the lender in ascendancy, the way the investment property business operates has changed dramatically from the way it operated in the mid-1970s. The change has been exaggerated by the record inflation of the late 1970s. Easily available, positive leverage, the backbone of the investment property business for the last 30 years—has all but disappeared for the time being. But all the myths about real estate being what one developer called "the ultimate pot of gold" are based on the existence of positive leverage and long-term, fixed-rate debt. All the rules of thumb and folk wisdom about the investment are grounded in the way the business ran when such mortgage money was plentiful.

Investors still use the words leverage and mortgage, but they mean something different today than they did five or even three years ago. The language of real estate is changing, the deals are changing, the tax code has changed, and the relationships among the players in the business—brokers, appraisers, lenders, developers, and investors—are shifting. To get a better sense of how the business works today, one needs a sense of what it was like in the "good old days" before inflation and interest rates took off—and what it may return to if inflation and interest rates stay down.

THE GOOD OLD DAYS

Nothing New

The income property business in this country, just like the stock market, has had a stormy history characterized by crashes, scams, immense profits—and immense losses. History is a great teacher. Any pension officer looking in wide-eyed wonderment at real estate owes it to himself to read Alan Rabinowitz's excellent history of the real estate business, *The Real Estate Gamble: Lessons from 50 Years of Boom and Bust.*

Rabinowitz contends that, with the exception of condominiums, there have been no real innovations in the investment real estate business in the post-World War II era. Some question whether condominiums are even really part of the income property business, much less an innovation. "They're just vertical sub-urban tract housing," insists one investor. In either event, Rabinowitz argues that in the investment property business, "the differences between one time and another are primarily in the intensity and scale of use of relatively familiar, time-tested financing mechanisms."[7]

For example, was the crash of the real estate investment trusts in the mid-1970s a new phenomenon? Absolutely not, writes Rabinowitz. The "same avoidable conflicts of interest and gross overestimates of value" characterized the great mortgage bond scandals of the 1930s.[8]

Much of the new income property in the 1920s had been financed by selling tremendous amounts of mortgage bonds to the general public. The mortgage-bond market grew 10-fold from 1921 to 1931, and thousands of issues were written, involving billions of dollars and hundreds of thousands of individual investors.

With the Depression, 60 percent of these issues were on the verge of default in 1931, and the newly formed Securities and Exchange Commission started examining the practices of the mortgage companies that had issued and serviced them.

Certain respected mortgage companies had deposited all the proceeds from their bond sales into their own accounts and invested them at their own discretion. They would finance the building's construction—and speculate with the rest of the money—while they were legally the trustees of that money. All through the 1920s, the major mortgage companies had concealed the possibility or fact of default from investors so as not to frighten away new investors. When the mortgage market did weaken, it collapsed suddenly.

In default, the mortgage companies were still in control and ignored their roles as trustees. Dissident shareholder groups could not challenge them for control of the defaulted bonds since the trustees possessed the only lists of shareholders and refused to release them. With millions of dollars of bonds in default, the average individual holding was $2,000. A rival group that tried to gain control would find it impossible to notify all the shareholders. The bondholders were at the mercy of the mortgage companies. The end result was the mortgage companies continued to drain all the money they could out of the buildings, and the bond-holders received little if anything.

Individual investors lost billions of dollars in the collapse of this market and the subsequent looting by the mortgage companies of whatever value remained. Yet, notes Rabinowitz, no one active in the real estate business today appears to remember or even know about that terrible collapse.[9] People in the real estate business have notoriously short memories for disasters, so it behooves a pension sponsor to remember them for them. It will give him a healthy skepticism.

It is not my purpose here to provide a history of the investment real estate business, but to show how it has changed over the last 15 years to reach its present condition. Most of the people in the business today entered it within the last 15 years. Their attitudes and decisions are colored by the assumptions that evolved over that time, and it is the present practitioners of the real estate craft that pension officers must deal with.

The 1960s and Early 1970s—A World Without Inflation

During the 1960s and early 1970s, both the economy and the investment property business were more simple and stable than they appear to be today. The issues appeared more clear-cut and problems more solvable. Inflation stayed below 2 percent a year until 1966 when it hit 3.35 percent. It moved higher and varied more in the early 1970s, prompting President Nixon to introduce wage and price controls in 1971. But the general feeling throughout the period was that although the nation would suffer from occasional spurts of high inflation, considered at the time to be 6 percent a year, inflation could be controlled and would eventually return to lower rates. Inflation protection was not an over-whelming consideration in investment decisions as it is today. Interest rates were also lower and less volatile than today.

The investment property business was relatively stable, although a collapse in the market for limited partnerships and tax shelters in the early 1970s "lost the usual billions of dollars for the general investor," according to Rabinowitz.[10] Nevertheless, it was a good time to be in the business. There were beneficial tax laws and positive leverage.

Since no one worried much about inflation, no one looked at real estate as an inflation hedge. "When I first started in this business," recalls a man who now runs a commingled real estate fund, "you used to buy real estate the same way you made a mortgage. If a property was producing $100,000 cash flow, you capped it at 10 and paid a million bucks for it." And if you were a lender who was going to make a mortgage on the property for 75 percent of its value, you would multiply that $1 million by .75 and write the owner a check for $750,000.

Everyone assumed that the property's cash flow would remain stable or increase gradually over the next 5 to 10 years. When the owner sold the property in 10 years, he would get more for it than he had paid, but not enough to consider such future appreciation at the time he bought the building. No one expected to make a bonanza on capital appreciation or increased rents unless they owned an extraordinary building in an extraordinary location.

For example, historically, owners have collected extra rent from their shopping center tenants. Once a tenant's gross sales reach a certain volume each year, he must pay a percentage of these sales to the landlord. This extra rent is written into the lease, and various types of tenants pay different "percentage rents" or "overages" as this extra money is called. In the late 1960s or early 1970s, when someone bought a shopping center, the overages were not even included in the official cash flow from the center. They were considered an undependable source of income, a bonus like capital appreciation, that the owner could possibly collect, but which he might not. So overage rents were capped at 15 while the official cash flow was capped at 8.

Leasing on all types of income property was straightforward. Owners wanted the longest leases they could get from their tenants—10, 20 or 30 years—and rents were fixed for the term of the lease. Owners were most concerned about the credit rating of their tenants. A tenant with a triple-A credit rating from Moody's was the best, and the higher the credit rating and the longer the lease, the more valuable a building was.

A landlord's expenses were just as stable as his rents. Inflation was low, so there were no major forces pushing expenses dramatically up, and there was no OPEC driving his energy costs up yet. In some cases, tenants would share some of the expenses of running the building, but these were fixed annual payments beyond which the landlord picked up the costs. In shopping centers today, for example, every tenant is expected to pay part of the increases in the owner's real estate taxes and to pay part of the "common-area maintenance" (CAM) of the public areas of the center, such as heating and cooling. In the late 1960s, CAM was figured as a fixed annual charge to each tenant, based on the size of his store. The landlord felt these fixed charges would be enough to meet any cost increases.

Financing

Real estate finance during this period was also a straightforward proposition. If a developer wanted to build a new office building, a commercial bank would lend him the money for the construction in a short-term loan with a one- to five-year maturity. When the structure was completed, the developer would get a long-term mortgage from a life insurance company, usually with a 30-year term, and pay off his construction loan with the proceeds.

The construction loan was, and still is, called "interim financing" and the long-term mortgage, "permanent financing" or "the takeout" because the long-term lender is said to "take out" the construction lender on the project. Most often, the developer would arrange a commitment from the long-term lender before he had even approached the construction lender or sunk a shovel in the ground. Once he had his commitment, he could shop the banks for the best deal on construction money.

Construction lenders preferred to lend against takeouts. What if the builder could not find permanent financing after he completed the project? He would probably default on his loan, and the bank would get involved in a messy restructuring, or actually be forced to foreclose—a fate it dreaded.

But takeouts on good projects during this period were not hard to get. Life insurance companies were anxious to make long-term mortgages on investment property. They had been steadily increasing their mortgage holdings on such property through the 1950s and 1960s, and their holdings rose rapidly during the 1970s. Life insurance companies viewed the long-term mortgage as a branch of the fixed-income world. If the yield on AT&T 30-year bonds was five basis points higher than what they could charge on a mortgage that month, they would buy the bond—and vice versa.

Once they had made a mortgage, they wanted to be certain that the building owner would not try to prepay it when rates fell slightly. So they added a lock-in of 10 or 15 years, similar to the call protection they wanted on their bond holdings. If an insurance company was going to make a 7 percent 30-year mortgage, they wanted to lock in that return as long as possible.

Owning real estate did not appeal to insurance companies at this time, and they had only 3 percent of their assets invested in property ownership. Since both owning and mortgaging gave stable rates of return in that stable world, why go through the grief of ownership to get a slightly higher return? They did not want to create a management or acquisition staff for such an incremental return.

This concern with stable yield brought about the blossoming of something called "the credit deal." Actually, the credit deal had long been a fixture of the real estate business and flourished happily until inflation and high interest rates drove it out of favor later in the 1970s. But for years, it was a favorite deal of all long-term lenders.

In a credit deal, the lender would look for the security of his mortgage not to the property itself, but to the credit of the tenant occupying the building. If a borrower owned a warehouse leased entirely to Goodyear Tire & Rubber for 30 years, any life insurance company would be happy to write a mortgage on that building. It was unlikely that such a financially strong company as Goodyear would default on a lease and, hence, the borrower on his debt service.

The most popular version of the credit deal was the "triple net" credit deal. This meant that not only did Goodyear pay its rent, it paid all the costs of running the building, including the insurance and real estate taxes. The owner just collected his checks, much like collecting interest payments on a bond he had purchased. Mortgage lenders loved these deals. Goodyear was more likely to make the real estate tax payments dependably than the building's owner. Triple net leases meant more security.

The term "triple net lease" is still used today, as is the term "net lease." The number of "nets" inserted before the word "lease" used to indicate specifically just what expenses the tenant paid in addition to the building's operating expenses. In a triple net lease, he paid everything. In a net lease, he might only pay insurance or real estate taxes. But the meanings are garbled today. Anyone who uses the words *net* and *lease* means the tenant is paying for something extra, but it is unclear what it is.

Today, as in the past, not all net leases are credit deals. A building can be net leased to Tony's South Side Garage, but Tony is not much of a credit tenant. It is unlikely that any but a small local lender or Tony's brother would want to loan or buy property occupied by Tony.

The 1960s and early 1970s were also a popular time for a financing technique called a "landsale-leaseback." Landsale-leasebacks are another form of financing and were usually done by insurance companies when they had lent the borrower as much as they legally could as a first mortgage on his property but he still needed money. If his credit looked good and the building was profitable, the lender would buy the land under it and lease it back to the borrower for a given period of time, at least for the term of the first mortgage and more often for 60 years or more. The payments on the ground lease would be subordinated to those on the first mortgage, just as if it was a second mortgage. Hence the term "subordinated landsale-leaseback."

The yield to the lender on such subordinated landsale-leasebacks would be computed so that it equalled what he would have made if he had made the owner a mortgage instead of buying the property. The annual payments would be enough to give the insurance company its needed yield and amortize its investment in the ground over time.

Everyone was happy. The borrower got his extra money. The lender got another stream of income off the property. At the end of the lease, the owner would have the right to buy his property back, usually for some nominal amount of money set 60 years before and perhaps only adjusted once during the course of the lease. After all, the lender had already received his return of capital and yield over the life of the lease, and he saw no value in keeping the land.

Building Empires—Tax-Free

These were the days of 100 percent financing, when an insurance company often would lend a developer so much money on a property that essentially he had no money in the deal. Sometimes, he actually made a profit on the financing alone.

All deals were positively leveraged, and the willingness of insurance companies to lend at such favorable rates meant that developers could create property empires. They would start with a small lump of capital and use it as a down payment on a building. They would then arrange such a large mortgage on it that they could take their capital and use it as a down payment on another building, arranging favorable financing on that one, too. This could continue indefinitely—and it did. One successful real estate developer told me he had been able to assemble his enormous portfolio of buildings primarily because he was lucky enough to have started in the business during this period.

Besides positive leverage, developers had other important forces on their side. The costs of building or buying property were reasonable. In many markets, income from buildings was steady or rising, and operating expenses manageable.

The tax benefits of building and owning investment property until 1976 were, as one developer noted, "extraordinary." A developer had a tremendous incentive to build all types of investment property because he could get big tax write-offs on his income taxes from construction loan fees and interest costs. He could deduct the construction loan interest and real estate taxes during the period of construction. He could also deduct prepaid interest, consisting of all the origination fees, discount points, and other loan charges he had to pay to his lenders. These front-end deductions would offset the income from finished properties he owned. The developer could finish the year owning, for example, four extraordinarily profitable buildings and one under construction while not paying any income taxes to speak of.

The conclusion was that as a developer, you always needed to have a project under construction so that the tax write-offs from construction could be applied to the income generated by your completed buildings. It could be said that the government essentially made you a present of each building you built because, with proper planning, you never paid taxes on its income.

The developer's existing buildings also contributed to his impoverishment for tax purposes. The developer could use accelerated depreciation schedules and write off 10 or 15 percent of the building's cost in one year. Since depreciation is merely a bookkeeping entry, not a real expense that costs money, accelerated depreciation was another valuable tax write-off.

The allure of accelerated depreciation and construction write-offs was that a developer could defer the taxes on the profits he was making from his buildings until he sold the building. Then he would pay his taxes on the profit from the sale at the much lower capital gains rate. Or if he was determined to avoid taxes, he could always use a tax-free exchange and swap his building for someone else's larger property, deferring taxes on the gain from his building once more. The country was lucky developers did not cover it with investment property. They certainly had the incentive both from the tax laws and the free lending habits of life insurance companies.

The general public saw what developers were making and wanted to share in the benefits, particularly the benefits of tax shelter. The 1960s saw Wall Street stockbrokerage firms respond to this demand by offering tax-shelter real estate syndications to the general public. Each participant would put up several thousand dollars, and the syndicator would use it to buy or build investment property.

As typically happens in such situations, the demand for investment property from these syndicates outstripped the supply of good, stable properties to invest in, and the syndicates got involved in borderline, more risky deals. When such properties suffered from the loss of a tenant or a business downturn, the syndicate did not have the cash needed to repair the damage, and the value of the building— and the syndicate's cash flow from it—plummeted. The syndicate markets crashed in both 1962 and the early 1970s with a halcyon period in between. They—and another kind of real estate vehicle, the real estate investment trust—would crash spectacularly in 1974 and 1975.

But before dealing with the REIT debacle of 1974, which ended this relatively stable and prosperous age for the professional real estate investor, it is appropriate to spend some time describing just who the players were during those golden times.

Developers

The key figure during the golden age was the developer. He was the man who came up with the ideas for new real estate projects, found the site, the architect, and the construction company to build it, and persuaded an insurance company and bank to finance the construction. He then directed the construction and owned the resulting building. Developers know how to organize deals. They did not— and still do not—know how to build buildings. That is the job of the contractor and the architect. The developer keeps an eye on construction by hiring a construction supervisor to keep an eye on the contractor.

The developer has always been the most exotic and idealized member of the real estate community, the embodiment of the entrepreneurial spirit, dashing around the country doing deals. Developers have broad sweeping ideas and egos to match. They think they are geniuses and can bluster enough to convince lenders to give them the money to build their dreams. If their dream later turns into a nightmare in the middle of its lease-up phase, it is less their problem than that of the lender. Real estate loans are nonrecourse loans. If a property goes bad and the developer defaults on his mortgage, the only thing the lender can go after to cover his loss is the property itself.

Typically, in this earlier era of 95 percent financing, the developer had hardly any money in the property to begin with. If the lender foreclosed, it was not disaster by any means. The developer had invested a small amount of money in a property and lost both, but he could equally as well have made a fortune. It was worth the risk to him.

Lenders tried to push the balance of risk more in their favor by demanding that their developers personally guarantee their mortgage loans. Then, if the property went bad, the lender could demand that the developer use his other resources to keep the mortgage current and the property in shape. The problem was, and still is, that everything a developer owns is usually tied up in property. His personal financial statement will show that he is worth $1.5 million because of all his equity in his property, but really he can only raise $5,000 in cash in an emergency. If he defaulted on a mortgage, all a lender could go after would be his interests in other properties which, in turn, would be equally as heavily financed by other lenders. Their rights were probably ahead of those of the lender in distress. Chances are, if one lender found he had to go after the developer for a default, the other lenders were chasing him for defaults on their properties. None would get anything but the property each had underwritten in the first place. Personal guarantees for most developers were, and still are, not worth the paper they are printed on—as guarantees. But lenders get them anyway, since if the developer defaults, the lender can swap the guarantee for title to the property.

If personal guarantees did not work out, the injured lender would do nearly anything to avoid foreclosure and be forced to write off the loan as a loss. He would try to restructure the deal by postponing interest payments or lending the developer more money to extricate himself.

This was great for the developer. Not only did he have a chance to make a tremendous amount of money if a deal turned out well, his lender would do anything to keep him from going bankrupt. If he did go bankrupt, he could always walk away from his deals and move to another section of the country, or work for another developer until the lenders forgot about his previous debacle and started lending to him again.

With this perspective on how developers look at life, it is easy to see why a typical developer will still build anything anywhere as long as the lenders will make him a mortgage. As one San Francisco lender noted, "A developer would build the Taj Mahal in Oakland if he could get the money."

Because developers work like this, the number of new investment properties built in a given year in this country is not a function of the demand for space in a given city, but of the availability of money to developers. Developers develop as long as they can borrow. Total new construction is a function of how much the lenders believe the stories the developers have been telling them about the desirability of a specific area. Xerox does not approach developer Jones and ask him to build an office building so they can rent 200,000 square feet of it. Instead,

Jones sees other office buildings going up in a specific area and sees that office space is in demand. He guesses he can build office space and lease it. He might approach Xerox with the idea of leasing a major part of his proposed building and he might try to find other potential large tenants. Or equally likely, he might just approach a lender, tell him his story about tight space, and see if he will believe it—and make him a loan.

Lenders

On the other end of the emotional and financial spectrum from developers sit the lenders. Historically, people who work for real estate lending departments at banks and insurance companies have been looked down upon by nearly everyone else in the investment property business. They are considered dull and stupid "deal-breakers," the people who come up with reasons why deals should not work and are paid to find the flaws. In their underwriting, lenders check to see that any deal they fund meets all their dozens of guidelines. Are projected lending costs within their limits for that area and type of building? Are there enough parking spaces to meet their standards?

A good deal of the complaints about lenders' pickiness is just sour grapes by people who view the lending officer at a bank as their obstacle to wealth. Lenders always try to find a reason not to do a deal because they know how much they have to lose if it goes bad. It is no wonder they never receive much sympathy from developers, though the sympathy increases as the amount of available mortgage money shrinks.

Nevertheless, the developers are often justified in their complaints. The top men at real estate lending departments know what they are doing and are often sophisticated and easy to do business with. But many of the middle managers are nothing but glorified clerks with little or no understanding of the real estate business.

Underwriting a real estate deal requires a great deal of detailed, boring work. Projections on markets, rents and costs all have to be researched and rechecked. Fifty-page leases have to be read, line by line. The analyst must draw up elaborate spread sheets of rents, tenant reimbursements for costs, and expected rent increases over the next five years as well as perform other mind-numbing calculations. Developers inflate their construction costs, and the underwriters must deflate them.

A real estate analyst at a bank or insurance company can learn a great deal about property by doing this grunt work, and many successful real estate professionals started their careers at banks and insurance companies. But they left after five years for bigger challenges and far more money. Banks and insurance companies pay less than anyone for real estate talent, so the talent doesn't end up there. The people who stay "go to sleep," as one ex-banker puts it. To make much money at real estate, an individual has to be comfortable taking risks and must be an entrepreneur. Most lenders are risk-averse.

To be fair, someone has to deflate the overoptimistic rent projections and simply wade through all the deals that go through a lender's shop. It is just not half as romantic as being a developer.

So a bank or insurance company lending department consists of a handful of qualified top managers and an unwashed horde of clerks. The short supply of good real estate managers is a real problem for these institutions, which they remedy by having nearly everything anybody does go through a committee for approval. Lenders move very slowly compared to everyone else in the investment property business. They have been known to take six months or more to approve a loan. As more and more lenders are interested in buying, not lending, they are having problems because, as one real estate developer put it, "all the best deals are done very quickly." If an owner is selling a building at a distress price because he needs money fast, the first buyer with the minimum acceptable amount gets the building. Institutions have missed these deals and get stuck with the mediocre ones because they have retained their slow, lender's attitude while entering an entirely different market—the equity market.

When institutions force themselves to move fast, they can really get into trouble. In the early 1970s, many banks and insurance companies sponsored real estate investment trusts to make construction loans. The competition among them to find properties and put out money was intense, and they had to move fast, making all sorts of mistakes and overoptimistic assumptions in their underwriting.

REITs advised by banks appeared to be particularly poorly run. Banks historically have had more trouble with their real estate lending programs than insurance companies because they do not pay attention to basics. They typically write their construction loans against takeouts provided by insurance companies. So they do not analyze closely whether or not the project makes sense in the marketplace. They figure they are covered by the long-term lender's takeout. He does the analysis, and if the project fails, it is his problem.

The bank is right. It is the long-term lender's problem. But bankers seem to use the same assumption when they write construction loans on projects without takeouts, which is what the bank-run REITs did in the early 1970s—and what many banks did on office buildings in 1980 and 1981.

Outside of the people who come up with the ideas for real estate projects—the developers—and the people who give them the money to do it—the lenders—there is a group of other players in the investment real estate business, most of whom serve developers, owners, or lenders, or all three, and are paid by fee or commission for their efforts.

Brokers

A real estate broker is anyone who tries to put deals together and gets paid by one of the parties if he succeeds. He gets paid only if the deal gets done. Usually a real estate broker is the agent of the seller and it is his job to find a buyer. If he can get the two parties to agree, he collects a commission from the seller based on the sales price of the property. Residential brokers and salesmen almost always collect 6 percent of the sales price, but with the elite brokers who handle investment real estate, the percentage is negotiable ranging from 3 percent for a $5 million deal to 1 percent or less for a deal over $100 million. Three percent of $5 million is still a $150,000 fee and 1 percent of $100 million is $1 million—all for getting two parties to agree, which sounds easy but is brutally difficult. Real estate brokers also can be hired to lease up office or shopping centers, and for those efforts they collect a percentage of the annual rent.

Brokers who deal in the big investment properties that large pension funds like are few in number. Perhaps only several hundred are truly active, and of them only a dozen do the really big deals.

Between 1965 and 1975, investment property brokerage was a good business. There was much money from insurance companies, plenty of new building, and lots of people buying and selling investment property. There were the real estate investment trusts and the syndications to do business with.

To be a big, successful real estate broker, you needed then, as you do now, to be well-connected. You need to know who is in the market for what kind of building and where you might be able to find it for them. More than anything, a good broker has nerve. If he thinks someone has the money to buy or lease his client's property, he will show up and pitch him. He works only for commission, and unless a deal is cut, he makes no money for all his efforts to sell a property. A deal can be bad for both buyer and seller involved, but that is not the broker's concern, though he is most often the seller's agent. He only cares about getting that deal done and at the highest price possible. The higher the price, the larger his commission.

One of the big problems with brokers, particularly when business is slow, has always been that they often do not control the deals they pitch. A broker will approach someone he thinks is a potential buyer of a property, convince him to buy a specific property, and then approach the owner of the property and convince him to sell. The owner may not be interested in selling, but the broker will keep on working on him by trying to get the potential buyer to raise his offer or make some concession.

The broker will work on the owner until the day of the supposed closing. If the broker cannot convince him to sell, the broker will simply not show up at the closing, leaving the expectant buyer and his attorney to sit there and gnash their teeth. They will never hear from him again. Such performances are not confined to small brokers in small deals. It happens with big-name brokerage companies on multimillion dollar deals and only reinforces the poor opinion most owners already have of brokers.

Anyone can be a real estate broker, and nearly anyone is. All you need is the ability to pass a state licensing exam and to convince people to list their properties with you. Most real estate brokers do not know what they are talking about when they pitch a potential buyer on a property. They have no more than a passing interest in the property itself, being anxious only to close the deal and are an unreliable source of information on the building in question.

The handful of good brokers who do big investment deals are the exception. They present professional submissions on properties to prospective buyers, find the information the buyer asks for, and act as a true and steady go-between. They have the confidence or at least the respect of both parties to the deal and almost act as consultants to both sides. But there are only a handful of such brokers. The rest are flakes. Pension officers will find this out on their own as more and more of these brokers troop through, offering to find real estate deals for the fund.

Mortgage Brokers and Mortgage Bankers

The roles of mortgage broker and mortgage banker are merging together among the larger firms in these businesses. But for years they had been separate.

Mortgage brokers are another form of real estate broker, but instead of finding buyers for a seller's property, they find financing for their clients' projects. The mortgage broker represents the developer or owner, finding him financing and collecting a fee of 1 or 1½ percent of the loan amount. Until 1974, mortgage brokers lived in a golden age, just like real estate brokers. Lenders were eager to lend, and many developers were looking for money. When real estate investment trusts became popular in the early 1970s, the mortgage brokers pitched them for money, too. Besides connections, mortgage brokers need only a telephone and a grasp of real estate finance to be in business.

Mortgage bankers, on the other hand, actually lend their own money to developers, so they need some financial credibility. A mortgage banker arranges long-term financing for developers with an insurance company, but then he himself lends the developer construction money from his own funds. Mortgage bankers have lines of credit at local banks. They borrow on these lines, hike up the rate, and then lend the money on a short-term basis to their clients, making their profit on the spread.

Of course, the developer could avoid this higher-priced money by going directly to the bank for his construction financing, but the mortgage banker offers him the allure of one-stop shopping. Not only will he do the short-term financing, but he promises good rates on long-term financing from an insurance company. Historically, many insurance companies have not wanted to do all the underwriting on every loan they made. They could not afford to open mortgage offices in every city they wanted to do business in. So they would sign on a mortgage banker in a given city as their correspondent. His firm did all the underwriting and for an annual fee, serviced the loan. If a developer wanted to apply for a loan from that particular insurance company, he had to go through the mortgage-banker correspondent. The insurance company refused to deal with the developer directly.

Some insurance companies, such as Connecticut General, did all their mortgage lending through correspondents. Others, like Prudential, used none, and still others, like Aetna Life, had correspondents in one city but took direct submissions in another. More and more, though, insurance companies are doing deals directly and cutting off correspondents, thus saving themselves the cost of their fee.

Appraisers

Appraisers have always been the frustrated intellectuals of the income property business. Everyone listens to what they have to say, but no one really takes them seriously. Appraisers did a good business between 1965 and 1974 because so many deals were being done that required appraisals. The REITs were papered with them, and no one really questioned the appraisers' approaches to valuing a piece of property. Inflation was low, the economy stable, and the real estate markets ordered.

The job of appraisers is to estimate what a property would sell for if it was sold by a willing seller to a willing and fully informed buyer, neither of whom is under pressure to do business together. This value is known in the trade as the "fair market value" of the property. It is also supposed to represent the value of the property when it is put to its "highest and best use"—which usually means whatever the development plans are of the fellow who hired the appraiser. If it is a vacant piece of ground and the developer intends to build a warehouse on it, the appraiser cannot assume that the land's highest and best use would be as a shopping center site.

The problem with appraising has always been that it takes high-sounding words and noble goals and lays them thickly over the reality of trying to come up with a number that makes sense and pleases the client at the same time. Appraisers can be hired by anyone who can come up with their fee. After someone pays an appraiser $25,000 to value a property the owner believes is worth $32.5 million, the appraiser had better be close to $32.5 million or he has lost the man's business forever. There are not that many big developers and lenders today, and if the appraiser alienates any of his clientele, he is hurting himself.

To avoid blatant pandering by appraisers, most lenders and developers hire only appraisers who are members of the Appraisal Institute, or "MAIs" as they are known. Tne Appraisal Institute is a trade association that certifies appraisers after they have worked for five years as apprentices and then passed a series of difficult exams. Yet in spite of this rigorous education, the standard joke in real estate circles is that MAI means "Made As Instructed." The value set in a real estate appraisal is usually 10 to 40 percent off what the property actually sells for, and more than one developer likes to say that he never believes an appraisal unless a certified check is attached. People do not believe appraisers, and it is understandable. They are no more capable of determining what a property is worth than any other informed person considering the same property.

An appraiser uses three methods to evaluate a property. First, he looks at the property's income and expense statement and sees if it makes sense to him. Then he caps the property's cash flow at the cap rate that seems right. This is the same way everyone in the income property business evaluates property, but when an appraiser does it, it is called the "income approach" to value.

His second method of valuation is called the "market approach." He snoops around the property and tries to discover what other comparable properties in the neighborhood have sold for and what their cash flows are. He calls up his fellow appraisers, real estate brokers, and other professional connections to see what he can dredge up and will send out one of his subordinates to visit comparable properties and pose as a prospective tenant to see what the rents are. Then the appraiser guesses what his client's property must be worth based on what everyone else's is worth.

The final method of valuation, "reproduction cost," is found by estimating how much it would cost to completely rebuild the property at today's construction costs. The appraiser knows the going cost of construction per square foot, does a little multiplication, and comes out with this value.

The appraiser now has three values for the same building, and if he is lucky, they are all fairly close. If not, he jumbles them altogether and comes up with some plausible story about why they are different. Perhaps the area has not been "discovered" yet as a prime office market, or the cost of construction is unnaturally high or low today. Whatever the story, the final number for fair market value is typed in big letters across the middle of the first page of the appraisal: FAIR MARKET VALUE: $5.4 million. Whatever the number is, it is usually close or identical to the number indicated by the income approach to value. The fair market value for a piece of income property is its cash flow divided by the cap rate. The other two methods of valuation merely provide some extra support for the income method.

Appraisals leave out a lot. The fair market value number is a static number, valid as a value for the property today. In computing this number, the appraiser does not consider the effect of inflation or of raising rents on the property's future value. Nor, in comparing it with the value of other properties, does the appraiser consider how those properties were financed as opposed to his client's. Financing, as we have seen, plays a big role in how much a property is worth, yet appraisers act as if every property in the world, and the "subject property" itself, were all held by their owners free and clear of any mortgage.

Appraisers do not consider how good or bad management makes one property worth far more than another. They act as if properties were intrinsically worth the values they put on them. How comparable can a comparable property really be when each property really is a separate business?

If the same appraiser values the same property year after year, the property's fair market value tends to march upward. Appraisers loathe marking a property's value down after they marked it up only two years before, and especially loathe it if the same owner has been holding the building all along. It smacks of treason, even if the market for that particular property has collapsed.

Despite all the problems with appraisals, they will always be with us. An appraisal is a qualified, limited, biased view of a property's worth that is nevertheless necessary because it is a third-party point of view. Most appraisals are done to convince a lender that the property he is about to lend millions of dollars on is indeed worth what he thinks it is worth. All developers and owners commission an appraisal before they visit their lenders or try to convince someone to become a partner and put up money for some deal. In the lender's case, he can file the appraisal away and know that if the loan ever goes bad, he has that third-party opinion to back up his decision. Appraisals are sales tools, then.

Appraisals are often pretty. They have colored maps with numbers on them indicating the comparable properties and the property being appraised. They have photographs of the property and all sorts of exhibits—income and expense statements, rent rolls, lists of comparables, engineer's reports on the condition of the building or architect's projections if the property is land to be developed with a new building.

How does a professional real estate investor, developer or lender read an appraisal? Cynically. Consider the hypothetical case of an investor who wants to buy an office building. To support his asking price of $5.4 million, the current owner has given him a copy of an appraisal he had done last month when he refinanced the building. The appraisal shows the building to have a fair market value of $5.4 million.

The investor looks at the photos of the building. Very nice. He flips to the section on the income approach to value and goes over the income and expense statement the appraiser has come up with. The expenses look too low to him. No wonder the building is shown to have a $5.4 million value. Probably a more accurate figure is $4.9 million. He next takes a look at the "rent roll"—the list of tenants, the terms of their leases, the rent they pay, and what expenses they pay. He pays special attention to when the leases expire because that is when he can raise the rents and force up the building's cash flow. The leases look too long for his taste. They do not roll over for another three years. He had been hoping to roll them next year. Maybe he can push up the cap rate because the leases are not great.

He then skips to the thick appendix in back, which has details on all the other buildings the appraiser is comparing to the building being appraised. The reader scans the tables of rents and selling prices. The appraiser's rent numbers look lower than what he thought was the going rate, but that is not unusual. The appraiser probably dragged them out of one of his file drawers from an appraisal he did three months ago in the same area. The reader makes a note to send one of his subordinates over to some of these properties, posing as an interested tenant, to find out what the real rates are. He pays no attention to the replacement cost section. The thing is built already. Who cares how much it costs to replace?

The owner has given him the appraisal, supporting his asking price, but both buyer and seller know that the property will be sold for less. Appraisals, especially when commissioned by an owner, always present a property in its most optimistic light. From 1965 to 1975, no one but a dummy ever bought a property for its appraised value. He would buy for less, then hire his own appraiser to appraise it for more than he himself paid for it so he could get a larger loan from a lender.

All lenders knew that their potential borrowers bought the property for less than appraised value, but they would make their loans based on a percentage of appraised value anyway. They could lend out more money that way. This practice led to the strange conclusion that the "fair market value" of a property was always higher than what the market itself had said the property was worth only six weeks before—when the fellow who had commissioned the appraisal had bought it.

Investors need third-party opinions on property values, but obviously formal appraisals have a limited use and must be read for what they are intended to be—a story supporting whatever the fellow who commissioned the appraisal feels his property is worth.

Others in the investment property business think appraisers have a cushy job. If a deal is made or dies, people still need appraisals, and he still gets paid for his work. A good appraiser will make as much as a good, independent money manager in the pension field.

Lawyers

Real estate attorneys are a particularly insufferable branch of the income property family tree. No one likes them. Like developers, they have giant egos; but unlike developers, they do not make money for the people who stick with them. They only eat up legal fees. Attorneys collect fees whether a deal gets done or not, and they are notorious deal-killers. If a client gives an attorney a complicated joint venture to look over, the lawyers had better find something wrong with it—or what was the point of having a lawyer look at it in the first place?

Because they spend most of their time on the picky points of real estate law, attorneys think of themselves as wheeler-dealers. They are not. They are experts on the picky points of real estate law and are not qualified to comment on the best spot for a high-rise office building in downtown Philadelphia. Unless they no longer practice law and are now real estate developers themselves, their advice on anything not related to the law should be ignored.

The real estate business has always been good to lawyers. There are more and more of them in practice every year.

Property Managers

Property managers have always been the unsung heroes of investment property, though they are the people who make the investment work and the foundation of the entire business. Property managers actually run the property. They rent out the space, pay the bills, handle the day-to-day problems of running a building, and generally try to squeeze as much income out of a building as they can. If they can use a lower-wattage lightbulb in the hallways or turn down the heat by two degrees at four in the afternoon, the good property manager will do it. Out of lower-wattage lightbulbs, lower heating bills, and other thrifty habits are great properties made.

Owners view their buildings as inflation hedges and believe that rents will keep up with inflation over the life of their ownership if expenses are kept in hand. It is the property manager who actually makes this happen by haggling over leases with reluctant tenants and ruthlessly cutting every cost he can find. He is living proof that investment real estate is a nickel-and-dime business. With his finicky attention to cost cutting, if he can increase a building's cash flow by $50,000 a year, he has actually increased the market value of the building by $625,000, assuming a cap rate of 8.

For someone who is indispensable to property investment, the property manager has the least prestige of anyone in the income property business. If you tell someone you spend your day trying to figure out where to get a better deal on heating oil in bulk or you tell them you put together multimillion-dollar real estate deals, the latter sounds more impressive. The former is more important. Real estate financiers and developers have always earned the kudos and glamour in the business, though their roles in making property work as an investment are greatly overrated.

Owners, especially institutional owners, tend to underestimate the importance of property management. An investor will own a 100-unit apartment complex and have it managed by some half-illiterate couple to whom he gives a rent-free apartment and $8,000 a year. The property is worth $5 million, and the owner entrusts its management to someone willing to work for nothing. Apartments need more intensive management than most income property since management must appease so many tenants at once—all of whom can move in and out on a month's notice.

Many institutional investors will hire local management firms to run their properties in different cities. These firms usually charge 3 to 7 percent of gross rents and will do an adequate job. But it is axiomatic in the investment property business that an owner who runs his own property does much better than hired help. The hired property manager has no incentive to chop costs since he is paid a fixed fee no matter what he does above some acceptable minimum performance. But an owner who manages his own property knows that every dollar he saves goes into his own pocket.

Some owners try to give hired managers incentives by giving them a percentage of any cash flow the property generates over a fixed minimum. This encourages the manager to raise rents and cut costs. It also encourages him to skimp on necessary maintenance so that he can boost cash flow. The best manager is the owner's own employee.

Professional Designations

People in the real estate business like to consider themselves professionals. As a result, practitioners of both the residential and income property trades can now earn up to 41 professional designations. This was the 1981 count, according to Lynn N. Woodward and Marcella Roberts, writing in the Winter 1981 issue of the *Real Estate* Review.[11] Property managers, residential and income property appraisers, mortgage bankers, brokers—nearly everyone in the business has a trade organization that will be happy to grant him some title in exchange for a small fee, some modest course work, and an exam. The association often requires that participants have some experience in their profession, but that is analagous to mail-order colleges which give their students course credit for "experience in life."

These "initialized merit badges," as Woodward and Roberts call them, do not prove that their holders have even minimum competence at what they are doing. But all those initials look nice after a name.

The appraisers and assessors can earn the most designations, the authors report. In Canada and the U.S., they can earn 24 designations: SRA, SRPA, SREA, RM, MAI, SR/WA, ARA, CRA, AACI, RPA, R-1, CA-R, CA-S, CA-C, CAE, AAE, CPE, RES, ASA, IFA, SIFA, IFAC and CMI. The authors cited one midwestern appraiser who had nine designations after his name.

Doctors, lawyers, and accountants have been satisfied with their simple MD, JD or LLB, and CPA. The multitude of real estate designations indicates a group of people stretching for some sort of professional mark to separate them from the herd of their competitors doing the same thing they do for a living.

So when someone from a real estate firm walks into your office and hands you a gilded card full of initials, do not be impressed.

THE REITS

This was the world of real estate from 1965 to 1975. Happy property managers, developers, brokers and lenders—with all their designations—doing deals in an environment where, as one lender put it, "everyone thought it was their God-given right to get a 30-year fixed-rate mortgage." Leverage was positive. Inflation was increasing, but appeared controllable, and capital for real estate development was in ample supply.

In 1968 and 1969, a new vehicle for real estate investment became popular—the real estate investment trust, or REIT for short. It was one in the long line of financial contraptions designed to allow the public to invest in income property. Little did anyone know what horrors the REIT concept would bring and that the REITs' eventual collapse in 1974 and 1975 would be the most devastating since the mortgage-bond scandals of the 1920s and 1930s.

The REIT was not new to the real estate business, but in 1960 Congress loosened the tax law on these trusts to make them a more attractive way for the public to invest in income property. A REIT could own real estate or make mortgages and would not have to pay income taxes if it distributed 90 percent of its income to its shareholders. The tax law also required the REIT to keep at least 75 percent of its assets in real estate equities, mortgages or cash. Trusts could not manage their own properties, nor could they deal in property—that is, develop properties and then sell them off for a profit. The trust was designed to develop new property or buy existing buildings and then just hold and manage them for the benefit of the shareholders. The affairs of the trust would be handled by an advisory company that would be paid a management fee for the service.

To raise capital to buy its properties, a REIT would issue common stock to the general public and could also borrow money from banks, or float bonds or commercial paper. The value of the real estate held by the REIT or its mortgages would back all its financings. The structure of the REIT ideally suited the needs of passive investors, such as the small, individual investor and pension funds. These investors wished to own property and collect its income but wanted nothing to do with it beyond that.

There is nothing the matter with the idea of a REIT. What happened in the 1970s was that investors put unrealistic expectations on their REIT holdings, and the advisors to the REIT were greedy. Together, they brought disaster on themselves.

The last thing the real estate community in the early 1970s needed was another source of mortgage money. Capital was plentiful, lenders eager to make mortgages, and developers obliging them by building and borrowing freely. When mortgage money flows, builders will build anything anywhere, and in the 1970s, with REIT money, they did.

The public liked REIT stock, so the number of REITs grew. By 1963, three years after REITs had received their tax advantage, new and existing trusts had raised $200 million, Rabinowitz reports.[12] By 1969, the REIT blossomed. He estimated that between the beginning of 1969 and the middle of 1971, almost $5 billion in new REIT securities were on the market, representing the bulk of all REIT stock then outstanding.[13]

REITs broke down into two general categories—equity and mortgage REITs. Equity REITs bought property and held it for their investors, raising their money largely through common stock offerings and long-term debt. Mortgage REITs made long-term mortgages and construction loans. They raised their money in the stock and bond markets, just like the equity REITs, but the mortgage REITs that made construction loans also borrowed money from banks. Many trusts were hybrids, doing mortgage, construction and equity deals, or some combination.

The REITs that made mortgages or construction loans outnumbered the equity trusts. Of the industry's assets, 80 percent were in such trusts and of these, the bulk specialized in construction lending. They made construction and development loans with maturities of less than three years, financing these loans by borrowing from banks. They would borrow from the bank on a line of credit, then turn around and lend the money out at a higher rate as construction loans to developers, making a profit on the spread.

The construction-and-development REIT was by far the most popular type of REIT because everyone involved with it—lenders, developers, trust advisors, even the shareholders—could make a great deal of money very fast. The more a construction trust borrowed and then lent out, the more money everyone would make.

The investing public loved the construction-and-development REITs because they paid ever-increasing dividends. All REITs were in a difficult predicament. To keep their tax-exempt status, they had to pass on 90 percent of their income directly to their shareholders. This meant the REIT could never finance its own growth through retained earnings because it could never keep much of its profits each year.

How could the stock of a REIT compete with Xerox or IBM or other growth-company stocks where the company plowed everything back into the company? Clearly, REITs were not growth-stock companies, in an era when growth stocks were booming. To compete with growth stocks, the REITs paid big dividends.

The problem was that real estate does not throw off a great deal of cash flow. Certainly, an equity REIT that owned and managed property for its shareholders would produce a respectable cash flow, but nothing that would increase dramatically year after year. Real estate yields depend on rents, and rents were only negotiated once every five or 10 years during the early 1970s. And then, increases were relatively small. So equity REITs did not attract great investor interest.

To make the yields from real estate attractive to the investing public at that time, you had to "turn a horse into a cow," as one astute observer put it. "Real estate can't throw off cash flows to compete with the dividends from big, growing companies," he said. "So you had to fool with it to make it look like it did." That is exactly what the construction REITs did. They turned real estate into a high-yielding investment—a horse into a cow.

The construction REITs would lend out construction money, without a takeout, at two points over prime, when prime was 12 to 14 percent. But the completed building would only generate a 9 percent return when capped free and clear of debt. Such a loan was negative leverage, and a tremendous debt service burden on the property. The underwriters at the REIT knew it, but they thought inflation would increase rents so much that by the time the property was completed, it would rent for far more than they had originally projected. A permanent lender could easily be found to take them out.

Unfortunately, everyone had the same idea, and the resulting oversupply of new space blunted their ability to pass along rent increases. They would be stuck in the end.

But they didn't see that far ahead. They just knew they were making 14 to 16 percent on loans and their dividend income was soaring.

Because of these high-rate loans, a construction-and-development REIT generated much more cash than an equity trust. Borrowers also paid loan fees to the trust, and that was cash that could be paid out as dividends. The bigger the trust and the more loans it made, the higher its fee income and the bigger the dividends it could pay. The public would flock to the stock. The stock would go up and the REIT would issue even more common stock or bonds, using the proceeds to make more construction loans and, of course, to pay higher dividends.

All REITs were very profitable for the advisory companies that ran them. After fees and expenses, 90 percent of a trust's income had to be paid out to the shareholders each year if the trust wished to keep its tax-exempt status. But that left 10 percent after fees for the advisory company to play with. That 10 percent was after the trust had paid the advisor 1 to 1.3 percent of assets as their annual advisory fee and all their other expenses, including the trust's appraisal and management business they had channeled to companies owned by their friends.

The construction trusts were the most profitable for advisors. First, developers paid the trust each time they received a loan. Second, the trust was positively leveraged. As long as it could borrow money at one point over prime and lend it out at two over, using as little of its own money as possible, the trust made money. Many large banks set up their own construction REITs. Since the REIT borrowed most of its money from the bank that had founded it, it had a virtual guarantee of continued existence. No bank would destroy a REIT that bore its own name.

Finally, because the trust had so little of its own money in loans to developers, it could spread that money a long way. It could borrow great sums from the bank, lend it out as loans, and watch its assets soar. Since the advisory company was paid a fee based on a percentage of the trust's assets, the advisor was all in favor of running a construction REIT.

Commercial banks were especially fond of setting up and advising construction-and-development REITs, precisely so they could earn all this advisory fee income. Rabinowitz writes that by June 1972, 25 major banks had set up REITs as subsidiaries.[14] The bulk of these REITs were construction-and-development trusts.

Before the invention of such short-term trusts, banks had been the principal source of construction money for developers. But they were limited in how much business they could do by banking regulations and the shortage of good deals. The construction REIT solved both these problems. These trusts could lend as much short-term money as they could raise and could be counted on to at least look at deals that the bank real estate department considered too risky to touch.

The construction-and-development REIT could also tap the capital markets to raise its capital, floating common stock and bond issues to raise its money for mortgages. But the largest source of lendable capital for these short-term trusts was the banks themselves. At the end of 1975, the REIT trade association reported that commercial banks provided 55 percent of the total credit available to all REITs while shareholders' equity followed in a far second at 19.3 percent. It was lucrative for a bank to lend to a REIT. The bank would collect fees for just making a loan to the trust. Then it would collect interest that varied over the term of the loan, depending on the prime rate.

The REIT sponsored by the bank and the bank real estate department competed for the same business—construction loans to developers. But because the REIT was living off borrowed money, its rates were consistently higher than those of banks, a deficiency the REIT made up by offering to lend the developer 100 percent of his construction money as opposed to the 75 or 80 percent the bank would lend. The rate differential served as a form of financial natural selection. The strong developers with good projects and some cash to put into their deals would go to the banks and pay one point over prime. The poorly capitalized developers with no cash and no place else to go for money would go to the bank's REIT and pay two to four points over prime. And the REIT would be glad to have their business.

The more money the REIT lent out, the richer the advisors, the developers, the bankers, the shareholders and the investment bankers became. Construction-and-development REITs were money machines. Equity trusts languished. They were simple real estate holding companies. But construction REITs were throwing off plumes of cash flow to everyone. Equity REITs were besieged by investment bankers telling them to convert themselves into construction REITs, get their stock climbing, and then float a new issue to raise even more money. More than one well-run but boring equity REIT followed this glittery path. One developer recalled such a trust in Ohio in 1969 that took the plunge and started making condominium conversion loans. "I think it only took them eight years to recover," he remembers.

The problem with the construction-and-development trusts was that the only way they could keep making money was to keep making loans. Dozens of REITs started chasing the same developers, asking if they wanted to borrow more money, which is roughly equivalent to asking an alcoholic if he wants another drink. The quality of developers the REITs dealt with started to fall and so did the quality of the deals. The construction REITs started lending on just about anything that was put up, not just traditional income property, but specialized properties like nursing homes and ice-skating rinks. They did hundreds of millions of dollars of land and land-development loans, some of the riskiest deals a construction lender can do. The trust would lend the developer the money to buy a piece of raw land and install sewer and water lines in it. Unlike a shopping center, land generates no income, so there is no cash flow to cover the mortgage payments. If the developer defaulted, the lender would be stuck with a difficult piece of property to sell. Investors would not want it because it generated no income. Only another developer would be interested and he would drive a hard bargain since he would know he was the only buyer.

Construction REITs could have taken some of the risk out of their wild loans if they had at least demanded that their developers have takeouts. Then there would be a long-term lender in the wings waiting to refinance the property and pay off the construction loan. But construction trusts were so anxious to lend they did about 50 percent of their loans without takeouts, according to a report on the trusts issued in 1976 by The First Boston Corporation.[15] If the developer defaulted, they would be stuck.

The construction REITs disregarded all the rules of prudence in their underwriting. They would lend millions of dollars to build major office buildings when not a single tenant had leased space nor a lender issued a takeout. They would lend the developer 100 percent of his construction costs and then lend him the money to pay the interest on the loan. They would lend him 105 percent of construction costs, and he would use his 5 percent bonus to buy a boat for himself and a mink coat for his wife from the first draw on the loan. The construction trusts had to make concessions or the developer would take the deal to another trust.

A great number of these 105 percent loans were made out of sheer ignorance because the trusts were staffed by greedy and inexperienced young men. The committee system which normally restrains the enthusiastic neophytes in a lender's office totally broke down at construction REITs. One veteran of the times recalls a meeting between two young MBAs who worked for a construction REIT and Judd Kassuba, the famous apartment developer who went bankrupt in 1973 but was the darling of the REITs before that. The fledgling loan officers apologized to Kassuba because they had only been able to convince their loan committee to make him a $2 million construction loan on his next project when he had asked for $2.3 million. They were surprised when he eagerly accepted the loan anyway, not realizing, of course, that he had massively inflated his costs of construction on paper and had only hoped to get a loan for $1.8 million. Their loan actually funded 105 percent of his actual construction costs. He would make a profit on his construction loan and not have a penny of his own money in the project, while the construction lender thought he was using his own money to cover 15 percent of the costs. These lambs had been fleeced.

The construction-and-development REITs flourished from 1969 until the middle of 1974 when one simple event brought the whole system to collapse. Short-term interest rates hit a record high. They triggered a chain reaction that brought the whole pyramid down.

As short-term rates rose, so did a developer's loan payments to his construction lender. His loan's interest rate floated as much as four points over the prime rate. Every time prime changed, the developer's payments grew or shrank, and in 1974 they only grew. A construction loan that bore an 11 percent interest rate when the prime was 7 percent suddenly became a loan with a 16 percent rate, and developers just did not have the cash to make such payments. They had not budgeted for such a problem. Often a developer had applied the proceeds of one generous loan to the needs of another project. Now he defaulted on both.

Meanwhile, all the furious building caught up with the developers. Everyone had built offices in Atlanta and condominiums in Miami, and now there was so much space available in so many cities that rents fell and buildings stood empty. If developers could not lease up their buildings or collect their rents, they could not pay their construction loans and they defaulted. By early 1975, Chase Manhattan Mortgage & Realty Investors, the construction REIT sponsored by that bank, announced that 37 of its projects, totalling $125 million, were not making their interest payments and were in default. The Chase REIT was only one of many.[16]

The construction REITs were swimming through a sea of defaulting developers. If they could not collect their mortgage payments from their borrowers, how could they make dividend payments to their shareholders? REITs started postponing dividend payments in droves. Rabinowitz reports that in one two-week period in August 1974, five REITs announced they were postponing dividends, including two large trusts—Larwin Mortgage Investors and American Realty Trust. The shareholders responded. By the spring of 1975, the index of REIT shares had dropped from its 1972 level of 100 to 21.[17]

Bigger problems than disgruntled shareholders and falling stock were looming. If the REITs could not pay their dividends, they certainly could not pay back their banks whose loans to them also floated over prime. But if the REIT did not pay back the bank, technically it would be bankrupt. While a freestanding REIT might falter, one owned by a bank could not. No bank could stand the thought of a REIT named after it filing for bankruptcy. The disgrace, not to mention the write-downs of all those loans, would be too much. So the REITs could blackmail their bank lenders and sponsors into giving them more money or restructuring their existing loans to avoid a big write-down.

It all came home to roost at the banks. The REIT would foreclose on a property, and the bank would swap one of its loans to the REIT in exchange for the property. The bank would take the property and post it on its own books as worth the face value of the loan and accrued interest. In many cases, it was clear that the property was not worth anywhere near what the bank was declaring it to be. Much of the property was raw land or half-finished condominiums, neither of which had a prayer of ever producing any income. Nevertheless, the bank inflated the value of all such properties so the bank and not the REIT would absorb the losses. In November 1975, Chase Manhattan Bank bought $85.5 million of non-income-producing real estate from its trust as part of a large purchase of $160.6 million. In February 1976, the *New York Times* estimated that $3 billion of such loan swaps were in the works.[18]

By 1976, it was becoming clear that few of these properties would ever recover and become decent investments. The accountants and the SEC were busy promulgating rules requiring the REITs and the banks to take their write-downs. As a result, many REITs went technically bankrupt, and their banks posted huge real estate losses. Some are still trying to unload the properties they swapped with their REITs more than seven years ago.

The carnage was incredible, as shown by this list of disasters collected by Rabinowitz:[19] Of the $22 billion in loans banks had made to REITs, one-half— $11 billion—were in default. A study of 32 trusts that had each issued more than $1 million in stock in 1972 showed that by May 1976 three were not traded, 27 were selling at an average of 40 percent of the price at which they had first been offered to the public, and 21 had eliminated dividends completely. REITs had floated $7.5 billion in stock and borrowed $22 billion from banks, but between

1974 and 1976, 80 percent of the stock value had disappeared and more than half the mortgages were in default.

The construction-and-development trusts were the hardest hit, although equity trusts and those that made long-term mortgages also had some problems because of the overbuilding. They were having trouble filling up their buildings with tenants. But they sailed through comparatively unhurt. Only the construction-and-development trusts had violated all precepts of financial management and were destroyed for it. In a nutshell, they had borrowed short-term money on their bank lines of credit, and lent it out longer term to developers. Because the interest rates on both loans fluctuated with the prime rate, when prime went through the roof, they were killed. The interest expense on their bank credit lines overtook their income from developers' loans. When rates hit a peak and the developers stopped paying at all, the whole REIT caved in.

The REIT collapse occurred at the same time the stock market collapsed in 1974 and 1975, but the two events are not directly connected. They were just simultaneous disasters, each set in motion by high interest rates followed by recession.

The investment property business virtually shut down. A layer of heavy smoke settled over the business, as if the Vandals had just finished sacking Rome. Investment property entered the Dark Ages.

THE DARK AGES: 1976 AND 1977

The only sign of life in the investment property business during these two years was the sound of frustrated lenders gnashing their teeth as they stared at their lists of foreclosed properties. Though there are no statistics on what the chief type of foreclosed property was, it appears that raw land, half-finished condominiums, and empty resort communities outnumbered the commercial foreclosures. Roughly half of all the loans the construction REITs had made were either on multifamily housing or raw land. Since many cities were glutted with apartments and condominiums and raw land was the riskiest loan a trust could make, it was not unusual that such properties dominated the rosters of the dead and dying.[20]

Lenders compounded their problems with foreclosed properties by being exby being extraordinarily pigheaded about selling them off. There were so many defaulted properties in 1976 and 1977, that a buyer with cash could pick up some real bargains, but only if he could penetrate the obstinate policies of the lenders, particularly the banks. Banks desperately wanted to unload their foreclosed properties, but they also wanted to get all their money out of them. As a result, they placed ridiculously high prices on their properties, regardless of the fact that some would need 10 years of intensive labor just to break even on operating expenses. The banks also insisted that if a buyer wanted one of the halfway desirable properties, he would also have to purchase one of the dogs along with it.

There were not a great number of takers for such high-priced, double-edged deals, and the bankers were left to brood on their own. Many just kept on trying to restructure their loans with their REITs to their own benefit, playing with property-value numbers that had nothing to do with the reality of what they now owned. Banks had neither the skill nor the desire to fix these defunct deals themselves, but they did not have the nerve to dump them, so they and the properties just sat. Eventually they would be forced to take the loss, but they postponed it as long as possible.

A few banks and their REITs were more enterprising and tried to clean up their mess. Some properties they just sold off. Others they turned over to "workout specialists," people who claimed to be able to breathe life into dead income property by cutting expenses to the bone and figuring out how to make money on the property. Often, a REIT or bank would sell the property to a workout investor. "Sell" was a misnomer since it was the lender who put out the money. In exchange for taking over the property, the buyer would get a break on the existing mortgage, a suspension of interest payments until the property was back on its feet, and often more money from the lender. Many of the foreclosed properties were unfinished, and the new owner would complete the building, using another loan from the bank. After several years of intense labor, the new owner would have an operating property, and the lender would have an income-producing loan once again.

Workouts were the only deals being done in 1976 and 1977. The last words any lender wanted to hear were "real estate." The banks licked their REIT-inflicted wounds and laughed at requests for construction loans. Insurance companies cut back their lending in favor of long-term bonds where rates were hitting record highs. Insurers had their own problems with the equity and mortgage REITs they had sponsored, and there were few customers for the long-term mortgage money they did have. It is difficult to seriously talk about a long-term loan when a property is half-finished and in default to the construction lender.

Many developers were bankrupt. Those that were left could neither buy nor build because there was no mortgage money for any but the safest and highest-quality deals. Many cities were glutted with empty, new buildings.

The ultimate nail in the coffin was the 1976 Tax Reform Act. Under the guise of quashing tax shelters, the Act destroyed three of the main incentives for building new income property. It eliminated much of the value of accelerated depreciation by changing the recapture rules. Instead of writing off 10 or 15 percent of a building's value against its income each year, an owner was stuck with straight-line depreciation, which restricted his write-off to 2 or 3 percent a year.

The Act also prohibited developers from deducting in one lump sum the interest on their construction loans and the property taxes they paid during construction. They would have to amortize these expenses over 10 years. Finally, the law prohibited developers from deducting their prepaid interest charges, such as loan-origination fees, discount points, and additional interest charges. These, too, would have to be amortized, but over the life of the loan. The new rules were phased in gradually, affecting only commercial real estate in 1976. Residential construction felt the changes in 1978.

The three changes applied only to individuals, not corporations, so individuals were discouraged from building, while corporations and institutions were given an advantage. If the moribund state of the investment property market had not been discouragement enough to investors and developers, the Tax Reform Act of 1976 provided more.

"The whole nature of the game changed radically," says one developer. "The tax write-offs were nowhere near significant, relative to the size of the investment." He cites a hypothetical case of a $10 million project that he built for all-cash in 1977 because he could not find a mortgage—a situation that is becoming more prevalent in real estate everyday. "What's the only write-off I had available?" he says. "I could depreciate the building over 50 years or so, so that means I could write off 2 or 3 percent of the building's value each year. I got a $300,000 annual write-off against a $10 million investment. It was nothing." This developer argues that the tax write-offs up front encouraged construction because they compensated the developer for the first years of his building's operations when cash flow was just starting and was low.

The Tax Reform Act of 1976, combined with the sick state of the investment property business, discouraged developers from building. This was good news for owners of existing income property. Their rents and rate of return could only climb because they had no new competition. And that is exactly what happened in 1978 and 1979.

SUPPLY MEETS DEMAND: 1978 AND 1979

While the real estate markets were glutted with property and nothing more was built, the economy continued to grow. Eventually its normal growth generated demand for space, and people started to rent the half-empty office buildings littering America. Eventually even Atlanta, the queen city of overbuilding, found that its sea of unpopulated office and apartment buildings started to fill up. After three years of misery, owners could actually start raising rents a bit.

As space started to move, lenders started lending again on both new and existing income properties, but nothing like what they had been doing in 1972. Volume was way down, and underwriting was grim. Construction lenders demanded takeouts and concrete proof that 50 percent or even 90 percent of a project's space had already been rented—before the ground was broken. They demanded that the developer put in 20 or 30 percent of the cost of construction from his own funds, a criterion only the strongest of builders could stomach.

Rates were onerous, and positive leverage almost nonexistent. An investor would try to buy an existing building at a cap rate of 9, only to find that the only long-term mortgage he could get would be at 12 or 13 percent. That was negative leverage, which meant he would be better off buying the building entirely with cash. Since few investors had that kind of money, they would take the high-rate loan, hoping to turn their leverage right side up again when rates fell and they could refinance the property. More often, they did not even have to worry about negative leverage. The interest rate on the mortgage would be so high that the building could not generate enough cash flow to make the mortgage payments. Thus, they could not proceed.

Neither construction nor long-term lenders would lend on raw land or multifamily housing unless the buildings were condominiums, and even then they were stingy on their loan amounts and terms. No one made rental apartment loans unless it was to convert an existing rental building to condominiums. Condominiums came into their own in the mid- to late 1970s, and although there are several reasons for their popularity, one of the most important has to be that rental apartments lost their allure for investors. Apartments did not generate enough income for the investment of time and money involved. So investors bailed out by converting them to condos. Rents were so low that the building's capitalized value as a rental project was far lower than its value as condominiums.

Lenders made it difficult to get loans on other properties, too. They had been burned badly by REITs and now were so conservative in their underwriting that they made few loans. Since real estate is a business of small entrepreneurs, it started to split in half. The largest, best-capitalized developers could get construction money and permanent financing, albeit on difficult terms. But the smaller developers and owners were shut out and forced out of the business. The real estate market took a big step toward dominance by big developers and institutions.

Money was scarce and expensive not only because lenders were cautious, but because the money market and the long-term bond market were offering them better opportunities for their money than real estate lending. Rates were higher than ever before, and if they did put out money in real estate mortgages, the lenders expected to make what they were making in the bond market—and then some. If that mortgage rate was 13 or 14 percent and rendered most deals immediately unfeasible, so be it.

But then things changed. Investment real estate began to earn back its golden aura. Because essentially nothing had been built since 1975, space in many cities became tight. Even Atlanta, where apartment and office vacancies had been 15 or 20 percent in 1975, had vacancy rates of less than 5 percent by 1979. At the same time, the high rates that insurance companies earned in the bond and money markets indicated that record-high inflation had hit the country. Inflation pushed up interest rates, and it also pushed up the cost of operating a building. Heating oil, replacement carpet for the lobby, janitors—the cost of everything was climbing. But because a building's tenants finally had no place else to go, owners were able to pass these increased costs along. Office and shopping center owners found they could raise rents with a freer hand than ever before, and they could force tenants to pay expenses once borne entirely by the landlord.

As a result, investment property gained a reputation as being one of the few investments that generated a rate of return greater than the rate of inflation. The properties that had been sitting dead for five years at banks and REITs now actually started to show some cash flow, much to the surprise of their reluctant owners. Even the worst properties were renting up, not because of brilliant property management, but because the demand for space had finally reached and was now surpassing supply. Everyone was talking about how real estate was a "hedge against inflation," as if when inflation climbed, real estate returns would follow lockstep behind it.

This is a useless way of looking at real estate investment. Inflation does not give property value, shortages of space do. Inflationary costs can only be passed through to the tenants if demand outstrips supply. The reverse was the case from 1973 to 1977. But then demand caught up. Everyone wanted to own income property, and the prices of existing property began to climb. But there was so little mortgage money available and at such high rates, investors who could buy with cash had the advantage over other buyers. Foreign investors, institutions, and commingled funds had more cash than most and found themselves in a great bargaining position. The commingled funds started to grow and buy up property for their clients.

Mortgage money was expensive and in short supply. This had happened before, and developers and investors had waited for rates to fall and money to loosen. This time, they waited in vain. Not only did mortgage rates refuse to fall, mortgage money at any price started to disappear. The real estate lenders had decided that they did not want to be lenders.

THE DROUGHT: 1980 TO 1982

Long-term lenders were earning 14 percent interest on new mortgages and a few fees upfront, but by owning property, their borrowers had an "inflation hedge." So life insurance companies took a startling step. They started adding equity kickers to their traditional long-term mortgages. In addition to his mortgage payments the owner had to pay 25 to 50 percent of the property's cash flow to the insurer. If and when the property was sold, the lender would get a similar percentage of the sale proceeds.

Mortgages with equity kickers, or "participating mortgages" as they are sometimes called, blurred the line traditionally drawn between debt and equity in investment real estate. A participating mortgage is not a true mortgage, but it is not true ownership either, in the sense that the insurance company controlled the day-to-day affairs of managing the property. The insurer was a passive partner, merely collecting its piece of cash flow and sale price and letting the other owner, the operating owner, run the property and make the decisions.

Participating mortgages had always been a part of the real estate business; but when inflation was low and lenders were competing to put out the most money, they had never been able to force such mortgages on their customers. And the lenders had not wanted to, since they shied away from ownership of property on all levels. But inflation changed that, and now they were anxious to put kickers on every loan they wrote. Only a handful of insurers were writing such mortgages in 1979. By 1981, unless a long-term loan with a five-year call was acceptable, loans with kickers were the only type of permanent financing a developer or owner could get.

The extensive use of the mortgage with a kicker marked a new phase in the investment property business. The entire business had been built on a foundation of cheap, easily available, long-term mortgage money. With it, owners could build real estate fortunes, controlling millions of dollars of property with only pennies of their own money. Now, lenders were saying they wanted a piece of the deal, too. Developers and owners raged. You cannot make a fortune if your once-docile lender keeps raking off chunks of cash flow and still quotes you such a high mortgage rate that you are negatively leveraged.

However, on the long-held and sacred real estate principle that 60 percent of something is worth more than 100 percent of nothing, developers and owners acquiesced. They had no choice. Where else were they going to get their money?

Once insurance companies decided they were going to buy property, they did more than just issue participating mortgages. They went out and bought entire buildings. As insurance companies were once the lending power in the investment property business, they soon became the buying power. They were the largest purchasers of income property, buying not only for their own account, the general account, but for their pension accounts as well.

They hit a snag in 1980 and 1981 because their cash flow for real estate fell. Short-term interest rates hit record highs during 1980 and 1981, and pension funds stopped buying long-term, fixed-income products from their insurance company money managers, preferring instead to invest the money in short-term paper. This sapped the insurance companies' own cash flow, as did a run on policy loans. In 1980, thousands of policyholders borrowed against the value of their life insurance policies, since the rates on such loans, 6 to 8 percent, were far below current short-term rates at the time. Policy loans died down in the second half of 1980 and were much lower in 1981, but the loans combined with pension fund withdrawals from long-term bond products trimmed the money insurance companies had to invest in property for their own accounts.

Because the times were so unsettling, insurers were also becoming more cautious about committing to lend or participate in a project two or three years in advance. Instead of real estate, they invested in high-yielding, short-term instruments.

All these factors cut the amount of money they were putting into real estate and mortgages in their general accounts. But while their own real estate funds were pinched, insurers found that pension funds were channeling ever-increasing amounts of money into their commingled real estate funds. The overall result was that as the amount of money insurance companies as a whole invested in real estate fell, more and more of it was supplied by pension funds through the insurers' separate accounts.

Pension fund sponsors considered real estate an inflation hedge and favored the handful of large commingled funds, most of which were run by insurance companies, with bigger contributions. In July 1981, for example, Prudential Insurance announced that in the last quarter of the year, it planned to take in $1 billion in new contributions to its commingled real estate fund, PRISA. Pension funds actually gave PRISA "only" $800 million, but it took Prudential just 60 days to raise the money. It was the largest amount of money they had ever raised from their clients for that account in one quarter.

In their pursuit of property, insurance companies and their commingled funds dominated the market. They had some competition from foreign investors and public syndications, but not much. The amount of foreign money chasing U.S. real estate has always been grossly overestimated, and although syndications were growing and raised over $1 billion in 1980, they could not compete with a PRISA that could raise $800 million in three months.

They were all chasing the same things—the largest, newest, most prestigious office buildings and regional shopping centers. The all-cash buyer was picky and conservative. Only prime property for him. This left out small shopping centers, apartments, anything that was built in a city with a population of 100,000 or less, and often anything that was not located in one of the nation's 10 largest metropolitan areas. As a result, the real estate market continued to split into tiers, a phenomenon that had begun right after the REITs collapsed. High-quality properties worth $25 million or more and located in good locations had many potential buyers. Large institutional buyers and foreign investors avidly sought out these properties. The rest of the investment property business was, as one developer put it, "Death Valley." The all-cash buyers would look at little if anything worth less than $25 million. Considering that the $5 million to $25 million range includes nearly all income property except regional shopping centers and big urban office complexes, the all-cash buyers were ignoring the vast majority of available income property. The public syndications would consider such smaller income property, but not the big institutions. Properties worth less than $5 million had been purchased by individual investors and small, private syndications, but as high interest rates hung on through 1981, these buyers disappeared, too.

The only way the owner of anything worth less than $25 million could sell his property and raise some cash would be if he had a low-interest mortgage on his property with a fairly large balance. A potential buyer could assume the mortgage and would not have to come up with a great deal of cash, cash that only the big institutions and syndicators seemed to be able to put their hands on. Owners without such mortgages could sit with their property for sale forever and never move it.

The real estate business became very strange. The vast majority of the business was starving for capital, and the few buyers who ventured into this arena with substantial cash could pick up some bargains. Good $10 million shopping centers were priced to yield 13 percent or 14 percent. But the prices of regional shopping centers and big office buildings—any prime property worth more than $25 million—

went through the roof. In 1978 a buyer could pick up a good regional shopping center at a cap rate of 9. By 1981 prices for such centers had climbed to a cap rate of 5 or 6. Institutional buyers started complaining that there was a shortage of the type of property they wished to buy.

The very largest developers and owners were greatly amused by the institutional chase after their properties, especially since it was making them rich. Once existing property became scarce, institutions tried to buy buildings under construction or before the developer had even started building. The institutional hysteria to own real estate at any price triggered a building boom in the types of prestige income property that institutions loved.

One developer, a happy participant in this process, described it as follows. Assume you are a big developer. You weathered the REITs, you have a nice portfolio of income property, and you want to build an office building. This is 1980, the prime rate is on its way to 20 percent, and because of the desire to own, commingled funds are willing to buy prime real estate at a cap rate of 5½. Wonderful. You have a big line of credit at a major bank, and they make you a construction loan on your office project at some interest rate floating over prime, which means your cost of money weaves between 13 percent and 22 percent throughout the year.

Construction costs, interest on the loan, and leasing the place up cost you $125 a square foot. It is a 100,000-square-foot building and on the day the building is totally leased and occupied, you have sunk a total of $12.5 million into it. The going rent is $20 a square foot, and it costs you $7 a square foot to operate the building. So you, the developer, are making $13 a square foot on this building, which is roughly a 10 percent return on the $12.5 million cost.

Now, a commingled fund comes along and offers to buy this office building at a cap rate of 5½. That means they will pay $23.6 million for a building that cost you $12.5 million to build. You make $11.1 million in cash on a building that cost you $12.5 million and three years to build. With a profit margin like that, you have a tremendous incentive to immediately start another building, which you do.

The buyer was willing to pay so much for this building because he believed that the rents from his real estate would increase much faster than his costs and that, in turn, his 5½ percent return would increase to 15 to 20 percent over time. The year 1980 was much like the 1960s in the stock market when pension funds and other institutional investors were paying 30 or 40 times a company's earnings for its stock. "They were buying futures," the developer who relayed this example says. "And as long as the buyers will buy futures, as long as they'll buy to yield 5½ while the developer can build to yield 10 or 15, the developers will keep on building."

The developers stopped building in the late summer and early fall of 1981, not because the institutions stopped buying futures, but because the interest on construction loans was so high that no one could afford to build them, even with the high prices being paid. The prime rate had stayed between 18 and 21 percent for most of 1981, and no deal would work at those consistently high rates.

While a 21 percent prime rate stopped big developers from starting big projects, it sabotaged those developers who were in the middle of big projects but had not yet lined up permanent financing or a buyer. After all, it had been a seller's market. Developers had been waiting to the last minute to line up financing to see if they could squeeze even more money out of buyers or possibly not have to sell at all. Two years before, when they had started construction, everyone had expected mortgage rates to fall and money to loosen by 1981. It hadn't.

Instead, the interest on their construction loans was eating them alive. The panic-stricken developers tried to sell off their properties before their construction lenders foreclosed.

Insurance companies, commingled funds, and other all-cash buyers had the pick of whatever they wanted. Prices on much property dropped. Some insurers, in a Machiavellian frame of mind, refused to buy properties outright and would make the developer an 18 percent long-term mortgage equal to 75 percent of the property's value. There was no way the developer could meet those payments, but what other choice did he have? When he defaulted, the lender would take over the property in lieu of the mortgage, essentially getting a property for 75 percent of what they would have had to pay if they had purchased it outright.

Some insurance companies almost stopped offering mortgages with kickers. They started buying property outright, shutting the developer out completely. Construction shut down, except for the very largest developers who already had commitments from institutional buyers. Late 1981 was the time that Prudential's commingled account, PRISA, went on its $800 million buying spree. The all-cash buyers bought up everything they could before pension funds cut back the stream of new cash flow to property in 1982.

1983 AND BEYOND

The Market Turns

At this writing in early 1983, the new office markets in several cities are overbuilt. Many office buildings were erected without permanent financing, and now rents are starting to fall and vacancy rates climb. Pension funds have cooled on real estate. A number of funds have reached their target level of real estate holdings and are cutting back on new cash flow. Others believe that real estate values have peaked.

The pure fixed-rate mortgage has reappeared in the shorter-term form of the bullet loan, referred to earlier. There is talk that the traditional 30-year mortgage should revive soon. But as discussed earlier, its future hinges on what interest rates and inflation do.

The Changing Roles of the Players

Everyone in the income property business has been affected by the changes that began in 1979, triggered by high inflation. If inflation continues to be a fact of life in the future, these changes should intensify. For them to reverse, the mortgage lenders would have to start making 30-year, fixed-rate mortgages in great volume and at reasonable rates, such as 10 percent interest. And they would have to continue making them for at least several years.

The relationship between developers and lenders has changed. As long as mortgage money is scarce, the smaller and weaker developers will continue to go out of business, but the larger developers will not disappear at all. Instead, they will be acquired by, or ally themselves with, life insurance companies and other institutions. The insurance companies will offer to fund the developers' projects and give them a reasonable profit, in exchange for the right to buy everything they produce. Many will become mere manufacturers of real estate for the big institutions.

The larger and stronger developers will be able to force the financing institutions to do joint ventures with them, allowing the developer to keep a part-ownership in whatever he produces. The developers who do hold on to their independence and even flourish will do so because of their connections. When a developer controls a deal or has expertise in a particular type of desirable property, an institutional investor will need him.

One American shopping center developer reports a conversation he had with the manager of a British pension fund that wished to stop doing joint ventures with developers and wanted to own everything itself—except for regional shopping centers.

"So I asked him why," recalls the developer, "and he said the fund had tried to buy into the shopping center business and found it couldn't do it. There were six guys in the country who built shopping centers," he chuckles, "and one of them was me."

Inflation and high interest rates have had other effects on other groups in the income property business. Some it has forced to change, but others will be able to keep on doing things the way they had always been done. For example, the role of the construction lender will not change. Banks will still make construction loans that float over the prime rate, and the prudent ones will still require the borrower to arrange a takeout. The construction lending business will continue.

On the other hand, the roles of mortgage bankers and mortgage brokers have already been torn apart. They no longer can survive by arranging only mortgages for developers. They look for buyers or arrange equity deals. Those that have tried to hang on to pure mortgage-financing work will not be around much longer. Their business no longer exists.

Between these two extremes, other real estate professions have been changing more moderately. Each profession is following the path of the income property business itself, splitting in two. A small elite serves the giant institutional investors, and the great masses hustle for business in the capital-starved reaches below. To a certain degree, this division has always existed. A handful of professionals dominated each profession and did the really big deals. But now that the number of people with capital has shrunk so dramatically to a handful of insurance companies and syndications, the number of professionals in other fields must shrink accordingly.

If there is only a handful of big buyers, they can have tight relationships with only two or three appraisers or property managers in each city where they own property or do business. The institutions will just play off the various firms in a given profession in one city to see which one gives them the best price for a given deal. An appraiser, for example, either cuts his fee to get that institutional business or he does not do business at all. At this writing, outside of the institutions, the rest of the income property business is dead.

Consider the case of the real estate broker. As the number of buyers has diminished, so has the need for a real estate broker. An owner is perfectly capable of calling up the half-dozen insurance companies in the market and asking them if they are interested in buying his property. He does not need a broker if his property is the type that interests institutions. If his property is small and risky, he does not need a broker either since the broker would be unlikely to sell it anyway. At this writing, there are no buyers for those small properties. To stay alive, the brokers go searching for sources of money and most are convinced that pension funds have it. They will do anything, promise anything, to get the pension fund to give them money. A number of real estate brokers now advertise themselves as property "consultants" to pension funds, offering to advise pension funds on what properties to buy in exchange for a fee. They would advise the fund to buy the Brooklyn Bridge if they thought they could collect a fee out of it. These are desperate men. It is either getting the money out of pension funds or leaving the business.

If the buyer of smaller properties—those priced well below $25 million— suddenly reappeared, the roles of real estate professionals would revert to their historical norms. At this writing, the appearance of the smaller buyer would seem nothing short of miraculous. Where would they come up with the money to buy property? Unless long-term interest rates fell to about 10 percent, and the long-term lenders became anxious to lend again, the smaller investor has no source of financing. Syndications of individual investors are flourishing and buy properties priced under $25 million, but they are small relative to the capital needs of this market. Property owners also help sales by financing the sale of their properties themselves. But what the income property market needs is new capital—capital which historically has been provided by long-term mortgage lenders. Unless they come back in volume to the business they abandoned, the income property business on all but the largest deals will stay dead.

Other Effects of Inflation

Inflation has triggered other changes in the income property business, changes that will persist until property investors believe that inflation is permanently gone.

The disappearance of the traditional 30-year mortgage is the one big, visible sign of the changes inflation has forced on the income property business. There are others. One of the greatest, on par with the phaseout of pure mortgages, has been a redefinition of what cash flow from a building is and how investors value it.

Cash flow is still rental income minus the building's operating expenses and debt service. Investors still buy buildings by capping the cash flow, just like they did 10 years ago. But while the procedure has remained the same, the definition of all the component parts has changed. Income, expenses and debt service do not mean what they used to in the income property business.

We have seen how "debt service" is different. It is no longer the regular payments of interest and principal paid on a mortgage to the mortgageholder, usually an insurance company. Instead, debt service has become a payment of profits of the building to a part owner of the property. It is still paid to the insurance company, but the insurer is no longer a mortgageholder. Compliments of the participating mortgage, or mortgage with a kicker, the insurance company is now the owner's partner.

The definition of "income" and "expenses" has similarly changed. Income has always meant revenues from rents and still does, except rent can now be adjusted far more often than it could 10 years ago. The landlord's income is more sensitive to changes in market rents and in recent years, that means both rent and income could increase more often. This rental readjustment has been abandoned in markets that are overbuilt or where demand for space has fallen. There, owners give tenants whatever they want including long leases and a free year's rent, just to fill up the space. But outside these markets, the new trends hold.

The entire nature of leasing has changed. Landlords originally wanted long leases but today, they want short ones so they can raise rents more often. Office and shopping center leases used to run five to 10 years. Now the landlord is trying to get them down to two- to five-year terms or at least arrange them so that every year or two there is an automatic increase in rent. The rent escalates each year according to the Consumer Price Index or some other index, such as the prevailing market rent at the time. In Manhattan, some office rents are hiked every time the local janitor's union gets a pay raise.

Not only has the type of rental income changed but, with certain properties, what is included as income. This is true of shopping centers in particular. Back in the late 1960s and early 1970s, overage or percentage rent was never included as part of a center's official cash flow when the owner was setting a price on the property. Inflation changed that. Because inflation pushes up sales volume, tenants find they are reaching the volume figure that triggers overage rent more frequently than ever. At this writing, overage rent is considered as dependable as base rent and is included in all cash-flow projections used to price a building. It is capped at the same rate as the base-rent income.

The nature of operating expenses is also changing. Landlords used to pay far more of the operating expenses of their buildings than they do today. They are now laying them off on their tenants. Shopping center tenants, for example, used to make a fixed payment every year to cover the cost of common-area maintenance and real estate taxes. The landlord picked up the rest. Today, the tenants must pick up a fixed percentage of the common-area maintenance. There is no cap on what they must pay. And the landlord in shopping centers and in office buildings is passing along more of his other expenses to his tenants— expenses, in some cases, that the landlord historically has always paid. In some new office buildings, for example, the landlord is demanding that tenants pay for their own heat, real estate taxes, and utilities, whereas historically they had only paid for utilities.

This attempt to push more of the cost of running the building onto the tenants and to raise their rents more frequently has been caused by both inflation and the lack of competition in the building market. Landlords started passing on their operating costs because high inflation was pushing their costs up faster than the landlords could raise rents, or even set them in the first place. Developers found they could not even predict their operating costs before they finished a building. How could they raise financing or find a buyer with no projections on cash flow? At the same time, because nothing had been built between the crash of the REITs in 1975 and 1979, developers could force their will on their tenants. The disgruntled tenant had no place to go.

As one developer put it, cash flow from good income property has begun to "pure up." The owner is becoming insulated from the effects of inflation on his income stream, making that income more stable and desirable as an investment. He is moving to a "more net-leased position," from "gross leases," as those in the trade would say. The developer who brought up this point argued that the income from a well-leased piece of property resembles that of a bond in its dependability. This is particularly true of new shopping centers because of the history in that business of sharing expenses between landlord and tenant. Shopping centers went to a more net-leased basis back in 1974, whereas it took office developers until 1978 or so to start passing on costs to tenants.

The stability of property cash flow helped depress yields. An investor in 1981 could buy a newly leased shopping center at a cap rate of 5½ and find that he had a more dependable income stream from his center than if he had purchased one in 1965 at a cap rate of 8. The quality of the cash flow is much better today. It would be as if Exxon borrowed in the 1981 bond market at 2 percent instead of 15 percent because the company had agreed to adjust the bond's interest payments each year to protect the bondholder from inflation.

There are by no means a great number of commercial properties sporting such net-leased cash flows. The interest in shortening leases and passing on expenses to tenants is only recent, and most of such valuable properties have been built within the last 10 years. They are far outnumbered by the many old shopping centers and office buildings housing tenants with 20-year leases with no escalator clauses and only a nominal liability for the building's expenses. These leases often plague fine old buildings in great locations. They are terrible investments because they have terrible leases. If a pension fund starts buying property on its own, the pension staff should be prepared to see many proposals to buy such crippled buildings cross their desks.

They should also be prepared to sift through great numbers of old landsale-leasebacks and net-leased credit deals, both of which are poor investments because of their leases. The leases run until what seems like the next Ice Age—99 years was not unusual. Many have rents that do not change at all over that time or increase by some significant amount only once every 10 years. When these leasebacks were done in the 1960s, no one thought inflation would top 10 percent by 1979.

The old, triple-net, credit-leased buildings are in the same league as leasebacks. In a triple-net credit deal, a high-quality company like Exxon agrees to lease an entire building from the owner and pay virtually all the operating expenses. The lease generates steady and dependable income but there is little inflation protection. The tenant may pay all the operating expenses, but he will also pay the landlord the same rent for 35 years with perhaps some minor increase once every 10 years.

Buying a building leased to Exxon for 35 years at a yield of 6 percent is much like buying a long-term, 6 percent bond at par. If the owner wants to discount the price to yield the new owner a market rate of return, then it might be worth talking about. But most holders of such leases are institutions that do not want to take such a write-down and be forced to post a loss.

Credit leases, ground leases, and long-term leases—all of them once provided the steady, long-term cash flow the investment property business flourished on in the 1960s and early 1970s. But at this writing, they are worthless unless their owners are willing to sell at a big discount. That is how much inflation has changed the desired type of cash flow in the real estate business.

And it has created another problem: Just how should an ever-changing cash flow be valued? The methods of valuing real estate in this country assume that a building's cash flow remains constant for several years at a time with only minor variations. When leases did not roll over more than once every five years, cash flow did not change. An appraiser or investor could value the property by capping the cash flow and the result would be accepted as the property's value.

At this writing, the income stream on many buildings, particularly those with the new, net leases, increases all the time. When the landlord scores the "big hit," as one developer called it earlier, and is able to raise his rents 25 percent in one year, that is a big boost to income. When escalator clauses kick in once a year or the tenants pay increased amounts of the building's expenses, all work to raise cash flow. It is really inaccurate to freeze cash flow at a point in time, cap it, and label the result the building's value, because the very next year that income will increase, assuming someone has not yet built a competing building next door.

Appraisers have tried a number of ways to cope with this problem. Some of the more mathematically inclined have tried to discount the increased cash flow over the base year back to the purchase date, or have fooled with internal-rate-of-return analysis or other techniques. But the income property community has not embraced sophisticated financial analysis of a building's earning power primarily because they cannot predict next year's cash flow, much less cash flow in 10 years. A few of the insurance companies and big property buyers use it, but that is it. Most appraisers stick with the traditional valuation techniques. They take the cash flow, divide it by a cap rate, and post the result as the property's value. They then spend a good part of their discussion section explaining that the cap rate reflects the increased cash flow the property will enjoy from future rent hikes.

The appraisers' approach is more in the spirit of how the market is dealing with the valuation problem. Everyone, with the exception of the sophisticates mentioned above, still uses the traditional technique. Rather than worry that the cash flow number will change next year and what kind of techniques they should use to reflect this value, they adjust the cap rate. Because the property will be expected to throw off more cash flow next year, the buyer should pay more for it this year. He should be willing to take a lower yield today. As one developer quoted earlier said, investors are buying "futures." When an investor buys a building to yield 5½ percent when the going rate on risk-free Treasury bonds is higher, he must be expecting great jumps in cash flow over the next five years.

And the appraisal business continues on, undisturbed. Adjusting the cap rates may not be elegant, but it works.

What's Happening to Leverage?

After the lengthy explanation of leverage earlier in this chapter, the reader may be annoyed to find it apparently killed off only pages later. Why waste time explaining leverage if the long-term, fixed-rate mortgage is now vanishing? Because everything moves in cycles in the real estate business. At this writing, the fixed-rate, 30-year mortgage, with no kickers, is gone, but it will be back if inflation stays down. It is the favorite form of positive leverage in the business, and just because it has disappeared does not mean the real estate community has abandoned positive leverage. They just use some different techniques to leverage themselves or to keep control of their properties until rates do fall and they can refinance on favorable terms. Using someone else's money to control a piece of property is still the fastest way to riches in real estate. With an impetus like that, some very gifted minds are working on how to leverage, or at least hold onto, what they have, the disappearance of the long-term mortgage notwithstanding.

The result has been a strange collection of mortgages with equity kickers and conversion clauses, balloon payments, and bobbing amortization schedules that typically get dragged out of the closet when interest rates are prohibitively expensive.

Convertible Mortgages

Convertible mortgages are neither pure debt nor pure equity. They are structured as either a first or second mortgage in which the lender has the option of converting his loan to an equity position in the future. They are attractive to institutional investors because they allow them to option a property they like, but have doubts about. Perhaps they like a property but are unsure that the owner is going to get good rent increases when the leases turn in five years. So they will make the owner a convertible mortgage and keep an eye on him. If the property rents do pick up, they will convert in five years and pick up a piece of the ownership, perhaps as much as 60 percent. If the property proves disappointing, they will just remain mortgage lenders and collect cash flow from their mortgage investment.

From an owner's viewpoint, convertibles are good deals because he does not have to give up any ownership—at least immediately—in order to cash out some of the equity in his building. He also retains control of the building. The lender does have the right to convert his debt to equity, but the owner prays that will not happen. The conversion option buys the owner time to think up ways of getting out of the deal. He hopes the institution will have a change of heart and decide that it doesn't want to own buildings like his. Maybe his new rents will disappoint them, and they will not convert, or interest rates will suddenly fall and the institution decide to keep its mortgage and forgo ownership.

There are two problems with convertibles. First, there are not many buildings that both attract large investors and can support a convertible mortgage. Owners have already squeezed all the leverage they can out of their buildings by laying on as many mortgages as a building's cash flow can support. There is nothing left for a convertible.

Second, because of the right to convert, a convertible bears a lower interest rate than a pure mortgage. If the lender decides he does not want to convert, he has lost that extra income. He is paying to postpone his decision to buy or pass up the building.

The Wraparound

Because of the shortage and expense of long-term mortgage money, any deal that gets done usually involves leveraging off the existing mortgage on a property. It is much like the way inhabitants of war-ravaged cities rebuild on the same sites, using the ruins of the old walls as the foundations for the new. If a $25 million property has a $15 million mortgage on it at 8 percent and a constant of .10, the owner will go through all sorts of financial contortions to keep it when he tries to refinance. The last thing he wants to do is pay off such a mortgage when the going rate on new mortgage money ranges from 14 to 18 percent. (Remember, the constant is the ratio of annual mortgage payments to the outstanding mortgage balance and must be less than the cap rate for a deal to be positively leveraged. The lower the constant, the better.)

To keep that lovely old mortgage, he will add second and third mortgages on top of it and if he is really lucky, he might find a lender to make him something called a "wraparound mortgage." "Wrap" loans, as they are often called, are nothing new to the income property business, becoming popular when mortgage money is scarce and expensive. They are great deals for both the property owner and the wrap lender.

There are three parties to a wraparound mortgage: the owner of the property, the first-mortgage lender, and the wraparound-mortgage lender. The wrap lender issues a mortgage on the property that is larger than the existing first mortgage and subordinate to it. He then takes responsibility for making the mortgage payments to the first-mortgage lender. He "wraps" his mortgage around the existing mortgage, hence the origin of the name. The property owner makes his mortgage payments to the wrap lender who, in turn, pays the first-mortgage debt service and keeps the balance of the payment for himself. That is a wraparound mortgage. Why would anyone execute such a strange arrangement?

A wraparound mortgage is a ballet of interlocking leverages in which the borrower and the wrap lender benefit at the expense of the first-mortgage lender who is helpless to stop them. Wraparounds play games with the amortization schedules of the first mortgage and the wrap loan, and by doing so, they create that most wonderful of situations—a high-yield, low-risk investment.

The first requirement for a wraparound is a good piece of income property with a first mortgage that is five to 15 years old. This is to assure that the first mortgage has started to amortize. Most long-term mortgages are amortized over a 29- or 30-year schedule. But the first years of mortgage payments are applied mostly to interest due on the loan, not to principal reduction. After about the 10th year, the situation reverses. More and more of each mortgage payment is applied to reducing the outstanding balance. This flip-flop from paying off interest to amortizing the principal is what makes a wraparound work.

Consider a building worth $25 million with a $15 million first mortgage that is old enough to be amortizing well. The wrap lender makes the owner a 12-year, wraparound mortgage for $20 million, which is 80 percent of the property's value. But because the wrap lender is taking responsibility for paying the $15 million first mortgage, he writes the owner a check for only $5 million. This is the difference between the balance on the first mortgage and the balance on the wraparound. But the owner makes payments on the wrap loan as if he had borrowed the full $20 million.

These mortgage payments will not cripple the owner because even though the wrap has a 12-year term, it is amortized over a 30-year period, and at the end of the term the entire unpaid balance of the loan is due. This last gigantic payment is typically called a "balloon," and the term "balloon loan" is used to describe any loan where the term is shorter than the amortization period, leaving a big chunk of the loan due on the last day. By amortizing the loan over 30 years, and using a balloon, the wrap lender makes the mortgage payments affordable even when the interest rate is high. Sometimes he can make them even more affordable by writing an interest-only wrap. That means the owner only pays the interest on the loan for 12 years, and the entire loan is due in one, giant balloon on the last day of the loan.

However it is structured, the mechanics remain the same. The owner makes the wrap lender payments on the wrap mortgage, most of which are applied to interest on that loan. The wrap lender then turns around and makes payments to the first-mortgage lender, which are mostly applied to principal. So the balance on the first mortgage is decreasing faster than the balance on the wrap. Or looking at it another way, the difference between the amount due on the first mortgage and the amount due on the wrap is growing.

Wrap loans mature in 10 to 12 years for a good reason. That is when the wrap loan itself begins to amortize substantially and that is the last thing the wrap lender wants. So after 12 years, the loan comes due and the owner must pay off the balloon. He does this by either getting a new mortgage and using the proceeds to pay the balloon or else selling the building and using that money to pay off the wrap lender.

The wrap lender then takes the money and pays off the first mortgage, keeping the rest for himself. Because the first mortgage was amortizing faster than the wrap over the last 12 years, the outstanding balance on the first mortgage is very small. In fact, after paying off the first mortgage, the wrap lender has much more money than the $5 million he had originally advanced the owner. He may have $10 million or even $12 million—all because one loan amortized faster than the other.

This is a good deal for the wrap lender. Not only has he received a good yield on his loan for the last 12 years, he gets this big cash bonus at the end of the loan. He may make an annual return of 11 percent as his mortgage yield, but when the effects of the big pay-off at the end of 12 years are added in, he has earned another 6 to 9 percent return. Not allowing for the time value of money, that means he enjoys a total annual return of 17 to 20 percent over the life of the loan.

This is often a better return than can be earned by owning the property outright. Wraps are subordinate to the first mortgage, so they are riskier than holding the first mortgage. But the amount of the first-mortgage debt service is usually substantially smaller than that of the wrap. If the owner did default, it would be on the wrap loan. The wrap lender could force the owner to sell and use the proceeds to pay off the first mortgage and the wrap. The wrap lender would still come out ahead.

From a property-owner's point of view, wraparounds are a good deal because they increase his leverage and are cheaper than straight first mortgages. Because the wrap mortgage feeds off the underlying first mortgage, the wrap lender can offer an interest rate less than the going rate on new first mortgages. As one happy wrap lender put it, "We're making a yield on money we did not lend," and in such a situation, the lender can share his good fortune with the owner in the form of a lower rate.

The one drawback to wraparounds falls on the wrap lender himself. He has a tax problem. The money he collects from the owner as a wrap-mortgage payment is mostly interest and he must post it as interest income. Interest income is fully taxable unless he has some offsetting tax deduction from another investment. At the same time, the wrap lender is using that interest income to make his mortgage payments to the first-mortgage lender. So not only does he have taxable interest income, he may not have enough cash to pay the taxes on it. He is using it to pay the debt service on the first mortgage.

This is one reason why wraparounds are not done more often and a good reason why they are particularly suited to pension funds, which are tax-exempt entities. But even though pension funds have a real advantage over the taxable competition as wrap lenders, few investment advisors offer them. Wraps are difficult to understand, at least difficult to understand when compared to a straight-out purchase of a property for cash. And pension funds have been interested only in owning property outright, not in getting involved in something like a wrap, which they perceive as a complicated financing scheme.

As a result, most wraparound loans have been done by smaller lenders or syndicators on deals in the $2 million to $10 million range. Balcor/American Express, a public syndicator based in Skokie, Illinois, has offered wrap syndications to small pension funds for several years and in the fall of 1981 came out with a commingled fund that has the ability to make wraps. But at this writing, this is the only fund available to large pension funds for wrap lending, and Balcor does not even bill it as a wrap fund. It primarily makes convertible first mortgages and has the authority to make wraps.

At this writing, in its public syndications and with this commingled fund, Balcor adds an equity twist to its wraparound loans. The firm asks its borrowers for a piece of the deal, sometimes as a percentage of cash flow, sometimes a percentage of the property's sale price if it is sold to pay off the wrap. And sometimes they ask for both, along with the right to have the first crack at buying the property when and if it does go up for sale. Pity the poor owner. He is being corralled into giving up more of his ownership again.

The Indispensable Developer

At this writing, just about the only owners capable of holding out a good chunk of ownership from the predations of the institutional lender are those developers who have such expertise in developing a particular type of income property that they are indispensable. Unless they put the deal together, there will be no deal for an investor to buy. In the end, these developers have the best leverage of any developer or individual owner.

Some developers are more indispensable than others. Thousands of people know how to build and lease single-tenant warehouses. Institutional investors can hire these people to build warehouses for them, or even start doing them on their own. They are simple deals. But only a handful of developers do regional shopping centers, those giant malls with more than one million square feet of rentable space. If an institution wanted to own one of these malls, and they were the investment rage among institutions in 1979 and 1980, then they had to deal with one man—the fellow who built it or the person he sold it to. And if the owner did not want to sell, the institution was out of luck.

Regionals are not the kind of income property an institution could hire an unknown to build for them. Big tenants come into a regional not only to get into a particular retail market, but because they trust the judgment and management ability of the developer. They have done business with him at other centers he has developed. And if a pension fund or insurance company wants to own a regional center, they will have to do business with that developer, too. He is truly indispensable.

  To show how much, consider how one regional in Texas was built and a half-interest sold to a group of pension funds in 1980. In 1978, the developer, well known in shopping center circles, had started hearing complaints from some of the major retailers who were in other big malls that he owned and ran. Apparently they wanted to enter a particular market in Texas, but the owner of the largest shopping center there would not rent to them. He refused to expand his 900,000-square-foot mall and to rent the new space to these retailers. In addition, the owners of the stores already in the center found him difficult to deal with, and he was disliked by them all. The owner was not interested in selling, so there appeared to be no remedy for everyone's dissatisfaction with the man.

That is, there was no remedy until the developer in question heard these complaints. He immediately approached the retailers he knew who were complaining that they could not get into the mall and received assurances that they indeed wanted to enter that Texas market. "Then, what we did," he recalls with a chuckle, "was finesse the owner into a sale."

Directly across the street from the existing center was some vacant land owned by an oil company. The developer talked them into selling him an option to buy the land. Then he approached the owner of the existing center and told him that unless he sold he would build a new center right across the street and populate it with the retailers who wanted to get into the market.

"He didn't want to sell," says the developer, "but he didn't want us to build across the street, and he believed we would do it, so he did sell. He got a good price for it."

The developer then started on his next challenge—the three department stores who were the major tenants in the existing center. The "majors" or "anchor tenants," as they are sometimes called, are the prima donnas of every shopping center. They attract the customers to the center, and in passing to and from the majors, the customers shop at the smaller shops lining the mall.

All majors know they make a center work, and they use that as their negotiating wedge with the developer. No department store sitting in a mall in a good area wants to see its competitors move in next door. So before the major agrees to rent or build in the center, it gets the developer to agree not to rent to its competition and also to grant the major all sorts of concessions on things like maintenance costs, parking allocations, and access to the store from the mall.

Since regional malls can have as many as five major tenants, each must make peace not only with the developer but with each other. The resolution of all their infighting and haggling are agreements describing who gets what, called "reciprocal easement" agreements. With the center in question, the developer had to reopen these agreements in order to let in the new majors, an event that was greeted by the existing majors with as much enthusiasm as the discovery that the bubonic plague had broken out in Texas for the first time in history.

It took months to renegotiate the reciprocal easements. "It's like being a guy with five wives," the developer says, "you have to keep them all happy, and you can't give any one of them everything. And of course they want everything— more parking, more convenants, more control over this and that. It's very complicated."

But basically, the existing tenants were resigned to their fate. They reasoned that the competition was going to come into their market no matter what they did, so they might as well let them locate in their existing center rather than watch them build across the street. At least it would increase foot traffic in their center. The existing majors and the interlopers made their peace.

All this squabbling with retailers, optioning land, and "finessing" the owner into agreeing to sell went on months before the developer had actually figured out how he was going to get the money to buy and expand the center. He knew that institutional buyers were interested in regionals. So he took the letters from the new majors, promising to rent in the expanded center; the newly renegotiated reciprocal easement agreements; and his plans for expanding the center. He started looking around for money. In the course of his search, he talked to a major New York bank. They sent some of their real estate staff down to look at the property, and they decided to buy into the deal.

As their contribution to the deal, they would put up most of the money. The developer originally had decided that he needed $15 million in cash to buy the center and expand it from 900,000 square feet to 1.5 million square feet. "But we had some cost overruns, so the bank really had to come up with $24 million," he says. He declined to be more specific on why such a modest-sounding item— as "cost overruns" could effectively double the cost of the deal. Usually "cost overruns" is a polite way of saying that disaster struck a project because interest rates went from 9 percent to 18 percent overnight. Since the developer's construction money is tied to the prime rate, his interest costs ate him alive. He had to turn the deal over to the lender.

But in this case, whatever the source of the cost overruns, disaster did not strike. The center had, as the developer put it, "tremendous upside potential." Tenants were selling enough merchandise to generate gross revenues to them of $160 a square foot, but they were paying only $4 a square foot in rent. Originally, the developer thought he could raise rents to $13 a square foot but found that tenants would tolerate $16.50 because their sales were so good. So the cost overruns did not break the deal.

In exchange for its $24 million in cash, the bank would get the first cash flow off the center each year until it had been paid an amount equivalent to a 10 percent return on its money for that year. After the bank received its preferred 10 percent, it and the developer would split the remaining cash flow equally. And if the center was sold, they would split the sale proceeds equally.

As his part of the deal, the developer would direct the expansion and lease up of the center and manage it once it was complete. He would also put up $500,000 in cash, which he had received as part of the deal as his "developer's fee."

For $500,000 of money he was paid by the bank and the ability to put together and manage a regional shopping center, he now owns half of an asset that will probably be worth $40 to $50 million when completed. He will be receiving perhaps a million dollars a year in cash flow and a share of the property's future appreciation with only his expertise and no money in the deal. Now that is leverage.

When this is pointed out, the developer just smiles and points out that there would have been no deal at all if those major retailers had not groused to him in the first place. "And they complained to me because I've been doing business with them for 15 years," he says. "I know what I'm doing and believe me, my education is street learning and cost millions of dollars in mistakes." This is a touching testimonial until one remembers that this developer flourished in the heyday of the fixed-rate mortgage and the "millions of dollars in mistakes" were probably borne far more by his lender than by him. But nevertheless, he has a point. He is indispensable.

As was noted at the beginning, this deal involved pension fund money, but that fact comes into play as almost an afterthought. The big New York bank had not used its own funds to do the deal, but had used money from a commingled fund it had set up for pension funds. Each of 16 pension funds had put up $1.5 million to buy into this deal. The developer did not know—nor care—where the money was coming from and only was informed of its source when he closed the deal with the bank.

"We had this cocktail party afterwards and I found out my limited partners were going to be all these pension funds of major U.S. companies," he says. "Some of them were interested in meeting us, but most of them couldn't care less. And," he adds, "none of them has ever seen the center."

Deals in Perspective

Convertible mortgages, wraparounds, joint ventures between indispensable developers and pension funds—these are only some of the different types of financing techniques being used to finance real estate development and ownership at this writing. But there are others: landsale-leasebacks and credit deals with kickers and escalator clauses, and convertible mortgages with fluctuating interest rates. Many deals sport mortgage payments that consist of only interest. The principal is due in a huge balloon at the end of the loan.

But as money becomes scarcer, so do the clever deals. At this writing, income property financing is less a negotiation between equals than the granting of a favor by those with money—the institutions—to those without it—the current property owners. Even indispensable developers can become dispensable if they need cash badly enough. Unless present owners have the resources to wait until institutions tire of this position, or the fixed-rate mortgage returns, the owner must give them what they want. Where else can he go?

TAXES AND MEDDLING GOVERNMENT

The disappearance of the pure long-term mortgage was the big event of the investment property business between 1979 and 1982, but there are other more subtle forces that are also shaping the business. Two worth mentioning are the Economic Tax Recovery Act of 1981 and the increased meddling of local governments in real estate development.

The Tax Reform Act of 1976 removed the important tax benefits of owning and building income property, particularly the big deduction for construction-loan interest. The tax law was changed again in 1981 and 1982, but the 1981 Act had more of an effect on income property. It did not restore any of the tax benefits real estate lost in 1976, but it did add a few minor new ones.

The 1981 Act lowered the highest tax on investment income from 70 to 50 percent and reduced the tax rates on capital gains from 28 percent to 20 percent. Investors were allowed to depreciate property acquired after 1980 over 15 years instead of the 40- to 60-year range used before the law was changed. Using straight-line depreciation, an owner could deduct 6.7 percent of the value of his property each year ($\frac{1}{15}$) instead of 2.5 percent a year ($\frac{1}{40}$).

Although each situation must be considered individually, under the 1981 Act, an investor using the 15-year straight-line depreciation schedule could be better off than if he had still been bound to the accelerated depreciations rules of the 1976 Act. The 1981 Act generally made owning existing property a better deal than before. But it did not add any direct, new incentives for building new income property.

Besides taxes, another force shaping the income property business is the growing ability of government at all levels to control development.

The trend toward government control started in residential real estate about 15 years ago when the suburbs began suffering from traffic jams, poor zoning, and the continuous growth of fast-food restaurants and gas stations along the main roads. The local sewer-and-water systems were overwhelmed as developers added new homes to the system without paying enough to have it expanded. When the system did have to be expanded, the necessary tax increases shocked the local citizens. As a result, over the last 15 years they have successfully demanded that the growth of their towns be more rigidly controlled.

On residential property, this means that homebuilders must conform to much stricter zoning and building codes. They must donate land for parks and schools and pay high fees to hook up to the sewer-and-water system, assuming, of course, the municipality does not insist they build their own. Estimates vary, but homebuilders estimate that such regulations tack on 20 percent to the cost of building a new home, a cost that the developer simply passes along to the homebuyer as a higher price.

In many ways, these developers deserved such a fate. One city-planning official talks of how a typical developer would drive up in his Cadillac to city hall, throw some blueprints on the table, and demand that he get permission to build next week. The city could not get a straight answer out of him regarding the standards of construction he would use on his roads or in his homes. Five years later, all the roads in the subdivision caved in during a heavy rain, and the city had to fix them.

But in curtailing developers, the cities have gone to the other extreme. One Chicago suburb demands that developers sod the lawns of every home they build, at a cost of $1,500 a house.

The desire to control has carried over from the residential sector to the income property business, greatly increasing the cost of development. No longer can a shopping-center developer pick up 100 acres of empty land on the edge of town and start building a regional mall there three months after he has bought the property. First, there are not many sites left for regionals. They have all been built on. Second, on those sites that are left, the local municipality will demand public hearings, land concessions, environmental impact statements, and other studies before they will even consider the developer's request to build. They may not approve it even then. After two years of studies, the developer may find that he cannot build on his land after all.

Prudential Insurance Company refuses to buy raw land for exactly this reason. One of the senior vice presidents in real estate complained that city regulations and special interest groups meant it could take "hundreds of thousands of dollars and five years or more just to find out how you can develop your property."

Prudential has a deep pocket and could absorb these costs if it wanted. But consider an independent developer stuck in the midst of such municipal deliberations. The interest expense on his high-priced construction money adds up. That extra two years of waiting for city approval is more than enough to drive him into lethal cost overruns that kill the deal before it has a chance at life.

It is not only the municipal governments that exercise such control. In 1977, the Pyramid Corporation of Syracuse, New York, was stopped by the governor of Massachusetts from building a regional mall outside Lenox, Massachusetts. The mayor of Pittsfield, a neighboring town, had complained that the competition would destroy his city's downtown shopping district; the governor backed him up.

This government control of private property is starting to resemble the situation in Great Britain, though it is much worse there. In fact, over the last five years, it has often been noted that the U.S. income property business is following in the path of the British real estate business. In that country, insurance companies and pension funds dominate the real estate business because years of high inflation and tight government control of development have driven everyone else out of the business. Institutions, particularly pension funds, are the only ones with any money to lend, and they do not lend, they buy property and hold onto it forever.

The parallels between our system and theirs outweigh the differences. Since they have had 20 more years of dealing with high inflation than we have, their system provides an early view of what ours will look like if high inflation stays a major fixture of our economic life and the government continues to get more involved in property.

NOTES

1. Alan Rabinowitz, *The Real Estate Gamble: Lessons from 50 Years of Boom and Bust* (New York: The American Management Associations, 1980).

2. Ibid, pp. 8–9.

3. Ibid, p. 10.

4. Samuel Zell, "Pension Fund Perils in Real Estate," *Real Estate Review* 5 (Spring 1975), p. 64.

5. Ibid, p. 64.

6. Ibid, p. 63.

7. Rabinowitz, *The Real Estate Gamble*, p. 158.

8. Ibid, p. 10.

9. Ibid, p. 56.

10. Ibid, p. 160.

11. Lynn N. Woodward and Marcella Roberts, "We Need an Advanced Real Estate Degree," *Real Estate Review* 10 (Winter 1981), p. 9.

12. Rabinowitz, *The Real Estate Gamble*, p. 182.

13. Ibid, p. 210.

14. Ibid, p. 213.

15. Ibid, p. 228.

16. Ibid, p. 216.

17. Ibid, p. 216–17.

18. Ibid, p. 218.

19. Ibid, pp. 207, 219 and 223.

20. Ibid, p. 227.

6 | THE BRITISH

Malcolm Forbes (of *Forbes*) asked me if we were buying U.S. real estate for our clients because the U.S. was the last bastion of capitalism. I told him, "On the contrary, Mr. Forbes. We're buying because the United States is moving toward socialism and that's the best time to be a property owner."

—*a real estate consultant for British pension funds*

SMALL AND CROWDED

Great Britain is a small and heavily populated country, and this fact has strongly shaped the investment property business in that country. To get an idea of the population density, imagine if the entire United States were as heavily populated as the state of New Jersey or Rhode Island. Roughly 13 million people live in the London metropolitan area alone, and as one British property consultant put it, "when you remember that all of Canada has something like 22 million people in it, you know we're cramped."

It is difficult for an American, used to sprawling cities like Houston or Los Angeles, to understand how organized the British must be to live in such close quarters harmoniously. To American eyes, they make extraordinary attempts to control land use. This is done by all levels of government but mostly by local government, under something called "town planning." Town planning is not like "urban planning" in the United States, where a city planner draws up pretty pictures of what the well-planned city should look like but has no power to enforce those plans. British town planning is more like what would happen if the zoning boards in American cities went wild—if suddenly they had life and death control over any construction or any change made in existing property. If they did not like a project, they could kill it, with no questions asked.

In Great Britain, "every scrap, every square inch of space is zoned as to how it can be used," says the consultant quoted above. Before it can be built on or the existing property use changed, the town planning board must approve the change, a maddeningly long process controlled by what one consultant labeled "an infinite bureaucracy." Before an owner can convert an apartment into an office he must get special approval from the town planning commission; this can take from two to three months, even if the apartment is in an area already authorized for offices. "Town planning is much, much worse than the government control you have in America," says a British property consultant. It is his opinion the United States will catch up with the British over the next 10 years as local governments here increasingly control what can be built within their limits. "As the planning laws get tighter and tighter," he predicts, "you're going to be driven mad."

Whether his prediction will come true, it certainly appears that the United States is following in the steps of the British in government control over property development and use. But since the British have had town planning since before World War II, the United States has a long way to go to catch up. American developers today complain it takes them five extra years to complete a project; the local government demands concessions or refuses to approve the zoning. In England, because of the town planners, it took the developers of a large shopping center in northern London 20 years to finish it. All the private interests involved in such a project had to be protected.

Town planning protects the existing property owner and is one of the major reasons that real estate in Great Britain has been a good investment for the last 20 years. The town planners keep anyone from building any new space; the owners of existing property will never have any competition. They may have other problems, and their property values fall. Pedestrian patterns may change, an area may turn into a slum, or it may become the fashion to rent in a different part of town. But for the most part, the owner will never have to worry about large expanses of vacant or underutilized land suddenly blossoming with competing space and driving his rents down.

In the United States, many downtown areas and small community shopping centers lost business when regional shopping malls were built on the outskirts of town. This rarely happens in Great Britain; the planners will not allow malls to be built. The major shopping streets in town or the "high streets," as they are called, will always be the major shopping districts.

Because the town planners have so effectively knocked out the competition, existing income property in England has a locked-in, protected value: it is less risky to own British property than to own property in the United States. The British feel that the Americans are slowly following in their footsteps and that U.S. real estate is also becoming less risky. According to one British property consultant, his British clients are interested in buying U.S. real estate not because the United States is the last bastion of capitalism, but because it is moving away from capitalism.

"We're buying U.S. real estate because the U.S. is preaching the economics of conservation and no-growth; you are starting to control what can be built," this man says. "By definition, you can't make money investing in real estate in a laissez-faire economy because anyone can build what he wants. And you can't make money investing in real estate in a communist economy because they won't let you. But in-between, when the country is going from laissez-faire toward communism, that's the time to invest in real estate. It's the first page of economics: if you control supply and allow demand to go ahead, rents will rise."

INFLATION

While town planning has guaranteed profits to existing British property owners, inflation has complicated their lives by eroding the value of their rental income and increasing their operating costs. Inflation came in ever greater waves to Great Britain. Inflation averaged 2.3 percent in the 1950s, 3.8 percent in the 1960s, and really started to climb in the late 1960s, reaching a height of 27 percent in 1975. Inflation averaged 12 percent in Great Britain in the 1970s; it hit them with double-digit power roughly 10 years before it struck the United States. Besides generating a great deal of loose talk about how real estate was "an inflation hedge," the increasing inflation had some profound effects on the British real estate business—effects not unlike what the United States is going through today as a result of its bouts with high inflation.

Inflation helped push up rents and changed commercial leasing. British leases typically run for 25 years, but every five years or so the landlord has the right to reopen the lease and increase the rent. These five-year bump-ups are called "reversions": they have been a fixture of British real estate for many years. By the mid-1970s, town planning had stopped the construction of competing space and inflation was pushing up interest rates and return demanded by an investor; the landlord was able to dramatically increase his rents at each reversion. He was also able to pass more and more of his operating costs along to his tenants. Tenants today pay all the costs of running their building either directly or through a service charge. Taxes, insurance, and interior and exterior repairs are paid for by the tenant. He sends his landlord a quarterly check that is essentially a pure return on his investment in the property. Why should the landlord allow inflation to erode his return by forcing him to pay for these ever-increasing operating expenses?

As we have seen, the U.S. leasing market is starting to undergo the same changes. Either leases are shortening or the landlord is allowed the right to reopen and raise the rent every three to five years. And more of the operating expenses are being paid for by the tenants.

The British income property business also preceded the American system in another important change—the crippling of the long-term commercial mortgage market. The British had a vigorous, and large, mortgage business in commercial properties until 1969 when climbing inflation started making fools out of mortgage lenders; they began dropping out of the market. Today, mortgage money is available in Great Britain, much like it is available in the United States at this writing. That is, if the borrower is willing to pay a high rate for a fixed-rate, long-term mortgage, someone or some institution will lend money to him. But such mortgages make no economic sense for a borrower.

High interest rates killed off the British real estate developers in much the same manner they have decimated American developers. Except in the British case, the death blow was delivered in 1974, not 1980. The British income property business suffered the same kind of disaster that befell the American property business in 1974. In both countries, real estate had been booming and lenders had overextended themselves when suddenly, interest rates climbed dramatically. Because the interest rates on their construction loans were tied to the prime bank lending rate, the developers found they could not make their loan payments; they started going bankrupt. The lenders had to step in to clean up the mess and wiped out developers in the process.

Unlike American mortgages, which are secured only by the value of the underlying property, British mortgages have always been recourse loans: the loan is secured not only by the property, but by the borrower's personal assets. A British lender can go after a defaulted borrower with more verve and venom than his American counterpart can, and in 1974 he certainly did. The result was that only a handful of large, well-capitalized developers survived. The American income property business at the time was also littered with the bodies of dead developers, but here the histories of the two countries diverge. The American insurance companies after 1974 were still willing to make long-term, fixed-rate mortgages to those developers who had survived. The British lenders would not. They had been moving away from long-term mortgages for five years and now they really had had enough.

Those English developers who were strong enough to have survived the debacle now found that they could not get the long-term money they needed for permanent financing on future projects. Just like their American counterparts are doing at this writing, they turned to institutions not to lend them money, but to buy them out. They gave away 40 and 50 percent of their equity to get favorably priced long-term money from the institutions. Many were forced to become building contractors for institutions; the developer would have the idea for a building and would handle the building's construction, but would have to turn over 75 or 80 percent, if not all, of the ownership to the institution that had provided the money.

At first, these institutions were mostly insurance companies, which unlike their American counterparts, have a history of buying property for their general accounts. But eventually more and more British pension funds became interested in owning property, either through commingled funds called "property unit trusts" or directly on their own.

THE PENSION SCHEMES IN PROPERTY

The British pension plans or "schemes" as they are known in Great Britain, discovered property investing along the same path U.S. pension funds are now taking; the British started down it about 10 years earlier. The British funds started out knowing nothing about property. Then they began investing in various commingled funds, and eventually the larger plans began buying and financing property directly for their own accounts. Finally, some of the most aggressive and largest funds started developing property on their own, first in Great Britain itself, then in Europe, and now in the United States. While large U.S. pension funds are still trying to figure out which commingled fund is "best" for their plans, their British counterparts are building industrial parks for their own accounts or, in the case of the British Coal Board Pension Scheme, buying up entire portfolios of U.S. real estate from publicly traded real estate investment trusts at several hundred million dollars a shot.

At this writing, the British pension funds average just under 20 percent of their assets in property ownership; many of the large funds have the goal of using 30 percent of their assets to buy property. U.S. pension funds, on the other hand, average roughly 3 percent of their assets in real estate equities; the large funds talk of holding 10 percent in property.

This enthusiastic embrace of property by the British funds does not mean that the sponsors of British pension funds have any more understanding of the income property business than their American cousins. Instead, they have simply realized that property does something for their portfolios and they should own some of it. Like their American counterparts, the British pension officers believe that if something is worth owning, it is worth hiring somebody else to buy and run it while you keep a fiduciary eye on them. So the British sponsors have hired either commingled funds, known as "property unit trusts" in Great Britain, to run their money in property, or in the case of the larger funds, they have hired an outside consultant to invest in property for them. Only a handful of the very largest funds have set up their own in-house staffs to invest in real estate; among these largest funds, only the Coal Board fund invests aggressively.

Many funds, mostly smaller ones, have no property holdings at all. One survey of funds showed that those with less than 3,000 participants held only 3 percent of their portfolio in property.[1] Nevertheless, it is far more common in Britain than in the United States to find a large pension fund holding property directly for its own account: a much greater percentage of all British pension plans hold some property.

The Civil Service and some of the larger companies had started pension plans earlier, but like American pension funds, most British funds came into being after the Second World War. The funds invested mostly in fixed-income securities until the 1950s when the post-war boom pushed up the stock market; they became infatuated with common stock. By the late 1960s, the British pension funds were investing just like their American counterparts. Both held most of their assets in securities, stocks and bonds, though in the British case, the funds held stocks and government securities, known as "gilts" which is short for "gilt-edged securities." The same climbing inflation rate that was, at this point, killing off the long-term mortgage market was also crippling the corporate bond market; only the government could find buyers for its debt.

During the 1960s, the British funds also started investing in real estate, first through making mortgages and then by buying property. There was not a great deal of British pension fund activity in real estate during the 1960s. Some of the larger funds started making long-term mortgages; they could get a better yield on them than on common stocks or gilts. When rising interest rates made fixed-rate mortgages poor investments, they stopped making them.

Owning property appeared to be a better investment than lending on it. But the large funds were loathe to start their own real estate investment operations and learn about property by trial and error. The small funds simply lacked the resources to do so even if they wanted to. This problem was remedied in 1966 by the creation of the "property unit trust." An actuary, an accountant and a real estate consultant decided to pool together pension fund money and use it to buy property. The pool would be a nonprofit cooperative owned by the pension funds: they would hire management and acquisition people to run it. Pension funds could sample real estate ownership with a small contribution to the trust.

This first trust was called the "Pension Fund Property Unit Trust," known by the whimsical acronym of PFPUT (POUF put). Originally, the trust was most popular with smaller funds; soon, it had a full range of pension fund members from the smallest to the largest funds in Britain. The PFPUT salesman did not have trouble selling the trust to pension funds: they were interested, unlike their American counterparts who would shy away from real estate entirely when the American commingled fund salesmen came calling in the 1970s. Cecil Baker, the actuary involved in setting up PFPUT, believes that these different responses had their roots in the different investment policies of insurance companies in both countries. British insurance companies had been buying property and common stock for themselves and their pension clients since the 1950s; U.S. insurance companies held their assets in mortgages and bonds. Until the 1970s, British pension funds were largely administered by insurance companies; British funds were more comfortable with property than American funds, because they had owned it indirectly for 15 years.

There were other reasons the British funds would be more enthusiastic about owning property than their American counterparts. As we have seen, town planning made British real estate less risky to own than American property. The British tax system also favored the pension fund owners. Unlike the United States, there is no tax deduction for property depreciation in Great Britain. As a tax-exempt investor, pension funds do not mind in the least, but the lack of depreciation deductions dampens the ardor of the individual taxable investor for owning property. The pension funds found there would be no competition to buy properties from individuals or syndications of individuals seeking tax losses. Their only competition would be with insurance companies buying for their own accounts and corporations.

But perhaps the biggest inducement to investing in property was the rate of wage inflation in Great Britain. Wages took off with amazing speed in the 1970s, increasing 12 percent a year in the first four years of the decade and climbing 20 percent and 29 percent in 1973 and 1974, respectively. Like American pension funds, most British funds pay a worker a fixed benefit at retirement, based on his final salary. If his salary was climbing to the stars, then the pension fund had to attempt to find an investment that would climb along with it. Property, with its regular rental increases, certainly provided an ever-increasing stream of investment income, though whether its increases could match those in wage agreements was unknown.

With these inducements to owning property, when the mortgage market evaporated after 1974 the British pension funds were willing to begin playing the role of the all-cash buyer along with the insurance companies. The large funds, such as those of the nationalized industries—the Electricity Council, the Post Office, the Coal Board, and British Airways—either set up their own real estate departments to bring in property or else hired outside consultants to handle their property investments for them. Competition among the funds and insurers for English property became intense; in the late 1970s some of the larger funds, such as the Post Office and the Coal Board, as well as some property unit trusts, began buying American property.

The property unit trusts became the most popular method for pension funds of all sizes to invest in property. At this writing, there are roughly 30 such trusts with more than $1.9 billion in assets. As the larger pension funds become more intrigued with owning property, they are gradually redeeming their interests in the property unit trusts and investing in property directly on their own. By 1977, private British pension funds held roughly 15 percent of their assets in real estate equities, up from 5 percent only 10 years before. And today, the larger funds are talking about an asset mix for their portfolios of one-third common stock, one-third gilts, and one-third property.

Although the British funds are more sophisticated than U.S. funds in property investing, in nearly every other aspect of pension fund investing, the British are at least 10 years behind. Most British fund sponsors know nothing about modern portfolio theory; there is no monitoring system that is uniformly used to measure pension fund investment performance. Many funds are managed by stockbrokers who are paid in commissions for their work—at a commission level that would shock American pension officers.

There is no "prudent man rule" in Great Britain; pension trustees are expected to behave as fiduciaries and invest conservatively. But there is no British pension law like ERISA hanging over their heads and threatening them with fines and lawsuits if they do not behave themselves. In fact, there are no laws at all barring conflict-of-interest situations with plan trustees, sponsors and money managers. Nor are there any laws requiring the fund trustees to disclose to their participants what they are doing with the pension money: the trustees can buy anything they want for the fund and do not have to tell anyone about it. If a union or corporate pension fund goes bankrupt, there is no government agency like the U.S. Pension Benefit Guaranty Corporation that will pick up the plan's obligations and make certain the workers get at least some of the benefits they were promised. In short, compared to the U.S. pension business, the British are still crawling through the Dark Ages.

Since pension funds have become a major force in the British capital markets, a number of studies and articles have come out, arguing that the government should have more control over what the funds are doing with their money. At this writing, the most recent study of the pension system was conducted by a committee chaired by former Prime Minister Harold Wilson. After several years of work, in 1980 the committee members concluded that the pension funds were adequately policing themselves but should probably disclose more about their investment activities.[2] The Wilson Committee submitted no draft legislation.

So life in the British pension community lumbers on in the dark. It is difficult to get any sense at all of how the funds' investments are doing simply because they will not tell anyone, not even their plan participants. Their annual reports to their beneficiaries tell them only that the plan's investment performance for the year was "above average, good, or disappointing." The sole number indicating any type of investment performance will be a figure for "gross income from investments." From the numbers that are available and from conversations with pension officers, Baker of PFPUT concludes that in recent years property has shown a better return for pension funds than common stocks; neither property nor stocks has quite matched the inflation rate, but both have far outperformed returns from gilts. The difference in performance has been so vast that some pension funds are starting to abandon the gilt market entirely, concentrating the bulk of their holdings in stocks and property.

Over the large collection of funds, however, money is still channeled into the three types of investments: stocks, property and gilts. Property has become an accepted part of British pension fund investment strategy: it is one more way the funds diversify their holdings. The U.S. pension business may be 10 years behind the British in real estate investing, but if inflation continues, we could gain on them quickly.

NOTES

1. The National Association of Pension Funds, *Survey of Occupational Pension Schemes—1979*, p. 7.

2. "United Kingdom's Financial Institutions Shouldn't be Nationalized, Panel Says," *The Wall Street Journal* (June 26, 1980), p. 24.

7 | WHAT TO EXPECT FROM REAL ESTATE INVESTMENTS

Under the English common law, the transfer of ownership of real property was completed by the ceremonial passing of a clod of dirt from seller to buyer. Remembrance of this archaic practice would serve today's institutional investor well, for the image of holding dirt in one's hand quickly dispels the attitude that real estate can be approached in a remote, abstract manner.

—from a pamphlet on real estate investing written by Thorndike, Doran, Paine & Lewis—investment counselors[1]

One of my pet peeves is the tendency of pension funds to look at real estate as some sort of CPR program, coming to breathe life into their rate of return. Here comes real estate: Just inject some money and it gives cash flow and stability.

After a buildup like that, we're often accused of not being heart surgeons.

—a manager of real estate for pension funds

THERE IS NO DATA

It is impossible to make dependable generalizations about how income property investments will affect a pension fund's portfolio. No one can predict how any investment will turn out, but income property in particular defies analysis. Each building is unique, a business unto itself; and there are many different types of property investing. An investor can write traditional mortgages, do wraparound loans, own existing office buildings, or develop amusement parks; each is a different investment with different risks. Which one is the "typical property investment strategy" that should be followed and analyzed to decide "what real estate can do for a portfolio?" There is no such animal.

When someone speaks of "what real estate can do for a pension portfolio," he usually means the return a fund can expect when it buys a property for cash and intends to hold it for years. But the studies that claim to analyze the results of this strategy, or any other real estate strategy, are meaningless at best and often misleading. The data from the past simply does not exist and today's cannot be gathered: there are no accurate studies of past returns on income property investment of any kind. Nor are there any studies that can help a pension sponsor predict what buying and holding property, or adopting any other real estate strategy, will do in the future.

This is worth repeating: There are no real estate indexes or rate-of-return studies that accurately quantify how real estate investments have performed in the past or describe what they can be expected to do in the future.

This is not a reason to not invest in real estate, but it is a good reason to avoid real estate "studies." Nevertheless, these studies are proliferating, a true example of supply rising to meet demand, regardless of merit. If pension officers think they need such studies, the marketplace will happily provide them, particularly if the fund or its investment advisor is willing to spend $20,000 to $50,000 to commission the work.

Real estate indexes differ completely from studies or indexes of securities prices. Studies of rates of return on stocks and bonds are accurate; they are useful to pension officers doing asset allocation work on their portfolios. Analyses like the famous Ibbotson-Sinquefield study have documented to the 100th of a percent the rates of return on common stocks, bonds and treasury bills over the last 50 years.[2] They draw legitimate conclusions about how stocks and bond returns vary over the long term. Roger Ibbotson and Rex Sinquefield did their study by analyzing data on common stock trading on the New York Stock Exchange and data on the public bond market. This data has been collected for years. The securities markets are public auction markets and information on share prices, dividends and coupon yields are easily available. To do their study, Ibbotson and Sinquefield amassed this huge file of data and computed the year-to-year changes of stock and bond prices.

It is impossible to do this for real estate. Reliable long-term data on either residential or income property does not exist. In his history of the real estate business, Alan Rabinowitz constantly laments the lack of such information: there is no data on the value of property during the Depression, during and after the tremendous collapse of mortgage bonds in the 1920s, and so forth. He is forced to base his conclusions about real estate values on reports in newspapers and old real estate journals.[3]

Real estate is not traded on an exchange like stocks and some bonds; no one has been collecting data on it in one spot. Even if someone had been attempting to do so and do it properly, the complexity and amount of the data he would need would overwhelm him and doom the project. To compute the rate of return on stocks and bonds, one needs to know the price the security was purchased at, the price it was sold at, and the dividend or coupon rate it paid while it was held. But with real estate, the price someone paid for a building and what he eventually sold it for are likely to be the least important indicators of how much the investor made on the investment.

What if he had to replace the roof? What if he bought the building for $5 million and sold it for $10 million, but had to take back a mortgage for part of the purchase price? He certainly did double his money on the sale, but what did he make? The researcher would need to know the loan terms and the collateral involved. What if the owner did a joint venture with a partner on the building, but the other partner received a 10 percent preferential rate of return? What is the value of that preferential return compared to a straight 50/50 split of the profits between the partners?

With all the variables affecting a property investment, the creator of a real estate study would spend days trying to estimate what one deal made for its owner. There is only one way to figure out what someone made—tracking the cash flow in the deal. The data gatherer would have to know how much cash the investor used to buy the property, how much cash he put into the property to run and repair it, and how much cash he took out each year in cash flow. He would also have to know how much cash the investor collected when he sold the property. By subtracting how much the investor put into the property from how much he took out, one can figure out his profit. Divide that by the total cash he had into the deal when he bought it, and the result is the total return he made on his money.

There are a few problems with this method. First, to compute a return, the investor must have sold the property. That is the only way to know what its market value is. Second, there is a tremendous amount of detailed data to collect for each deal included in the study. Third, and most importantly, the data does not exist. Real estate investors have no reason to disclose the intimate details of their deals to anyone and they do not; anyone trying to do a study would be stymied by his inability to get any data to work with.

One pension fund consulting firm tried to collect detailed data on income property in commingled real estate funds. It wanted to create an index that would show which types of properties were the most lucrative investments and which commingled funds the best performers. "They sent us a stack of forms to fill out that was six inches thick," said one manager of a commingled fund. "We wanted to participate in this study and were even helping fund it. But they wanted to know all these details about the operations of our buildings, broken down by categories. In the end, they had to give up because no one would fill out the forms."

That sensible real estate indexes cannot be created does not stop academics and consultants from trying to devise them. Pension fund sponsors would love an Ibbotson-Sinquefield study for real estate, and the market is looking for one as if it were in pursuit of the Holy Grail.

In one case, a real estate investment advisor went over data on mortgage loans made by 15 insurance companies since 1951.[4] He picked out the cap rates the insurers used to appraise the properties before lending on them and decided that that cap rate was a good proxy for real estate yields since 1951.

Property not only throws off cash, its resale value changes over time; an owner's total return consists of cash yield and the profit he makes when the property is sold. So the study's author had to find some data on resale values. He decided to use data from the Marshall Valuation Services. Marshall provides appraisers with data on the replacement costs of property, such as how much it costs per square foot to build a wood-frame building in 1981. Arguing that the value of a piece of a property eventually must be equivalent to its replacement cost, he used the Marshall data as a proxy for the property's resale value.

His study concluded that for the 28 years between 1951 and 1978, property had a total average return of between 13 and 15 percent; the return was remarkably stable. The rate of return on common stocks and bonds bounced around far more, or had higher "volatility," as investment jargon would put it. This study "proved" that owning income property over this 28-year period was as perfect an investment as one could get. Its return was not only higher than what an investor could have earned owning stocks and bonds, it was far less volatile.

But in reaching this conclusion, the author made a critical error of judgment; his proxies for yield and appreciation do not work. For his yield proxy, the author used the cap rate appraisers use to value properties for mortgage loans. Unfortunately, a cap rate does not give any idea of what the real long-term yield on the property is. It only says what the yield is when the property was purchased; even then it is a poor indicator of a property's cash return. It does not take into account the effect of financing on yield. It never considers the impact of major repairs an owner had to perform. Appraisals are also inaccurate by nature, being educated estimates of value created for an audience that only wants to see property appreciate. The cap rates could be 15 to 30 percent or more off of what the property would really sell for. Imagine if the Ibbotson-Sinquefield study of publicly traded securities was done with data on sales of securities that was 30 percent off. How much credibility would that study have?

The study runs into further problems with the proxy it uses for property appreciation. First, Marshall Valuation Services shows how the cost per square foot of construction has increased over time, but Marshall breaks its data down by the type of construction, such as wood-frame or reinforced concrete, and not by the type of building, such as office building or shopping center. Since the the data on yield was collected by type of building, the two sets of data are incompatible and the study's author had to make a number of assumptions and adjustments to use both in the study.

Second, the Marshall data only shows how the cost of a particular type of construction has gone up. It does not take account of what the author calls "functional or locational obsolescence." If an old warehouse has columns but industrial tenants want and can get wide, freespan spaces, that warehouse is functionally obsolete. If it is located in an inner-city neighborhood but potential tenants prefer the suburbs, it is locationally obsolete. In both cases, this warehouse is worth little, if anything, since no tenant but a poor one wants it. Yet this study would show its value appreciating because the cost of building new warehouses has gone up over time.

This is a critical omission. Since the value of a property depends primarily on the amount of comparable competing space located nearby, how can a study of property values ignore obsolescence and location? Short of a collapse in the real estate market, poor location and obsolete features are the two major forces pushing a property's value down. The study's author has left out the major forces that would depress a building's value. His study does not pick up the ruined property values in central St. Louis or Harlem. Insurance companies do not loan on buildings in bad neighborhoods; his data do not pick up how the decay in the central sections of many major cities is destroying property values. This is a serious flaw. In his study, real estate values can go only one way—up. What this study has proved is not that property has been an ideal investment, but that the cost of construction has increased steadily over the last 30 years. It also provides us with a history of cap rates used by mortgage loan appraisers at insurance companies.

This study is typical of the new studies that routinely appear every two or three years. They use appraised values, or estimates, or computer simulations to make broad generalizations about how real estate investments perform. The Frank Russell Company index, for example, consists of data on 694 properties owned primarily by commingled funds. Since the properties are rarely sold, the data on their performance is really the history of how the funds' appraisers have marked up the funds' values over time and how the accountants have computed property yields.

None of these studies would harm anyone if their creators did not imply that they were as accurate and legitimate for real estate as the Ibbotson-Sinquefield study is for securities. Some authors even hint that their real estate indexes are equivalent in accuracy and importance to the Standard & Poor's Index of 500 stocks. It is here that the studies move from being irrelevant to becoming misleading. Their authors start claiming that there are relationships between the securities and real estate markets: they argue that real estate returns are negatively correlated with the stock market. Some even try to compute a beta—a statistical measure of risk used in securities investing—for real estate. This is all nonsense. In addition, real estate indexes are philosophically off-base. Since each real estate deal is unique, having a total return figure for industrial warehouses or shopping centers is so general as to be useless.

These criticisms fall on deaf ears in the pension community. The fund sponsors are determined to find some way to analyze their real estate holdings. They have their portfolios neatly divided into equities, fixed income, and cash and they are eager to create a category labeled "real estate."

Many pension sponsors have concluded that, over the long term, real estate will show a rate of return that is higher than bonds but lower than stocks. So, they reason, real estate as an investment is really 75 percent a fixed-income investment and 25 percent an equity investment. This way of looking at property is promulgated by many commingled fund salesmen who use it to explain to their prospects what rate of return they could expect from the fund. The analysis infers that real estate investments are really hybrids of stocks and bonds; all three markets are interrelated. This simply is not true. The return on long-term, high-quality bonds is not directly related to a collapse of the value of office buildings in Boston: yet that is what this analysis says.

The authors of real estate studies encourage this kind of thinking among pension funds. They have created their studies to pander to the pension sponsor's love of numbers. After they sell the pension sponsor their real estate index, some hope they will be able to sell funds their services as real estate investment managers. Fund sponsors would do well to avoid advisors promoting studies: if these advisors take such studies seriously, they have the wrong idea of what real estate investing is really about. They are far too removed from the "hands-on," opportunistic approach to investing that real estate requires.

About the only real estate "index" that is of any use to a pension sponsor is one that he can create himself using data on the values of interests in commingled funds, known as unit values, and the cash flow the properties in these funds have thrown off. The managers of commingled funds publish both these figures quarterly.

An "index" of commingled fund figures will not tell the pension officer anything about how the real estate in the fund is behaving. But it will tell him something about what kind of an investment commingled real estate funds have been. He can compare their returns with the projected returns on other real estate investments he has been offered; if he absolutely needs a number to estimate the returns real estate throws off, the historical performance of the commingled funds is as good as any. At least money changes hands between the commingled fund and its pension clients based on those published values.

Rather than filling their heads with indexes and computer studies, pension sponsors should keep a few down-to-earth ideas in mind about real estate returns. First, they should remember that commercial real estate mortgages tend to generate dependable cash flows; historically, they have shown a higher rate of return than that earned on corporate bonds. If the mortgage lender must foreclose, he actually takes over a property he can sell to satisfy the debt. If a company defaults on a bond, the investor can end up with nothing.

Second, an owner of income property collects cash flow from the building's rents and perhaps some capital gains if and when he sells the building. If the building is managed correctly and disaster does not strike, the building's owner makes more money than its mortgage lender. The "ifs" are big ones here: it is always riskier to be an owner than a lender.

Beyond these simple statements, the study of the returns one can expect from income property fades into witchcraft. This is certainly a hardship for fund sponsors trying to fit real estate into their asset allocation studies, but income property does have some other general characteristics that can guide them in their decisions.

LEARNING FROM EXPERIENCE

Boom and Bust

The income property market moves in boom and bust cycles, commonly caused by overbuilding combined with recession. These two forces triggered the 1974 collapse in the office markets; they are behind the losses suffered by some office building owners in 1982 and 1983. Sometimes busts occur in only one type of income property in a given city, such as office parks in Atlanta. Other times they affect all types of income property in a number of cities. Busts normally last several years, during which time everyone assiduously avoids investing in income property; the financial press fills with horror stories about all the money being lost in real estate. In the meantime, a few shrewd investors are buying up everything they can lay their hands on for pennies on the dollar.

Not all slumps in demand for a particular type of space turn into busts, though they can lead into them. A bust is triggered when owners and lenders panic, throwing their properties on the market all at once. Sellers far outnumber buyers, and the value of the "busted" property plummets. Busts affect different propertyholders in different ways: owners of uncompleted, unleased property involved in a bust will sustain great losses. But owners of uncompleted property that is already leased or owners of existing, leased properties will only be mildly affected.

A bust in office buildings can be sweeping an area, but unless an owner of a fully leased office building is forced to sell to raise cash, he can painlessly weather it. Assuming his leases do not come up for renewal or his major tenant file bankruptcy, he can sit there and collect his rents. During the bust no one builds office space; after the bust is over, there is likely to be an office shortage. If he is lucky and his leases come due during the shortage, the owner will be able to raise rents. His property will appreciate as if there had never been a bust at all.

A pension fund that finds itself in this position can easily survive a bust and even profit by it. It makes no difference if the so-called "market value" of a property slides during a bust as long as the fund does not sell. The fund can continue to collect its rents. If it wishes, it can sell the building at a good profit when there is a shortage of competing space in five years. During the bust itself, the fund can pick up bargains in distressed property, though few are likely to be so shrewd.

Of course, if a pension fund found itself owning uncompleted, unleased property in the midst of a bust, the fund is in the same dreary straits as other hapless property owners. Busts are just one of the risks of being an income property developer or development lender.

Cycles

Booms and busts do not occur in predictable cycles; economists have not discovered any underlying economic forces that consistently trigger changes in real estate values. Income property values fail to move in sympathy with fluctuations in the stock and bond markets: the securities market and the income property market are two entirely separate and unrelated businesses. Certainly, both are affected by powerful economic forces, such as inflation and recession. The question is whether they both are affected in predictable ways. The answer appears to be no.

The value of an income property depends on local demand for that type of space; the value of a stock ultimately depends on the earnings of the company that issued it. If at times real estate values and securities prices move together, it is either a coincidence or the result of some overwhelming bull or bear market that is affecting all investments. The recession of 1974, for example, drove both the stock market and the value of certain properties into the ground, but for two independent reasons. Corporate earnings fell, so the stock market collapsed. Demand for space dried up, so the value of income property without strong leases evaporated.

Several authors of real estate studies suggest that stocks are countercyclical to income property: when the value of one is up, the other is down. Property, they imply, is a good investment for pension funds to own since it softens the swings in value of a pension fund's securities portfolio.

Unfortunately, these studies base their conclusions on only a few years of observations and on data that, as we have seen, is incomplete and misleading. Using the techniques of these studies, one can pick any number of different five-year time frames and predict with equal authority that income property and stock values move in the same, not opposite, directions.

For a pension fund, income property investments diversify and help a portfolio not because they are countercyclical to stocks, but because they are such a different investment from securities. Income property is independent of the securities markets and gives a pension portfolio more variety and diversity than, say, an investment in foreign securities. Foreign and U.S. securities respond to outside forces in much the same manner. But income property is in a world of its own. It is this diversity that makes income property a worthwhile investment for a pension fund. As for what it can be expected to do, the fund just has to make the investment and find out on its own.

Buying Right

Investors introduced to income property in the late 1970s did not realize that it was a boom time for all types of real estate; property values had exploded. The result was that a whole group of investors, including many pension fund sponsors, believed that property only appreciated and never lost value. It was the ultimate inflation hedge, throwing off cash flow and appreciating enough to beat inflation no matter what the economic climate. To make money on income property, all the investor had to do was buy a beautiful building and hold it indefinitely. At this writing, the collapse of the new office market in certain cities is dissuading investors from this naive belief.

Property values rise and fall over time. Some values collapse in a bust and never recover their initial value, as many properties held by REITs 10 years ago did. Others gradually lose their value, as some downtown retail property does when the new regional shopping mall opens two miles out of town. With the high-quality, fully leased properties that pension fund real estate managers buy, such a grim outcome is unlikely. Sometimes rents will not meet the target rates, and the property will not appreciate that year. But over 10 or 20 years, it is likely that most of these properties will increase in value, although perhaps not as much as their owners would like. That is where pension fund buyers face one of their biggest problems.

In many cases, they have paid so much for a property that they cannot hope to make a rate of return that matches that of other investments, much less beats the rate of inflation. More than anything, how an investor buys a property determines what kind of return he will make on it. He must, as they say in real estate, "buy it right." If he pays too much for it or cuts a poor deal in some other way, he must live with that mistake for as long as he owns the building. He can hope that rents will soar so he can recoup his extravagant purchase price. But if they do not, he has lost out: he is not going to make as big a profit as he had anticipated.

Paying too much for a property is one way of not buying right. Paying off favorable mortgages and using all-cash to buy is another mistake. Not trading on tax advantages that cost you nothing but mean something to the existing owner is still another. Not insisting that the existing owner repair the roof or pay the taxes rather than leave them to you are still other ways of buying wrong. In fact, "buying right" just means cutting the deal as much to your advantage as possible.

Over the last several years, many pension funds did not buy right. They purchased property through the commingled funds that bought "wrong." They bought properties entirely for cash, and did not try to positively leverage their positions. They bought at cap rates ranging from 5 to 9 when high-quality, long-term bonds were yielding 16 percent; Treasury notes, the riskless investment, yielded 14 percent. A 7 percent cap rate was not a competitive yield unless, of course, the funds expected to raise rents so high that in 10 years they could sell the property for far more than they had paid for it.

Considering that operating costs should continue to rise and that the landlord in this country still pays most of them, investors must quadruple rents when leases come up in order to make a 10-year return competitive with that of 10-year Treasury notes. Operating costs increase daily, but leases often run for five to seven years: the owner may increase his income annually through escalator clauses, but he has only one chance every five years to significantly increase cash flow. If he cannot raise his rents substantially when the leases expire, he has missed his opportunity to improve his return possibly for as long as 10 years. Chances are, that unless there is a total lack of competing space, he will not be able to quadruple rents; it is certainly not something he should plan on. If that arbitrage really existed, people would be building in great volume.

Yet, in buying property over the last few years, many pension fund real estate managers assumed they could do the impossible. They used internal-rate-of-return analysis (IRR) and sophisticated cash flow studies to show that even though they were paying a 9 percent, cash-on-cash return for a property in 1981, over a period of time the building would show a compound annual rate of return of 20 percent. Rents would surely quadruple when the leases came due, they reasoned, and make up for the fact that they overpaid for the property in the first place. They counted on the future to save them from today's mistakes.

The IRR analyses were really cover-ups, whether intentional or not. Any deal where the going-in cash return is 9 percent, before management fees, but the internal rate of return is 15 or 20 percent, deserves some hard questioning about just what rents on that property could realistically be expected to do over the next five years.

In a property market where prices are high but so are rates of return on long-term bonds, a pension fund would be better off not buying property at all, unless the fund or its manager was willing to negotiate hard on deals. A fund should bring to the negotiating table the same skills as the real estate investor and developer who claims to make 20 percent on his money on every deal the day he buys it. He haggles hard over the purchase price and takes advantage of existing financing, borrowing money from banks and private investors when to do so would give him positive leverage. He structures the deal for maximum tax write-offs and brings in his own property management team to start cutting fat off the operating budget immediately.

When his tax benefits run out, or he sees that properties like his own are in favor with investors, he sells and reinvests his money by buying more out-of-favor properties at bargain prices. Sometimes he will buy a property, knowing another investor is interested in it, and play a game of arbitrage, buying the property and reselling it to this other investor for a profit in less than six months.

These are only some of the techniques an investor can use to squeeze as much return as possible out of a deal. For the investor who does this, real estate definitely is a fine investment. This is a far cry from the typical pension fund real estate manager who buys the most impressive piece of property in town, pays the owner's asking price for it—entirely in cash—and plans to hold it forever, hoping that it will just keep appreciating. Pension funds do not have to squeeze every drop of return out of a deal, but they could certainly be far more aggressive in buying their properties than they now are.

Pension fund real estate managers often behave like the insurance company that bought an industrial warehouse in 1980. The warehouse was triple-net-leased to Continental Can, and at the price the investor paid, he would earn 8 percent on his money. There were a few bump-ups in rent over the next 20 years, but nothing much: all the new owner could expect to make on this property was 8 percent.

After the closing, the seller asked the buyer why he had agreed to pay so much for the property when at the time, he could have bought Continental Can common stock to yield 11 percent.

"Inflation," responded the buyer.

"What's the difference between the yield on Continental Can stock discounted at 11 percent and discounted at 8 percent?" the seller said.

"I don't know," came the reply, "but we decided to put a certain percentage of our assets in real estate of this type."

Risk v. Reward

No matter which type of real estate investment a pension sponsor wants to try, there is a definite trade-off between risk and reward. Some deals are definitely more risky than others and should pay a correspondingly higher rate of return. This does not mean they really will, just that the investor expects to make more money because he knows he is taking more risk.

This risk and return trade-off exists, but it cannot be measured. It is impossible to say that one deal is x percent riskier than another and hence an investor can expect y percent more return for his willingness to participate. Instead, real estate investors use common sense and some general guidelines to estimate how much risk they are exposed to in a given deal and what they should bargain for to compensate them for assuming that risk.

Assuming the underwriting is done correctly, and the owner has some of his own money invested in the building, it is always less risky to be a lender than an owner. Lenders have first rights to the cash flow from a building and the first order of business for any owner is to make his mortgage payments. Lenders typically write mortgages for only 75 to 80 percent of a property's appraised value, but the loan is secured by the full value of the property. If the borrower defaults, the lender can foreclose on the loan. Though foreclosure is messy and difficult, the lender can eventually sell the property and use the proceeds to satisfy the balance due.

An owner, on the other hand, is in a riskier position. He must generate enough income off the property to make his mortgage payments or else lose the property and the money he has invested in it in foreclosure. Fending off foreclosure is his biggest challenge. The owner only collects his return on the building after making his mortgage payments. He is responsible for all the problems the property has, from cleaning up the lobby after the water pipes burst to finding a new major tenant when the old one suddenly breaks his lease.

In exchange for his efforts, the owner receives the cash flow remaining after debt service is paid and the proceeds if the property is ever sold. He enjoys the tax benefits of being a property owner, consisting primarily of the depreciation write-offs; he also has control of a substantial asset. He can use his real estate as collateral to borrow money for other projects. The owner assumes more risk than the lender, but as a result he makes a greater return. Until 1979, the only return the lender received was the repayment of his mortgage principal plus interest. At this writing, lenders are now demanding and getting cash flow over and above their debt service as well as the right to a share of the proceeds if the property is ever sold.

These concessions certainly increase the lender's return on his mortgage, but they are less a bonus than compensation for the interest-rate risk that lenders feel they assume when they make mortgages today. In the days of 2 percent inflation and interest rates that moved 50 basis points in a year, not in a day, lenders did not need to demand extra return. At this writing, interest-rate risk is far more substantial; lenders demand and receive extra return to compensate for it.

Besides the division between mortgage lender and owner, a deal's risk can be broken down in another major way. There is a division in risk between owning a fully leased building and owning another that is under construction. If an office building has been fully occupied for five years, the owner of that property is in a far less risky position than the owner of an office building under construction down the block. The lender who holds the mortgage on that existing, occupied office building is in a less risky position than the lender who is financing the construction of the half-completed one.

Development is a risky business. The developer carries all the worries of construction. What if the operating engineers or masons go on strike? What if the cost of reinforced concrete doubles or the soil proves difficult to sink pylons in? If he has cost overruns, where will he get the extra money? His construction loan is tied to the prime rate; every time prime climbs a point, it costs him thousands of dollars in extra interest expense. Unless he has signed up tenants before he started construction, or "preleased" the building, as it is called, he must bear the risk that the building will be more difficult to rent up than he first thought. Building an office building "on spec," that is, on speculation and without major tenants lined up, is far riskier than building one where IBM has agreed to rent 80 percent of the space before the first shovel of dirt is turned.

The developer and his lender bear far more risk than an owner of a fully occupied building; they can be assured of a far larger return on their money if they manage to complete the building without a hitch. But there are risks in owning existing buildings, too. Buying a building where the major tenant has just indicated he will not renew his lease next year is more risky than buying one where all the tenants are happily paying rent and have no intention of moving.

In fact, there are gradations of risk in lending on or owning any type of property. Single-family home mortgages are safer investments than commercial mortgages. A building leased to IBM is a safer investment than one leased to 14 local tenants. And it is always safer to build and lease a warehouse to Firestone Tire for 20 years than to build a giant amusement park outside Orlando, Florida. But that amusement park, if it does not go bankrupt first, has a chance to become a far more lucrative investment than the Firestone warehouse will ever be.

GETTING STARTED

There is no right or wrong way for a pension fund to invest in property, but a fund can follow some logical steps to make the whole process easier. First, the fund trustees must ask themselves some questions, beginning with why do they want to make an investment in real estate? What do they expect it to do for their portfolio?

If the answer is they think real estate is an inflation hedge that will save the portfolio from poor returns, they have the wrong idea. Well-located and managed real estate can be a great investment and beat inflation, but it is difficult to find and buy right. Real estate returns as a whole do not march lockstep upwards, always a few feet ahead of inflation; it is not some super investment that always outperforms stocks and bonds. A pension fund should invest in income property, not because it is an amazing investment, but because it will help diversify the fund's holdings out of the securities business where 100 percent of the fund's money has been since day one.

The second question trustees must ask is, just how involved do they want to get in real estate? Do they envision real estate as 30 percent of their portfolio or 10 percent? Do they want to get directly involved in running their property, or do they prefer to be passive investors? Most funds cannot answer these questions until they have had some experience with property to begin with; the logical thing for a fund to do is to start making some small real estate investments and see how comfortable they feel. But where to start?

There are two preferable routes open to a fund. It can hire its own real estate staff to buy property for the fund directly, or it can give its money to a commingled real estate fund where it will be pooled with money from other pension funds and used to invest in property. The fund sponsor can also use both approaches, investing some money directly and some through commingled funds. The choice depends on just how involved the plan's trustees and staff want to be with their real estate investments.

The commingled approach is the easiest: the pension fund sponsor needs to know nothing about real estate. He gives the commingled fund his money, and they handle everything, sending him quarterly reports about how much his investment is now worth. In return, the commingled fund manager collects a percentage of the commingled fund's assets as an annual management fee, usually 1 to 1¼ percent, plus assorted other fees. The problem with the commingled approach is that the pension fund has absolutely no control over how the pool is run or what properties it buys. The fund sponsor learns nothing about real estate investing; because of the management fees involved, he makes less on his real estate investments than if he had invested directly in property.

On the other hand, by investing in a commingled fund he gets an immediate participation in a diversified real estate portfolio, assuming it is an established commingled pool; he will never have to worry about managing the buildings himself. Because commingled funds are such effortless investments, they have been the most popular way for pension funds to invest in property. The next chapter deals with their benefits and drawbacks.

Another popular approach to investing is for the fund to hire an advisor who will run an individual account. After spending several years investing entirely in commingled funds, several of the larger funds are taking this route: they have more control over what they invest in and feel they are learning more about real estate investing. But often, advisor-run portfolios are no improvement over commingled funds; pension funds using advisors could find that they're actually making less money on their real estate than if they had stayed in the commingled funds. The arguments supporting these contentions are detailed in chapter 9.

If a pension plan really wants to control its own investments and learn about property, it would be better off setting up its own in-house staff than hiring an advisor. The staff could start out doing small, low-risk, management-free deals and then gradually work up to the riskier and more lucrative deals as the fund becomes more comfortable, a process that can take years. If it is done right, direct investment should make the fund more money than if it had given its money to a commingled fund. There are no management fees, and the pension fund has control over its properties. It can run them as tightfistedly as it wishes.

The problem with the direct approach is that it requires a pension fund sponsor who is truly interested in property and willing to learn about it through experience. He must handle all the daily problems of running an office building or keeping track of payments on a portfolio of commercial mortgages; he must deal with the crisis when an investment does not work out and must be cleaned up or sold off. Either the sponsor and the pension staff learn how to manage property, or they hire an in-house staff of professional property investors. Often, if a sponsor decides to hire a staff, he must completely realign his methods of paying for investment advice; otherwise, he cannot hope to attract the right kind of people.

With direct investing, all the fund's hopes for a good return from real estate will be pinned on the handful of deals it can afford to invest in. If one of them goes bad, it can really depress the return from a real estate portfolio. If, instead, the pension fund had given its money to a commingled fund, it might mitigate such a problem. When a property in a commingled fund goes bad, its effect on the total real estate portfolio is dampened by the returns from the 50 or 60 other properties in the pool. Diversity in a real estate portfolio is as much a virtue as diversity in any investment portfolio.

There is also a size problem with direct investing. No pension fund is too small to invest in real estate, but some are too small to invest directly and must use commingled funds instead. If a pension fund holds less than $1 million in assets, it makes no sense to hire someone to manage a real estate portfolio that may total only $100,000. There is not much anyone can buy in the income property market for $100,000; it would cost the fund that much to hire someone to manage its portfolio to begin with. Such a small fund can invest only through commingled funds or syndications designed for pension plans.

The larger pension plans are the ones who have the option of doing it on their own. The question then becomes, how big does a fund have to be to invest directly in property? There is no definite answer for this. Some consultants say a fund should have $100 million in assets before it can start a direct investment program. But this is an arbitrary number, and everything really depends on the individual situation. The pension fund of a real estate company, for example, can invest directly in property at a much lower level of assets; it has cheap access to real estate advice. Perhaps a $10 million pension fund may be lucky enough to have a pension officer who has worked in the real estate business. He can certainly do some low-risk deals that require no management, such as well-secured mortgages with equity kickers or sale-leasebacks. If he hires an outside consultant to advise him on the deal and also reviews it with the real estate department of the bank that serves as his pension fund trustee, he should get sufficient competent advice on these simple deals.

Again, it all depends on the situation. The most important consideration is that the fund staff and trustees do not get in over their heads, taking on risks they neither understand nor are capable of handling. The trustees must be willing to take responsibility for their own real estate decisions. This is not something that comes suddenly to a pension fund board of trustees. It takes time for them and their pension staff to become comfortable with real estate. What some pension funds have done is start their real estate program by investing in commingled funds. Once they become comfortable with that, they start a small, direct investing program. They have arrived at the point where they are too unsure of themselves to invest all their real estate money directly, but they are tiring of commingled funds and want to make a better return.

There is no right or wrong technique for investing in property—commingled investing, direct investing, or a combination of the two can make equally good sense for a fund. Again, it depends on how much of a commitment the fund trustees want to make to real estate. If they want to invest 20 or 30 percent of the fund's assets in property, then it is probably worthwhile for them to start a direct investing program and learn about property from experience. But if a fund sees property as a minor part of the portfolio, perhaps 10 percent of assets, then it should probably stay with commingled funds and not bother to learn.

However a fund decides to invest in and manage its real estate, the board of trustees still has one final question to ask: how much risk is the pension fund willing to take on its investments? This is a personal decision each fund's board must make and a difficult one to make since risk is hard to define, much less measure. Such decisions are virgin territory for U.S. fund sponsors, but this is certainly not the case for some pension funds in other parts of the world. The National Coal Board Superannuation Schemes, the two pension funds for the British coal-mining industry, have been investing in property for about 30 years; they were making property investments years before other British funds even considered real estate. The Coal Board's experience with real estate investing can give U.S. funds some guidance.

In 1980, I had the opportunity to interview these funds' director-general of investments, Hugh Jenkins, about their extensive property holdings. He told me the following.

THE COAL BOARD

In 1980, one-third of the Coal Board's $4.3 billion in pension assets, or $1.4 billion, was invested in property. The funds own 80,000 acres of farmland in Australia. They own and manage roughly two dozen major shopping centers in the British Isles, many of which they built themselves; they are now one of the top shopping center developers in Great Britain. In the United States, the Coal Board owns roughly $350 million in real estate, ranging from the Watergate Hotel in Washington, D.C., to timberland in the state of Georgia. The funds picked up much of their U.S. property by buying up the stock of a publicly traded REIT, converting it to private ownership, and then absorbing the REIT's property into the funds' own portfolio.

The Coal Board funds, when taken together, are the second-largest pension fund in Great Britain. The fund is run out of a central office in London, and the operation is not a typical pension fund management system by either British or U.S. standards. First, the fund's asset mix is weighted toward real estate. Common stocks make up 48 percent of the portfolio; 20 percent is in gilts and corporate bonds, 2 percent in venture capital, and 30 percent in property. Second, and more unusual, the Coal Board has no outside money managers. The large British pension funds, particularly the public ones, tend to manage at least some of their money in-house, but no one has embraced this philosophy with as much enthusiasm as the Coal Board. "We are unique in that we do 100 percent of our own management in everything," said Jenkins. "Nobody handles any of our money. We handle it ourselves and have a long history of being entrepreneurial."

The fund resembles an investment conglomerate more than the passively run portfolio typical of most pension funds. Jenkins has special departments to handle venture capital, common stocks, bonds and gilts, and real estate. The property department consists of more than 30 people, most of whom have extensive experience or professional training in real estate. It is "the largest part of the empire," as Jenkins put it. In contrast, it takes only 11 people—seven analysts and four managers—to run the 48 percent of the funds' assets invested in common stocks worldwide.

The Coal Board is pleased with its investment results. The fund's stock and bond portfolios regularly outperform those of other British pension plans. From 1968 through 1980, the fund's total rate of return almost matched the rate of inflation, which averaged 12 percent a year in the 1970s. On average, most British and U.S. pension funds have not been able to do this; a big part of the Coal Board's success must be credited to its real estate holdings.

The Coal Board first approached real estate investing by doing small, simple, low-risk deals and then working its way up to riskier and more lucrative ones. The people on the staff learned as they went; they never made the jump to riskier real estate until they felt comfortable with what they already were doing, even if it took 10 years. The entire real estate investment operation, from selection to management, has always been run entirely in-house.

The Coal Board started investing in real estate about 30 years ago when it was a tiny, new fund. In 1954, the fund discovered it could make twice as much money by doing high-quality leasebacks than by buying government bonds (gilts). Gilts were showing a running return of 2½ percent, but leasebacks to triple-A-rated corporations were yielding 5 percent. The fund would buy a store owned and occupied by a high-quality retailer located in a prime shopping area. The fund would then lease the store back to the retailer on a triple-net basis for 99 years; the fund could charge a rent that yielded it 5 percent on its money.

To the fund, this was a great discovery. It could double its money while increasing its risk only slightly; it was "sensible" and "simple logic" to make such deals, Jenkins said. In doing these deals, the Coal Board became the first British pension fund to invest in property and was the only major fund in property until the 1960s.

The Board continued to make leasebacks for four more years and was so pleased with them that the trustees decided to invest 10 percent of fund assets in real estate. They also decided to try some more adventurous and potentially lucrative deals; they came to their first major crossroads. What were they going to do next?

The fund considered buying existing income property, just like U.S. funds are doing today, but decided that could not be the main thrust of their real estate strategy. Even in the late 1950s, said Jenkins, the type of high-quality property the fund wanted to own was too expensive. It would have had to accept lower and lower yields while assuming more and more risk. The fund decided to take a different path: if it could not buy decent property for good yields, it would build it. Unfortunately, the fund's staff knew nothing about real estate development, so the Board decided to do the next best thing. It would finance real estate developers.

In 1958, the Coal Board started. It would put up all the money for a project. In exchange, the developer would guarantee the fund a minimum yield on its money; the developer and the fund would split the equity equally. Now, the fund was not making 5 percent on its real estate; it was making 6½ percent plus an equity kicker. For 10 years, the Coal Board did these joint-venture deals, and as Jenkins put it, "Some of them turned out very well, and some turned out not quite so well. But overall, we came out quite ahead of the game."

More important than the properties it acquired, the fund's staff learned a tremendous amount about real estate investing. "What this whole period enabled us to do was go up the learning curve in terms of what we could do and what risks we were exposing ourselves to," said Jenkins. One of the big revelations was that they were putting up 100 percent of the money for deals but getting only 50 percent of the equity. The developer was walking off with the other half without putting up anything but his expertise. That expertise was necessary for the success of the deal, but was it worth 50 percent of the equity? The fund decided it was not and began negotiating much harder. At the same time, the long-term mortgage market was starting to disappear; as the sources of money dried up, developers had to accept more onerous terms from those, like the Coal Board, that had it. By 1968, a joint-venture developer with the Coal Board was getting only 25 percent of the equity in a deal, "if he was lucky," said Jenkins.

By 1968, the Board had also made another discovery about real estate developers. Unless they received cast-iron guarantees from their developer-partner

that he could finish the project and pay them their preferred return, then effectively, they were financing themselves. The developer could have a good idea
and be a good manager, but because he had little or no money, he made a bad
partner when a project got in trouble. Jenkins described the situation from the
fund's point of view:

If the development is going to cost more than you thought because you can't tie down
the construction costs due to inflation, then you're going to have to pick up the tab, not
him.
If the rents which you achieve are less than you expect, then you take it on the nose, not
him. And what is worse, if it takes you three times longer than you thought to lease the
building and get it to produce income, you're taking the risk on that, too.
So, you're effectively taking three major risks in financing somebody who can't shelter
you from those risks. Now you should ask yourself the question: "Should I do this in
spite of the fact that the man is saying to me, 'Don't worry. I will cover you?' "

Increasingly, the answer became no. It got to the point that the fund would
only do deals it would like to do anyway, regardless of any guarantees the
developer could or could not give. They would only get involved in a project if
they were prepared to take 100 percent of the risk themselves.

But if they took 100 percent of the risk, they wanted 100 percent of the deal;
they started paying the developer a fee for his idea and direction, but no longer
gave him part of the equity. The developer had essentially been demoted from
a joint-venture partner to a general contractor. There was no long-term mortgage
money around; what else could a developer do? He had to dance to the tune of
the Coal Board. The Coal Board, in turn, still did joint ventures with selected,
strong British developers who had the option of getting their money elsewhere
if they wanted. But the rest of the developers were treated like employees, not
partners. After 10 years of joint-venture deals, the Coal Board was in the development business on its own.

Their first major project was a 180,000 square-foot shopping center, a regional
mall by British standards, which they did in 1969. The center has done "fabulously
well" for the fund, according to Jenkins, who said the income stream from the
property has gone "straight up" since the fund built it to yield them a cash flow
of 10 percent a year, 15 years ago. The center cost £1.5 million to build, but
the fund's real estate staff estimated it was worth over £50 million in 1980.

The fund continued to develop shopping centers and other income property
throughout Great Britain for the next six years, rarely buying anything if it could
build it, when the great recession of 1974 hit the British real estate business.
The business collapsed in a pile of defaulted loans, overbuilding, and bankrupt
developers, the latter ceaselessly trying to sell their properties before the banks
took them over. In short, the situation was exactly the same as it was in the
United States. As Jenkins described it, "The property companies (developers)
had to liquidate their portfolios in order to deal with their debts; a lot of them

had borrowed money up to their eyeballs on a short-term, roll-over basis."
Suddenly, the real estate market was glutted with property.

By this time the Coal Board fund had been investing in real estate on its own
for 20 years. Its portfolio of properties was doing well: they were not stuck with
short-term loans. But Jenkins and his staff immediately realized that a bonanza
of a lifetime had fallen into their laps. They dropped development work where
they could and poured all the cash flow they could muster into purchasing real
estate that developers and lenders were forced to sell. In 18 months the fund
bought about $300 million of "the best property we'd ever seen," according to
Jenkins. "I will never have the opportunity to do that again," he said. "It was
beautiful." The fund picked up some magnificent shopping centers cheaply, as
well as the Coal Board's prize property—2½ acres of land developed with
250,000 square feet of office space along a prime stretch of Oxford Street,
London's main shopping street. "Money couldn't buy that property today,"
Jenkins said.

After its great buying spree, the fund was never the same. No longer was it
a simple real estate developer and sometime purchaser of existing property. It
was a full-fledged real estate company, looking for opportunities wherever it
found them. By the late 1970s, that meant the fund had to look beyond Great
Britain. Existing property there was overpriced, and development sites were
becoming scarce and more expensive. The fund also felt it should diversify its
holdings; most of its investments were in London and southeast England. So,
in 1978, the Coal Board decided to invest in U.S. real estate, which appeared
to be more reasonably priced.

The Board's experience in the United States mirrored its history in Great
Britain: the fund tried to move cautiously until its staff understood the types of
markets and risks they were dealing with. But it took them a great deal less than
20 years to find out. The fund hired a real estate consultant and arranged to have
the Morgan Guaranty Trust Company review any deal the fund came up with.
They started looking for deals and bid on a number of prime buildings, of which
the Seagram's building was a typical example. "We were number six out of
seven bidders, and at those prices I would not have wanted to be number one,"
said Jenkins.

It was rough going. There was not much property available at prices they
wanted to pay; in a short time they concluded that the marketplace for income
property in the United States was almost as narrow as it was in Great Britain.
Everyone was chasing the same properties. "But we just kept banging away,"
said Jenkins. To gain some experience, they put up $2 million of equity to build
an office building in Florida with an American developer who was a good friend
of Jenkins. The project turned out well for the fund but was, as Jenkins put it,
"miles below" the size deal they should have been doing. Nevertheless, they did
gain some experience. They also decided that they either had to make a big stake
in the United States and acquire a base of quality property or they might as well
not be investing in the country at all: it was not worth the effort.

The only way to acquire a base of properties quickly was to buy someone else's portfolio, and that is exactly what the fund did. They discovered the publicly traded REIT advised by the Continental Illinois National Bank. The Continental REIT was a well-run trust that had survived the 1974 real estate collapse. It held good properties, had no skeletons in its closets, and was selling at a substantial discount to the appraised value of the property it held.

After a small bidding skirmish with some Arab investors interested in buying the REIT, the Coal Board was able to acquire 96 percent of the REIT's stock. Suddenly they had about $350 million in real estate, an instant U.S. real estate portfolio, 18 months after entering the U.S. real estate market. That was in 1979. In 1981, they tried to buy another REIT, this one advised by Connecticut General Life Insurance. The REIT was publicly listed and traded near $30 per share, which was less than the value of the equity in the properties. The Coal Board offered shareholders $33 a share or a total of $267 million. The REIT's Board of Directors insisted this was inadequate and went looking for another buyer. They found it in Prudential Insurance Company, which offered to pay 25 percent more. The Coal Board dislikes bidding wars; Prudential bought the REIT for a total cost of $335 million and then merged it into PRISA, one of its commingled real estate funds for pension funds.

Since 1981, the Coal Board has been buying properties individually, but is still taken with buying entire REITs. As of September 1981, the fund held 5.5 percent of RAMPAC, a California REIT, though it was unclear whether this was merely a passive investment or the first step to a takeover. As of 1981, the Coal Board has not tried developing any property in the United States, but that could change. They are definitely in the U.S. real estate market for the long term.

After this investment history, one gets the impression that the Coal Board must have a truly amazing collection of trustees to be permitted to operate like entrepreneurs. They must be investment supermen. But this is not the case. The trustees are a mixture of men, much like those on pension boards in this country. In 1980, they ranged in investment sophistication from the financier who had been on the board for 25 years to a coal miner who had been there seven.

What Jenkins and his staff have done is build up the trustees' confidence in them so they trust what the staff recommends. "The trustees will follow you as long as you've got a business plan and they can see the direction you're going," said Jenkins. "We take them along with us. We promise them certain things and tell them our objectives when we get into them. They can see we can handle each degree of risk which we assume because if the thing did blow up, they wouldn't let me do it again, or they'd sack me."

Yet with the careful attention paid to the trustees, they are by no means a rubber-stamp group. They make the final decisions. When the staff recommended the fund buy the Continental Illinois REIT in 1979, the trustees debated it extensively, arguing over what the fund saw in the REIT and what they could do with it. Jenkins brought in outside real estate consultants and the trustees of the REIT to talk to his board and help them form an opinion. After the purchase was approved and the fund was able to buy the REIT, he brought in more external consultants and advisors to let his board know that what the staff had said would happen with the investment was indeed happening. "You build up a level of confidence with your trustees," he said, "and if you do that, they're prepared to follow an aggressive, entrepreneurial strategy."

In trying to apply the Coal Board's experiences in real estate to their own situation, U.S. pension sponsors may laugh and think that no one will ever get to this point with a U.S. pension fund. This could definitely be the case. The Coal Board's entrepreneurial and self-willed investment program makes it a maverick among British and U.S. pension funds. The investment program is headed by a man who is well-schooled in real estate investing and who says that the principal pleasure he gets out of his job is "changing direction in our investments and seeing if we can manage them in-house." This is hardly the education and attitude most pension sponsors and officers have toward their funds' investments, either in Great Britain or here.

U.S. funds have other problems: they have ERISA and the prudent man rule, which do not exist in Great Britain. Jenkins believes that few trustees are what he calls "mentally robust" enough to bear the anxiety of running an investment operation with both these laws hanging over them. So the trustees just follow the herd. He also pointed out that although large British funds have a tendency to invest much of their own money in-house, most U.S. funds are run by outside advisors. If a fund cannot even manage its securities portfolios in-house, how could it handle an entrepreneurial real estate operation?

Finally, both U.S. and British funds are typically run by people on the lowest levels of the corporate totem pole. Jenkins is unique in that he is a department head of the Coal Board. He has real power and influence and is well-paid, unlike his counterparts on both sides of the Atlantic who handle the pension fund from somewhere in the bowels of the treasurer's office. "If you think of your pension fund as something that should be run by a man number six from the bottom of the page on the annual report, you'll get a pecking-order problem," said Jenkins. "He'll be so low down the echelons that you can't afford to employ people who will do an adequate job for you."

With all these problems, the United States may never have a pension fund run a real estate investment operation like the Coal Board's. After all, Great Britain has only one. But then again, maybe we will. In any event, the experiences of the Coal Board show that a pension fund can become a powerful force in the real estate business.

I asked Jenkins what advice he would give U.S. pension sponsors who are considering investing in real estate. Calling the question a difficult one to answer, he said that the one thing he had learned in British real estate is that if you bought the best real estate you could find, you would not go far wrong. Unfortunately, he said, the best real estate is also the most expensive real estate and the largest. So if you cannot buy the best because it is too expensive, build it instead, whichever is cheaper.

"Every time we've played that philosophy, it's worked. But if you start buying small pieces of real estate, it doesn't work," he said. That is why in its U.S. investing strategy, the fund's minimum equity investment in a property is $5 million. In 1980, when I talked to him, they were looking at shopping malls and would not consider buying a local community center with a food store and drugstore in it. They wanted regional malls with a minimum of 800,000 square feet of gross leasable area and had just purchased one in Florida for $40 million, a center Jenkins called "a beautiful little money box."

The "buy or build the best" philosophy means that even investments that prove unwise can be salvaged. For example, consider the first real estate investments the Coal Board made, the leasebacks on prime retail properties. The leases ran for 99 years, yielded 5 percent, and had no rent escalators since inflation was 2½ percent. Those deals made sense in 1954 but look ridiculous today. Because the property involved was the best, the fund got back its original investment two or three times and "made out alright," according to Jenkins. Fifteen or 20 years into the lease, the tenant would typically want to improve or expand the building and either extend his lease or buy out the landlord. The property was now worth far more than when the deal was first done; the Coal Board could negotiate a big cash settlement for terminating or extending its lease. Jenkins noted that if the fund had leased the buildings without rent escalators for 14 years, instead of 99, they would have made much more money, but, he commented, "that's life." Nevertheless, the fund made far more money doing leasebacks at 5 percent than buying gilts at 2½ percent. The latter just plummeted in value and sat there.

This strategy of only dealing with the best quality properties has served the fund well in its other real estate holdings. Jenkins is pleased with the investment results of the existing properties the fund bought and is particularly pleased with the return generated by the development arm of the fund.

In addition to his preference for quality, Jenkins believes that a pension fund should not invest in real estate unless the fund intends to channel a great deal of money into property and invest the money directly. This cuts out funds that were considering putting in $10 million here and there in a direct investment program or those who were interested in commingled real estate funds.

"I suppose it comes back to being very self-centered about my own judgment," Jenkins said. "I'm prepared to put my money where my judgment is and vice-versa. But with commingled funds, somebody else is exercising all the decisions, added to which a large chunk of that money is going to be taken up by management costs." He did qualify his statement by saying that the quality of a commingled fund depends on the track record of the people managing it. So presumably, if a pension fund put its money in a commingled fund run by talented real estate investors, it would be a mediocre but acceptable way to invest in property, in his opinion.

In applying Jenkins's remarks to U.S. pension funds, one must remember that he is running a $1.4 billion real estate company for a pension fund that has been investing in property for 30 years, and for the last 15, as an entrepreneur. Only a handful of pension funds internationally can lay claim to a similar position. If he opts for running the fund as a sophisticated property investment company, it is because that is the way he has been doing it, and doing it well, for the last 10 years. If any pension fund had this large a property portfolio, it should invest aggressively and directly; it will make far more money than if it had contributed the money to a collection of commingled funds.

But it took the Coal Board 30 years to get where it is today. When they took their first steps into property investing, they did small, conservative leasebacks, and they did only those for four years before deciding to advance to more daring deals. It took them several years before they decided to commit as much as 10 percent of their assets to property. Since most U.S. pension funds are at the level of sophistication the Coal Board had 30 years ago, they should start out with small, careful steps, too, learning as they go.

Regarding his comments on commingled funds, they are certainly accurate. But some pension funds, actually most in this country, are willing to give up some part of their returns in order to invest in real estate without having to manage property. A pension fund should not avoid real estate entirely just because it cannot put 30 percent of its portfolio, or at least $100 million a year, into real estate. Smaller funds and those that are far less aggressive than the Coal Board can enjoy the diversification real estate gives their portfolios by going into commingled funds. If they have to give up some of their return in exchange for higher fees, that is the price involved.

But investing in commingled funds has its own problems. It may appear to be the trouble-free alternative, but the pension fund participants in these funds pay for this convenience.

NOTES

1. Thorndike, Doran, Paine & Lewis, Inc., *Real Estate and the Institutional Investor* (Boston: 1980), p. 3.

2. Roger G. Ibbotson and Rex A. Sinquefield, *Stocks, Bonds, Bills, and Inflation: The Past (1926–1976) and the Future (1977–2000)* (Charlottesville, Va.: Financial Analysts Research Foundation, 1977).

3. Alan Rabinowitz, *The Real Estate Gamble: Lessons from 50 Years of Boom and Bust* (New York: American Management Associations, 1980), pp. 2, 3, 71, 92.

4. John McMahan Associates, Inc., *Institutional Strategies for Real Estate Equity Investment* (San Francisco: 1981), pp. 1, 14, 15.

PART THREE

Pension Funds in Real Estate

8 | THE COMMINGLED FUNDS

> Once you get over the break-even point on running one of these com-
> mingled funds, the margins are unbelievable on the amount of money
> you can make. And you don't have any capital at risk.
>
> *—the manager of a commingled fund*

> In 1979, there were about 60 commingled funds. In 1982, there were
> close to 135. We figured new ones were being added at the rate of one
> a week.
>
> *—another commingled fund manager, 1982*

POOLS OF MONEY

Commingled funds are the most popular method used by pension plans to invest
in income property. The funds are likely to hold on to that title for the next 10
years, if not forever, because they make it easy for pension plans to invest.
When a pension sponsor wants to broaden his plan's exposure to real estate, he
merely increases his participation in the fund he is in or buys into two or three
more.

There are a variety of commingled real estate funds and at this writing, new
ones appear every week. In this chapter, I will not dissect each of the funds,
but describe how they operate in general and offer plan sponsors some guidance
in analyzing them.

Commingled funds are simply pools of money made up of contributions from
a number of different pension plans. The money is managed by a professional
money manager, be it a bank, insurance company or independent investment
counselor. The pension plan contributes money to the pool, and it is mingled
together—or "commingled" with the assets of the manager's other pension clients.
Because they consist entirely of pension money, the commingled funds are tax-
exempt.

Commingled real estate funds are only one type of commingled fund. Others
are organized to invest in stocks, bonds or short-term investments. There are
many specialized funds, such as those that invest in foreign stocks or deep-
discount bonds.

In the vast majority of commingled funds, the money manager collects a fixed
fee for handling the fund's investments. The fee is normally expressed as an
annual percentage of the market value of the fund's assets and ranges between
0.1 percent and 1.25 percent. The lower fee would be charged for a commingled
fund that is easy to manage, such as a portfolio of short-term instruments. The

larger fee would be charged for a commingled real estate fund, which is far more complicated and requires intensive management.

Most commingled funds are discretionary accounts, meaning the fund manager has complete control over how the money is invested. The fund managers typically are qualified plan asset managers (QPAMs) under ERISA, though in the case of some real estate funds they are not. Regardless, all have fiduciary responsibility for the pension money they manage in those funds.

Technically, the term commingled fund applies only to pools managed by banks; but when it comes to real estate, the term is applied to nearly any pool consisting of pension money and run by a professional real estate manager. Money run by insurance companies or independent investment managers; or pools organized as limited partnerships, tax-exempt corporations, private real estate investment trusts, or group trusts—all are called commingled funds. In spite of their different managers and legal structures, they are really much alike, both in how they are run and in what they invest in.

Commingled funds of all kinds are familiar to pension plans. They have been a fixture of the institutional money management business for years. They were originally begun in bank trust departments to handle pension accounts that were too small to be individually invested. The small pension account would find its assets split between two commingled funds, one investing in common stock and the other in bonds—or equities and fixed income, as they are respectively known in the pension community.

As the trust department and its pension management business grew, the bank would add more specialized commingled funds, such as one to invest in foreign securities or the stock of small companies. These specialized funds would be used by both large and small pension clients to diversify their portfolios. If a pension plan of any size wanted to invest 1 percent of its assets in foreign stocks, it could do so by contributing money to the bank's commingled foreign stock fund. The pension client would enjoy the benefits of owning part of a diversified portfolio of foreign securities, even though the amount it had invested was far too small for a manager of foreign securities to run as an individual account. The commingled fund management fees were one-half or one-third of what such an independent manager would charge. Commingled funds were, and still are, good ways for pension plans to diversify their investments.

Stock and bond commingled funds have been in existence for years, but real estate commingled funds are late bloomers. Several large banks did run commingled mortgage funds for their pension clients in the 1960s, but it appears no one had a commingled fund that bought real estate for pension funds until Wachovia Bank & Trust Co. in North Carolina started one in 1968. Wachovia was followed by a handful of other banks and insurance companies in the late 1960s and early 1970s: Prudential Insurance Company, First National Bank of Chicago, Equitable Life Assurance, and Aetna Life Insurance, among others. The independent money management firm of Rosenberg Capital Management started offering commingled real estate funds in 1975.

At the time these funds were started, few pension sponsors were interested in real estate. Their stock and bond portfolios were doing so well in the early 1970s that real estate paled by comparison. When a pension plan could make 15 percent a year on its stocks, it was not interested in the 8 percent returns posted by the commingled real estate funds. When the stock market plummeted in 1974, common stocks lost their allure, but unfortunately so did real estate—whatever allure it had to begin with. The collapse of the REITs in 1974 convinced many pension fund sponsors that all real estate investing was risky, and they avoided it further, though the commingled funds had made it through the REIT catastrophe relatively unscathed.

There was so little pension plan interest in real estate in 1976 and 1977 that few, new money managers entered the field: and less than 20 commingled real estate funds existed, most of which had $60 million or less in assets, a small amount for a commingled fund. If a pension sponsor really wanted to invest in real estate using the largest and most prestigious of the commingled funds, he could put his money into PRISA, which was run by the Prudential Insurance Company.

During this period, Prudential's real estate staff thought properties were overpriced and found it difficult to reinvest PRISA's existing cash flow much less take on new money. They turned new clients away and limited the amount of money that existing clients could contribute. In spite of the line to get in, pension fund interest in property was insignificant. The entire commingled real estate industry had $2 billion in assets, and the total amount of money that pension funds were talking about contributing to real estate funds totalled less than $200 million a year, a tiny amount in pension terms. Total pension assets at the time were roughly $300 billion: the $200 million they would contribute to real estate was less than the annual cash flow from stock dividends on one $7 billion pension fund, of which the nation had several.

Pension sponsor interest in real estate did not pick up until late 1978 when the commingled real estate funds started posting tremendous rate-of-return numbers. In 1977, PRISA had a 9.88 percent rate of return, but in 1978 it hit 14.4 percent, followed by 24.7 percent in 1979, and 24.3 percent in 1980. PRISA was not the only commingled real estate fund showing such returns. Most funds had them.

They were riding the wave of the great space shortage in commercial, industrial and office space. No one had built such properties since 1974, and now rents were starting to reflect the lack of competing space and were climbing. At the same time, inflation had hit new heights. The pension community connected real estate's returns with inflation, deciding that real estate must be the ultimate inflation hedge. The commingled real estate funds outperformed every other investment the pension funds held and inflation, too. For the three years through 1981, a study of 19 commingled funds showed they had an average annual return of 18.2 percent before fees compared to a 14.4 percent return for the Standard & Poor's 500 and −2.6 percent for the Salomon Brothers Bond Index.

The same study, conducted by Evaluation Associates of Westport, Connecticut, showed that 13 commingled real estate funds had a five-year, average annual return of 14.9 percent compared to 8.2 percent for the S&P 500 and −1.3 percent for the Salomon bond index.[1] Only 13 of the 19 funds Evaluation Associates studied had five-year records to begin with, but those numbers showed real estate outperforming everything and continuing to do so. The best year for many was 1981.

Pension sponsors started paying attention and contributing to these funds; they grew from $2 billion in assets at year-end 1978 to roughly $14 billion at year-end 1981—still a minuscule amount of total pension fund assets, but a start. The line of pension clients waiting to get into PRISA lengthened and another formed at the door of Equitable Life Assurance's Separate Account Number 8, the next largest commingled fund after PRISA. Both funds found that they could commit on hundred-million-dollar deals overnight, even though they had nowhere near that amount of cash in the fund. They would simply let the word out that their funds were open for some new money from pension funds and wait a few weeks while eager new clients wrote checks.

This new interest of pension plans in real estate was not lost on the money management business, and though most pension clients preferred to give their money to the well-known commingled funds, the number of new commingled funds multiplied. In 1979, there were about 65 commingled real estate funds on the market. By 1982, there were about 135, with new ones being announced every week.

In April 1983, *Pensions & Investment Age* magazine surveyed the pension fund money management community and identified 64 firms that specialized in real estate investing services for pension funds.[2] Five years earlier, only a handful of managers had offered real estate investing at all.

Those who thought they could take business from the funds with lines were mistaken. Prudential opened more commingled funds, including a PRISA II, and in 1981 announced it was going on a $1 billion property buying spree for its pension clients. Equitable's Number 8 became a more aggressive buyer of property and branched into joint-venture development projects to invest the pension money it took in. The lines at Prudential and Equitable disappeared, and both funds mushroomed in size. The Real Estate Separate Account, RESA, of Aetna Life Insurance also grew rapidly as did the series of funds run by Rosenberg Real Estate Equity Fund (RREEF).

As of June 30, 1982, four managers dominated the real estate investing business and still do at this writing—Prudential, Equitable, Aetna and Rosenberg. Of the more than $19 billion that pension funds held in real estate equities in mid-1982, 51 percent was run by these four managers. Prudential alone ran $4.4 billion of pension money in its PRISA accounts, followed by Equitable with $2.3 billion, Aetna with $2 billion and Rosenberg with $900 million.[3] (See Table 8.1.)

The remaining 131 or so commingled real estate funds had only 25 percent of the business to carve up among themselves. The result is that dozens of

Table 8.1
20 LARGEST MANAGERS OF REAL ESTATE EQUITIES FOR PENSION FUNDS
(June 30, 1982)
($ millions)

Managers	Assets
Prudential Insurance Newark	$4,422
Equitable Life New York	2,300
Aetna Life Hartford, Ct.	2,000
Rosenberg Real Estate Equity Fund (RREEF) San Francisco	900
Citibank New York	791
Coldwell Banker New York	625
John Hancock Boston	600
Morgan Guaranty New York	500
Travelers Insurance Hartford, Ct.	500
United Trust Fund Miami, Fl.	500
Corporate Property Investors New York	456
Wachovia Bank and Trust Winston-Salem, N.C.	377
First National Bank of Chicago Chicago	332
Libra Real Estate Corp Chicago	300
Boston Company Real Estate Corp. Boston	275
Metropolitan Life New York	230
JMB Institutional Realty Chicago	225
Interfirst Bank Dallas Dallas	212

Table 8.1 *Continued*

Managers	Assets
North Carolina National Bank Charlotte, N.C.	210
First National Bank of Boston Boston	200
Total	$15,955

Reprinted by permission. *Pensions & Investment Age* (September 13, 1982), p. 23. Crain Communications.©

Assets for JMB Institutional Realty were not listed in the table compiled by *P&IA* and were provided by JMB.

commingled real estate funds are scrambling for business and not making much money for their managers. But at this writing, new funds keep appearing because, compared to what a manager can make running stocks and bonds for a pension plan, running a commingled real estate fund can be lucrative.

FEES

Commingled real estate funds charge much higher fees than commingled stock or bond funds. Stock or bond fund managers typically collect an annual fee of 0.3 or 0.4 percent of assets. Real estate fund managers charge three times as much, from 0.9 to 1.25 percent of assets, for a commingled fund that buys real estate for pension funds; and twice as much, 0.7 percent, for a fund that writes participating mortgages. The fund managers claim that it takes more effort on their part to manage a real estate fund than a securities fund and still more effort to buy real estate instead of writing mortgages, all of which is true.

Pension sponsors used to balk at these fees but now accept them. Some pension sponsors may feel that these fees are a fair price to pay for being able to invest in a professionally run real estate portfolio without knowing a thing about the investment. But more likely, the pension sponsors are simply unaware of how much they are really paying in management fees.

The formal management fee is only the most visible fee. Some real estate fund managers charge their clients annual service fees and entry fees when they make a contribution to the fund. Others collect a share in the proceeds of each property that is sold, subject to a preferred return to the pension clients.

Some managers play games with expenses. In many funds, the manager is fully reimbursed for all his expenses in running the fund, including the cost of acquiring the properties, appraising them, and administering the fund. But other managers do not charge the fund for expenses. Instead, they manage the fund's properties and then bill the fund for this service at the market rate charged by independent property management firms. The fund managers confuse their clients by not fully disclosing all these fees or by burying them in corners of their brochures or in the footnotes to the funds' operating statements. A manager will list the formal management fee as an expense in the fund's operating statement while the remaining fees are coyly hidden under titles like "property expenses" or "administration."

The total fees and the cost of administration billed to the commingled fund each year can easily eat up 15 to 20 percent of the annual investment income the fund collects from its properties. This is before the manager is reimbursed for the expenses of acquiring the property or selling it.

These high fees appeal to money managers because, after they hit break even, the returns promise healthy rewards for their efforts. One manager of a bank commingled real estate fund estimated that in the late 1970s the break-even point for his fund was $100 million of assets under management. When the fund passed that mark, it became a real money-maker for the bank. It did not take many more people to run the fund at $200 million or $300 million; fee income would double and then triple because the fee was a percentage of assets under management.

The funds are profitable for their managers because of the type of property they buy. Commingled funds buy the highest-quality properties leased to the best tenants with the least amount of management to be done—and then they hire an outside firm to manage the properties that need it. They are rarely under pressure to sell any property. By investing this way, the fund manager keeps his expenses low and fee income high. The manager of the bank commingled fund mentioned above had a particularly vivid example of how this works:

I used to get perverse and think about a big office building we had net leased entirely to a Fortune 500 company for their headquarters. It was a super $10 million asset.
We had to do nothing. No management. No administration. We didn't even have to go and look at it, the tenant did such a phenomenal job of maintaining it.
So once a year I would go out and look at it when I wanted to go see my wife's folks. Do you know how much fee income that building generated each year? $120,000. Our fund's fee was 1.2 percent of assets.
It was the most glaring example of collecting fee income for doing nothing.
Of course, some deals we did were bombs, and we had to really kill ourselves working on them. But imagine if you got 10 deals like that headquarters building in a $100 million portfolio. You'd generate $1.2 million in fees for doing nothing.
Not a bad business.

With margins like this, it is no wonder that banks and investment managers are eager to start up commingled funds and have already done so. But at this writing, only 20 or 25 have more than $100 million under management, and even though the break-even point must vary, it is unlikely to vary by much since most funds are carbon copies of each other. The majority of funds are sitting with anywhere from $10 million to $50 million of assets under management and scraping along, running operating losses until they reach their magic break-even point, if they ever will. Their funds are so small they cannot afford to hire the type of real estate people who could do a decent job of running the fund. And the competition for pension money is so stiff that most do not have a good chance of getting much money.

A number of these funds were formed by investment managers, particularly banks and insurance companies that advertise themselves as full-service pension managers. They had to offer a real estate fund or risk losing clients to the competition. It was expensive to start a fund so a number of these managers are now sponsoring funds in partnership with existing real estate firms.[4] The real estate firm finds the property; and the bank markets, administers and acts as trustee for the fund. Other large banks and insurance companies with funds are allowing smaller banks and managers to offer the funds to their own clients.

Part of the problem with the smaller commingled funds is that pension sponsors prefer the large, established funds. In terms of organization and investment strategy, most commingled funds are copies of the largest commingled fund, PRISA. Because the largest funds have substantial real estate holdings already, a pension sponsor gets better diversification by investing in them. The sponsor also has a natural inclination to believe that the larger funds are better-run than the smaller ones, simply because they are larger. If the First National Bank of Nowhere is offering a fund with the same investment strategy as PRISA, the bank could have a brilliant real estate team; the plan sponsors will still prefer to give their money to the larger fund, which is why the four largest real estate managers have 51 percent of the pension fund real estate business.

In spite of the mimicry in the commingled fund business, there is one organizational difference splitting the business. A growing minority of fund managers have chosen to organize their funds as closed-end funds as opposed to the open-end approach taken by PRISA. A "closed-end fund" is one that closes its doors to new pension money once it has reached a certain level of pension assets under management. It does not allow new pension clients to buy into the fund.

The fund manager then invests the money in real estate with the intention of selling the entire portfolio in 10 years or so and distributing the proceeds to the pension clients. Closed-end funds are designed to be self-liquidating, though the date of liquidation can be postponed. In contrast, the open-end funds can accept or decline new money from pension clients at any time and have no limit on how large they can grow.

Open-end and closed-end funds can be far more alike than different. They may have the same investment strategies, fee schedules, and problems, with one exception: the closed-end managers have a different approach to allowing pension plans to buy into and cash out of their funds. Otherwise, the two types of funds are nearly identical.

A few managers offer both closed-end and open-end funds; but only a handful, such as Rosenberg Real Estate Fund, JMB Institutional Realty and Coldwell Banker, offer only closed-end trusts. Although the number of closed-end funds is growing, they are far outnumbered by their open-end competitors, both in number of funds and the amount of money they run.

HOW OPEN-END FUNDS WORK

The typical, open-end commingled fund is a simple organization. It has a staff of administrators to keep the records straight, a marketing man or two to bring in pension fund money, and a handful of people who make the fund's property investments.

At banks, the funds are run in the trust department by a real estate staff that is typically separate from the one in the bank's real estate lending department. Insurance company funds are run by the same real estate staff that finds property for the insurer's general account; independent money managers usually create a special division or company to handle the commingled real estate fund. At real estate companies which start such funds, the company's staff works on both the fund and the firm's other business.

Regardless of who sponsors them, most commingled real estate funds have the same investment strategy. They buy complete ownership in the highest-quality and most prestigious income property they can find and then rarely sell it. Most would never consider buying a property with the intention of selling it within two years and making a profit. For example, PRISA I, which had assets of $3.98 billion on September 30, 1982, had sold only $36.8 million of property in the previous 12 months, or less than 1 percent of its total holdings. This is typical of its total sales in earlier years. At this writing, few properties, once parked in a commingled fund portfolio, ever find the exit.

The typical management fee system encourages this behavior. Managers are paid an annual fee based on the amount of assets they manage. The bigger the assets, the larger the fee. The fund's staff is not rewarded for running a portfolio that makes a big return for the clients but for one that simply gets bigger and bigger. Unless a property is pulling the fund's rate of return to dangerously low levels, the manager has no reason whatsoever to sell. So he does not.

Shopping centers, office buildings and industrial warehouses are the mainstay of the commingled fund portfolio. They must be the best properties, located in the best areas of the nation's largest or fastest-growing metropolitan areas, which means that all the funds are chasing the same top 2 percent of the property market. They are not interested in the remaining 98 percent of the nation's real estate nor are they typically interested in any type of deal that is not a straight purchase. Most commingled funds do not write mortgages of any kind, including landsale-leasebacks. They avoid buying raw land, nursing homes, or any type of specialized property, although a few will buy apartments, hotels, and farms. Several funds manage their own properties, but most hire outside firms to run individual buildings.

Most fund managers do not develop properties for their own account, and avoid investing in properties under development. The closest most get is building an addition to a property they already own, or buying a preleased building that is nearly completed from a developer who has a construction loan without a takeout. Instead of searching for a permanent loan, he sells his building to the commingled fund.

Sometimes the larger funds break these rules. Instead of demanding 100 percent ownership of a property, they will settle for half and will do joint ventures with developers. Equitable's Separate Account Number 8 has done a few joint-venture developments as has Prudential's PRISA I, but not many. Both avoid developing property on their own.

Fund managers argue that development work is too risky for a commingled fund consisting of pension fund money. They also think management fees are too low to justify getting involved in development projects. Development work is labor-intensive, and if they are collecting 20 percent of cash flow to manage a portfolio of existing properties, they would probably require 30 or 40 percent of the property's eventual cash flow and a piece of the deal for doing development work.

Commingled funds typically do not borrow money to finance their property purchases and some are oblivious to the merits of existing, favorable mortgages on the properties they acquire. They prefer to buy entirely with cash and the percentage of their property that carries mortgages is low. For example, as of September 30, 1982, PRISA had an average loan-to-value ratio on its properties, expressed as a percentage, of about 10 percent. Historically, there is a reason for this aversion to mortgaged property. Until 1981, pension funds could not own mortgaged property without incurring a tax on the income from such property. Pension sponsors and managers of commingled funds were afraid to buy mortgaged property, even though commingled funds run by banks and insurance companies were exempt from the tax, known as "the unrelated business income tax." Commingled fund managers also like to argue that mortgaged property is too risky for pension plans to own, a claim that makes little sense as was demonstrated in chapter 5. But most pension sponsors still believe it.

In their search for property, commingled fund managers rarely if ever buy a property for under $1 million, preferring to buy in the $1 million to $10 million range. The largest funds can buy much larger properties. Flooded with cash from enthusiastic pension plans in 1980 and 1981, they were able to make some huge purchases.

PRISA, as both the largest fund and the one with the most incoming cash, went on a spending spree. Among its giant purchases in 1981 was the CIT Building in Manhattan, which it bought for $90 million. In 1982, the fund paid $110 million for seven office buildings and three warehouses owned by the Vantage Companies of Dallas. The fund's gargantuan deal was the purchase of the entire Connecticut General Mortgage and Realty Investment Trust in the summer of 1981: Prudential Insurance Company, PRISA's manager, spent roughly $335 million to buy the trust, and put its 93 properties into PRISA.

ERISA instructs plan sponsors and fiduciaries to diversify their portfolios and in this spirit, PRISA had set limits on the percentage of its portfolio it could hold in different types of property. In 1980, so many large properties were available that PRISA was bumping into its own limits; Prudential started PRISA II, which was specifically designed to be an undiversified real estate portfolio. The new fund's first purchase was an $85 million hotel in San Francisco. In 1981, it bought the headquarters of Emigrant Savings Bank in New York for $50 million. But the giant purchases of PRISA I and II and those of the other large funds are the exceptions in the commingled fund business. Most funds look for properties priced closer to $15 million than $50 million.

Besides setting a minimum on the size of a deal they will consider, commingled funds set minimums on the amount that a pension plan must contribute if it wants to invest in the fund. Most funds accept minimum contributions ranging between $100,000 and $500,000. Even if the minimum is met, funds will often refuse to accept money from a pension plan if the amount involved is more than a certain percentage of a pension plan's assets. Such limits vary anywhere from 10 percent to 33 percent of plan assets: fund managers set them because they do not believe it is appropriate for pension plans to hold more than these percentages in property. Since the minimum at most funds is at least $100,000, and assuming a 20 percent limit, this rule cuts out pension plans whose assets are less than $500,000. If a $500,000 minimum applies, the cut-off point would be a $2.5 million plan.

Plans falling below these limits must either seek out the funds with $50,000 minimums, where the pension plan need be only $250,000 to participate, or resort to participating in syndications where the minimum contributions are usually $2,500 to $5,000. Syndications are not considered commingled funds, but have some features in common with them. They are discussed briefly later in this chapter.

A commingled fund will also limit the amount of a pension plan's contribution and will not accept any that give a client too big an interest in the fund. Most have rules that a plan cannot hold more than a 10 percent interest in the fund. The manager wants his commingled fund to be diversified in its clients.

The commingled fund has an appraiser revalue the properties in the portfolio each quarter and estimate how much the properties have appreciated or depreciated in value. Smaller properties are valued by an in-house appraiser, but larger properties will be appraised by an outside firm. Once a year, the fund brings in an outside appraiser to value all properties.

The manager computes the income return from the fund each quarter by dividing the cash flow from the properties by what they were appraised at the quarter before, or if they are new properties, their purchase price. The sum of these two numbers—the income return and the change in appraisal values, expressed as percentages—is the total rate of return for the fund for the quarter.

Each pension plan's account at the commingled fund is expressed in the number of units of the fund it owns, a unit being equivalent to one share in the fund. Each quarter, the unit values are increased by the amount of the total return and the pension funds dutifully enter that increase in their records as the investment performance of their commingled real estate fund for the period. Usually, the pension plans do not see any of this total return in real money. The manager of an open-end fund typically does not distribute any of the properties' cash flow to his pension investors, though the pension plans may have the option of withdrawing this income regularly.

If a pension sponsor wants to buy into a fund, he will be sold new units priced at the unit value for the most recent quarter. Some funds allow pension plans to buy in each quarter, others, once a month, with the money changing hands at the current unit value. This is why these funds are called open-end funds. They are open to pension plan contributions.

When they invest in an open-end fund, pension sponsors are told that it is an illiquid investment. There is no secondary market in units of commingled funds, and if a pension plan wants to cash out of the fund, it is at the discretion of the fund manager. Most fund contracts say that pension plans are permitted to withdraw their money by having the fund manager buy back their units at their current value. But the manager is not obligated to redeem their units although most will, if there is enough cash available to and it has not been committed to some other purpose. A manager is under no obligation to sell property in order to redeem units. PRISA has no contractual obligation to ever honor redemptions, a Prudential official told *Institutional Investor* magazine in June, 1982.[5] But, he added, the fund had a "moral commitment" to do its best to honor them.

It can take from 90 days to a year for a pension plan to withdraw money from a fund, even if the fund contract indicates that plans are permitted to ask for a redemption quarterly or monthly. It could possibly take longer than a year if a fund is strapped for cash, and at this writing, PRISA is taking six months or more to cash out clients. Some fund sponsors are more specific about the limits on redemption than others, with the Smith Barney Real Estate Fund being the most straightforward. The fund permits plans to cash out of the fund but gives itself two years and three months to honor their requests.

FUND VARIATIONS

Participating Mortgage Funds

Although most commingled funds are typical of the open-end funds just described, a few have different investment strategies. The largest group consists of the participating mortgage funds, which do not buy real estate but instead use their money to make mortgages with equity kickers. There are about 20 of these funds at this writing, compared to 130 equity funds; these mortgage funds are a small part of the commingled real estate fund business.[6] For every property these funds write a mortgage on, they collect, in addition to their mortgage payments, 30 to 50 percent of the property's cash flow, and a similar percentage of the proceeds when the property is eventually sold.

Participating mortgages are new to the commingled fund business. Aetna Life Insurance started the first one in 1981, the same year Prudential Insurance started one. Balcor/American Express, a real estate syndicator in Skokie, Illinois, also markets such a fund which, in addition to making participating mortgages, will also make wraparound loans with equity kickers. The Balcor fund is the only commingled fund that makes wraparound mortgages, an investment well suited to pension funds, as was explained in chapter 5.

Participating mortgage funds were created in 1980 and 1981 when long-term bond rates were over 12 percent. Commingled real estate fund managers felt they needed some product to compete with bond yields and found it in this new mortgage fund. At this writing, the participating mortgage funds generate a higher cash income than the typical equity real estate fund.

Pension plans can be very attentive to cash return when it comes to property investing. Metropolitan Life Insurance found this out in late 1980 when it bought the Pan Am Building in New York for $400 million. The company intended to sell interests in the building to pension plans, but the plans were not interested. The initial cash return was too low for them, and many would only participate if the insurer would match their investment in Pan Am with a property that showed a better cash return. At this writing, the Pan Am Building has no pension investors. By appealing to a desire for cash income, the participating mortgage funds have enjoyed modest success, enough that Aetna Life Insurance Co. started a second fund.

Other Variations

Outside of the participating mortgage funds, there are a few other funds with different investment strategies. JMB Institutional Realty and the First National Bank of Chicago have each sponsored a commingled fund that invests only in residential apartments, an investment completely ignored by the majority of commingled fund managers. They do not want the management problems of running a property where all the tenants can leave overnight, nor are they fond of playing residential landlord. Equitable Life Insurance once had the misfortune of acquiring an apartment building in Indianapolis through foreclosure. Every year, the chairman of Equitable received letters from Wendell Willkie's widow, complaining about something in the building.

But the managers of the new apartment funds, which were started in 1982, believe that rental apartments will be such good investments in the 1980s that their investment potential will outweigh the headaches. In recent years, it has been difficult to afford a home; people are forced to rent and these fund managers reason that housing demand will overtake supply and push up rents still further.

One fund has been buying apartment properties since the mid-1970s, but in this strategy and in everything else it does, it is a maverick among commingled funds. The Smith Barney Real Estate Fund buys apartment buildings out of foreclosure at cut-rate prices with as much favorable mortgage financing as it can find. It then installs its own property managers, shapes up the buildings, and raises rents, turning the buildings into very profitable investments for the fund. The fund also buys industrial, office and retail properties using the same technique. Everything it buys it intends to sell. No other commingled fund uses as much leverage, buys out of foreclosure, or intends to sell what it buys, and no other fund has the investment performance of the Smith Barney fund. It has one of the highest rates of return of any commingled fund for any time period.

Some funds cater to the politics of a particular audience. In 1981, both Prudential and Aetna started funds that would make participating mortgages only on income property constructed with union labor. These were responses to requests from union pension funds, especially in the construction trades.

Other funds buy properties in only one region of the country, such as the North Carolina National Bank fund, which specializes in properties in the Southeastern United States or the fund started by Rhode Island Hospital Trust that invests primarily in New England properties. Such funds are usually sponsored by regional banks, and their preference for real estate located in their area of the country is less a well-thought-out investment strategy than an announcement of their limitations. They do not know any other market.

Several other funds are distinct, not in what they invest in but in how they are organized. Corporate Property Investors in New York is a private real estate investment trust. Most of its shareholders are pension funds, and the REIT is treated by the pension community as a commingled fund. The same is true of a private REIT for pension funds started by LaSalle Partners in Chicago.

Coldwell Banker organizes its funds as limited partnerships, and Rosenberg Real Estate Fund (RREEF) runs theirs as individual tax-exempt corporations. Metropolitan Life Insurance runs a commingled fund that breaches the norms of both organization and investment strategy for commingled funds. The Met's fund invests primarily in properties under development and buys them or issues mortgages on them in partnership with the Met's general account. The commingled fund takes a small position, going as low as 5 percent of the deal, and consequently holds a highly diversified portfolio of interests in new properties.

Manufacturers Hanover Trust sponsors a fund that buys vacant land it believes has the potential to be developed one day. Agricultural Investment Management of Bannockburn, Illinois, runs a fund that invests in farms, and Travelers's commingled fund has been making farm mortgages for years. It also does mortgage and equity deals. As the commingled business grows, more of these specialized or unusually organized funds should appear. But for the most part, the world of commingled real estate funds lacks variety: the handful of funds trying something different is dwarfed by the funds offering the same thing.

A REASON FOR EXISTENCE

Commingled real estate funds serve a definite and good purpose in the pension fund community. They allow pension plans to invest in real estate with great ease. A pension sponsor can invest $5 million in PRISA and find that he suddenly has a share in a \$4 billion, diversified real estate portfolio run by the largest real estate company in the country. True, he must give up a big chunk of his investment income in fees, but in exchange he has no headaches. He does not worry about running the properties, buying them, selling them or leasing them.

The fund manager assumes all the fiduciary responsibility under ERISA, makes all the decisions, takes all the blame, and actually promises a pension sponsor the chance to get out of the fund if he has a change of heart. The fund will redeem his units, turning real estate from an illiquid to a liquid investment, or at least giving the illusion of doing so. Investing in real estate through a commingled fund makes a great deal of sense for many pension plans.

On the other hand, there are drawbacks. None of them is serious enough to warn pension plans away from these funds, but knowing about them in advance can save plan sponsors from unpleasant surprises. The decision to invest in or avoid commingled funds depends on what the pension investor wants. He must decide what he is willing to give up or put up with to get the effortless diversification and professional management that the commingled funds promise.

THE PROBLEMS WITH COMMINGLED REAL ESTATE FUNDS

The basic problem with commingled funds is that they are completely entangled in conflicts of interest with their managers. This shows up primarily in how the funds value their real estate portfolios. Because the manager selects the appraiser who values the properties, he can control how the value of the portfolio is determined, but his management fees are directly tied to whatever that value is. By changing the value, he can change his fees. This does not mean that managers are playing games with the value of their portfolios, just that they have every reason to. They can be tempted to make subtle judgments about the property's values that favor their position.

All commingled real estate funds use the same system of valuing their properties, which, in turn, is an essential part of computing the rate of return on the fund. Each quarter, the commingled fund managers supply their pension clients with a number that represents the total rate of return on their investment in the fund for that three months. The total return consists of the cash flow the properties generated for the quarter plus how much the properties appreciated, known as "unrealized appreciation."

The cash flow number is fairly straightforward. The cash a property generates can be counted. But how much the property has appreciated in a quarter is a pure estimate. The fund hires an appraiser or has one of its own appraisal staff go over all the properties in the fund each quarter and estimate how much they are worth. Appraisals are notoriously inaccurate: it is not uncommon for them to be 15 to 30 percent off what the property actually sells for.

Often, fund appraisers tie their estimates of a property's value more to their own underlying assumptions about the rate of inflation than to the real income-producing ability of the property. If an appraiser thinks the inflation rate next year will be 10 percent, he will tend to assume that good income property will be able to post increases of a least that amount on new leases. At the same time, each appraiser has his own opinion on the strength of the market for a given property. The result is that different appraisers can come up with radically different values for the same property.

One former manager of a bank commingled fund described how his fund would hire two, reputable, outside appraisers to value its properties. "They would fight to see what the other guy did as an appraisal for a given property so they would know where they should come in at. But we wouldn't let them see it," he recalls. "So the numbers the two of them came up with—from the same data—were totally different, 30 percent apart. It was wild."

Nevertheless, fund managers act as if the total return number they hand out is God's word. They quote it to the hundredth of a percent and give it all the legitimacy that they would assign the quarterly return for the S&P 500, which can actually be measured. The fund's quarterly report will announce that its "unrealized appreciation" for the third quarter was 3.04 percent. It would be far more accurate to write that the appraiser guessed that the property increased in value anywhere from 1 to 10 percent in the last quarter, and management is fairly certain that the property has not lost value.

Pension fund sponsors do not understand that in order to realize a property's appreciation and show an accurate rate of return, they must first sell the property. No one knows what he has made on a property until he has sold it. While he owns it, he will have some sense of how good or bad an investment it is but certainly will not know to the hundredth of a percent until he sells. An astute real estate investor and developer offered the following analysis of unrealized appreciation:

This form of valuation isn't wrong, it's just unrealistic.
It's similar to buying art. You buy it at $1 and the next year you think it's worth $2. But the only real benefit from the appreciation goes to your insurance company because it costs you more to insure.
You're not a seller, so who cares if it appreciates?
I can prove to you with great ease that properties have special values but the only way to realize the value is to sell it. It's like saying that a woman's greatest asset is a man's imagination. She looks much better dressed than undressed.
There's an illusion.

Few funds have sold any property, and then only in small amounts, so it is difficult to draw conclusions about whether or not unrealized appreciation can be turned into realized profits. Audit Investments conducted a survey of the operating statements for 18 commingled funds from 1976 to 1980; the survey showed that in three out of four years, the funds that sold property sold it at more than appraised value. Only one year was a loss year.[7]

A few large funds had a bad time. Equitable's Number 8 account showed a loss on property sales in three out of the five years, and Fund F at the First

National Bank of Chicago showed a loss on its property sales in all four years. But all these sales were minuscule compared to the size of both funds: most likely the funds were selling off properties that had not worked out, so the loss is understandable. The funds were cleaning house. But it can be argued that some of the funds that sold property consistently at a profit did so, in part, to demonstrate that their appraisals were accurate estimates of property values. At least one commingled fund manager said this was one of his fund's major motives in selling.

Funds could afford to demonstrate the accuracy of their appraisals at their leisure; until 1982, few funds had any need to raise cash quickly, so they had no need to sell. In fact, the only times a fund would need cash would be if it had overcommitted to buy property, or if a number of clients wanted to withdraw their money and the fund manager felt it would be wise to honor their requests.

A demonstration of how a commingled fund manager might react to both situations was given by PRISA during 1982. Through the first nine months of that year, a small number of the fund's clients were trying to withdraw their money. Total requests were $260 million through September 30, 1982 or about 6 percent of PRISA's $4.2 billion in assets. But PRISA had already committed most of its available cash flow to purchase new property; it would have had to sell some of its current holdings or borrow money to cash out its clients promptly. Although PRISA had said it would try to honor withdrawal requests quarterly, it had no obligation to honor them at all.

The value of the fund's properties fell during 1982, a dramatic reversal of the 14.8 percent increase it had posted in 1981. For the first nine months of 1982, the appraisers depreciated the portfolio by 1 percent. PRISA refused to sell property to raise money unless the property could be sold at or above appraised value. One real estate investor reported that PRISA refused to sell property unless it could do so at a cap rate of 8: the fund needed that much return to meet its appraised values. "I told them 8 was not the market and we did not transact any business," this man said.

For the first nine months of 1982, PRISA sold only $24 million in property, all of it at or above appraised value. This was nowhere near enough to honor the withdrawal requests. PRISA did not cash out any clients until the end of September 1982 when it disbursed $78 million. That payment reduced outstanding withdrawal requests at the time from $260 million to $182 million. It was taking six months or more for clients to withdraw from the fund.

PRISA refused to sustain a loss on a property sale in order to cash out a client. So would most other commingled funds if they were in a similar position: to honor the requests would hurt the return of the clients who remained in the fund. But such a policy also puts the clients who want to withdraw and collect their unrealized appreciation in cash in a difficult position. They must wait until the manager has enough cash from internal cash flow or until he can sell property at a profit.

This leads to a strange scenario. What would happen if a great number of pension funds decided that real estate had peaked? They all wanted to cash out of the same fund at once. If the fund did not have the cash to pay them off, it would have to sell property or wait until it collected cash flow from other sources to honor their requests. But if great numbers of pension clients were asking to withdraw simultaneously, it would be likely that real estate returns were falling and investors were panicking. It would be the worst time to sell property. At the same time, new contributions to the fund would have probably dropped. If the fund manager did not have enough cash flow from the properties themselves to pay off the clients, he would be in trouble.

The manager would be forced to postpone withdrawals and hope the clients requesting their money would change their minds. Otherwise, he would fall further and further behind in his attempts to cash them out. The only way he would ever honor all requests at the promised rate of return would be if the value of some of his property dramatically climbed and he could sell it at a big profit. He could also cash them out if he suddenly collected new cash flow, either from new pension contributions or from increased rents. He would only be saved if everything dramatically improved—an unlikely event.

This may be pushing the whole scenario too far, but it is possible the clients requesting withdrawal could never be cashed out. They would get reports showing how much their units were worth, but they could never collect their money. By the very act of trying to collect their appreciation in cash, they would be assured of never collecting it. At this writing, no commingled fund is in such a predicament. None may ever be, but there is an intriguing logic behind it.

The problems funds have with withdrawal requests stem from using real estate appraisals to set unit values. Melnikoff, the creator of PRISA, argues that the criticisms of the use of appraisals in open-end funds are exaggerated. He contends that the inaccuracies in individual appraisals tend to balance each other out so that with the larger open-end funds, such as PRISA, the unit values the fund posts are accurate indications of what the portfolio is worth. He compares the appraisals at commingled funds with mortality tables. No one knows how long one individual will live, but mortality tables are accurate and important tools for life insurance companies. Similarly, individual appraisals may be inaccurate, but together they give an accurate picture of a portfolio's value.

Melnikoff raises an interesting point. But there is one crucial difference between mortality tables and collections of real estate appraisals. Mortality tables are based on actual events: millions of people die each year and their age at death has been measured. But at this writing, real estate in commingled funds has never been sold in significant enough quantities to tell if the appraisals support the sales prices in aggregate. It can also be argued that real estate appraisals have an upward bias because appraisers tend to overestimate a property's value to please their clients. Until sales confirm or disprove it, it is reasonable to believe that all commingled funds are overvalued.

If this is not the case, and Melnikoff is right, then there's the question of just how big a commingled fund would have to be before the inaccuracies in its appraisals balanced each other out. Would the funds with less than $500 million, which includes most commingled funds, have serious errors in their unit values? Commingled funds rarely sell property and few clients ever cash out of the funds: perhaps it makes no difference at all if their fund values are accurate or not. They'll never be tested.

The participating mortgage fund managers have even more problems with valuation techniques than the equity funds. With equity funds, an appraiser can review each property quarterly and estimate how much it could be sold for. But how much would someone pay for a participating mortgage? How much more— or less—is the mortgage worth today than it was three months ago?

The Balcor participating mortgage fund solved this problem by leaving the valuation of the portfolio entirely in the hands of the trustees of the commingled fund. They can value the portfolio any way they see fit as long as they are consistent and apply the technique uniformly to all properties in the fund. Aetna Life Insurance tried to be more concrete. It values its fund by discounting the stream of mortgage payments and the fund's estimated share of the equity to the present, using a rate commensurate with other investments of similar risk.

This procedure is fraught with problems. Just what interest rate should the fund use to discount its cash flow? Supposedly, it should use one that is borne by an investment with commensurate risk to a participating mortgage, but no one can tell what investment that would be. Each participating mortgage is unique. Secondly, since 1979, interest rates have been so volatile that from one month to the next it is difficult to estimate what any investment should be returning.

The third problem is the estimates themselves. No one can accurately estimate how much money he is going to get out of a participation in a building's cash flow. It depends on what the building's rents will be over the next 10 years. Nor can anyone predict what the property will be worth in 10 years when it is sold and the fund lines up to get its cut of the sales price.

Yet the valuation method hinges on these estimates. The managers that use this method are applying questionable discount rates to questionable cash flow estimates, claiming that the end result is the fund's investment performance for the quarter. The valuation practices of these funds are more farfetched than those of the equity real estate funds. Nevertheless, the pension plan clients of all these funds receive their total return numbers from their commingled managers and treat them as if they were some absolute measure of investment performance, equivalent to the total return numbers they post for their stock and bond portfolios.

These valuation techniques are totally foreign to the real estate community, where a property's value is completely determined by capitalizing its cash flow: no one cares what the market value of a participating mortgage is. Investors have their properties reappraised if they are trying to refinance or sell them, or simply to get another opinion on what the property is worth. Unrealized appreciation did not even exist until the managers of commingled real estate funds dreamed it up, and it was greeted with laughter and disbelief when it first appeared. Melnikoff recalls that Prudential's top real estate staff nearly threw him out of the room when he first suggested quarterly property valuations for PRISA using this technique.

The legal source of these valuation practices is U.S. banking law. The law requires banks to value their commingled funds quarterly and report the results to their clients. With commingled stock and bond funds, this is not difficult: there is a public market that sets the value of these securities. With real estate, the fund managers settled on unrealized appreciation as the valuation solution. Unrealized appreciation also provided the managers with a method to equitably handle the contributions that pension clients made to the fund at different times during the year.

This latter problem could have been avoided by setting up closed-end instead of open-end funds. Closed-end funds do not allow new clients to buy into them after the initial offering is made; there is no need to make quarterly valuations of the fund for that purpose. The funds still provide the valuations in order to report to their clients on the progress of their investments and to set the managers' fees. But no money changes hands based upon these valuations, at least going into the fund. U.S. banking law forbad banks from running closed-end funds until 1982. The Comptroller of the Currency then permitted three banks to open closed-end funds: First National of Chicago, Bank of America and Crocker National Bank. There has been no rush to set up closed-end funds or to convert open-end to closed-end funds.

The managers of real estate commingled funds find themselves in a unique and enviable position in the world of pension money management. If a stock manager has a bad year because the market is down, he cannot disguise that from his clients. They know what the market has been doing, and to the dime. But with a commingled real estate fund, the clients have no way of knowing if the rate-of-return figures are accurate. The fund manager cannot hide a property's cash flow, but if he wants to mark up his values a little more aggressively to show a better return than a competing fund, no one can stop him.

Admittedly, the late 1970s and early 1980s were a boom time for real estate and its value increased remarkably. But at this writing, values are falling, particularly on office buildings, which were popular with many commingled funds. Some funds, like PRISA, have had to mark down their portfolios: 1982 was one of the rare years they ever had to do so. The temptation is to avoid writing the property down. Instead, the appraiser will not show it appreciating as aggressively. No appraiser doing steady work for a commingled fund wants to devalue a property after several years of marking it up. It is viewed as treason.

All these possibilities for abuse do not mean that commingled fund managers are consciously meddling with their total return numbers to mislead their pension clients, only that they have strong motivations to do so and little to stop them. Fund managers are fiduciaries. They must be worthy of trust because rules cannot be written down for every function they perform. But fiduciaries are also human and their natural inclination must be to inflate values.

Fund managers have one final and good reason for tending to inflate property values. The management fees they collect are based on the market value of their portfolios; when values go up, so do their fees.

Consider a hypothetical, billion dollar real estate fund with 1 percent management fee. The fund manager collects $10 million a year from this fee. Now assume it is 1980 and the fund's appraiser or an outside appraiser reports that the fund's portfolio appreciated 15 percent, which was not an uncommon figure for that year. The portfolio is now worth $1.15 billion and the management fee climbs to $11.5 million. Because the appraiser said the portfolio appreciated 15 percent, the fund manager collects $1.5 million more each year in fees. Those fees are paid in cash.

If the appraiser had said appreciation was only 14 percent, the manager would have received $100,000 less in extra income. The appraiser's estimate means real money to the manager, and this situation is a conflict of interest between the manager and his clients with a capital "C." Again, this does not mean that fund managers manipulate their asset values to increase their fees, only that they have good reason to do so.

Only a few funds have shunned the practice of tying fees to appraised values. Among them are the funds run by Coldwell Banker and Smith Barney, which tie their fees to combinations of the cost of the property purchased, capital contributions by pension plans, and cash flow. For example, the Smith Barney Real Estate Fund collects 2 percent of each capital contribution made by a pension plan to its fund and then a certain percentage annually thereafter. The manager also collects 25 percent of the cash flow distributed to its clients in excess of a 9 percent return to them. But none of the manager's income comes from values based on unrealized appreciation.

A Closer Look at Performance Numbers

A commingled fund's total rate of return consists of unrealized appreciation and income return: the two figures are incestuously related. Each quarter, a fund's appraiser will value each property by capitalizing its rents at what he considers to be the market cap rate. The amount the property's value has increased or decreased since the last valuation is the unrealized appreciation or depreciation for the quarter. The appraiser cannot compute a property's value without a cap rate, which is his estimate of the yield that investors are willing to accept on that general type of property.

The income portion of the fund's quarterly return is computed by dividing the cash flow from the properties by their value at the beginning of the quarter and expressing the result as a percentage. But this is just unraveling what the appraiser did to figure unrealized appreciation in the first place. Then, he started with cash flow, divided it by a cap rate, and came up with a property value. Now, he starts with the cash flow, divides it by value, and comes up with the cap rate again. Except this time around, he calls it income return or yield. The quarterly income return a fund posts is really the cap rate its appraiser used that quarter, divided by four.

Both income and unrealized appreciation are the creations of the appraiser. The fund's properties are certainly generating increasing amounts of cash for their investors, but the income figures the commingled funds post do not indicate what the investors are making on their cash invested in the fund. They are not cash-on-cash returns. Instead, they are a history of the cap rates that the fund's appraisers have been using to value the properties.

Often, the income figures for commingled funds will be within basis points of each other for a given period. This shows that for the most part, the funds buy properties the real estate community considers remarkably similar in risk and that the cap rates for such properties are well-known by the fund's appraisers at any given time.

Sometimes one fund will show a much higher yield than the others. This occurs for one of two reasons. The fund may own properties that are considered risky; they are capped at higher rates than real estate held by other funds. Apartments and income properties in smaller cities, for example, typically are capped at higher rates than the big prestigious properties most commingled funds prefer to buy.

The unusually high income may also be due to a manager's ability to run cash when short-term rates are high. One fund showed a high income one year because it had a substantial amount of pension fund money that it had not yet been able to invest in property; it held the money in money market instruments. Since the yields on short-term investments from 1979 through early 1982 were 15 or 16 percent while the cap rates on real estate were 9 or 10 percent, the fund manager showed a high income figure.

While the income numbers of commingled funds are remarkably similar, especially when compared over five-year periods, their total return numbers will often differ dramatically. Other than substantial cash holdings, the only source for these differences is unrealized appreciation.

For example, in 1980, Prudential's PRISA had a total return of 23.3 percent for the year while Equitable's Number 8 showed only a 12.5 percent increase. Both had roughly the same income, 8.5 percent for PRISA and 8.2 percent for Number 8, but they differed wildly in unrealized appreciation. PRISA's appraisers said their property appreciated by 14.8 percent, while Equitable's showed an unrealized appreciation of only 4.3 percent. Probably, a high percentage of property leases came up for renewal in PRISA and the building managers re-negotiated them at substantially increased rents. Since a property's value is a multiple of its cash flow, the value of the property climbed. Number 8 simply had fewer leases rolling over.

But in addition to this obvious reason for such a dramatic increase in value, there may be a more subtle element. As explained in chapter 5, appraisers use three methods to set a property's value: replacement cost, market value, and the income approach. The latter uses cap rates and is considered the best method for valuation. But an appraiser will increase the value indicated by the income approach if the other methods show it may be warranted. How significant such adjustments are in setting values at commingled funds is unknown. Among the funds, PRISA has a reputation for aggressively marking up its property values whereas other funds, such as Equitable's Number 8 and Fund F at the First National Bank of Chicago, are considered more conservative. But the general accuracy of all appraisals at the commingled funds is basically unknown.

Commingled real estate funds also use a wide variety of techniques to compute their rates of return, making it impossible to compare one fund's performance with that of another. One longtime observer has called these performance numbers "an accounting minefield." One fund will use compounded, time-weighted rates of return, while another will just average its returns or use some totally homegrown method. The funds sometimes will not compute the income per unit, nor will they allocate return between income and unrealized appreciation per unit in any intelligible way.

Some funds compute their rates of return based on gross assets of the fund, that is, assets before management fees have been deducted. Others compute returns after fees are deducted. Some managers bill the commingled fund for management fees and deduct the fees from investment income. Others bill their pension clients directly and the management fee never shows up as a commingled fund expense.

If a pension customer could figure out what the total fees are, he would be able to adjust the performance numbers so he could compare the funds on equal footing. But it is nearly impossible to unearth total fees in some funds. Special fees or administrative fees will be tacked on to the management fee but will not be included in the fund's expenses or will be hidden under some catchall category. One fund will express its fees in dollars per unit and another in percentage of net assets, but neither will provide enough additional information for the reader to convert both into the same measurement system and compare them. Worse, the same fund may compute some of its fees in dollars per unit but show others as a total expense and provide no data to convert one into the other.

A handful of funds throw another wrench into the comparison process by charging their clients fees based on the performance of the fund. The manager collects a fee when the properties are finally sold, but until that time the fund carries it as a liability on its balance sheet. How should such an incentive fee be factored into a fund's fee schedule?

Commingled funds have a strong aversion to the calendar year. Each fund has its own fiscal year based on the day the fund started. PRISA's fiscal year starts October 1; Fund F's, on December 1; and Aetna's RESA, on July 1. It is impossible to compare quarterly results among the funds when each has its own version of when a quarter begins and ends. Pension plans that rely on consultants to disentangle this information will be disappointed: the consultants have the same problems with the data as a plan sponsor, and each consultant will come up with different return numbers for the same funds.

In an excellent article written in 1981, Thomas Richardson, Jr., then of the Wells Fargo Bank real estate fund, brought up a number of these criticisms and argued that all commingled fund managers should use the same accounting system.[8] All fees should be disclosed and deducted at the fund level, not charged to individual clients. All funds should use the same techniques for computing rates of return, and there should be standard appraisal techniques. At present, these sound suggestions remain just wishful thinking. Until the pension clients raise a clamor about the mess, the managers have no reason to change their ways.

Property Allocation

Commingled fund managers have a conflict of interest in how they assign properties to the fund. Often the manager will run other real estate pools or buy property for other clients. When he comes across a good deal, he must decide which account will get it, though all of them would want it. It is a definite problem.

The British Coal Board, which manages two pension plans for British coal miners, solved this allocation problem for its two plans by creating a real estate pool. Both plans jointly own the pool, which handles all their real estate investing. The Coal Board thus avoids the dilemma of parceling out properties between its two "clients." But few money managers with a number of different accounts have chosen to run all their clients' money through a joint pool; most are faced with allocating among them.

The insurance companies have the most obvious problem because they are the largest private real estate investors in the country, investing on their own behalf through their general accounts but also running the largest commingled real estate funds for pension plans. The insurers' real estate expertise was what enabled them to create large commingled funds and attract pension clients in the first place. Unfortunately, when it comes to property, insurance companies and their pension clients share the same long-range investment goals. The insurance company's account, known as the general account, needs more income than the commingled fund because the general account must pay off insurance claims. So, though general accounts bought small amounts of real estate over the years, the overwhelming percentage of their real estate assets have been mortgages.

But between 1979 and 1981, insurance companies began to view property as an inflation hedge and bought more of it for their general accounts. In doing so, they ran right into the investment goals of their commingled funds. Both wanted to own big, high-quality income properties or issue shared-appreciation mortgages on them. When such a property fell into an insurer's net, which account got it?

Generally, the insurance company employees who actually buy or write a mortgage on a property on behalf of the insurance company have no idea which account will get the investment. The insurance company pays one price for the property, and someone back at the home office decides where it will go. If it is a risky property still under development or a bit exotic, the general account gets it. Otherwise, the allocation procedure steps in.

Different insurance companies have different techniques of dividing up properties. At Prudential Insurance, the two accounts take turns. The general account gets one, then PRISA does, depending on how much money each has available to spend. The general account also gets properties under development, while PRISA buys only existing properties or those that are near completion. At Aetna Life and Travelers Life, if the separate account has the money, it always has priority over the general account. Equitable Life has an allocation committee: each account has a representative, and if both want the property, a senior official in the real estate department arbitrates. He considers who got the last good deal and whether the property would be a logical choice for the account, given the types of property it already holds.

The only insurance company that effectively avoids the allocation problem is Metropolitan Life Insurance. Its real estate separate account shares its investments with the Met's general account and can elect to take a specific interest in what the general account acquires. But the Met has also started a traditional open-end commingled fund; the insurer is right back into the conflict of interest it originally had avoided.

At this writing, the allocation problem at insurance companies has diminished considerably. Many life companies do not have enough cash flow from the general account to buy much property. In early 1982, one real estate man at Equitable Life noted that most of the money the general account had for real estate equities was being used to expand and renovate the property the account already owned.[9] Once insurance company cash flow picks up again, the allocation problem should re-emerge as an issue.

Insurance companies are not the only fund managers with allocation problems. Private money managers have them too. A manager may run syndications for the public, manage an open-end commingled fund, and also start a series of closed-end funds for pension clients. At any one time, all three could be in the market at once with the latter two in particular looking for the same properties. Other managers run a commingled fund but also have individual pension plans as clients. Who gets the good deals—the fund or the individual client? To a certain extent, any money manager who sets himself up as a real estate manager for individual pension plans runs into a logical dead end. How can he serve the best interests of each client exclusively when they all want to own or mortgage the same thing?

There are also real estate managers who run two commingled funds at once. One may be open-end and thus always in the market, and the other a closed-end fund that buys properties over a certain time period and then withdraws. But while the closed-end fund is out looking for property, it is in direct competition with its open-end sister.

All insurance companies and real estate managers downplay the conflicts among the different accounts they run, claiming such conflicts are not a problem. These conflicts may not be a problem for the real estate managers, but they are one for the pension client who knows that his commingled fund manager does not have all his loyalties in one place. He has several clients who all want the same thing and he has promised each that he will devote his energy exclusively to serving their particular investment needs. But he cannot.

The Problem of Success

There is one conflict-of-interest problem peculiar to insurance company separate accounts. Because of ERISA, separate accounts find it difficult or impossible to buy property that their general accounts hold the mortgage on. PRISA, for example, cannot easily buy a property that the Prudential general account has written a mortgage on, nor can Equitable's Fund Number 8 buy one with an Equitable mortgage. Along similar lines, Aetna's Real Estate Separate Account cannot buy a property developed by Urban Investment and Development Corporation; Urban is an Aetna subsidiary. These are all conflicts of interest forbidden under ERISA and are known as "prohibited transactions."

It is possible for the separate account to buy a property mortgaged by its parent, but only if the account receives a special exemption to do so from the U.S. Department of Labor, which administers the prohibited transaction section of ERISA. The account must file for an exemption for each property, and it can take six months to a year for the Labor Department to approve or deny the request. So, the separate accounts do business with their competitors. PRISA buys properties with Equitable mortgages, and Number 8 buys those mortgaged by Prudential.

This situation puts insurance company separate accounts in a peculiar position. Their general accounts are the leading source of long-term mortgages and real estate capital in the country. They are the nation's largest real estate investors, with billions of dollars of mortgages and strong relationships with many major developers. Those mortgaged properties and their developers are precisely the properties and people an insurance company would want to buy or do business with for its separate account. But it cannot, precisely because the general account is so comfortable with them: ERISA forbids it.

The insurance companies have been too successful at real estate investing for their pension clients' own good. The problem will intensify as the sources of long-term real estate capital disappear and big institutions become an even more important source of money. The possibility of colliding with a "prohibited transaction" will increase.

Lack of Information

Commingled fund managers do not clearly disclose all their fees or explain where their rate-of-return numbers come from. They also refuse to give clients details about the properties held in the fund, identifying properties in fund reports not by name and what they cost but by property type, square footage and location. A property will be identified only as an "863,000 square-foot shopping center, Tampa, Florida," or a "36,000 square-foot multi-use warehouse, La Jolla, California." The fund will also list the cost of these mystery investments. The only things such listings are good for is to figure out what percentage of the fund is invested in industrial, retail or office property and how geographically diversified the fund is.

Equitable's Fund Number 8 used to list the names and purchase prices of its properties in the fund's brochure but took them out in the interests of secrecy. Equitable did not want a potential buyer to know how much a property had cost, presumably because the buyer might then come in with a lower offer. But the lack of property information certainly does not help the pension investor who is supposed to be the principal audience for the brochure.

At most funds, when a pension customer wants further information on the portfolio the managers are closemouthed. The customer may get a list of properties with names and costs, but he certainly will not get an exhaustive report on each property in the portfolio. As mentioned earlier, one pension sponsor interested in investing in a commingled real estate fund asked each fund manager to show him the worst deal in their portfolios. This is a perfectly legitimate question from an investor considering handling over $2 million to $10 million to the fund; he was refused this information by several major funds.

The funds' refusal to disclose information is no reason for pension plans to stop demanding it. Vincent Martin, formerly with the Coldwell Banker funds and now managing partner, TCW Realty Advisors, Los Angeles, advises pension officers to analyze each property in a commingled fund portfolio in depth, as if they were purchasing it directly themselves. He said, "No one can make reasonable and prudent investment decisions without adequate information. The lack of such information is, without a doubt, the biggest single shortcoming of the commingled fund industry today."[10]

Property Management

Commingled managers tend to hire local property management firms to manage all their property in a given town. The rents will get collected and the stairwells cleaned, but the property will not be managed as well as if the employees of the fund were running it. It is axiomatic in the real estate business, on all property, that owners make the best managers. Property management is a nickel and dime business; if a good manager saves five cents a roll on toilet paper by buying it in bulk from a different distributor or really negotiates hard to cut down on services he must provide tenants, he is a valuable asset. Anything that improves a property's cash flow increases the property's value. A $50,000 savings added to cash flow each year and capped at 8 can add another $625,000 in value to a building.

Local managements who are merely hired by the owner have no incentive to kill themselves managing a building. They will get paid no matter what they do. The owner's own people, however, find their salary and possible bonuses tied to how well the building is run; they do a better job. A few commingled funds try to improve the management of their buildings by hiring outside firms and giving them a bonus or a piece of the cash flow depending on how well the properties do. The outside manager thus has an incentive to increase cash flow and be a better manager. He also has an incentive to inflate cash flow by postponing repairs or cutting down on maintenance that should be done but is not obviously needed. The owner will not know that the roof has a leak in it until big water stains appear on the ceiling and he sees them the next time he inspects the building. The manager knew about the leak for months, but by doing nothing, he kept the property's cash flow up and thus increased his own income.

Some commingled funds do joint developments with developers and have them manage the finished buildings. If a developer's own return depends on how well the project is managed, he has an incentive to do a good job. If he has a great deal of his own money in the project, he has the best incentive to manage well. That incentive wanes the less money and less importance he attaches to the project, and if it is low enough, he can manage the property just as badly as any hired outside manager.

Cashing Out

Commingled fund managers give their pension clients a double message on the liquidity of their investment in the fund. On the one hand, the manager insists that real estate is an illiquid investment and that no pension plan should invest in a commingled real estate fund with the intention of cashing out of it several years down the road. On the other hand, if the pension plan wants to withdraw from the fund, the manager will buy the plan's units back, providing the account has enough cash and the manager has no other plans for that money.

To the pension plan, then, an investment in a commingled fund is illiquid— until the day the plan sponsor decides it can be liquid. Fund managers are finding this to be a dangerous attitude to foster.

Until 1982 the funds had no problem with their withdrawal policy because few plans wanted to withdraw. Returns on commingled real estate funds were topping those of stocks and bonds; pension plans wanted to get into the funds, not leave. If a plan did want to withdraw from the fund, all it needed to do was notify the fund manager that it wished to cash out during the next quarter. Since so much new pension money was coming into the account, the manager could easily honor the requests to leave.

In 1982 the tables started to turn. Pension plans decided real estate had peaked or they wanted to diversify into other funds or make real estate investments on their own. Some plans had done so well in property that their percentage of assets invested in real estate had exceeded their targets; they wanted to cut back. About 30 of PRISA's 400 pension clients decided to withdraw $260 million from the fund in the first nine months of 1982. This was only about 6 percent of PRISA's $4.2 billion in assets, yet, for the first time in its history, PRISA could not honor their requests. It had already committed its available cash and had underestimated the amount of cash it would get from new pension contributions to the fund.

This situation would never have occurred if the commingled fund managers had insisted that their funds were illiquid. Once a pension plan was in, it stayed in. If the plan wanted to cash out, it would have to find another plan to purchase its units.

But the commingled funds did not do that. In order to market themselves to a pension community frightened of real estate's illiquidity, they said they would allow them to withdraw their money. At this writing, PRISA, at least, has suffered the consequences.

Pension plan sponsors can be fickle investors. When they sour on an investment, even though they may adjust their portfolio only slightly away from it, their decision will rock that particular part of the investment market simply because the plans are so large. If a $5 billion pension plan changes its asset mix from 10 percent real estate to 8 percent, and all of its real estate holdings are in one or two commingled funds, those funds are going to receive a request for a $100 million withdrawal between them.

Pension plans often move as a herd. Presumably, if the $5 billion pension plan submitted a request to withdraw, other pension plan sponsors would feel the same way and would also be trying to withdraw. The manager might be forced to sell property to honor the requests. Technically, there would be nothing in his contract with his pension clients that said he must honor withdrawals, and he could refuse to do so. But if he did not come up with the money, he would have some angry customers and might cause his existing clients to distrust his promises about liquidity, thus triggering further withdrawal requests.

The Closed-End Solution?

Closed-end managers like to claim that their funds are organized to avoid the withdrawal requests, conflicts of interest, and other problems that bother open-end funds. It is true they have some advantages over open-end funds, but they also have disadvantages and it is not clear that one form of fund is superior to the other.

As the reader may recall, the principal difference between open-end and closed-end funds is that open-end funds always accept new contributions from pension plans but closed-end funds do not. They take in money only during a subscription period, and then are closed to new contributions—hence the source of their name, "closed-end."

The closed-end fund manager buys property intending to sell it all 10 or 12 years down the road and distribute the proceeds to the unitholders. Closed-end funds are designed to die, though the pension clients can vote to postpone property sales and extend the fund's life. Open-end funds never die: they keep on taking in new money and live forever.

The design of closed-end funds gives them one clear advantage over open-end funds. They do not sell their units to pension plans based on appraised values, like open-end funds do. Since all the pension plans that participate in a closed-end fund come in at its beginning, the value of a unit in that fund consists of the total cost of all the property bought by the fund divided by the number of units. No plan buys units whose value is computed using unrealized appreciation, the common procedure at open-end funds. No money changes hands between manager and pension client at this market value, at least going into the fund. But here, the advantages of these funds end.

During the life of a closed-end fund, its manager values the fund's properties the same way that open-end funds do; the closed-end manager has the same valuation problems as his open-end competitors. Like the open-end manager, many closed-end managers compute their management fees as a percentage of appraised value. Like the open-end funds, the clients use these appraised values as their rates of return. And like the open-end funds, the closed-end funds give their clients a mixed message about liquidity. The funds claim they are illiquid, but they allow clients to cash out. The only difference is that some of the closed-end funds make it more difficult than open-end funds to withdraw.

For example, the management of Rosenberg Real Estate Fund will not consider requests to withdraw from one of its funds during the first two years of the fund's existence. After that, the plan that wishes to withdraw can offer its shares to any other pension plan for 60 days. If it finds a buyer, they negotiate the selling price between them. If no one is interested, the units will be offered specifically to subscribers of other RREEF funds for another 60 days. Again, the price will be negotiated if another plan wants to buy. If the units still cannot be sold, the manager of the RREEF fund involved can buy the shares back if he wishes, providing he believes his purchase will not hurt the fund's other unitholders. He can buy the units using the fund's available cash or sell property to raise the money. He repurchases the units at 90 percent of the market value of the shares; the remaining 10 percent, along with its proportionate share of income and appreciation, will not be paid to the seller until the fund is liquidated.

Ultimately, the RREEF manager will cash plans out of the fund at market values based on unrealized appreciation, just like open-end funds do. But he will not do it for the first two years of the fund's life; he will not do it until at least six months after the request is made; and if he does redeem, he will withhold 10 percent of the return until the fund is liquidated. What he is telling his pension clients is that the market value of their interests is the number he posts for them every quarter, unless they want to withdraw their money. Then the market value is only 90 percent of the posted market value. Open-end funds do not have the option of making it so difficult to withdraw, because the only way a client can realize his total return is by cashing out of the fund.

Both closed-end and open-end funds could avoid the problems of withdrawals if they would encourage their pension plan unitholders to buy and sell fund units among each other. A plan that wanted to cash out of one fund and buy into another could buy through such a market. The British pension funds have a small but active secondary market in the units of their commingled funds, most of which are open-end funds.

A secondary market would complicate the lives of the managers of the existing commingled funds. When offering new units to the pension community, they would have to compete with the secondary market in their existing units. They would run the embarrassing chance that their units in the secondary market would sell at a discount to the new ones they were offering. But the commingled funds would never have to worry about liquidity and withdrawal requests; pension plans would be assured of a market for their units, albeit at possibly a poor price.

Closed-end fund managers claim that their funds are better than open-end funds because they self-liquidate. Ten or 12 years after they are created, closed-end funds will start selling off their property and distributing the proceeds to their clients. A pension plan gets its capital back in the normal course of affairs, unlike open-end funds where the client must withdraw to retrieve it. But there is sometimes a catch here: the funds do not always liquidate.

For example, at some closed-end funds run by RREEF, the fund will end at the end of its 10th year unless 60 percent of the pension plans in the fund vote to continue its existence. The fund will then be continued for another two years, at which time another election will be held. If 60 percent vote to extend the fund's life, it goes on for another two years. This process can go on indefinitely, making the closed-end fund a de facto open-end one in a limited sense.

This is a peculiar clause. The pension plans are paying RREEF to buy and run their real estate, yet RREEF is letting them decide when to sell, an important investment decision. By passing the responsibility to liquidate the fund on to the clients, RREEF must believe that selling a property at the right time is not all that important. From a marketing viewpoint, this policy makes a great deal of sense. If pension plans want to stay in the fund, why should RREEF liquidate it? It will only have to start up a new closed-end fund and hope to recapture these clients as customers. Why not just keep them happy by maintaining the fund as long as they want?

This may make sense for marketing the fund, but not for handling its investments. As long as real estate is doing well, the pension plans will vote to keep the fund going. But as real estate goes into one of its slumps and the rents from the funds' properties stagnate, the plans could vote to liquidate, forcing RREEF to sell into a depressed market. Pension plans as a whole have a terrible sense of timing. One only has to remember how many of them sold huge chunks of their stock portfolios at the bottom of the market in 1974, entirely missing the 1975 bull market, one of the biggest runs in stock market history. These are the same people who are going to decide when to sell off office buildings and shopping centers, investments they know far less about than stocks.

Certainly, RREEF needs some flexibility on when it can liquidate the fund. If the fund's 10-year life span comes to an end in the middle of a real estate depression, RREEF does not want to be forced to sell just because of an arbitrary date requirement. But RREEF could insist on giving itself the option to wait for a better market to sell. There is no investment need to drag the clients into the decision.

A pension plan can cash out of the RREEF fund even when 60 percent of its cohorts have voted to extend the fund's life. RREEF says it will allow such dissidents to withdraw from the fund without penalty; they will be paid the full market value of their units. But such market values are based on appraisals and unrealized appreciation, just like those at open-end funds. The plan that wants to withdraw is stuck with the same problem it had tried to avoid by going into a closed-end fund in the first place: it is being paid back its capital based on appraised valuations.

In addition to the problems they share with open-end funds, closed-end funds have some unique problems that put them at a disadvantage with their open-end competitors. Closed-end managers lack flexibility to buy and sell property when they wish. Each fund is open for pension contributions for only a fixed period of time and then closed to new money; the manager then uses the proceeds to buy property. That money is all he will receive to invest and he must invest it at about the time he receives it, regardless of the market. If the closed-end manager comes across a desirable investment in the middle of the fund's life, he cannot buy it because he lacks the money. He is also required to sell all the property at or around the liquidation date, regardless of the market at that time, unless he can convince his clients to postpone the process. An open-end fund doesn't have these problems. It can buy or sell property when it wishes; it is always open to new contributions from pension plans and is not required to self-liquidate.

When a pension plan buys into a closed-end trust, the trust has not yet bought any property, so the plan sponsor does not know what properties he is actually buying. The smaller closed-end funds also lack the diversification of the large open-end ones because the closed-end funds lack the money to buy as many properties. Small open-end funds have the same problem, but they at least have the option of growing larger and improving their diversification.

A closed-end manager can work around his flexibility and diversification problems by continually opening new closed-end funds and urging participants in the older ones to buy into the new. But this is more cumbersome than just running an open-end fund. In the long run, the organization of the closed-end funds does not make them intrinsically any better or worse an investment than open-end funds.

THE ONLY CHOICE

From the above discussion, it is clear that commingled funds of all types are far from the perfect vehicle for pension plans to invest in real estate. Their fees are often impossible to determine and compare. They have simple-minded investment strategies and refuse to disclose details of what they are investing in. They are beset with constant conflicts of interest with their clients. Their rate-of-return numbers are based on real estate appraisals, and they allow plans to buy into the fund, at least open-end funds, at unit values that are likely to be inflated. Over all hangs the chance that if the real estate market falls sharply, the funds will be hit by problems they were not designed to handle. They are not perfect.

But how big are these problems for a plan with a true, long-term investment outlook and no desire to get actively involved in real estate? If the plan intends to keep its money in a commingled fund for 10 or 15 years, it does not make much difference if it slightly overpays to get into the fund or must take a year or two to cash out at a decent price. It is highly unlikely that any financial panic that hits commingled funds is going to sink them. These funds are not the REITs of 1974. Though their operational problems are annoying, they are by no means fatal. For many pension plans, commingled funds are the only way they can invest in property. If it is a choice between commingled funds or no real estate investing at all, the commingled funds, warts and all, are better than nothing. The diversification that real estate offers a pension plan simply outweighs the funds' problems.

For small and medium-sized pension plans, commingled funds are the only choice; the plans lack the assets to invest in real estate effectively on their own. They are stuck with commingled funds, and the truly small plans, those with only $500,000 in total assets, do not even have that. Most commingled funds have minimum contributions of at least $100,000, although a few accept as little as $50,000. Using a conservative rule of thumb that a pension plan should put 10 percent of its assets into real estate, this $50,000 minimum means that plans with less than $500,000 in assets are shut out of the commingled fund market.

These plans could invest in real estate through public syndications designed specifically for small pension plans and which accept minimum contributions of $5,000 or even $2,000. Syndications are limited partnerships, and the fate of the pension plans as limited partners is wholly tied to the abilities of the general partner, the "manager," to run the pool. The reputation and track record of the syndication manager is the most important thing to check in going into a syndication.

Syndications are a different world from commingled real estate funds and beyond the scope of this book. There are far more of them than commingled funds. Outside the largest half-dozen public syndicators, a pension sponsor is far more likely to run into goofy general partners and poorly selected investments than he would in the commingled fund world. At least at commingled funds there is the comfort of knowing that fund managers are the leading banks, insurance companies and real estate firms in the country. It is unlikely they are going to do something flagrantly disloyal to their clients.

Syndications are expensive: it is typical for the investor to pay 30 percent of his contribution to the syndication in fees. Unless a plan sponsor is investing with a well-known syndicator with a strong track record, he is better off waiting to invest in real estate until his plan is large enough to enter a commingled fund.

PICKING A FUND

Given all the problems commingled funds have, how should a pension sponsor choose one, or two, for his plan?

In making their choices, pension sponsors should remember that the vast majority of commingled funds have the same investment philosphy, structure and problems. With few exceptions, they all look alike. What distinguishes one from the other is the quality of the staff.

At this writing, there are roughly 135 funds. In trying to analyze them, the pension sponsor should avoid the trap of organizing them by investment performance, with the fund with the "best" record on top followed by the others in descending order. Fund performance numbers are largely make-believe and performance numbers among funds cannot be compared. Some funds' rate-of-return figures include fees, others do not. Some figure return on gross assets, some on assets after fees, or after the assets of the short-term portfolio have been deducted. Who can tell which fund has had the best performance? Hire two consultants to unravel these mysteries, and they will come up with exactly opposite conclusions.

The sponsor's best bet is to look at one of the quarterly comparisons of some of the largest funds put out by pension consulting firms and reporting services. The sponsor will end up with all the data on the larger and more well-known funds in one place, as well as some ideas about how they differ. It will be a great deal cheaper and more enlightening than hiring a pension consultant to study the commingled funds and make a recommendation. The consultant is probably starting with one of the reporting service's numbers anyway.

With all this data there is really no systematic way to pick the best fund, or eliminate one fund and choose another. Your decision will be based more on impressions and rules of thumb than numerical analyses of the funds. For example, one sponsor set down 14 criteria to sort through managers. His plan intended to invest $200 million in real estate before 1993; he wanted to make certain that the commingled funds he picked were large enough to handle his contributions. He screened out managers using criteria such as their size, the number of professionals on staff, and how geographically diversified their holdings were. In addition, a sponsor should pick a commingled fund that has a minimal number of the conflicts and problems plaguing the industry. The fund should also have an investment policy that is more aggressive than buy and hold. The buy-and-hold philosophy will certainly make money over the long run, but a more aggressive strategy will make much more.

In selecting a fund, the most important thing to consider is the reputation of the fund manager and his track record at managing real estate investments. You are going to be giving him your plan's money, and he will have complete power over what will be done with it; give it to someone you have a good reason to trust. This usually means giving it to a fund run by an insurance company or real estate firm that has more than a 10-year history of long-term mortgage lending or real estate investing. Or give it to a new firm made up of people with substantive, appropriate experience—people who created a history of successful real estate investing at an insurance company or property firm. People are the most important part of any real estate firm or commingled fund. They make the decisions that make the fund money. Do not worry if the fund is an open-end or closed-end fund. If the people who run it are good, the fund's structure will make no difference in the long run.

Avoid funds sponsored by banks, unless the funds they offer specialize in short-term or intermediate-term real estate loans. Banks are short- to intermediate-term lenders, not long-term equity investors, and the two are separate businesses. With few exceptions, they do not have strong real estate staffs to draw upon. The banking community's last major foray into the investment property business was with the REITs in the early 1970s: we all know what happened to them then.

Some banks have realized that they do not have the experience or staff to run a commingled fund that buys properties; they have teamed up with real estate firms to do so. The bank serves as trustee, and the real estate firm runs the real estate. These could be good funds to invest in as long as the real estate firm is really making the decisions. If the firm must run its deals past the bank for approval, avoid the fund. It is really a bank fund in disguise.

Avoid new funds that have been started within the last three to five years by investment bankers, securities firms or money managers without prior, demonstrated records as real estate principals. Lacking such experience, they are merely trying to supply what they deem to be in vogue. These people know nothing about the real estate business. Unless their funds are staffed with well-known real estate people from insurance companies or major property firms, you will be letting them practice investing in real estate with your plan's money.

Do not give your money to a manager who is running both closed-end and open-end funds at once, unless the funds have dramatically different investment objectives. For example, one could buy property and the other write mortgages. Without different strategies, the fund you are in will be in competition with a sister fund for the property the manager unearths.

Weed out funds that have shown operating losses for more than one year out of the last five. At this writing, we have just come out of a period in which real estate values soared. It would take a real knack for mismanagement to lose money consistently in that environment.

Pick a manager who is willing and eager to tell you anything you want to know about the properties in the portfolio. Ask for a full, detailed explanation of all the deals in the fund, particularly the one he considers the fund's biggest problem. Ask what he intends to do with it. If he refuses to discuss it or any of the other properties in the portfolio, or puts you off in any way, avoid the fund. When you are planning to give him millions of dollars in cash and full discretion as to what will be done with it, you have a right to ask as many questions as you wish.

Ask for a full explanation of every fee his fund charges and an estimate of how much such indeterminate costs, such as appraisals and legal fees, will run when he bills them to the fund.

Look for managers who pay themselves incentive fees rather than a flat charge based on assets. Their goal is then to make money for you, the fund, and themselves, not just to increase the size of the fund's assets. These managers will work harder for you. There are few commingled funds that pay themselves incentive fees, and the fact that so many do not is not necessarily a reason to rule them out if they have other attractive features. But incentive fees are a sign that the fund is likely to be more aggressive, and its managers better investors, than their competitors with fixed fees.

In reviewing any fund, talk to other pension sponsors with money in the fund and ask them about staff turnover. If each time you call you are getting someone new to talk to because his predecessor has left, avoid the fund. If it cannot keep its staff happy, the staff will not be doing a good job running your money.

The best managers have an investment strategy that goes beyond the buy-and-hold philosophy of most funds. They have actually sold properties over the last five years for intelligent reasons, such as the belief that the value of a specific property had peaked and its future rent increases were likely to be disappointing. The managers then took the sale proceeds and bought what they considered undervalued property.

Avoid funds that refuse to use leverage and buy properties entirely with cash, arguing that it is safer to do so. You need all the positive leverage and well-structured deals you can find in your fund. You do not need a manager who throws away one of the greatest benefits of property ownership out of some misguided sense that all leverage is inappropriate for pension plans. Also select a manager that distributes cash flow to his clients if they wish. You do not need to be stuck with years of paper profits only.

The best managers do their own property management. They refuse to contract out the work to local management firms, and by their refusal they add thousands of dollars each year to their properties' cash flow.

A plan sponsor who analyzes funds in this detail will find that the realm of acceptable funds shrinks appreciably. Only a handful meet most of these standards. The rest are not dangerous or badly run, they are just mediocre, with all the problems that infest the industry infesting them as well. But a plan sponsor who does not want to exhaust himself analyzing funds can certainly give his money to a large, well-known fund after a cursory look at the competition. His investment will most likely be safe. It will not be superbly managed, but it will not be badly run either. It will diversify his portfolio into real estate without his having to learn anything about property investing.

Most pension plans will limit their real estate investing to several million dollars invested in a commingled fund. It is the most painless way to go. But some sponsors will want to go beyond the funds. Perhaps they want to make property 20 or 30 percent of their portfolios. Or a sponsor may realize that his plan is going to get so large in the future that even 10 percent of assets in property will mean a $500 million real estate portfolio. Other sponsors may want more out of real estate than commingled funds can offer. They want more aggressive investing, bigger returns, and more control.

All these plans should consider investing in property directly, either by hiring an investment advisor to handle their account individually or by setting up their own in-house real estate staff. There are many problems with running your own real estate portfolio and although a handful of plans can prosper at it, many will find they are unable to handle direct investing. Nevertheless, a growing number of large pension plans that have invested in commingled funds for several years are now trying their hand at investing on their own.

NOTES

1. Linda Sojacy, "Open-end realty funds beat all other indices last year," *Pensions & Investment Age* (April 26, 1982), p. 2.

2. "Top 100 firms run $955 billion in assets," *Pensions & Investment Age* (April 4, 1983), p. 23.

3. "Real Estate—Profile Statistics At-A-Glance," *Pensions & Investment Age* (September 13, 1982), p. 23.

4. Among these funds are the following: a series of closed-end funds sponsored by Aldrich, Eastman & Waltch and State Street Bank in Boston; a participating mortgage fund run by Abacus Realty Advisors and American National Bank in Chicago; an open-end fund run by The Center Companies (formerly Dayton-Hudson Properties) and First Bank Minneapolis; a closed-end fund run by Bedford Associates, Inc. and Kemper Financial Services of Chicago.

5. Julie Rohrer, "PRISA's Surprising Shortfall," *Institutional Investor* 16 (June 1982), pp. 119–20.

6. "Real Estate—Profile Statistics At-A-Glance," p. 23.

7. Nancy G. Boyland, *Real Estate Funds for Pension Plans* (New York: Audit Investments, Inc., 1981). I went through the data for the individual funds to reach this conclusion.

8. Thomas Richardson, Jr., "Examining Realty Performance," *Pensions & Investment Age* (June 8, 1981), p. 22.

9. "Melnikoff predicts by 1989 $200 billion will be in realty," *Pensions & Investment Age* (March 15, 1982), p. 30.

10. Vincent Martin, Jr., "How Reasonable Are your Manager's Valuation Techniques?" *Pension World* (September 22, 1980), p. 99.

9 | DIRECT INVESTING

When institutional investors go to buy a building, the first thing they should do is hire an expert, experts agree.
—*from an article in* Pensions & Investment Age, *July 20, 1981*

The best way for pension funds to invest in property is to get in there and try to do it on your own.
Take your lumps and try to make some money.
—*a commingled fund manager turned real estate developer*

BEYOND COMMINGLED FUNDS

Though commingled real estate funds have their problems, the majority of pension plans will continue to use them as their principal method of investing in real estate. There is no easier and more efficient way to invest in property without knowing anything about it.

But some pension plans will want to go beyond commingled funds. They may want more control over their investments or seek a better rate of return. At this writing, there are more than 125 pension plans with assets of $1 billion or more and in less than 10 years, their numbers should top 200. Some of these giant plans will want to put 15 to 30 percent of their assets into real estate, but their sponsors cannot see investing $500 million or $1 billion through commingled funds. They will want to run their real estate themselves—either by hiring a firm to manage their accounts or by handling their property investments themselves in-house.

The first thing these plans will discover is that they have few role models to follow, particularly if they want to invest in-house. So few plans have tried to invest directly that any plan that does will have to cut its own path. This should not discourage a plan from investing directly, but it does mean that a plan's trustees and staff must be committed to real estate. They must be willing to work out the problems they will inevitably run into. Before they invest their first dollar, they will have to hire a staff to acquire and manage their property; it will take a good deal of time and money to assemble such a group.

There is no model method for pension plans to invest directly in property, no right way. There are big plans and small ones doing it, public plans and private ones. There are plans that buy regional shopping centers and others that do only credit-leaseback deals. There are mortgage lenders and at least one plan whose entire real estate program is leasebacks on fast-food restaurants.

To the question "Should we invest in real estate directly?" the answer must be "It depends on how much you want to invest and what type of real estate you're talking about." For example, if the trustees envision their plan becoming a purchaser of shopping centers and office buildings, they must have $75 million to $100 million a year to invest in real estate. They simply could not afford the high-quality staff they would need to buy such properties if they did not have at least that much to invest. Such properties cost $10 million to $50 million apiece, and the fund would need a good deal of money to adequately diversify.

This investment strategy cuts out all plans but the very largest from directly investing in property. But a plan does not have to opt for this ambitious approach. It could, for example, decide to invest only in leasebacks secured by property occupied by credit tenants. A plan could have as little as $5 million a year to invest in property and do so through credit leasebacks. Credit-leaseback deals can be very small, $1 million to $2 million. The security of the deal rests on the quality of the tenant, not the property itself; the plan would not need an expensive real estate staff. It would still want to be careful not to overpay for the property involved. But it could get by with a credit analyst who has worked for a mortgage banker or insurance company and done such deals before.

Whether a plan buys regional shopping centers or does leasebacks on ware-houses leased to General Motors, it must have a real estate investment philosophy. The trustees must decide if the plan will make mortgages on local warehouses, buy suburban office buildings, or become a credit lender. The plan must specialize.

The trustees should make this decision based on how much money the plan has to invest in property, how involved the trustees want to get in managing property, and how much risk they wish to take. Credit leasebacks are ideal for a small investment program where the trustees do not want to get too involved in management. Credit leasebacks require little management since the tenant typically does everything, and leasebacks are less risky than owning a multi-tenant office building. If the tenant breaks his lease and moves, the landlord will still collect his rent because the former tenant is typically financially strong enough to pay his rent on the space. But in exchange for these benefits, the deal's rate of return will be lower than that of equity deals.

In addition to devising an investment strategy, the plan trustees must also decide how they are going to invest. To invest directly, the plan either hires an investment advisor or it uses its own staff. If it uses its own staff, the trustees will have to learn enough about property to hire the staff and supervise them as they buy and manage property. If the trustees hire an advisor, he will handle everything and they will not have to learn a thing about property. Most plans whose trustees choose to invest directly choose to hire an advisor for exactly this reason. They want to avoid the problems of setting up their own operation.

Typically, such trustees are dissatisfied with the commingled funds but do not want to take the big step to set up an in-house operation. Instead, they hire an advisor and split their real estate holdings between him and a commingled fund. They do not consider the real estate investment strategy they want. They simply hire an advisory firm and let the firm make that decision for them.

A good investment advisor will force them to draw up an investment strategy that he can follow. But with so many people jumping into the advisory business, many will just give the trustees what they think they want, regardless of how appropriate it is for the fund. The result will be a potpourri of properties scattered around the country. They will be difficult to keep track of much less manage well.

THE ADVISORS

How They Work

The proof that a growing number of plans are giving their money to advisory firms can be shown by the great increase in their ranks. In 1979, one pension sponsor interested in hiring a real estate advisor came up with only three firms that would do it as a fiduciary. They were the Boston Company Real Estate Counsel in Boston; Merrill Lynch, Hubbard in New York; and McMorgan & Company in Palo Alto, California. In September 1982, *Pensions & Investment Age* magazine surveyed real estate advisors for pension plans and counted 151.[1] Clearly, the era of the outside real estate expert has arrived. It sometimes seems as if every large real estate firm, mortgage banker, real estate broker, and consultant has started a subsidiary for the sole purpose of managing real estate accounts as a fiduciary for pension funds. The firms often register themselves with the Securities & Exchange Commission as investment advisors and plan to run real estate portfolios for their pension clients the same way stock and bond managers run the funds' securities portfolios.

For example, in hiring a bond manager, a pension plan will give the manager a fixed amount of money and then allow him full discretion as to how to invest it, given the manager's investment style. The manager may clear some investment decisions with the pension fund, but for the most part, he makes the investments on his own and simply reports to the pension client each quarter on how the portfolio is doing.

The real estate managers often operate the same way. The pension client gives them $5 million or $10 million a year to invest in real estate. The manager picks the investments and, after a review by the fund's board of trustees, makes them. He manages the properties, decides when to buy and sell, and reports his results to the plan each quarter. Like the bond manager, the real estate manager collects an annual fee for this service, based on the amount of assets he manages for the fund.

Advisory fees vary, but typically they are based on the number of properties the advisor buys or sells or the number of mortgages he writes; he also charges a fee based on the amount of assets he runs. One advisor, for example, charges 1 percent of a property's book value when he buys or sells the property, plus his out-of-pocket expenses. If he makes mortgages for his client, he charges an annual administrative fee of one-eighth of 1 percent of their value. If he buys property, the annual fee is one-half of 1 percent of the properties' value. This administration fee does not include the cost of managing the individual buildings themselves, which is handled by on-site managers and billed directly to the property. This advisor bases all his fees on the property's book value, not appraised value, like commingled funds. But there are advisors who charge on the basis of appraised value, since it is so acceptable to pension plans in commingled funds.

Advisory fees vary more from advisor to advisor than commingled fees do. They are negotiated between the advisor and his pension client and are based on what the client wants the advisor to do for him. Some advisors charge a flat annual retainer but most charge fees based on some measure of assets under management.

Like the pension plan's securities managers, the real estate manager will take fiduciary responsibility for the investments he makes. This is of overwhelming importance to pension fund boards of trustees. If the real estate sours and the fund is sued for imprudent investing, the investment manager, not the board, takes the blame. All the board needs to show to exonerate itself is that it acted prudently in selecting and monitoring the manager, not that the individual investments were prudent in themselves.

The trustees' desire to shield themselves from the possibly perverse consequences of real estate investing is one of the main reasons these advisory firms exist. They promise protection. Developers and other real estate people who have talked with pension funds about possible joint ventures and financing know that the one thing that inevitably kills any deal is that the pension officer refuses to accept the responsibility for making the deal. He may love the deal, the trustees may love the deal, but unless they can find a third party who will serve as a fiduciary and who also loves the deal, they refuse to do it. They want a fiduciary to approve it. Since many real estate people do not want to be fiduciaries, the pension funds do not do business with them. The man with the deal has to submit it to the pension fund's real estate advisor who will then submit it to the fund.

Ironically, then, by hiring advisors pension funds are not showing that they are especially committed to real estate. They are committed enough to want to do better than commingled funds, but not enough to figure out if hiring an investment advisor is really the best way to do it. Many plan sponsors view hiring an advisor as just another way of diversifying their real estate holdings. They will hold money in both commingled funds and an account with a manager.

The Advantages and Disadvantages

Hiring an advisor offers a plan certain advantages over an investment in commingled funds. The pension plan trustees have greater control over what properties the plan invests in. They can instruct the manager to invest only in certain types of properties and to clear every transaction with them. This is a far cry from commingled funds where participants have only a vague idea what they are investing in.

The trustees need not worry about buying into commingled funds at inflated unit values. The' plan is now buying its own properties, and it buys them at actual cost.

Hiring an advisor is just as convenient as giving the plan's money to a commingled fund. The advisor will handle everything for the plan, and his administrative costs may be higher or lower than those of commingled funds, depending on how many clients he has to spread them over, how efficiently he runs his office, and what the market will bear.

For it to make sense for a pension plan to hire an advisor, the trustees must believe at least one of two things: that the advisor will make a better return with less risk than a commingled fund, or that if he is not a better investor, he is at least different. They must believe that hiring him will diversify the plan's real estate holdings.

Pension plans have been hiring advisors only since 1980, so there is no 10-year record available showing whether these advisors really outperform commingled funds or diversify a plan's investments. But from the way these advisory firms are set up and the type of people that run them, there is no reason to believe that they will outperform commingled funds. In some cases, hiring an advisor may actually work against a plan's best interests. The advisory firms are plagued with the same problems that beset commingled funds and have a few unique problems of their own.

Commingled funds and plan advisors share many of the same characteristics. Both charge their clients fixed fees for their services, and these fees eat up a substantial percentage of a property's cash flow—16 to 20 percent, or even more. Before a plan can collect any cash flow from its properties, it must pay the manager his fee, be it an investment advisor or a commingled fund.

Fees paid to advisors appear to be higher than those paid to commingled funds, but not always. Fees vary among advisors and commingled funds and are difficult to compare. Those individual advisors who do charge an annual management fee based on the amount of assets under management charge 1 to 2 percent. Commingled funds generally charge from 1 to 1¼ percent of assets.

Sometimes advisors will compute their management fees the same way as commingled funds. In these cases, all the fee-related problems that beset commingled funds also beset advisors. The advisor's fee will be based on the market value of the portfolio, which is determined by a real estate appraiser. But the advisor hires the appraiser; an agent of the advisor is setting the value that the advisor's fee will be based on. The higher the value, the larger the advisor's fee and the more business the appraiser can expect from him, just like at the commingled funds.

A pension plan with an advisor must battle the same conflicts of interest that commingled funds fight. The advisor is in the business of finding real estate for pension plans, and his pension clients must compete with each other for the deals he unearths. Which plan gets which deal? Which plan gets the best deals?

The fine points of investment strategy aside, all his pension clients are most likely eager to acquire the same type of deals.

This is the same dilemma that afflicts commingled funds run by insurance companies. The insurer must decide whether to put deals into its own account or into the commingled fund and, in fact, will have an easier time of making this decision than the advisors to pension plans. The insurer's general account can do riskier deals than its commingled fund, and that gives an insurance company at least one basis for dividing up deals between the two. But the advisor's pension clients are most likely all looking for the same thing, giving him no basis for allocation.

In several areas, a pension plan with an advisor is at a definite disadvantage to one invested in a commingled fund. For example, it can take months for an advisor to put together a real estate portfolio. He has to go out and find the deals. But a pension plan can instantly invest in real estate through a commingled fund by just buying a few units in it.

Another problem stems from the control that the plan trustees have over the advisor. They have hired the advisor because they wanted more control over their portfolio. But sometimes they decide to exercise it by second-guessing the advisor's decisions. The advisor wants to keep them as a client, so he listens to their opinions and tries to accommodate their prejudices. The plan ends up with an investment strategy that is an amalgam of the advisor's professional advice and the trustees' half-baked opinions. Those who know the least about real estate, the trustees, are essentially setting the policy. The portfolio will not be a disaster, because the advisor will not risk his reputation by presiding over one. But the plan will end up with a mediocre portfolio and investment performance, and to get that, they might as well have invested in a typical commingled fund.

This problem is not unique to real estate advisors. Stock and bond advisors and other investment counselors run into strong-willed and intrusive clients who will not listen to the advice they have just bought.

But the greatest and most obvious disadvantage to hiring an advisor is that an individually run portfolio is not as diversified as a commingled fund. A $10 million real estate portfolio run by an advisor may contain one office building, but the same investment in a commingled fund can give a plan an interest in dozens of properties. The portfolio run by the advisor is definitely more risky.

If that office building is hit by a hurricane or the major tenant walks out on his lease, the pension plan has $10 million of problem assets to handle. If the pension plan held that same building in a commingled fund with 19 other properties, perhaps only $500,000 of the plan's real estate investment would be in trouble. The other $9.5 million would be invested in the 19 other properties that were doing fine. It works the other way, too. That office building could be such a superb investment that its return dwarfs anything the plan could have made in a commingled fund.

If a plan invests in real estate with an advisor, it takes more risk than if it invests in a commingled fund. The trustees should have reason to believe that the advisor will make more money for their plan than a commingled fund would. But as will be argued, there is no reason to believe that. An advisor would have to be a consistently better investor than the people who run commingled funds, and there is no reason to assume that he would be. Nor will hiring an advisor to run only part of a plan's real estate give the plan the benefits of a new or different investment strategy, since most advisors invest exactly like commingled funds. They buy high-quality income property entirely for cash.

It is, therefore, possible that a pension plan that hires both an advisor and a commingled fund to run its money could turn in a consistently worse investment performance than a plan that had invested only in commingled funds. The plan with the advisor is assuming more risk by hiring him but is not getting compensated by a better return. Because the advisor has an undiversified portfolio compared to that of an existing commingled fund, his returns are more likely to be worse.

The larger the portfolio a plan gives to an individual advisor, the more diversified that portfolio can be. A $100 million portfolio is more diversified than one of $10 million. But as argued in more detail later, both plans would be better diversified and show better long-term returns by investing in commingled funds.

People and Fees

For a real estate portfolio run by an advisor to outperform commingled funds, it must be managed by better investors than those at the funds. But these more talented people will not become advisors to pension plans because they can make more money and have more control over their lives by being in business for themselves. How pension plans pay their real estate advisors discourages the better people from entering the business.

Pension plans pay their advisors to find and manage property for them. Sometimes an advisor is paid a flat annual fee and other times, some percentage of the amount of money he invests. Either way, it does not encourage him to be a shrewd investor on behalf of his client.

If the advisor collects a flat fee each year, he has no incentive to invest well because no matter what he does he will be paid the same. If he is paid based on how much he invests, he still has no incentive to invest well. He is only encouraged to make as many investments as he can since he is paid on the quantity, not the quality, of what he does.

These fee structures do not tie the advisor's compensation to the amount of money he makes for his client; he will handle the properties well enough to keep his client happy, but he will not make the extra effort to turn a fair investment into a good one. What is the point? He does not benefit.

Fee compensation schedules work adequately for a pension plan's stock and bond managers, but for real estate advisors, they are disaster. The best real estate investors work toward the day when they no longer work for someone for a salary, but get a piece, if not all, of every deal they do. They do not want fees, they want to own. If an investor is any good at investing, which usually means he is adept at buying property, someone will bankroll his efforts. They will set him up in business and split the profits with him. Good acquisition people are rare, and there are far more investors with money to put into property than good acquisition people to do it for them.

How do pension plans stack up in the eyes of these talented people? As one put it:

You may think that a fee of 1 percent of assets is a lot of money, and it is to many people. But I can do a deal and make 20 percent on my money the day I go into it. Now why should I sell my ability to make 20 percent on a deal to a pension fund for 1 percent? It makes no sense.

The real estate advisory company and its pension clients find themselves stuck with the marginal people who cannot find someone to bankroll them. They lack the expertise, the experience, the connections or the motivation to go out on their own. Instead they work for banks, insurance companies and pension plans.

Some of these people will be the movers and shakers of the real estate world in 10 or 15 years. They are just young now and are picking up experience working for an institution. They will leave as soon as they have stopped learning and someone else will pay them more money. But most are simply bureaucrats.

A man who runs an executive-search firm for real estate people once said there were two types of people in real estate, the entrepreneurs and the bureaucrats. Both types could make a great deal of money working for entrepreneurs, he said. But neither would make much working for other bureaucrats. When compared to what a really talented real estate investor can do, bureaucrats working for other bureaucrats will not make money for the client, either.

I do not mean to imply that these bureaucrats are bad investors, fools or incompetents, or that they do not behave in a professional or responsible manner. Like any group of people, many are proud of their work, competent, and conscientious. But they are no better or worse than the thousands of other real estate investors who are competing for deals with them.

It is illogical to hire such people to directly invest in real estate for a pension plan, when these same types of people already staff the larger commingled funds. Such funds always hold more properties than a plan could buy on its own; the funds are more diversified. So a plan's investment in a commingled fund should always outperform its advisory account over the long run, such as 10 or 20 years. Given the same quality of investment expertise, a diversified portfolio will outperform a less-diversified one.

If the advisory firm were truly staffed by better investors than ran the commingled fund, this would not be the case. The advisory firm would be likely to outperform the commingled fund over the long run. But the advisory firms cannot attract any better personnel than those that staff commingled funds, because neither offers the right kind of compensation.

It is difficult to offer incentive compensation to managers because ERISA forbids them from benefiting from investments they make for the plan. But as mentioned in chapter 3, some commingled fund managers already collect incentive compensation; they share in the cash flow of the properties owned by the fund. This area of the law is changing. A pension plan or advisor with good legal advice should be able to structure such an arrangement without violating the protections provided plans through fiduciary law or ERISA.

But even if pension plans did change their compensation schedules, they would still be at a disadvantage to other investors competing for real estate talent. No other moneyed investor requires his acquisition person to assume fiduciary responsibility for any investment he makes. He is exposed to the possibility of being sued for imprudent investing by thousands of pension plan participants and retirees he does not even know. A pension plan might be able to persuade him to bear that risk if they paid him well enough. But it is unlikely that the discussion between plan and advisor would ever get to that level since plans that hire advisory firms do not see anything wrong with the present fee and fiduciary arrangements.

Actually, people who own the advisory firm are the ones who really make the money. They add new pension clients without adding more real estate staff and can make 20 percent on their money, too, just like the real estate investor quoted earlier. They make their money off the fees their pension clients pay, not the profits of the property they buy for them. Marketing the firm to pension plans is more lucrative and important than acquiring property for existing accounts. From the client's point of view, this emphasis is all wrong.

Who Are These Advisors?

The real estate advisory business is very new. With the exception of companies that have managed commingled funds for several years, none of these firms has any track record in managing pension money. In fact, no one in the pension business has any idea who many of the people who run these firms are. The firms just start into business overnight and are staffed with people with real estate backgrounds. Anyone can announce his willingness to become a fiduciary and offer his services as a real estate advisor to a pension plan. You do not have to know what you are doing to be willing to take fiduciary responsibility for it.

A pension plan is far more vulnerable to the whims of its real estate advisor than to those of its stock and bond managers because real estate is illiquid. The vulnerability shows when a plan becomes dissatisfied with its advisor and decides to dismiss the firm and hire another. When a plan fires a securities manager and hires another, the new manager can restructure the former manager's portfolio to his own investment strategy in just days. He can simply sell the stocks or bonds he dislikes on the market and buy up his favorites instead.

With a real estate advisor, it could take the new manager months just to figure out what the fund had in its portfolio. Established securities managers who work for pension plans keep detailed records on their portfolios, but no one knows how the new real estate advisors keep records. If the previous advisor kept bad records, the new one will have no idea how the buildings have been maintained or who the tenants are and what their leases look like. He will have no inkling of the problems peculiar to each building.

Then there is the problem of what happens when the pension fund's advisor decides to leave the business; the firm does not want to run real estate for pension funds anymore. The company's owners want to develop condominiums, or do syndications for doctors, or simply dissolve their firm and go their own ways. The pension sponsor will be in the same position as if he had fired his pension manager. He will be out in the market looking for a firm to take over a portfolio of properties he and his trustees neither understand nor care to understand.

There is one final and more subtle problem that large pension plans face if they are using an advisor and competing for large properties. Sometimes, they will be cut off from some of the best deals.

The market for big real estate deals, such as $15 million office buildings, is really very small. Perhaps 60 people and firms across the country would have the money to buy such buildings, and all these people are competing for the same properties. If one of those organizations starts representing a large pension fund as an advisor, that firm's role changes. It runs real estate for pension funds but still buys deals for itself. So its competitors treat it gingerly. As one big real estate investor and developer put it:

If I want to offer a deal to the pension fund that firm represents, the advisor is going to be looking at my numbers and saying yea or nay on whether the fund does that deal.
But he is also motivated by the fact that if he says nay, he may be able to undercut me and get the deal himself for his own corporate account.
So why should I show my work product to my competitor? I won't. Life's too short.

This man explained that he had no problem dealing with the pension fund's advisor if the advisor was representing the fund and both he and the advisor were competing for the same deal. But when it came to submitting his own deals for possible sale to the fund, he simply refused to take the chance of running it through an advisor. He would take his deals elsewhere, to the other 59 investors perhaps. There he can get a sense of whether or not they want the deal without having to spell it all out to them and risk the chance of having it stolen. The pension plan, after hiring a well-known and well-connected advisor, could find itself shut off from a good number of the deals it hired the advisor to find in the first place.

A fund could avoid this problem by hiring an advisor that handles only pension accounts. But if it handles only pension accounts, it is likely to be a small and unknown firm without the connections that the larger and well-established real estate firm has. Either way, the pension plan is not getting access to all the big, lucrative deals that it wanted.

Is It Ever Right to Hire an Advisor?

Given the problems that pension plans have with advisors, is there ever reason to hire one? Rarely. The chief objection is that advisors invest as commingled funds do, with the same level of skill. But because advisors do not run diversified portfolios, they increase the risk that a plan takes in real estate without increasing return. Therefore, they are likely to show a lower return than commingled funds, and a plan should prefer the commingled fund to them.

But there are exceptions.

One would be if the advisor somehow did have a superior real estate staff. There are probably some advisory firms staffed by people who are truly talented in real estate acquisitions and management, but who like the low-key pace of working for such a firm. They are good at what they do; they just prefer a quieter life than doing their own deals would require. A firm with such people would do a fine job for a pension plan. The problem is finding them. These firms are rare and it would take intimate knowledge of an advisory firm to know that the plan had found a winner.

The advisor's fee structure sometimes points out good firms. If the advisor has tied his compensation to the performance of the plan's properties, he has the incentive to manage them aggressively and not spend his time out looking for other clients. If the people who manage property for this firm also have their compensation tied to the performance of the client's property, this firm would be worth exploring. At least they are encouraging behavior that benefits the existing clients.

A pension plan might hire an advisor because that firm is offering the plan some type of investment that it could not get at a large commingled fund. An advisor might specialize in landsale-leasebacks or wraparound mortgages on apartment properties. But there are few advisors really investing in a way that is substantially different from what the commingled funds offer.

Some observers argue that hiring an advisor is a good way for a pension plan to learn about real estate investing with the eventual goal of investing in property itself with its own in-house staff. The advisor is really just a tool for learning.

I would argue that the only way to learn about investing in real estate in-house is to invest in-house. Leave out the advisor. How would an advisor teach a fund about real estate?

He supposedly would help the plan learn more about property by spending time with the trustees and teaching them about property. But the advisor has less time to spend explaining property to his clients than commingled fund managers do. Commingled funds are typically sponsored by institutions and have large staffs. Individual advisory firms often consist of three or four people, all of whom are constantly on the road looking for deals and new clients. The last thing they have time to do is sit and hold hands with existing clients.

Presumably, the plan would also learn about real estate by owning its own property directly. The trustees could see how the property was performing on a quarterly basis. If it did well, they would learn about the profits in property investing and if it did badly, they would learn about losses. I would argue that they learn nothing. They merely receive their quarterly reports on their property investment performance from an advisor instead of an employee of a commingled fund. They learn nothing about managing property, the crux of the business. If the property does badly, the plan will be stuck with it. If its poor performance is due to the advisor's incompetence, the plan will have to fire the manager and hire another one to unravel the property's problems.

Pension plan trustees who really want to learn about property investing should start grilling their commingled real estate fund managers about their portfolios. Demand real information about what is happening with the properties. Demand that the manager sponsor regular seminars for his pension clients in which the fund's acquisition staff and property managers analyze one of the fund's properties in detail. Read books; sign up for real estate courses; and for corporate plan trustees, talk to people who work in the corporate real estate program.

But the only real way a plan's trustees are going to learn about what their plan can do with real estate is to start an in-house investing program of their own and hire their own staff to teach them.

Tips on Picking an Advisor

In spite of the arguments against hiring an advisor, many pension plans will do so anyway, usually out of some unexamined urge to have more control over their real estate portfolio or with the hope that the advisor will prove to be a superior investor to commingled funds. If a plan insists on hiring an advisor, the pension staff should keep a few things in mind when they start interviewing candidates for the job.

They should look at the track record of the advisor, short and uninformative though it is sure to be, and try to figure out whether his numbers have any relation to reality. The staff will have to measure his investment performance against that of commingled funds since the funds' performance numbers make up the only real estate index that is not total fiction. The advisor's numbers are not likely to tell the staff much, since it is impossible to compute real estate returns until an investor has sold off the investment.

So, they should ask to see specific deals that the advisor has done where he has sold the property. What did the client make on them? Ask to see deals he has done recently and those he did 5 or 10 years ago. He will show you his successes, but ask to see the failures. You want a complete explanation of the worst deal he ever did and how he is going to avoid making such mistakes in the future. If the advisor refuses to discuss such deals with you, cut him from your list. He will not be honest with you about your money once he gets it.

Find out who has worked for the firm before and who works for them now. Call those that left. Why did they leave and what are the backgrounds of the people who work there now? How long have they been at the firm? A pension plan should avoid a firm headed by men over 60 years of age who used to work for banks and insurance companies, since they are certain to be bureaucrats, not real estate investors. They will not want to change, and they will not have the energy to keep up with the competition.

On the other hand, companies headed by young MBAs five years out of school should also be avoided. You want a firm where people have 10 or 15 years of real estate investing experience, and you should be particularly picky about the person who acquires property. He is the most important man in the firm and should have at least 10 years of experience in acquisitions work including "workouts," which is real estate jargon for bad deals that needed to be straightened out. Interview him in depth about his strategies and his deals, both successes and failures. Ask him to what extent the properties for your portfolio will be generated by his other clients. This will give you some idea of the conflicts of interest he has.

Talk to whoever heads property management. What is his philosophy? You want to hire an advisor who manages his own properties and does not farm them out to local property companies to run. That in-house property management division should be headed by a real nitpicker who can give you a detailed description of every property he runs, its operating costs and problems without looking at a note. Next to the head of acquisitions, who will be making your investments, the property manager who will run them is the most important man in the firm. After talking with the property manager, visit his properties and see what kind of quality they have and how well they are run.

A pension officer should call the people the advisor has done deals for but should be aware that these people have their own interests. The client who likes the advisor may pan him to a prospective new client because he wants to keep the best deals to himself. The developer who has been financed by the advisor may praise him loudly because once the advisor signs your fund on, the developer has another source of capital for his deals.

Once a plan decides to hire an advisor, it should not give him $30 million and expect him to invest it in four months. It takes time to find the right deals. This does not mean that the plan should not set goals. The plan staff should tell the advisor what they expect of him over the next one, three and five years. Set up a reporting procedure and give the advisor the discretion to make investments that clearly meet the objectives you have set for him. The trustees should approve only property investments that are highly unusual or large. Periodically send out some of your pension staff to drop in on some of your properties unexpectedly, just to see how they are doing.

In hiring an advisor, plan sponsors should remember that they must pay his investment fee and administrative costs in addition to the expenses that are incurred by buying, selling and running property. No matter who runs the portfolio, those property expenses will always be there.

When a plan buys a property, it must pay for the real estate appraisal, the legal costs of drawing up the sale documents, and the cost of hiring an engineering firm to examine the building's condition. There are title fees and insurance fees and all sorts of extra expenses, some of which also are paid by the plan. Typically, the plan must pay commissions to real estate brokers who have arranged the sale of the property. Though the seller pays the broker's commission, the buyer actually does since it is tacked on to the price of the property by the seller.

Broker's commissions will be overt when a plan sells a property, but hidden in the sales price when it buys. If you want to see how much the broker costs you, go over the closing documents. His commission should be listed.

Once a plan owns a property, it must pay for the direct expenses of running it, such as utilities, real estate taxes, plowing the main drive in the winter, and maintaining the air conditioning and heating system. All these expenses are taken out of the property's cash flow, but if the building's revenue is down, the plan must pay for them out of its own pocket.

The plan must also pay property management fees to the individual managers of each building, fees that are paid out of a property's cash flow. It is nearly impossible to compare them. One building manager will charge 5 percent of a property's gross annual income to run the building. Another will charge less but then will bill the property separately for the cost of keeping its books or the manager's salary. The only way for a plan to know what it is paying is for its staff analyze the management contracts and compute the total cost of each.

To all these fees and costs, the plan with an investment advisor must then add on his investment management fees and administrative costs.

Whether a plan chooses to hire a manager or avoid them, it is important to remember that a manager is merely a plan's agent; he has a different attitude toward the plan than an employee. One real estate developer put it as follows:

Remember, these advisors are middlemen. They're agents, and there's a big difference between being a principal and an agent.

A principal has money in the ground and in buildings. He knows how he did on those investments over 20 years. But the agents don't have any money at all in the investments they make for pension funds. They'll make money irrespective of how the principal did. They're going to collect fees, and it's going to be great for them.

The more dollars the agent invests for the principal, the more money the agents end up making. I don't want to imply that he doesn't care how the principal does. In the long run he does, because if the principal doesn't do well, no more principal and no more fees.

But in the short run, he wants to bring in clients and make each deal. That's just a fact of life.

It's also worth remembering, when a representative of an advisory firm approaches your pension plan and assures you that now is a great time to invest in property, that values will only climb. He may really believe it, but his vision is also clouded by his own interest.

IN-HOUSE INVESTING

The Advantages

A pension plan that wants a better return than commingled funds offer should set up its own in-house real estate program. If done right, the plan will make more money on its holdings than a similar portfolio run by an investment advisor or a commingled fund.

The real estate staff will have only one client to work for, the plan itself. They will not be wasting their time marketing themselves to other pension plans or playing Solomon, dividing up the deals they find among many clients. They will have no conflicts of interest because they work only for the plan.

The plan will have total control over its real estate costs. The staff will know exactly how much property management and administration costs, and what actually gets invested in bricks and mortar. This is a refreshing change from the statements plans receive from commingled funds; there, listings like "administrative costs: $500,000" are shown with no explanation attached. Large pension plans will also find that major developers and other real estate firms will be more eager to do business with them as the plan's reputation as an investor that is easy to deal with becomes known. People who bring deals to the fund will know that they are not showing them to the competition, as with an advisor, but are dealing with an investor that acts on its own behalf. The quality and number of deals a plan sees will climb.

The plan trustees will start to learn about property, unlike the situation in which they hire an advisor or a commingled fund. Then, they just sit passively and read performance reports each quarter. An in-house staff, if it is any good, will handle most problems, but big ones will have to be presented to the board of trustees. The staff will have to teach them enough about real estate investing so they can make informed decisions.

With an in-house staff the plan can devise its own strategy and be as aggressive or passive as it wishes, electing to invest in buildings it must manage intensively or sticking to credit-lease deals where management is nil. The longer the staff keeps investing, the better it will get. It will become easier to invest money, to negotiate hard, buy right, and run well what it buys. The plan's real estate returns should improve over time. Nor will the plan ever have to worry about being abandoned by a manager who has decided to go into another business. The plan has its own staff.

An in-house operation will give a plan better investment results than a commingled fund or investment advisor because the plan will not be paying all the overhead that a commingled fund or advisor requires. The plan does not have to subsidize the large real estate operation of an insurance company or the other real estate operations of an advisor. It is only paying for its own staff.

But the real source of improved performance is the superior investment staff the plan can hire. If the plan pays better than commingled funds and ties the salaries of its real estate staff to the performance of the property managed, it should attract people who are better investors. This is an important point which will be discussed later.

The Disadvantages

With all the benefits of in-house investing, there are problems. In-house investors have the same major problem as those plans that hire advisors: their real estate portfolios will be undiversified until they become fairly large or contain numerous, small investments. The plan has all its hopes for real estate pinned on several properties, and if these properties have problems, so does the entire real estate portfolio.

This problem can be partially offset by having some of the plan's real estate money invested in commingled funds as a diversification backstop. If the in-house holdings have problems, at least the fund has some decent returns from its commingled investments. This same strategy can be used to diversify a portfolio run by an investment advisor.

Though both suffer from lack of diversification, in-house investors should have an edge over advisors. If the plan has properly structured its compensation package, its in-house staff should be better investors; a plan run in-house will show a better return than commingled funds or advisors can make. Of course, a plan that hires mediocre people for its in-house staff will show no better performance than if it had hired an advisor, and could possibly do worse. But barring such poor choices, the in-house staff will make the plan more money with less risk than an advisor. It will make more money than a commingled fund, though it will be taking on more risk by doing so.

Not all problems with in-house investing have such a silver lining. Pension plans will find that as in-house investors, they are more closely involved with their investments than they ever dreamed possible. If a building starts to lose tenants or needs an overhaul of its heating system, they are the plan's problems. There is no outside advisor who will work them all out and then send a bill to the plan later. The plan's own staff must wrestle with them, and the bigger ones will require the plan's trustees to get involved.

If the trustees change their minds about investing directly in property, it can take a long time to liquidate the portfolio, especially since they probably want to sell because their holdings are not doing well. Selling property that is in trouble or out-of-favor is always difficult, and the plan may lose money on the sales if the trustees want to sell quickly.

A plan must also change how it makes investment decisions if it wants to do well in real estate. All the best real estate deals are done quickly and by people who have the power to make a decision and write a check immediately. There are aggressive buyers competing with pension plans for property who can do just that. If the plan's in-house staff must clear all its decisions to buy and sell through a committee that meets once a month, it will never be able to move fast enough to do good deals and the plan might as well leave its money in a commingled fund.

Finally, the plan must beware of trustees who encourage the plan to invest in real estate directly and then volunteer to oversee the operation. They are paid little if any money for their services as trustees, yet suddenly they find hours of time to devote to "overseeing" the plan's real estate operations. Inevitably, they have "friends" in the real estate business which the plan soon finds itself doing business with.

These trustees are not being civic-minded. The plan may not be paying them for their work but the real estate people they steer business to certainly are. The trustees are being paid in the form of kickbacks, commissions, or promises of shares in future lucrative deals. This is especially a problem with union or public pension funds where the trustees change often and do not earn any money for being trustees, doing it as a service to their union or city.

Real estate direction from the board of trustees is not free. Consider paying them for any extra work they must do to oversee the plan's property investments. But make certain the real estate man hired to run the plan's real estate division has the real power to run it. The trustees' role is to approve or reject his investment philosophy, not to run the real estate portfolio for him. They must keep their hands, their connections, and their uninformed opinions out of his way.

Human nature being what it is and pension trustees being the nervous sorts that they are, this may be impossible. Few, if any, boards of trustees can maintain such aplomb. Then, few if any pension funds should set up in-house real estate operations to do anything beyond leasebacks.

Unless pension trustees give their real estate staff freedom and real power, the fund has no business trying to buy real estate through an in-house staff. The trustees can get away with browbeating a real estate staff that does only simple leasebacks. But it is an invitation to disaster to second-guess a man who is buying regional shopping centers for the fund.

Investment Goals and People

Once a plan's board of trustees decides to invest directly in real estate using an in-house staff, it must have a definite investment strategy. The fund should not behave, as one observer put it, "like a kid in a candy store," buying or investing in just about any property that some real estate broker shows up with to dazzle the trustees. The fund must have a strategy that is more defined than "we will buy and hold quality income property." What type of income property? Where? Why the office building in Dallas instead of the industrial warehouse in Los Angeles? The plan's board of trustees must sit down with its real estate staff and decide how such questions will be answered.

In setting an investment strategy, the plan trustees are in a chicken-or-egg situation. If they try to set an investment strategy without the help of a good real estate professional, they will not do a good job since they know so little about real estate. But whom they hire to run their real estate will determine what their strategy will be.

This is less of a problem than it first appears. The trustees should pick someone they are comfortable with. Whom they choose to run their money will say something about how much risk they are willing to take in their investments and what they want out of property. So the trustees' gut instincts do have a role. Certainly, if they hire someone they really distrust or think is too aggressive, their relationship will not last long and they will not listen to what he has to tell them.

To outperform advisors or commingled funds, a plan must hire better people than staff those organizations. For the largest plans, those with more than $75 million a year to invest in property, this means the plan should hire one, talented real estate acquisition person to run the real estate department. He should be paid lavishly and be given bonuses and pieces of the deals that he does for the plan. His income should be tied to the amount of money he can make for the plan.

It is legally difficult to devise an agreement that gives a real estate man a piece of the deal while still allowing the fund to dismiss him for good reason, but it can be done. Under ERISA, it is also difficult for that person, as an employee of the fund's sponsor, to share in the fund's real estate profits. It smacks of conflict of interest by the sponsor. The fund will need good legal advice to set up such an operation. It may have to create a separate corporation to run its real estate holdings and have the real estate staff be that corporation's employees. But given that certain real estate advisors and commingled fund managers already pay themselves incentive fees, a pension plan should be able to find some way to compensate its in-house acquisition person similarly.

Such legal complexities are only necessary if the plan is buying property or making mortgages with equity kickers. If it sticks entirely to credit-leaseback deals, it does not need top-flight real estate talent.

The Small Plans

Plans with less than $75 million a year to invest, which is nearly all pension plans, cannot hire expensive people to head their operations. They do not have enough for them to do and cannot pay them. Instead, they have to find a less-experienced investor who shows promise and have him direct the staff. This is risky since the young man or woman may show promise and little else.

Instead of taking this chance, it makes more sense for the plan to do simple deals that require less expensive talent. The king of simple deals is the credit leaseback. Credit leasebacks are really long-term mortgages secured more by the credit of the mortgageholder than by the property itself. Such deals are primarily business loans to the company involved, and all a plan needs is someone who knows how to underwrite a deal where the credit of the company and, additionally, the real estate are the security. A former banker or mortgage banker, either of whom has done a number of leaseback deals, will do fine. And he will not be overly expensive or require bonuses or incentive compensation to do a good job for the plan.

The problem is credit leasebacks are the one deal that will not outperform commingled funds or advisor-run portfolios, no matter who assembles them. They simply are far less risky than owning or mortgaging property, which are the bread and butter deals of advisors and commingled funds. So a portfolio of credit leasebacks has a lower rate of return. A plan that decided to specialize in such deals would have to do them to diversify its real estate portfolio and not in any hope of outperforming anyone.

In certain cases, a smaller pension plan can go beyond credit leasebacks in its in-house operation. The plan may be lucky enough to be part of a corporation that already has its own real estate staff for locating factories or building stores. If the plan is interested in the same types of properties, the corporate staff can handle the plan's real estate investing, too. For example, the H.E. Butt Grocery Company pension fund of Corpus Christi, Texas, had $40 million in assets and used $10 million to buy six, small shopping centers. The plan bought them because that was what the company knew best. The company had its own real estate staff to find space for its stores. It was only a small jump for that staff to start working for the pension fund in addition to working for the company.

But to use a corporate real estate staff, the plan must want to invest in what the corporate staff is good at investing in. The H.E. Butt fund was interested in neighborhood shopping centers. But the Pillsbury pension fund, for example, is not interested in investing in fast-food restaurants even though Pillsbury owns Burger King and has a corporate real estate staff filled with people expert in the business.

It is unusual for a plan to be able to share a corporate real estate staff. Unless they can set up such a beneficial arrangement or are happy with only credit-leaseback deals, most pension plans should avoid in-house real estate investing. They should stick with commingled funds and leave in-house investing to the largest pension plans, those with $75 million a year to put into property. The only other way smaller plans could invest in-house would be if they pooled their money with other pension plans until they reached $75 million and jointly hired a good real estate man and a small staff to run it. But at this writing, there are no such pools in this country that I am aware of.

Hiring a Good Real Estate Man

To run their in-house operation, a large plan or one of these theoretical pools of smaller plans needs a man with 10 to 15 years' experience acquiring real estate. He must be an acquisitions man, not one who has spent his time underwriting mortgages. Though the mortgage business has gotten far more complex in recent years, it historically has not required the knowledge of real estate that acquiring property does.

The person should not have spent his time largely at insurance companies or banks. Though some of the top-ranking real estate staff members there are good and worth attracting, most of the lower-level staff is not. Most likely, the man the plan is looking for will have been on his own or working for a private real estate company as head of acquisitions. He will be well-connected in the real estate business and have sources for all types of good deals.

The plan must pay him a great deal of money by corporation standards—at least $150,000 a year, plus bonuses and a piece of any deal he does for the plan. The idea is to tie his financial success to that of the plan's property and make him prefer working for the fund instead of going into business for himself or taking off with some friends and starting his own company. The plan is trying to entice an entrepreneur into working for it.

His salary level will drive both the pension officer and the personnel department wild. He will make as much as a senior manager at the company and three times as much as the pension officer to whom he technically reports. It may help to think of him like one of your company's top salesmen. If a company is well-run and has strong sales, the top salesman will be making a similar amount of money.

There is one consolation for the fund sponsor whose eyes are popping out at this salary level. All he needs is one good man. The real estate staff who will work under him will cost much less. But he is the one who is making the decisions. He can commit $60 million to $100 million in money to good real estate investments in a year, if he is given enough freedom to act.

Pension plan trustees who think they can cut corners by hiring a cheaper man to head their operation will pay for it in the end. There is no trick to investing in real estate badly. One pension sponsor who is familiar with real estate investments was traveling through Kentucky several years ago and came upon a new regional shopping center financed with a $20 million or $30 million mortgage from a teachers' pension fund. He was accompanied by someone familiar with the deal and asked what kind of equity kicker and slices of cash flow the fund was collecting as part of the mortgage.

His companion looked puzzled. Apparently the fund had provided the center with a traditional, fixed-rate, long-term mortgage at a time when other lenders were just starting to demand and get equity kickers. The mortgage interest rate was also a point or two below the market. A competent real estate man would have insisted on kickers and a better rate, but the man who made this deal cost his fund millions of dollars in lost cash flow. This fund will have no share in the increasing revenues of this center and will only make the 10 or 11 percent rate it wrote on the mortgage.

When the amount of money a fund can lose through stupid deals and mismanagement of its property is measured against the annual compensation of a good real estate man, it appears paltry. If he sells all the fund's apartment buildings into a rising market and makes the fund $350,000 more than if he had sold them three months later, he has earned his money for the year. The plan should measure the cost of the man against the amount of money he can make for them and not try to get by with cut-rate real estate people who will work for straight salaries of $50,000 a year.

A fund should also compare what it is getting from its one good man with what it could get from a real estate advisory firm. If an advisor is charging 1½ percent of assets a year to run a fund's property, he needs to be running only $10 million of property, which is one medium-sized office building, before he is making $150,000 a year in fees. This is the base salary a fund would pay an in-house real estate man to run a $75 million property portfolio.

By the time an outside advisor is running $75 million in property, he is making $1,125,000 in fees off the fund and may be billing the fund separately for a share of his company's overhead. The fund will still have to pay gas, electricity, taxes, and the other operating expenses of its properties, regardless of whether an in-house man or outside advisor runs them. It will still have to pay special expenses, like appraisals and title search fees, when it buys and sells property.

Basically, the $1,125,000 in fees that the fund is paying the advisor is covering salaries and part of the advisor's corporate overhead. A fund can run $75 million in-house for less than that. The head of the in-house real estate department will make $150,000 a year plus bonuses, fringe benefits, and a piece of the cash flow on the deals he does. He will cost $300,000 a year. He will have an assistant and a few clerks for another $200,000 in salaries and someone to head up property management at $100,000. With his bonuses and cash flow participations included, the property management man will cost $200,000 a year. The real estate staff will share offices with the pension fund and run up big telephone bills. But the whole in-house operation could probably get by on $750,000 a year, plus some bonuses paid five years down the road when the properties are sold and the heads of acquisitions and property management collect their share of the equity. The in-house operation is approximately one-third cheaper than an outside advisor.

It is also better. An outside advisor spends one-tenth of his time on the fund and nine-tenths on his other clients. He will cut adequate deals but not excellent ones, since his fees are not tied to how well the property does. He is likely to hire local management firms to run the fund's properties; a good in-house man will set up his own management staff who will do a better job. The in-house operation makes more sense.

How does a pension fund find such a person to run its real estate department? With a great deal of legwork. A good real estate investor has many opportunities to exercise his talents. Not only must the pension fund find him, the trustees must convince him to work for them.

As previously mentioned, the person should not have spent a great deal of time working for banks or insurance companies. He may have started there to learn the ropes, but has been out on his own with a private real estate company for years now, buying property. You do not want someone who thinks like a bureaucrat. You want someone who is aggressive, opinionated, persistent, and makes money. He will not be a team player.

He may be working for one of the big syndication firms like JMB Realty, Balcor or Consolidated Capital. Perhaps he is at one of the big, private development firms such as Gerry Hines or Melvin Simon, working right under top management and realizing that he has gone as far as he will go there. He will not be able to do things his way.

Snoop around. Talk to executive-search firms and the real estate departments at banks and insurance companies that run money for your plan. Ask them who are the best and shrewdest real estate people they have lent money to. The banks lend construction money, and they will know developers. The insurance companies lend long-term mortgage money, and they will know people who buy property.

Call up other people who have lent money to the man. Call up people who have been joint-venture partners with him or have worked as a general contractor for him on buildings he has developed. Go to buildings he owns or runs and talk to the tenants. Are his buildings good to lease in? Are they well taken care of?

When you have dug up a small pile of information on the man, call him up and tell him you need someone to run a real estate portfolio that will start out at $100 million and grow by $75 million to $100 million a year. Once he and the fund trustees set strategy, he will control the operation and get a piece of every deal he does. He will also direct property management or can hire someone he likes who will.

Even if the man is happy at what he does, it is not every day that someone calls him up and wants to talk to him about running his own real estate company funded by a continuous source of capital. Real estate people are always looking for money, and to be offered $100 million a year to invest as he sees fit would be heaven for many. You will at least get some interesting interviews with these potential headmen, if not actually find the one you want.

If he is not interested, he may refer you to someone else he knows who might be. Eventually, the persistent pension officer will develop a network of people and contacts, all of whom will be out looking for a headman for him. Not only will the officer learn a lot about what motivates real estate people, but he will probably find someone the fund would be pleased to hire.

He should emphasize in his interviews that the man who heads the real estate department at the fund will be autonomous—and the pension officer should mean it. This autonomy does not mean that the trustees should not hold him fully accountable for his deals or that he is free to act without their approval. Certainly, the trustees must understand and be comfortable with what he is doing and the real estate man must be willing to teach them about real estate investing as he goes. But it makes no sense for a fund to hire a talented real estate person and then hamstring him with committees who second-guess him on every deal he tries to do. If the man knows this will happen, he will not even express interest in running your in-house operation. And if he discovers it once he arrives, he will quit immediately. If the fund trustees cannot agree to a fair degree of autonomy, and few will, they have no business trying to set up a sophisticated, in-house operation.

The trustees and the head of the real estate department must jointly set a real estate investment strategy. The trustees must give him the authority to quickly make deals that fall within certain parameters. Set up a chain of command where he can get permission to do these deals right away, with only one or two signatures. All the best real estate deals are done fast, and your fund is competing against private investors who can write checks immediately if they like a deal. The sources of real estate capital may be dwindling, but these private investors are still out there and will always be. It takes only one other person with the money and the desire to do the deal to knock your fund out of it.

On deals that fall outside the guidelines, the trustees should make the decision to invest after the head of the real estate department has made a full presentation to them and answered all their questions. The board should trust their man's judgment and not lightly reject any deal he brings to them and believes in.

It takes a great deal of work to find the right person to run the real estate department, set strategy, and start making investments. Pension officers should compare the work they put into real estate to the work they did the last time they hired a new stock or bond manager. They had to decide on a stock or bond strategy and do asset-allocation analyses. They researched dozens of managers and intensively interviewed a half dozen or more. Often they visited the office of a potential manager and talked with the portfolio manager who would actually run their money. All this work was expended to hire a manager who would invest in stocks and bonds, an area the pension officer conducting the interviews knew a great deal about. It could take nine months to a year to hire such a manager, from the day the staff started researching potential managers to the day they actually hired someone.

Pension officers should not be surprised if it takes more than a year, and much more work, to hire someone to set up and run an in-house real estate department. After all, the pension officer is venturing into an investment frontier for his fund and will want to work as carefully as possible.

SOME SUCCESSFUL IN-HOUSE REAL ESTATE OPERATIONS

General Electric

The master of credit-leaseback investing by pension funds is the General Electric Pension Fund. In 1980, this fund had $500 million of its $800 million of real estate assets in credit leasebacks, and they are still the fund's principal type of real estate investment. The G.E. fund has been doing credit leasebacks for 30 years. It started doing them with gas stations in 1954 because the fund could make more on leasebacks than on bonds and have better collateral.

The G.E. fund has branched into other types of real estate at various times and not always successfully. During the early 1970s, the fund was drawn into the fad of financing second-home projects and financed the Big Sky Country resort in Montana and a project on Hilton Head in South Carolina, among others. "They all came back to bite us," says E.B. "Buck" Griswold who headed up the fund's real estate department in 1980.

In 1974, sky-high interest rates and overbuilding destroyed the market for vacation homes and the developers of these recreational communities defaulted on their loans. The G.E. fund found itself the unhappy owner of several resorts through foreclosure. The fund managed to sell off most of them and more than made up for its losses, including that of Big Sky, which it had had to write down from roughly $6 million to $1.00.

"It could have been worse," said Griswold. "It wasn't, because we had staying power and were doing quality properties with quality people. But basically, we got caught up in a fad."

The fund has been more careful since then. The fund considers itself solely a mortgage lender and it is sticking close to its credit orientation. It now does joint ventures with developers but only on large deals. There is a $10 million minimum for any deal it considers and its typical deal is $20 million. The fund is trying to position itself in the market as a lender that can do what insurance companies cannot, such as lending more than 75 percent of a property's appraised value. But the fund is primarily known as a credit-leaseback lender and sees a tremendous volume of these deals each year.

The entire real estate operation at the G.E. fund employs four professionals and is organized so they can move fast on a deal. The G.E. fund is run entirely in-house, and the senior investment managers are also the plan's trustees. They are supervised by a committee of senior executives at G.E., but together, the seven trustees run the fund. The plan never has the problem of its managers seeking approval from trustees unfamiliar with real estate investing. The people who run the money are responsible for it.

In the fixed-income department, which includes real estate, it takes two out of three trustee signatures to make nearly any investment commitment. "You're not a figurehead here," said Griswold of his staff. "If it's your ball game when it comes to investing, then you sign for it. If we make a decision as trustees, it's irrevocable. And the way they solve the problem of bad decisions is by firing the trustees."

Not only is the G.E. fund an example of a credit-leaseback operation, but an example of how one pension fund dealt with the need to make real estate decisions fast. It is also an example of a pension fund that knows exactly what its real estate strategy is. It is a mortgage lender that looks to the credit of the tenant or borrower over nearly every other consideration, and it does only big, high-quality credit deals. When the fund strayed from its strategy and made resort loans, it lost money.

The G.E. fund has had every opportunity to stray from its investment strategy if it wished, since General Electric also runs one of the largest financing companies in the world, the General Electric Credit Corporation. GECC does all sorts of real estate financing and equity deals from condominium conversions and office mortgages to second mortgages and recreational-lot receivables. It is an aggressive real estate investor when compared to the pension fund. Their operations are entirely separate and there is no thought of pooling their money since GECC uses company funds and the pension fund is a trust for employees.

The pension fund does not seek out the expertise of GECC. In fact, it works the other way around. GECC sends its staff to the pension fund to learn about the capital markets. Many people go through GECC as part of their management training at G.E. and rely on the pension fund staff to teach them about real estate investing.

Minneapolis Teachers

The credit-leaseback deal is the safest of leasebacks, but it is only one form of the structure. A pension fund can increase its return from leasebacks, while still avoiding the problems of managing a building, by doing leasebacks with tenants of lesser but still substantial credit.

The Minneapolis Teachers Retirement System is doing landsale-leasebacks on fast-food franchises such as Wendy's, Arby's, Ponderosa and Bonanza. The franchisee builds the restaurant and starts operations, and the fund then comes in and buys the land and the building, leasing it back to the franchise. In essence, the fund is providing a long-term mortgage for the property. The fund does little of its own work exploring the feasibility of the different restaurants because it feels that the good restaurant chains do such a thorough job of researching a location that anything the fund would do would be redundant.

In 1981, the fund held 40 percent of its $160 million in assets in such leasebacks and was so thrilled with them that Newell Gaasedelen, the fund's executive secretary, told *Pensions & Investment Age* that the fund would be delighted to send its sample contracts to any interested pension fund.[2] The fund wanted to create a secondary market in these leasebacks and was trying to drum up interest.

At this writing, the leasebacks have been a good investment for the fund and have earned it far more than it would have made in the bond markets, according to Gaasedelen. In 1980, the fund earned 14 percent on its leases. Gaasedelen considers them less risky than bonds because they offer inflation protection. The rent on the leases is always a combination of a fixed minimum and a percentage of annual sales, which the fund hopes will increase over time.

There is certainly no question that investing in leasebacks on hamburger stands is an unusual strategy for a pension fund. It sounds risky and crazy and could be, but not necessarily. If the franchise is a strong one with a national name and the company guarantees the lease payments, these leases resemble middle-grade bonds with inflation protection. If the company does not guarantee the lease, the deals are riskier. The security is the credit of the individual operator and the building itself. If a restaurant does fail, the fund can lease the building to another restaurant or company. The deals are also so small—$400,000 to $450,000— that the failure of one or two out of the 160 restaurants the fund owned in 1982 will not be a disaster.

The only real problem with the fund's strategy is that it has been too enthusiastic in doing these deals. It had 40 percent of its assets in leasebacks to one industry. If the fast-food business hits terrible times and one-fourth of the fund's restaurants have trouble paying rent, the fund would suffer. But this unlikely problem is the only real criticism one could level at this strategy. The overall investment risk of this fund is almost certainly lower than that of most pension funds.

The British Coal Board

The Coal Board's investment strategy was described in detail in chapter 7, but briefly, it is an example of how a plan can specialize in stages. The fund started out 30 years ago, doing leasebacks on quality retail stores in the best shopping areas of London. After doing only those deals for four years, the fund pushed on to something more lucrative. It started financing developers, and in 1958 it began doing joint ventures with them.

By the early 1970s, the fund was developing shopping centers on its own. The fund has done all types of real estate investing, but it has done them in stages, increasing its level of risk only when it felt comfortable doing so. The fund did not try to do credit leasebacks and joint ventures, purchase income property, and then start a few developments on the side—all at once. It moved slowly and deliberately, taking 30 years to become the shrewd real estate investor it is today.

MORE STRATEGIES FOR IN-HOUSE INVESTING

Joint Ventures

Funds that want to make more on their real estate than leasebacks provide but do not want to manage property should consider joint ventures. The fund will take more risk, but should make more money. It will also need a top real estate man at the head of its real estate department to successfully carry off joint-venture deals. This is no business for amateurs or committees—or for truly passive investors.

Joint ventures match up moneyed investors with developers who have ideas but no capital. Such deals are typically done with new projects. The pension fund puts up the money for construction and the long-term mortgage while the developer provides the expertise to design and build the project. The developer also contributes some of his own money, but in comparison to what the pension fund or other moneyed partner puts up, it is peanuts. The developer might contribute $300,000 to the pension fund's $30 million.

In addition to actually constructing the building, the developer will often manage it as part of his contribution. When the building is completed, the pension fund and the developer each have a 50 percent ownership in it.

Joint ventures flourish when mortgage rates are high because developers view a joint venture as a cheap source of both equity and mortgage money. The moneyed partner will provide the mortgage money at a lower rate than a lender would. The developer will have to give up half an interest in the property, but the difference in rate and terms can mean the project will now be financially viable, whereas with an outside lender it would not have been.

Joint ventures have much to recommend them. The fund ends up owning a half interest in a new, desirable property. Since the developer will own half the finished building himself, he will do a better job constructing it than if he were building to sell, benefiting both himself and the fund. Because he is part owner, he will also manage the building better than an outside management firm.

On the surface, joint ventures look like an ideal way for a pension fund to invest in property. The pension fund provides the money, of which it has plenty; the developer provides the expertise, of which the pension fund has none; and in the end, the fund owns half of a new income property.

But there is a great deal of violent feeling in the real estate business about joint ventures. Some real estate people swear by them and claim they are the best way for investors with little development expertise to invest in property. Others would never consider them. The usual criticism of joint ventures is that the moneyed partner starts out with the money and the developer the expertise. But by the end, the developer has the money, and the investor the expertise.

It is hard to generalize about joint ventures, primarily because each is unique and is the product of negotiations between the two parties. In one joint venture, the moneyed partner, or in our case the pension fund, may have a great deal of say in how the property is managed. In another, it may behave almost like a limited partner, merely providing the money and leaving all management to the developer.

The ownership interests are not always divided evenly. Sometimes the moneyed partner gets 60 or 70 percent of the ownership, and the developer 30 or 40 percent. Sometimes the moneyed partner does not even get straight ownership, preferring to structure the entire joint venture as a mortgage with an equity kicker, or a mortgage that can be converted to equity in the future or when the property starts generating a specific level of income.

In spite of the uniqueness of each joint venture, there are some problems intrinsic to the form itself. The most obvious is that the moneyed partner is putting up all the money and taking all the financial risk, yet he is only getting half the deal. Hugh Jenkins, who heads investments for the pension funds of the British Coal Board, said this is exactly the reason his funds stopped doing most joint ventures. No matter how the deal is cut, the partner that is putting up the money is taking all the risk.

If the building costs more to build than they thought or takes twice as long to lease, the joint venture must come up with the money to cover the cost. Each partner is expected to pay half but often, the developer simply will not have the money, regardless of all the promises he made to the contrary when the venture was created. The moneyed partner must come up with all the needed money. In exchange, he takes over the developer's half interest or buys him out at some previously set price. He also opens himself up to some potentially devastating lawsuits.

The developer will go down fighting. He will not sit back and allow his moneyed partner to run him out of the deal, especially if the developer has invested a year or two of work in it. He will sue the partner, charging him with colluding to force him out. He can do this and make it stick because if the moneyed partner is an institution, it has typically played so many roles in the venture that it can be accused of acting in bad faith and engaging in all sorts of conflicts of interest.

The institution will probably have worn at least three hats in the deal. Typically, the venture will have borrowed the construction money from a bank; but the institution, usually an insurance company, will have lent it the remainder of the needed money. The institution will have made the long-term mortgage to the venture. Often it will have bought the land under the project and leased it back to the venture as a way of lending even more money. In addition to these two loans, the institution will have put up part of the equity money for the project and will be a half owner, a partner.

The main goal of the two partners in the early years of the venture is to get the building completed, leased, and making enough money to cover the mortgage payments. They want to stay out of foreclosure. The developer is riding a knife edge. He probably does not have enough money to make up his share of the mortgage payments if something goes wrong. He will do everything in his power not to spend money on the project, so he is certain of meeting those mortgage payments.

But his institutional partner does not see things that way. The institution knows that if the developer cannot come up with his half of the mortgage payment, the institution can foreclose as the lender. By doing so, it will have acquired the other half interest in the property for the amount of the mortgage balance, which is far less than what the property is really worth.

Many institutions in the late 1970s and early 1980s did joint ventures with exactly this goal in mind. They prayed that the developer would overextend himself after the building had been completed and would default on the loan. Since the loan was typically 75 percent of the property's overall value, the institution would then pick up 100 percent of the developer's interest for only 75 percent of what it was worth. Suddenly the institution owned the entire project, and at a bargain price. But the developer is going to sue, charging his lender-partner with conniving to force him out.

One solution is for institutions to refuse to do joint ventures at all and thus stay out of development deals. There are plenty of deals to be done on existing properties and properties that have been completed but lack permanent financing. A fund can do these instead and leave development to the entrepreneurs, with no loss of return. It is possible to do just as well in the existing property market as with development properties, if the fund is a shrewd and careful investor.

Another solution is for institutions to become developers themselves, and insist that the developer do his job as a contractor instead of a partner. But then the fund gets involved in the risky and intensive business of developing property, which requires a large staff and great expertise. This is assuming, of course, that the developer would agree to work as a contractor for the fund in the first place, and there is no reason to assume he would. If institutional investors are anxious to acquire property, many would be happy to do joint ventures with this developer. Only when this source of institutional patsies dries up will this developer be forced to work for a fee and not a piece of the deal.

Perhaps the best solution is for the fund to continue to do joint ventures but only with developers who have so much money that they do not need a moneyed partner. They have other sources of money and substantial assets of their own. If the institution puts up $30 million, these developers can put up $10 million and can raise more if the venture needs it. These developers will joint venture with an institution because they realize they can get a better deal on their financing than if they had taken out a straight long-term mortgage.

An example of a successful approach to joint ventures is provided by a large, private company that does a great number of them with real estate developers; it is now considering doing a few for its pension fund. The company would never get involved in new property development without a joint-venture partner, according to the attorney who runs their pension fund. "There's nobody in this company that has experience in the real estate business," he said, "yet we do a large number of real estate deals because we do them as partners."

Before they do a deal, they review it with their bankers, lawyers and other colleagues. But they then make their own decisions. The attorney demonstrated his company's attitude toward joint ventures in this description of one of them:

We have these partnership meetings, and I go to them with Joe, who's the developer and one of the three partners in the deal. We discuss something, and then we vote, and I ask Joe, "How should I vote?" And he tells me.

Joe is very, very good at what he does. He has more money to lose from this deal in proportion to his net worth than my company does, so he's going to do his damndest to make it work. He's going to do what's best.

And I'm going to do what he tells me to do because that's why I got into a partnership with him in the first place. He knows what he's doing. When he tells me to take money out of the deal, I take it out.

When he tells me to put money in, I write a check. And it's all worked out very well. We've made a lot of money.

This arrangement demonstrates not only a successful joint venture, but how important trust is to such deals. This particular joint venture shows how far this trust can go when the partners work well together. The "Joe" in this deal has done a number of joint ventures with this particular company. They both want to make this deal work because they can make a lot of money or lose it. They also want to do more deals with each other in the future, so they are not going to stab each other in the back on this one. They like and trust each other.

In addition to a heavy financial commitment, trust is essential to a joint venture. If each party is concerned only with his interests in the deal and is not willing to bend to work out solutions to a problem, the two partners might as well dissolve the partnership. You cannot do a joint venture with someone you do not like and cannot work with. Unfortunately, you also do not know if you can trust somebody until you take the chance of doing a deal with him in the first place.

Joint ventures require more teamwork than straight deals. The partners must meet and resolve issues that affect them both. If one partner feels slighted or cheated by the other, it is a poison that destroys the joint venture. He starts acting in bad faith, and when real problems come up for discussion, the whole joint venture comes apart during one final, heated argument. A fund need not get into a venture where there is so much trust that the fund literally writes checks whenever the developer tells them to, but the fund's in-house real estate staff should have confidence in and trust the developer it is working with.

Although a fund trusts its partner, it should always retain legal control of the project. This is the advice of Vince Martin, managing partner of TCW Realty Advisors in Los Angeles and former head of Coldwell Banker's commingled funds, which have done numerous joint-venture deals with pension funds. "Never, never, never" should a pension plan be a passive investor in a joint venture, Martin said in a December 1981 speech. He also advised his audience of pension officers and trustees to not let the exotic loan structure of some joint ventures disguise the fact that their plan is putting up all the money, and taking all the risk.[3]

No matter how it is sliced, a joint venture is always more risky for a pension fund than investing in existing property. The latter is already built, leased and generating income. But in a joint venture, the partners must build and then lease their project, running the risk of cost overruns on construction and a depressed rental market when it comes time to lease the building up.

If the partners hit the rental market at its peak when rents are high and leases favor the landlord, they are set. They will rent the entire building at top rents and can make far more money than if they had just been dealing with existing property. But if they hit a down market when it is time to lease, they can be stuck with a half-empty building throwing off only enough income to meet its electric bills, a recipe for financial disaster.

Both partners share the construction risk, that is, the risk that cost overruns will force them to pour more and more of their own money into the property just to finish it. But for the moneyed partner, some joint ventures are less risky than others because the developer agrees to shelter him from leasing risk. The developer will guarantee the moneyed partner a fixed return no matter what happens to the leasing.

This guarantee, or master lease, as it is sometimes called, is only worth something if the developer has the money to back it up. Otherwise, when the building does not lease up, the developer will not pay up. The moneyed partner will essentially be left with all the leasing risk since he is the only one with any real money in the deal to begin with. The venture can end up as a one-man jaunt by the moneyed partner into the developing business.

Going It Alone

A pension fund can avoid the legal problems of joint ventures by never doing them. And it can avoid the risks of construction and leasing by never doing development deals. Instead, the fund can do all its deals alone and stick entirely to investing in properties that are fully leased and generating income; it can buy or mortgage existing properties. The closest it may ever get to a partnership with anyone is collecting its share of the cash flow when it writes a mortgage with an equity kicker.

There is a lot to be said for self-sufficiency and for concentrating on the existing property market. When it owns 100 percent of an existing, fully leased property, a fund has 100 percent control over that property. The fund will not have to suffer the whims of a developer or other partner, nor will it have to worry that the property will turn into a bad investment because the partner is mismanaging it. All mistakes, and successes, are the fund's own.

A fund can also buy newly completed properties. When interest rates are high, developers often build projects without arranging long-term financing, hoping that rates will fall by the time they finish. If rates do not fall, the developers are forced to sell their properties since they cannot afford the available mortgage money and they must pay off their construction lender. Pension funds can pick up new properties at fire-sale prices under such circumstances.

To date, the 1980s have been a prime time for buying property this way. Martin of TCW Realty advises funds to scrutinize the relationship between the prices they are paying for these properties and the risks they are assuming. If the fund is paying a retail price, that is, a price based on the property being fully leased and generating full income, then it had better be fully completed and leased. The fund should not buy a half-finished, unleased property at a price based entirely on its future rents. As Martin puts it, "If income is in its place, it's a retail deal. And if it's a development deal, you should get a developer's rate of return and have control."[4]

But buying properties out of development is only one strategy a fund can adopt. The country is filled with income property that has been operating profitably for years, and each is a possible investment for a pension fund investor. Existing buildings are often a better investment than new ones because they are cheaper to buy relative to the amount of income they spin off. And there is no construction or leasing risk.

Some Key Points

A discussion of all the investment strategies a fund can embrace as a sole investor is beyond the scope of this book. But there are a few points to keep in mind, regardless of what the fund buys or whether it purchases total or partial interests in buildings. Some have been mentioned elsewhere but are important enough to bring up again.

If the fund is going to buy property, unless it is dealing with a party in interest, the fund should avoid paying entirely with cash. As was argued in detail in chapter 5, the fund should hold on to any existing mortgages or financing concessions from the seller that will generate positive leverage.

A fund should also buy to sell. Because the fund has a 40-year investment objective does not mean that it buys a property and holds it for 40 years. Like stocks and bonds, there is a time to sell a piece of real estate.

Always manage your own buildings. As shown in chapter 5, it's the difference between a mediocre investment and a superb one. When you buy a building, cancel the existing management contract and put in your own people, either imported from your office or hired away from a local management firm. Offer them more than they were making at the management company and a piece of any increased rent that comes out of the building.

As you acquire more properties, you'll have to hire someone to supervise the property management staff. Hire the best you can find, again, by enticing him away from a local management company with a good salary and a piece of any building he supervises. Like your department head, he should have 10 or 15 years' experience in managing income property.

Pension funds will be surprised at how much property they will have to look at to find a deal worth doing. Don King, who runs commingled real estate funds for Rosenberg Real Estate Fund, has said he considers 1,000 properties a year, makes offers on 30 of them, and ultimately buys fewer than 10, which is less than 1 percent of the deals he's considered.[5] His funds are a national real estate investor, so he sees deals from all over the country. But any fund that invests directly can expect to be offered dozens of deals for every one that it is actually interested in.

Ignore the income-tax considerations of real estate and concentrate on buying deals with good cash flow that shows a healthy chance of increasing soon. From the pension fund viewpoint, the impact of income taxes on real estate prices is greatly overrated.

Pension fund officers have complained that their funds are at a disadvantage in the property markets because they are tax-exempt investors competing with taxable investors. Real estate generates tax deductions so the taxable investors are willing to pay more for it. Since pension funds cannot use the tax deductions, the funds always overpay. This can be remedied, the argument runs, if funds become partners with taxable investors. The funds can then pass along as many tax benefits as possible to their taxable partners in exchange for an extra cut of the cash flow. Though heard often, these arguments do not hold up when the actual tax benefits involved are considered, as well as what the fund must give up to pass such benefits on to its taxable partners.

Consider the case of a pension fund that buys only 100 percent interests in fully leased, existing properties. These properties are at least several years old and are stable, income producers. The only tax write-offs they generate are depreciation and mortgage-interest write-offs.

With the exception of apartment buildings, the only depreciation it makes sense to claim is straight-line, which is not much of a tax benefit and will not inflate prices much. The owner can also deduct mortgage-interest payments. But at this writing, so few mortgages have been written over the last three years that the mortgage balance has probably been greatly reduced. Its interest payments are not the tax benefits they once were. They are too small to shelter much income; their existence will not inflate the building's price substantially. Because the mortgage balances on these buildings are so low, an investor would need a good deal of cash, perhaps as much as 70 percent of the sales price, to purchase them. On a $15 million building, that is $10.5 million in cash. Pension funds are some of the few investors that have that kind of money. If they are competing primarily with each other for these buildings, no consideration of the buildings' tax benefits will be built into the prices. The market simply does not care about them.

Now, consider a pension fund that does joint-venture, development deals or buys partial interests in half-completed buildings. Again, the fund is likely to find that it is only competing with other tax-exempt investors for these deals. Tax benefits are not inflating prices because taxable investors do not have the money to compete. But the prices may be inflated regardless because the tax-exempt funds are competing with each other to pass along the tax benefits that do exist to the developer. He can play off one potential partner against the other, seeing which fund will give the most in its attempts to pass tax benefits to him.

In any event, unlike existing property, buildings under construction generate some sizeable tax deductions. The owners can capitalize the construction loan interest and certain other costs, amortizing them faster than the other costs of construction. These write-offs are much less than what they once were when a developer could deduct them as expenses, but they still exist.

A pension fund, as part owner, does not need these write-offs and could pass them all to the developer in exchange for more cash flow. It does this by writing a mortgage structured so that the fund collects a big piece of the cash flow as a kicker. Instead of being a 50 percent owner in the property, the fund becomes a lender that collects at least 50 percent of the cash flow and probably more.

The fund is passing some big tax benefits to the developer. The developer is now legally the sole owner of the property and can claim all the construction write-offs. He can also deduct all the "mortgage payments" to the pension fund "lender." Instead of paying shares of income to a part owner, the project is now making interest payments to a lender and interest payments are tax-deductible. If the pension fund is collecting 60 percent of the cash flow, the developer can write off that amount as interest.

Such participating mortgages are not restricted purely to development deals or joint ventures. A pension fund can use such a mortgage to shelter income to a taxable partner in any deal it does.

The only problem is that the pension fund has lost control of the property. The developer is legally the only owner. When disputes arise over how the property should be managed or when it should be sold, the pension fund has no real say. The developer's decisions rule. Trading off control of the property for a few extra points of return is a poor strategy in a development deal unless the fund totally trusts its partner, an unlikely occurrence. If the fund wants to make participating mortgages on existing buildings, it should realize that it is a true mortgage lender, not an owner. A fund should ignore the Byzantine methods its partners' attorneys devise to provide the developer and other partners with massive tax write-offs while giving the fund a few more dollars in return. Usually, such schemes require the fund to give up ownership: it is a bad swap.

Pension funds should stop fixating on income-tax problems and concentrate on doing deals with cash flows that have a reasonable chance of increasing. The name of the game in real estate is cash-flow return, not tax write-offs.

Developing Property

Beyond everything that has been discussed, there is one more strategy a fund can pursue. It can develop property on its own. To the best of my knowledge, there are no U.S. pension funds with in-house staffs doing development work for their own accounts. This does not mean that pension funds are not getting involved in development deals. They are—in the joint-venture deals described earlier—where the funds provide the money and the developer handles everything else. But they could go beyond this; they could buy land and build warehouses, office buildings or shopping centers on it, all on their own. They could develop property using their own in-house staffs.

The only funds doing such adventurous investing are foreign funds, such as those of Royal Dutch/Shell and the British Coal Board. The Coal Board, as previously mentioned, is one of the largest developers of shopping centers in Great Britain and may one day announce that it intends to start developing property in the United States.

Many U.S. observers feel that development work is completely beyond pension funds. It is too risky. There are enough other people doing it, why should a pension fund take such risks? This is an excellent point. Why should a pension fund take the risk?

In the vast majority of cases, it should not. Developing property is a quirky and wild business, especially in times of volatile interest rates. A pension fund would need an in-house staff of dozens to carry it off as well as the best developers. From the pension fund viewpoint, the only real reason to develop is that at times it is cheaper to build a building than to buy an existing one. This is the situation the Coal Board found itself in in Great Britain in the 1950s, so it started doing joint ventures and then building on its own. It was cheaper to build than buy.

The build-or-buy decision is probably more clear-cut in Great Britain than in the United States because the United Kingdom is so much smaller. There is far more existing property in the United States than in Great Britain. There is no reason a U.S. pension fund cannot find an existing building it likes for a price it likes.

Pension funds should get larger and more important in real estate financing over the next 20 years, and it seems probable that several of the largest and most aggressive funds will consider becoming developers. By then, the development business in this country should be more dependent on pension fund money, and some developers will have no choice but to work for pension funds. A pension fund could become a developer by hiring its one-time, joint-venture partners as contractors. In some cases, the fund may actually buy the developer, thereby acquiring the ability to do deals completely on its own. Several large foreign pension funds have already done this. In late 1980, the KLM Royal Dutch Airlines Pension Fund bought all the outstanding stock of North Hills, Inc., a development and management firm in North Carolina. Everything that developer builds will now be built for the pension fund.

CONCLUSION

Pension funds should continue to play a growing role in real estate finance in this country. But history is a crafty lady with many surprises up her sleeves. Americans may start buying life insurance in abundance, flooding the life companies with money to invest. At the same time, interest rates could fall to 5 percent, stay there, and inflationary expectations disappear. The insurers would be deluged with even more money as everyone paid off their high-rate mortgages. The 30-year, fixed-rate mortgage could once again become the dominant method of financing. Real estate would then return to an era like that of the early 1970s when every developer and owner could find a lender to finance his deals at affordable rates. Other sources of capital for real estate might also appear, and pension funds would find real estate finance to be crowded with competitors.

At this writing, this seems unlikely. The economy is short of capital with no relief in sight, and real estate must suffer from this shortage along with every other sector of the economy.

Most pension funds are not committed to real estate investing. Those that have expressed interest and invested have done so mostly by putting a few million dollars into commingled funds in order to diversify their plan's portfolio. Although their numbers are growing daily, only a minority of pension sponsors view real estate as a true investment alternative, as important to their portfolio strategy as stocks and bonds. The rest consider themselves securities investors; until they think of property as a real investment and not a toy, they will continue to merely dabble in it.

Pension funds are passive investors in everything they do, and their stock and bond strategies are often as stodgy as those involving real estate. Perhaps they will stay passive investors forever. All the forces surrounding them—the way people become pension officers, ERISA, their investment outlooks—encourage them to be passive and to settle for mediocre or poor investment results.

But if these forces change, particularly if corporate managements begin to realize how much pension funds cost and how much more profitably they could be run, then the funds could become more aggressive investors. They would have the chance to become important lenders, owners and developers of real estate in this country.

NOTES

1. "Real Estate," *Pensions & Investment Age* (September 13, 1982), p. 23.

2. Linda Savage Ruhe, "Food franchises give tasty returns to Minnesota," *Pensions & Investment Age* (April 27, 1981), p. 1.

3. Vincent Martin, Jr., "Real Estate Investing," *Employee Benefits Journal* 6 (December 1981), pp. 21–24.

4. Ibid, p. 23.

5. Lawrence Rout, "Quick $58 million transaction typifies new industry climate," *The Wall Street Journal* (June 24, 1981), p. 23.

BIBLIOGRAPHY AND OTHER SOURCES

THE PENSION FUND BUSINESS

News on Pension Investment Trends

1. *Institutional Investor*. 488 Madison Avenue, N.Y., New York 10022. *II* is a slick monthly magazine read by everyone on Wall Street. It covers investment banking, institutional investing, retail brokerage and certain foreign financial markets. Each issue contains one or two articles on pension fund investing, often with in-depth analyses and a great deal of gossip. Periodically, *II* runs articles on or devotes a big part of an issue to pension fund investments in real estate. A subscription to *II* is a must for anyone interested in the pension investing business.

2. *Large Corporate Pensions: Report to Participants*. Greenwich Research Associates, 135 E. Putnam Avenue, Greenwich, Conn. 06830. The premier survey of the investing habits of the nation's largest corporate pension funds. Each year, the Greenwich staff interviews hundreds of people responsible for investing pension fund money at these corporations. For its 1981 survey, the staff interviewed 1,074 people at the 1,600 largest American companies. Greenwich compiles the information into categories and publishes it as a report; no data on specific plans is included. Among its other analyses, the report breaks out the types of investments pension plans intend to make in the upcoming years based on the size of their plans and sponsoring corporations.

   In their overview essay, the authors usually lament that corporations are not paying enough attention to their pension funds' investing practices. They also marvel that in spite of the differences among plans in actuarial assumptions, benefit formulas and cash flow needs, they all have much the same asset mix. The authors conclude that pension officers are not assertive enough when they meet with corporate officials to set the pension plan's investment strategy.

   The Greenwich information is interesting but not directly useful for real estate managers. It is also expensive. *P&IA* briefly reviews the survey each year.

3. *Pension World*. Communication Channels, 6285 Barfield Road, Atlanta, Ga. 30328. A monthly magazine. Although some is staff-written, most of the magazine consists of articles written by people in the pension fund business, including money managers, plan sponsors, actuaries and attorneys. The magazine covers pension investing practices but also contains articles on pension benefit and funding issues and regulatory practices.

   Because the articles are often written by people with investment products to sell, they take on a self-serving tone. But they can be informative; they alert investment managers to what the competition is saying.

   Each year, the magazine devotes its September issue to articles on pension fund

Each year, the magazine devotes its September issue to articles on pension fund investing in real estate. The issue contains a variety of articles, lists of real estate advisors, and typically, a summary of the "Annual Survey of Real Estate Investing by Pension Funds" conducted each year by Money Market Directories, Inc. A subscription is worth having.

4. *Pensions & Investment Age.* Crain Communications, 740 N. Rush Street, Chicago, Ill. 60611. *P&IA* is the newspaper of the pension investing business. The magazine used to be known as *Pensions & Investments* and comes out once every two weeks.

P&IA has the latest and most comprehensive information on which plans have changed money managers; it covers the latest fads and trends in investment products. *P&IA* is often the first to report news in the pension trade. Everyone in the pension investing business reads it and a subscription is a necessity for anyone doing business with pension funds.

Periodically, the magazine runs special issues on pension fund investing in real estate. It packages all the real estate articles it has carried during the previous year and sells them to the public. Contact Ulla Goldberg, *Pensions & Investment Age,* 220 E. 42 Street, New York, N.Y. 10017.

News on Laws and Regulations Affecting Pension Fund Investments in Real Estate

1. *BNA Pension Reporter.* The Bureau of National Affairs, 1231 25th St., N.W., Washington, D.C. 20037. *The Pension Reporter* is published weekly. Its staff covers all aspects of the pension business but concentrates on the legal and regulatory proclamations coming out of Washington. BNA is readable and accurate; every good pension attorney subscribes.

2. *I.F. Digest.* International Foundation of Employee Benefit Plans, 18700 W. Bluemound Road, P.O. Box 69, Brookfield, Wis. 53005. The *Digest* comes out monthly and contains articles of interest to trustees of jointly administered, labor-management pension plans and union pension plans. Most of the articles are general and deal with benefits, not investments. But each issue also contains several pages entitled *Washington Update:* the section reviews recent regulatory and legislative actions affecting pension plans and is useful and well-written.

The International Foundation is a trade group for suppliers and sponsors of jointly trusteed and union pension plans; the *Digest* is one of their subscription services for members.

3. The Pension Real Estate Investment Association (PREIA). John Tuzzolino; Smith, Barney Real Estate Corporation, 1345 Avenue of the Americas, New York, N.Y. 10105. PREIA (PREE a) was officially formed in early 1982. It is a non-profit organization consisting of managers of commingled real estate funds and individual accounts for pension funds, as well as plan sponsors whose funds invest in property on their own.

The group is primarily educational in nature and meets regularly to hear presentations on technical and legal problems facing pension funds that are trying to invest in property. The group works with the Labor Department and other federal agencies to design regulations and laws that make it easier for funds and their managers to invest in property.

To join, one must have some knowledge of the real estate business. The group is not interested in brokers, lawyers and consultants looking for business. PREIA is a good source for the most up-to-date information on regulatory issues affecting institutional real estate investing.

Background Information on Laws and Regulations Affecting Pension Fund Investments in Real Estate

1. Chadwick, William J. *The Annotated Fiduciary: Materials on Fiduciary Responsibility and Prohibited Transactions Under ERISA,* 2nd ed. (Brookfield, Wis: International Foundation of Employee Benefit Plans, 1980). Chadwick is a former head of the Pension and Welfare Benefit Programs division of the U.S. Department of Labor. This division regulates pension funds and their investments. Chadwick's book is a 487-page volume containing the parts of ERISA and the regulations and interpretive bulletins issued by the Labor Department on fiduciary responsibility and prohibited transactions. He comments on these and also touches on relevant court decisions. A reference work for lawyers.

2. Gropper, Diane Hal. "The Ordeal of Jeffrey Clayton," *Institutional Investor* 16 (August 1982), p. 115+. At this writing, Clayton is the administrator of the Pension and Welfare Benefit Programs division at the Department of Labor. The department has cut back on staff and money to the pension division. The article describes how the division is dealing with it or, more accurately, not dealing with it, and how it is writing regulations and enforcing ERISA. The article is informative and worth reading. It turns the bureaucrats into human beings and provides insights into how pension fund investing is regulated by the government.

3. Hutchinson, James D. "Legal Standards Governing Investment of Pension Assets for Social Investing," *University of Pennsylvania Law Review* 128 (1980). Hutchinson describes the laws and regulations restraining private pension plans from investing for "social purposes." He is a former administrator of the Pension and Welfare Benefit Programs division at the Department of Labor.

4. Kaster, Lewis R. *Pension Trust Investments in Realty: Banks, Insurance Companies, Wall Street, Developers—a Course Handbook* (New York: The Practising Law Institute, 1981). The Practising Law Institute conducts seminars each year on the legal issues of pension fund investing in real estate. The PLI then collects the speeches, notes and outlines of its speakers and publishes them in a handbook. Another reference work for lawyers.

5. Knickerbocker, Daniel C., Jr. "Prohibited Transactions Excises After Reorganization: Ticking Time Bomb or Just a Dud?" *The Tax Lawyer* 34 (Fall 1980). A good, technical article on the penalties for engaging in prohibited transactions and how the Internal Revenue Service is enforcing the law. Good for lawyers to read.

6. Pianko, Howard. "Socially Responsible Investment and Union Involvement in Pension Investment," *Legal Issues in Pension Investment* (New York: Practising Law Institute, 1981), pp. 353–67. Notes from a seminar given under the sponsorship of the Practising Law Institute. A good rundown of the issues, laws and regulations involved. Also contains a bibliography.

7. "Special Supplement 298," *BNA Pension Reporter* (Washington, D.C.: The Bureau of National Affairs, 1980) A special supplement on the prohibited transactions rules of ERISA. Technical but good. For anyone who wants a detailed explanation of prohibited transactions.

8. U.S., Department of Labor, Pension and Welfare Benefit Programs. *The Prudence Rule and Pension Plan Investments Under ERISA* (Washington, D.C.: Office of

Communications and Public Services, Pension and Welfare Benefit Programs, 1980).

The logic behind the Labor Department's "prudence regulation." The department ruled that to prove a pension fund is investing prudently, it is unnecessary to show that each investment is prudent; instead the portfolio as a whole must be shown to be prudent. The department also argues that an investment is not imprudent just because it is risky. The pamphlet contains a speech by former administrator of the Pension and Welfare Benefit Programs division, Ian Lanoff. It also contains the prudence regulation and some commentary. Worth reading by anyone doing business with pension funds.

9. U.S., Department of Labor, Pension and Welfare Benefit Programs. *Standards for Exemptions from ERISA Prohibited Transactions Provision* (Washington, D.C.: Office of Communications and Public Services, Pension and Welfare Benefit Programs, 1980). This is the official word on prohibited transactions exemptions from the people who grant them. Contains speeches by the former administrator of the Pension and Welfare Benefit Programs division, Ian Lanoff, and copies of the relevant sections of ERISA. A short pamphlet worth reading by anyone doing business with pension funds. At this writing, the pension division is adhering to the philosophy laid down by Lanoff.

Descriptions and Investment Performance of Commingled Real Estate Funds for Pension Funds

1. EBF Marketing Inc., San Francisco, Calif. EBF published a manual describing 15 major commingled real estate funds in 1980.

2. Ennis, Knupp & Gold, Chicago, Ill. A pension consultant that tracks commingled real estate fund investment performance.

3. *Funds Evaluation Service.* A.G. Becker Company, Chicago, Ill. A.G. Becker, a pension fund consulting firm, tracks commingled real estate fund investment performance.

4. A.S. Hansen, Chicago, Ill. A pension consultant that tracks commingled real estate fund performance.

5. National Council of Real Estate Investment Fiduciaries (NACREIF). Blake Eagle, Frank Russell & Company, Tacoma, Wash. Frank Russell & Company is a pension consulting firm that gathers information on commingled fund investment performance and publishes it as the *FRC Property Index.* The commingled funds that provide the information formed NACREIF. (NAC reef)

When the association was formed in 1982, it had 15 members consisting of the leading managers of real estate commingled funds. The council also intends to educate pension fund sponsors about real estate investing and intends to ask plan sponsors to join.

The Russell Company keeps detailed information on commingled real estate funds; it is considered to be one of the leading sources of such information. At this writing, the firm only releases it to its consulting clients for a stiff fee.

6. *Pensions & Investment Age,* (September 13, 1982). *P&IA* has started running an annual issue profiling the managers of commingled real estate funds and individual accounts for pension funds. The profiles lack performance data; they do provide descriptions and addresses of each manager, as well as the total assets each runs.

In September of each year, *Pension World* runs an annual issue on pension fund investments in property. It sometimes lists managers of commingled funds and individual accounts. *Institutional Investor* periodically runs lists of pension fund real estate managers.

7. *Real Estate Funds for Pension Plans.* Audit Investments Inc., New York, N.Y. An investment service that occasionally publishes a booklet on commingled real estate funds. The booklet includes some commentary on how the funds operate, but primarily concentrates on investment performance. A good, all-round handbook on commingled funds. Audit published a 1981 edition, based on 1980 data, but did not publish a 1982 study.

8. *Real Estate Profiles.* Evaluation Associates, Inc., Westport, Conn. EAI provides its clients with detailed descriptions of the funds it analyzes, setting out the data for each fund on a four-page spread sheet. The service comes out quarterly and includes investment performance. A good, basic source on commingled funds.

General Sources

1. Drucker, Peter. *The Unseen Revolution: How Pension Fund Socialism Came to America* (New York: Harper & Row, 1976). Drucker argues that because their pension funds own so much common stock, American workers are actually the owners of American industry. In a sense, America is a "Socialist" country. An intriguing work.

2. Information Center, The International Foundation of Employee Benefit Plans, Brookfield, Wis. The International Foundation has an extensive library of materials on pension funds, including books, periodicals, research reports, government documents and bibliographies. Persons who are not members of the foundation can still use the library; the staff is happy to answer information requests made by phone.

3. Levine, Sumner N., editor. *The Investment Manager's Handbook* (Homewood, Ill: Dow Jones-Irwin, 1980). A book for investment managers, consisting of articles by 41 contributors on everything from setting investment objectives to using computers. Also contains articles on modern portfolio theory, ERISA and fiduciary law. Though designed for all investment managers, most of the articles are directly relevant to managers of pension money. A good reference work.

4. *The Money Market Directory* (Charlottesville, Va: Money Market Directories, Inc.). The *MMD* comes out annually and is the "yellow pages" of the pension investing business. It lists the names, addresses and contact people for several thousand pension plans, as well as for other tax-exempt funds, such as foundations and endowments. A second section lists similar information for money managers. Every real estate firm that intends to market itself to the pension industry needs a copy.

   Each year since 1980, MMD has conducted an annual survey of real estate investing by pension funds. Fund sponsors are asked about their plans for real estate investing and their attitudes about property. The survey is summarized each year in the September issue of *Pension World* magazine.

5. *Pension Facts.* American Council of Life Insurance, Washington, D.C. A booklet published annually and containing all types of data on pension plans, regardless of how they are managed. The 1982 edition contained a glossary and extensive bibliography, though most of the listings dealt with benefit, not investment issues. It also contained good descriptions of the various types of plans and a history of

the pension business. Worthwhile reading for anyone involved with pension funds.
6. Sandler, Linda. "Wall Street enters the pension fray," *Institutional Investor* 16 (November 1982), pp. 267–282. A good piece describing the state of pension fund investing in real estate and the attempts of money managers to enter the business. *II* periodically produces such wrap-up articles on pension funds' real estate activities.
7. Thorndike, Doran, Paine & Lewis, Inc. *Real Estate and the Institutional Investor* (Boston: 1980). TDP&L is an old-line money management firm for pension funds. This booklet is informative though misleading on the legal aspects of pension fund investing in real estate. Worth reading.
8. Twentieth Century Fund. *Abuse on Wall Street: Conflicts of Interest in the Securities Markets* (Westport, Conn: Quorum Books, 1980). A collection of essays by various authors who provide insight into how pension funds are managed and how that management is riddled with conflicts of interest. There are good pieces on commercial bank trust departments; corporate pension fund asset management; and the management of state, local and union pension funds. The Twentieth Century Fund is an independent research foundation, well respected in institutional investing circles. Recommended reading for anyone doing business with pension funds.
9. Zell, Samuel. "Pension Fund Perils in Real Estate," *Real Estate Review* 5 (Spring 1975), pp. 61–67. A classic. Should be required reading for all boards of trustees before they put money into any real estate investment. Zell deals with unrealized appreciation, liquidity in real estate, and leverage. Zell is a Chicago-based real estate developer and investor.

THE REAL ESTATE BUSINESS

1. Arnold, Alvin L. *Modern Real Estate* (Boston: Warren, Gorham & Lamont, 1980). A good textbook on the real estate business, designed for introductory real estate courses in college or for those going into the real estate business with no previous background. A good primer for a pension officer to start with.
2. H.E. Hoagland. *Real Estate Finance* (Homewood, Ill: Dow Jones, 1977).
3. Rabinowitz, Alan. *The Real Estate Gamble: Lessons from 50 Years of Boom and Bust* (New York: The American Management Associations, 1980). A history of the real estate business from the late 1920s. Rabinowitz uses newspapers, monographs, magazine articles and earlier studies to recreate the real estate business earlier in this century. His research is impressive and dense: this is not light reading. His thesis is that the real estate business goes through booms and busts based on the greed of the participants and the availability of financing. A good book for pension officers to read.
4. *Real Estate Issues*. The American Society of Real Estate Counselors, 430 N. Michigan Avenue, Chicago, Ill. 60611. An informative magazine with articles on all aspects of the income property business. Worth reading.
5. *The Real Estate Review*. Warren, Gorham & Lamont, 210 South Street, Boston, Mass. 02111. The *Review* is a quarterly collection of articles by different authors touching on all aspects of the real estate business. In one issue there will be an article on depreciation schedules under the latest tax code, another on demand for housing, and something on the mathematical fine points of appraising. Some articles are good, and some are not. But in each issue there is usually something of interest.

The magazine gives someone new to the real estate business a sense of how broad the business is and the types of issues that affect it. Other real estate magazines tend to be more specialized and of less use to someone who is not involved in the business on a daily basis.

6. Ring, A.A. *Real Estate Principles and Practices* (Englewood Cliffs, N.J.: Prentice-Hall, 1981). Another good textbook on the real estate business.

7. Thorndike, Doran, Paine & Lewis. (See Pension Fund Business—General Sources section of this bibliography for listing).

8. Twentieth Century Fund. (See Pension Funds—General Sources section of this bibliography for listing). There is an excellent essay on real estate investment trusts in this work.

9. Wendt, P.F. *Real Estate Investment Analysis and Taxation* (New York: McGraw-Hill, 1979). Designed for those who care to see how sophisticated cash flow analysis is applied to real estate. A detailed and technical book, well known in the real estate finance field.

10. R.J. Wiley. *Real Estate Investment* (New York: Ronald Press, 1977). The basics of the income property business.

11. Zell, Samuel. (See Pension Fund Business—General Sources section of this bibliography for listing). Also by the same author: "The New Real Estate Math: 1 + 1 = 1½," *Real Estate Issues* 7 (Spring/Summer 1982). This article deals with changes in the rental apartment markets, in which Zell is a substantial investor. It is worth reading by any pension fund sponsor considering investing in such properties.

"Neither a Lender nor a Lender Be," *Real Estate Issues* 6 (Spring/Summer 1981). This article discusses the changes that real estate finance will undergo in the 1980s and is also recommended.

INDEX

Aetna Life Insurance Co.: commingled funds, 212, 214, 215 (table 8.1); investment allocations, 235; participating mortgage fund, 223; and prohibited transactions, 81, 236

Actuarial valuations, 89–91

AFL-CIO, 96, 97

Agricultural Investment Management Co., 224

Alaska Teamster Employer Pension Trust, Local 959, 73, 76–77

Aldrich-Kopcke study, 11

All-cash buyers: compared to buyer with a mortgage, 123–24; in Great Britain, 184; pension funds as, 159–60, 278

Alliance Capital Management Co., 47 (table 2.3)

American Realty Trust, 152

Apartments, rental: bad deal involving, 116–17; and condominium conversions, 156; depreciation of, 279; as a pension fund investment, 219, 223–24

Appraisals, real estate: business described, 141–44, 146, 163; effect of inflation on, 166–67; use in commingled funds, 221, 225–33; use by investment advisors, 252; use in real estate studies, 188–89, 190

Arizona Public Employees Retirement System, 25

Asset mix, 26

AT&T, pension fund, 9–10, 31 (table 1.6), 51

Audit Investments Inc., 226–27

Baker, Cecil, 183, 185

Balcor/American Express: participating mortgage fund, 223, 229; syndications, 65, 171

Balloon loans, 169

Banks: class exemptions of, 81; commingled real estate funds of, 218, 219, 230, 245; as investment advisors to pension funds, 46 (table 2.2), 47 (table 2.3), 48, 49; as real estate lenders, 137–38; and the REITs 147, 149–50, 152, 153–54

Bank of America, 230

Batterymarch Financial Management Co., 47, 48 (table 2.4)

Becker, A. G., 16–18

Berin, Barnet N., 60–61

Beta, 49, 58, 190

Big Sky Resort, 270

Block trading, 14

Bond markets: and real estate lending, 156. See also fixed-income securities

Boston Company Real Estate Counsel, 250

British Coal Board. See National Coal Board Superannuation Schemes

Bullet loans, 128

Burroughs, Eugene B., 43

H. E. Butt Grocery Co., pension fund, 266

Buying right, 193–94

California Public Employees and Teachers Retirement System, 31 (table 1.6), 32, 96

Cap rate: and commingled funds 231–32; defined and use, 116, 119–21, 122, 189; effect of inflation on, 167; of shopping centers, 160

Cash flow: defined and use, 115–17, 119, 120, 125, 229; impact of inflation on, 131, 164–67; and tax write-offs, 280

Cash-on-cash return, 121–22, 232

Chase Manhattan Mortgage & Realty Investors, 151–52

CIT Building, 220

Clay-Brown provisions, 91–94

Closed-end funds, 218–19, 230, 239–42

Coal Board. See National Coal Board Superannuation Schemes

Coldwell-Banker: commingled funds sold through Smith-Barney, 64; fees on commingled funds, 74, 231; joint venture with AT&T, 11; structure of commingled funds, 85, 218, 224, 277

Commingled fund, 32n. 5

Commingled funds, real estate: compared to hiring an advisor, 251–54, 262; drawbacks of, 225–42; and ERISA, 85; in Great Britain, 182, 183, 240; growth of, 63, 157, 158–59; investment performance, compared to direct investing, 261–62; investment performance, computation of, 231–34; investment performance, data, 191; investment performance, through 1982, 18, 20, 22, 188, 190, 191; investment strategy, 119, 237–38; operation and history, 211–16, 215 (table 8.1); place in pension fund investment strategy, 198–99, 207, 224–25, 242–43, 263; profitability for managers, 216–18; salesmen of, 110, 111, 190; selection of, 243–46; and small pension funds, 65; as teachers, 259; varieties of, 222–24, 229; withdrawals from, 222, 238–42. See also Closed-end funds; Open-end funds

Commissions, brokerage, 75–76

Common area maintenance (CAM), 132, 165

Compensation, of in-house staff, 255–56

Competition, 117–19, 179

Comptroller of the Currency, 230

Conflict of interest: in commingled funds, 225; of pension funds in joint ventures, 274–75. See also Prohibited transactions

Condominiums, 129, 151, 156

Connecticut General Life Insurance Co., REIT, 205, 220

Connecticut state pension funds, 96

Construction costs, 115–16, 117

Construction lenders, 162

Construction loans: of construction union pension funds, 97–98; in Great Britain, 181; rates in 1981, 160; of REITs in 1970s, 147–53; underwriting, 132, 138, 155

Consultants, to pension funds, 72–73, 233, 244

Consumer Price Index, 16

Continental Illinois National Bank, REIT, 205

Corporate Property Investors, 224

Corporate real estate departments, 55, 112, 266

Cost-of-living adjustments, on pensions, 24

Cost overruns, 173, 277

Credit deals, 133. See also Leasebacks

Crocker National Bank, 230

Dailey, James, 81, 82

Deal, 110

Debt Service, 164

Defined-benefit plan, 20

Defined-contribution plan, 20

Depreciation, 119: in Great Britain, 183; as a tax write-off, 134–35, 154, 175, 279–80

Direct investing: Coal Board, 200–208; done badly, 103–8; in pension fund real estate strategy, 198–99, 246–50; using an investment advisor, 250–61. See also In-house investing, real estate

Diversification, 253–54, 255

Drucker, Peter F., 36

Economic Tax Recovery Act of 1981, 175

Employee benefit funds, 20

Employee Retirement Income Security Act. See ERISA

Endowments, 45

Equitable Life Assurance Society: pension fund assets managed, 46, 47 (table 2.3); and prohibited transactions, 81; real estate managed for pension funds, 212, 215 (table 8.1); Separate Account No. 8, 214, 220, 226–27, 232, 237

Equities. See Stock

Equity buildup, 119. See also Mortgages; Mortgages, participating

ERISA: and brokerage commissions, 75–76; dual administration, 71, 78; fiduciaries under, 38, 71–76, 225; funding under, 23; history of, 69–70; and incentive compensation, 74–75, 256, 265; no British equivalent, 184; and pension investments in real estate, 59, 69, 71–89, 236; plans covered, 23, 24, 68; prohibited transactions, 76–89; qualified plan asset managers (QPAMs), 72; and social investing, 94–96; strain of on trustees, 206, 282; on valuation of pension assets, 89–90. *See also* Prudent man rule; Prohibited transactions

Evaluation Associates, 213–14

Exxon Corp., pension fund, 31 (table 1.6)

Fair market value, 141

Farmland: in commingled funds, 219, 224; owned by Coal Board, 200; as real estate, 4, 109

Fast-food franchises, 272

Fayez Sarofim & Co., 47, 48 (table 2.4)

Federal employee retirement system, 23

Fees, 49–50: on commingled real estate funds, 225, 230–31, 233–34, 252, 254–56; incentive, 233, 245–46, 254–56; of real estate investment advisors, 250–51, 252, 254–56

Feldman, David, 9, 10, 11, 30

Fiduciaries: definition and role under ERISA, 71–76; and incentive compensation, 74–75, 256; responsibility of, and real estate investment advisors, 83–85, 251, 256; restrictions on, 38, 75–76

Financial Accounting Standards Board (FASB), 60

Financing out, 122

First National Bank of Chicago: Fund F, 212, 215 (table 8.1), 226–27; other funds, 223, 230

Fixed-income securities: held by pension funds in 1981, 26, 27 (table 1.3), 28 (table 1.4), 29 (table 1.5); held by pension funds through commingled funds, 211, 212

Florida State Retirement System, 26

Foreign investors, 159

Foundations, charitable, 45

Free and clear, 119

Functional obsolescence, 189

Gaasedelen, Newell, 272

General Electric Co., pension fund, 30, 31 (table 1.6), 270–71

General Electric Credit Corp., 271

Georgine, Robert, 96, 97

GICs, 11, 127–28

Gilts, 182, 184, 201–2, 207

Ginnie Mae, 64, 114

Glass/Metal Association and Glaziers and Glassworkers Pension Plan, 73

GNMA, 64, 114

Gochberg, Thomas, 92

Government control of land use, 175–79

Government National Mortgage Assn. (GNMA), 64, 114

Great Britain, real estate business in, 176–79, 281

Greenwich Research Associates, 22, 65

Griswold, E. B., 270–71

Gross, Stephen, 41, 60

Group trusts, 32n.5, 212

Guaranteed Income Contracts (GICs), 11, 127–28

Guarantees, personal: in development deals, 136; in joint ventures, 202–3, 277

Highest and best use, 141

Hotels, 219

Ibbotson-Sinquefield study, 187, 190

Illinois Teachers' Retirement System, 25

Inco, Ltd., 61

Income approach to value, 142

Income property: defined, 110, 113; investment performance of, 52, 114–15, 119, 186–97; investments of the Coal Board, 200–208; measuring risk of, 196–97; scope of book, 4, 114; valuation of, 115–29, 229–30. *See also* Real estate

Income property business: attitude toward fixed fees, 74, 254–55; and brokers, 138–40; effects of two-tiered market on, 162–63; future of, 161–77; in Great Britain, 178–85, 281; history of, 112–13, 127–137, 155–61; and lenders, 137–38; scope of book, 4–5

294   INDEX

Individual Retirement Accounts (IRAs), 4,
20, 21
Inflation, effect of: on commingled real estate funds, 213; in Great Britain, 176–
77, 180–81, 183–84; on income property
business, 128–32, 148, 157–58, 161–65,
166, 225–26; on income property values,
115–16, 117–18, 156; on pension costs,
60–61; on stock prices, 19
In-house investing, by pension funds, 50,
51, 200–208
In-house investing, by pension funds in real
estate: advantages of, 262–63, 267–68;
disadvantages of, 262–64; examples of
successful operations, 270–73; investment performance of, 261–63, 264; role
of trustees, 248–50, 263–65, 269–70,
271; staffing, 262, 263, 264–70; strategies, 264–66, 271–78, 281; as a way to
learn about real estate, 258, 262
Interest rates. See Inflation
Interim financing, 132
Internal rate of return, 167, 194–95
Internal Revenue Service. See IRS
Investment advisors: as fiduciaries, 2–73;
investment performance of in 1970s, 16–
20, 17 (table 1.1); operation of business,
44–51 (table 2.1), 46 (table 2.2), 47 (table 2.3), 48 (table 2.4)
Investment advisors, real estate: advantages
of using, 251–52; disadvantages of using, 252–54, 256–57; fees, 75, 217, 250–
52, 258, 260–61; as fiduciaries, 83–85;
251; and incentive compensation, 74–75,
254–56; investment performance of, 252–
54, 257–58, 259, 262; operations of, 250–
61; relationship with pension funds in
infancy, 64, 214; selection of, 257–61;
strategies of, 198–99, 258; as teachers of
pension funds, 258–59; trustee involvement with, 253, 260
Investment Advisors Act of 1940, 72, 74
Investment bankers, 150
Investment performance, of pension funds,
16–20, 16, 17 (table 1.1)
Investment performance, of real estate: in
commingled funds, 213, 214, 221–22,
225–34, 240; inaccuracy of, 56–58; in-

come property compared to residential,
114–15; on leasebacks, 265, 272; owned
by British pension funds, 185; and positive leverage, 122–27; prediction and
computation of, 121–22, 186–208; in
terms of risk taken, 196–97
IRS: and ERISA, 70, 71, 85, 86; on pension
fund valuation, 90–91

Jenkins, Hugh, 200–207, 274
JMB Institutional Realty, 74, 81, 218, 223
JMB Realty, 62
Joint ventures: of the Coal Board, 202–3,
273; as a pension fund investment strat-
egy, 273–77, 280

Kansas Public Employees Retirement Sys-
tem, 25
Kassuba, Judd, 151
Keogh plans, 4, 20, 21
Kickbacks, 263–64
King, Don, 279
KLM/Royal Dutch Airlines Pension Fund,
281
Knickerbocker, Daniel, Jr., 70, 86, 87
Kopcke, Richard, 11

Land: and commingled funds, 219, 224;
government control of in Britain, 176,
178–79
Land development corporations, 114
Land loans, 150, 153, 156
Landsale-leasebacks, 133–34, 166, 219. See
also Leasebacks
Lanoff, Ian: on exemptions to prohibited
transactions, 78–79, 82, 87; on social
investing, 95, 97, 98, 99n.33
Larwin Mortgage Investors, 152
LaSalle Partners, 224
Lawsuits, danger of in joint ventures, 274–
75
Lawyers: corporate, 53–54; real estate, 144
Leasebacks: at G.E. pension fund, 270–71;
investment performance of, 207, 265,
272, 273; made by the Coal Board, 201–
2, 207, 273; made in Minneapolis teachers fund, 272; in pension fund investment
strategies, 248, 249, 265; subordinated,

133; and unrelated business income tax, 93. *See also* Landsale-leasebacks

Leases, 117–19, 131, 164–66, 180–81

Leverage: changes in meaning, 44, 129; example of developer's, 174; negative, 126–27; positive, 122–26, 127, 134, 155–56, 167–71, 278; use by pension funds, 94, 220, 246; with wraparound mortgages, 168–71

Life insurance companies: British, 183; investment allocation problems of, 234–35, 253; as pension fund investment advisors, 22, 27–28, 46 (table 2.2), 47 (table 2.3), 48, 127; real estate lending of, 11, 127, 132–34, 157, 158; as real estate managers for pension funds, through general accounts, 12, 33n. 10; as real estate managers for pension funds, through separate accounts, 28, 32n. 5, 81, 218, 219, 236; real estate staffs of, 137–38, 140–41

Lillard, John, 62

Liquidity, of commingled funds, 238–39, 240–42

Locational obsolescence, 189

Lock-ins, 127, 132

Lorie, James, 19

Los Angeles Police & Firefighters Fund, 24

Manufacturers Hanover Trust Co., 224

Market approach to value, 142

Marshall Valuation Services, 188

Martin, Vincent, Jr., 237, 277, 278

Master leases, 277

MBAs: dislike real estate, 54–55; in real estate, 104, 108, 151, 259–60

McMorgan & Co., 250

Melnikoff, Meyer: on fund resistance to real estate, 52, 54, 55; on growth of fund interest in real estate, 13–14; on unrealized appreciation, 228–30

Mergers, 60

Merrill Lynch, Hubbard, 250

Metropolitan Life Insurance Co., 223, 224, 235

Money Market Directory, 104

Morgan Guaranty Trust Co., 204

Mortgage bankers, 140–41, 146, 162, 265

Mortgage bonds, 129–30

Mortgage brokers, 140–41, 146, 162

Mortgage constant, 122–23, 168

Mortgage correspondants, 140

Mortgaged property, risks of ownership, 124–26

Mortgages: bullet loans, 128; in Great Britain, 180–81; held by pension funds, 12, 27 (table 1.3), 28 (table 1.4), 29 (table 1.5), 33n. 9, 219; in joint ventures, 274, 275, 280; long-term, disappearance of, 127–29, 159; long-term, and positive leverage, 123–24; made by REITs in 1970s, 147–53; as real estate investments, 109–10, 132, 191; and unrelated business income tax, 91–94. *See also* other Mortgage listings; Land loans

Mortgages, convertible, 167–68, 171

Mortgages, participating: in commingled funds, 222–23, 229; defined and use of, 157–58; in joint ventures, 280; and unrelated business income tax, 94

Mortgages, residential: as a pension fund investment, 4, 114, 32; and social investing, 77, 95–97

Mortgages, second, 167–71

Mortgages, with equity kickers. *See* Mortgages, participating

Mortgages, wraparound, 168–71, 223

Motels, 103–8

Multifamily housing, 153, 156

Municipal Assistance Corp., 25

National Association of Realtors, 113

National Coal Board Superannuation Schemes: approach to real estate investing, 184, 200–206, 272–73, 281; compared to other British pension funds, 182; and property allocation, 234

National Co-ordinating Committee of Multiemployer Pension Plans, 96

Net-leased credit deals, 165, 166. *See also* Credit deals; Leasebacks

New York City pension funds, 25

New York State Common Retirement Fund, 25, 31 (table 1.6), 32

Noddings, Calamos & Associates, 47

Nonrecourse loans, 124

North Carolina National Bank, 224
North Hills, Inc., 281

Office buildings: effect of real estate cycles on, 191–92; and example of good leasing, 118; overbuilding, 151, 156, 161
Ohio Teachers Retirement System, 30, 31 (table 1.6)
100 perent financing, 122
Open-end funds, 218, 219–22, 230. *See also* Commingled funds; Closed-end funds
Overage rent, 131, 164

Pan Am Building, 223
Parties in interest, 76
Partnerships, limited: and Coldwell-Banker, 224; as commingled funds, 32n.5, 212; pension funds in, 83–85, 174
Pension Benefit Guaranty Corp., 70–71, 184
Pension Fund Property Unit Trust, 183
Pension funds: assets of, 13, 20, 20–26 (tables), 34n.17; benefits, 42; costs, 42; number of, 29; 100 largest, 30, 31 (table 1.6); ownership of, 36–38; scope of book, 4–5; 200 largest, 29–30; type interested in real estate, 63–64, 65; by type of sponsor, 20–26. *See also* listings that follow
Pension funds, British: the Coal Board, 200–208; real estate investments of, 15, 181–85
Pension funds, corporate. *See* Pension funds, private
Pension funds, Dutch, 15, 281
Pension funds, government. *See* Pension funds, public
Pension funds, insured, 21–22, 27, 29 (table 1.5). *See also* Pension funds, private
Pension funds, investments of: asset mix, 12, 26–28; assets, 13, 20, 20–26 tables, 34n.17; in bonds, 14, 19; conservative approach, 36, 37–38, 41; in farms, 224; in government securities, 14; history of, 13–14; operations, 35–39; performance in securities, 16–20, 17 (table 1.1); performance monitoring business, 40–41; and the prudent man rule, 39–41; social investing, 94–98; splitting the fund, 50–

51; in stocks, 14, 18–19, 26, 27, 27 (table 1.3), 28 (table 1.4), 29 (table 1.5); in stocks, through commingled funds, 211, 212; valuation of under ERISA, 89–91. *See also* Pension funds, real estate investments of
Pension funds, non-insured, 22
Pension funds, private: asset mix, 26, 27 (table 1.3); assets, 13, 21 (table 1.2), 21–22; cost-of-living adjustments, 60–61; costs, 42–43, 59–60; number of, 29; real estate holdings of, 22, 30, 31 (table 1.6); and social investing, 94, 95, 96–98; union funds, 36–37, 97
Pension funds, public: administration and investment management of, 23, 25, 26; asset mix, 26, 27, 28 (table 1.4); assets, 22–26; cost-of-living adjustments, 24; GAO study of, 24–25; number of, 29; and PERISA, 23, 24; real estate investing by, 26, 30, 31 (table 1.6), 32, 103–8, 264; social investing, 26, 95–96
Pension funds, real estate investments of: in apartments, 223–24; assets, 12–13, 22; attitude of pension officers toward, 52–59; and California state pension system, 32; and the Coal Board, 200–208; in commercial mortgages, 12, 33 (nn.9, 11); through commingled funds, 211–47; in convertible mortgages, 167–68; dangers of, 103–8, 115, 174; effect on fund, 60, 186–208; equity holdings, 12; in the future, 10, 11, 13–16, 65–66; and the G.E. pension fund, 270–71; in Great Britain, 181–84; history of, 3–4, 9–13; impact on real estate markets, 11, 14–15; and in-house investing, 248–50, 261–81; through joint ventures, 273–77; legal problems of, 68–94; through life insurance companies, 12; made by the largest funds, 30, 31 (table 1.6); made by small funds, 65, 265–66; made from 1980 to 1982, 65, 158, 159; and the Minneapolis teachers fund, 272; and net-leased deals, 165–66; in participating mortgages, 222–23; performance of, in commingled funds, 211–22, 225–34, 240; and prohibited transactions, 78–89; and property busts,

192; through real estate advisors, 248–61; in resorts, 73, 270–71; role of trustees in making, 200, 205–6; and social investing, 94–98; strategies behind, 114, 126, 194–200, 249–61, 278–80; and taxes, 279–80; in wraparound mortgages, 168–71, 223. *See also* Investment performance, real estate

Pension funds, union, 36–37, 97, 264

Pension law. *See* ERISA

Pension officers: and commingled real estate funds, 216, 218, 241; dislike real estate, 44, 52–59, 282; duties of, 42; low status of, 41–43, 206; and real estate advisors, 258–59; and real estate brokers, 140; and real estate studies, 187, 188, 190

Pension Real Estate Investment Association (PREIA), 75

Pensions & Investment Age, 215, 215 (table 8.1)

Percentage rents, 131

Performance monitoring, 40–41

Permanent financing, 123

Pillsbury Co., pension fund, 266

Plan assets regulation, 83–85

Population growth, 116, 117

PRISA: described, 13, 212, 215 (table 8.1); effect of prohibited transactions on, 81; fee income, 75; investments of, 205, 219, 220; investments of, how allocated, 235; investment performance, 213, 232; sales to pension funds, 52, 159, 213, 214; withdrawals from, 222, 227, 238–39. *See also* Prudential Insurance Co; PRISA II

PRISA II, 221

Professional designations, in real estate, 145–46

Profit-sharing funds, 20

Prohibited transactions: administrative exemptions, 77–83; class exemptions, 80–81; defined, 76–77; enforcement of, 85–89; how to deal with, 88–89; impact on real estate investments, 71, 80–83, 236; retroactive exemptions, 87–88; statutory exemptions, 77

Property management: at commingled funds, 217, 237–38, 246; described and impor-

tance of, 144–45, 146, 163, 278–79; fees, 261; identifying good managers, 260

Property unit trusts, 182, 183, 184

Prudential Insurance Co.: and land investments, 176; participating mortgage fund, 223; pension fund money managed, 46, 47 (table 2.3). *See also* PRISA; PRISA II

Prudential Property Investment Separate Account. *See* PRISA; PRISA II

Prudent man rule: defined, 39–40; effect on pension fund investing, 38–41, 58, 73–74; and fiduciaries, 71, 206; imprudent investing, 73–74; nonexistent in Great Britain, 184

Pyramid Corp., 176

Qualified plan asset managers (QPAMs), 72, 74, 212

Rabinowitz, Alan: on disasters in the income property business, 114–15, 130, 131; his history recommended, 129; on lack of data on real estate, 187; on REIT collapse, 129, 152

Railroad Retirement System, 23

Real estate: costs of buying, selling, operating, 260–61; cycles, 192–93; defined, 109–12; how pension officers can learn about it, 111–13; importance of acquisition work, 260; marketing it to pension funds, 59, 62–65; need for capital, 11, 12, 15, 53; people in, 53, 103–8, 145–46; state of pension fund interest in, 9–32. *See also* Income property; Income property business; Pension funds, real estate investments of; Investment performance, real estate; and following Real estate listings

Real estate, residential, 112–13, 114, 175–76

Real estate, special purpose, 113, 150, 219

Real estate brokers: commissions, 260–61; description of business, 113, 138–40, 145–46; and institutions, 104, 163; residential, 113, 139

Real estate consultants, 163

Real estate developers: the Coal Board, 201,

273, 281; effect of high interest rates on, 128, 158, 161; in Great Britain, 181; and institutional investors, 160, 162, 171–74; in joint ventures, 273, 274; and the REITs, 150, 155; typical behavior of, 134–37, 171–74. *See also* Real estate development

Real estate development: and commingled funds, 219–20; and pension funds, 15, 275, 280, 281; prices of property in, 278; risk of, 197. *See also* Real estate developers

Real estate equities, 12

The Real Estate Gamble: Lessons from 50 Years of Boom and Bust (Rabinowitz), 129

Real estate investment trusts. *See* REITs

Real estate lenders: British, 181; G.E. pension fund as, 271; and the REITs, 153–54; types of people, 137–38; and wraparound loans, 169–71. *See also* Life insurance companies; Pension funds, real estate investments of

Real estate studies, 186–91

Reciprocal easement agreements, 172–73

Recordkeeping, 256–57

Redemptions, from commingled real estate funds, 222, 238–42

REITs: bank-sponsored, 111, 138; as commingled funds, 32n.5, 212, 224; compared to commingled funds, 243; history of and operation before 1975 collapse, 114, 129–30, 135, 146–53; purchased by Coal Board, 205

Reproduction cost, 142

Resorts, 73, 270–71

Reversions, 180

Rhode Island Hospital Trust, 224

Richardson, Thomas, Jr., 233

Risk: in advisor-run portfolios, 253–54, 257–58; of being a fiduciary, 256; in commingled funds, 252–54, 257–58; in joint ventures and development, 202–3, 273, 274, 277, 278; measuring it in real estate, 196–97; and pension fund real estate investing, 200, 264, 272, 273, 281

Roberts, Marcella, 146

Rosenberg Capital Management, 212, 215 (table 8.1). *See also* RREEF

Royal Dutch/Shell, 281

RREEF: organization of, 214, 218, 224; property screening of, 279; termination and withdrawal procedures of, 240, 241–42

Frank Russell Co., 190

Salomon Brothers, 34n.17

Securities and Exchange Commission (SEC), 74–75, 130, 250

Self-dealing. *See* Prohibited transactions

Seller-leasebacks, 93. *See also* Leasebacks; Unrelated business income tax

Separate accounts. *See* Commingled funds, real estate; Life insurance companies

Shopping centers: Coal Board, 202, 207; development of, 171, 172–74; percentage rents and CAM, 131–32; yields from, 115, 159–60, 164–66

Smith Barney, Harris Upham, 64

Smith Barney Real Estate Corp.: commingled fund of, 74, 222, 223–24, 231; and unrelated business income tax, 92

Social investing, by pension funds, 26, 37, 77, 94–98

Socialism, 36

Social Security, 23, 60, 61

Stock: in commingled funds, 211, 212; held by pension funds, 26, 27, 27 (table 1.3), 28 (table 1.4), 29 (table 1.5)

Stockbrokers, 135

Stock market: effect of pension funds in, 14; performance of, 18–19, 192–93

Studebaker Corp., 69–70

Sultry Nights Motor Lodge, 103–8

Syndications, real estate: collapse of, 114, 115, 135; described, 243; and small pension plans, 21, 64–65, 221; as a source of capital, 159, 163; of wraparound loans, 171

Takeouts, 132, 150

Talley, Madelon, 25–26

Taxes: in Britain, 183; and wraparound

mortgages, 170–71; and write-offs from real estate, 134, 155, 175, 279–80

Tax-exempt corporations, 212, 224

Tax-exempt funds, 20. *See also* Pension funds

Tax Reform Act of 1969, 92, 154–55, 175

TCW Realty Advisors, 237, 277, 278

Teamsters Central States Pension Fund, 30

Town planning, 178–79

Travelers Life Insurance Co., 235

Triple net deals, 133

U.S. Department of Labor: on incentive compensation, 74–75; plan assets regulation, 83–85; prohibited transactions, enforcement of, 76–77, 85, 86, 87, 88; prohibited transactions, exemptions, 78–83; prohibited transactions, study of, 89; and prudent investing, 39–40, 73; role in pension regulation, 70, 71; and social investing, 95, 96–98; study of pension asset growth, 13

U.S. Government Accounting Office (GAO), 24

U.S. Steel and Carnegie Pension Fund, 50

Unrealized appreciation, 57–58, 120, 225–32, 239–40, 242

Unrelated business income tax, 91–94, 220

The Unseen Revolution: How Pension Fund Socialism Came to America (Drucker), 36

Urban Investment and Development Corp., 81, 236

Valuation: of commingled funds, 225–34; of pension funds, 89–91

Vantage Companies, 220

Wachovia Bank & Trust Co., 212, 215 (table 8.1)

Warehouses, 171

Willkie, Wendell, 223

Wilson Committee, 185

Withdrawals, from commingled real estate funds, 222, 238–42

Woodward, Lynn N., 146

Workouts, 154

Zell, Samuel, 120, 124–25, 126

About the Author

Natalie McKelvy is a financial writer based in Chicago. She worked in the investment property business as a financial analyst and mortgage banker in the mid-1970s, followed by stints as a reporter for *Pensions & Investment Age* magazine and the real estate section of *The Chicago Tribune*. She holds an MBA from the University of Chicago and is currently a speechwriter for the U.S. League of Savings Institutions, the trade association that represents savings and loan associations and savings banks.